THE FORCE OF FASHION IN POLITICS AND SOCIETY

The Force of Fashion in Politics and Society
Global Perspectives from Early Modern to Contemporary Times

Edited by

BEVERLY LEMIRE
University of Alberta, Canada

ASHGATE

© The Editor and Contributors 2010

All rights reserved. No part of this publication may be reproduced, stored in a retrieval system or transmitted in any form or by any means, electronic, mechanical, photocopying, recording or otherwise without the prior permission of the publisher.

Beverly Lemire has asserted her right under the Copyright, Designs and Patents Act, 1988, to be identified as the editor of this work.

Published by
Ashgate Publishing Limited
Wey Court East
Union Road
Farnham
Surrey, GU9 7PT
England

Ashgate Publishing Company
Suite 420
101 Cherry Street
Burlington
VT 05401-4405
USA

www.ashgate.com

British Library Cataloguing in Publication Data
The force of fashion in politics and society: global perspectives from early modern to contemporary times. –
 (The history of retailing and consumption)
 1. Textile industry–History. 2. Fashion–Social aspects–History. 3. Fashion merchandising–History.
 I. Series II. Lemire, Beverly, 1950-
 338.4'7687'09-dc22

Library of Congress Cataloging-in-Publication Data
Lemire, Beverly, 1950–
 The force of fashion in politics and society: global perspectives from early modern to contemporary times / Beverly Lemire.
  p. cm. – (The history of retailing and consumption)
 Includes bibliographical references and index.
 ISBN 978-1-4094-0492-7 (hardcover: alk. paper) 1. Fashion–History. 2. Fashion–Political aspects. 3. Clothing trade–History. 4. Textile industry–History. 5. Advertising–Fashion–History. 6. Retail trade–History. 7. Consumption (Economics)–History. I. Title.
 TT504.L46 2009
 746.9'2--dc22

2009053221

ISBN 9781409404927 (hbk)

Printed and bound in Great Britain by
MPG Books Group, UK

Contents

General Editor's Preface		*vii*
List of Figures, Maps and Tables		*ix*
List of Illustrations		*xi*
Notes on Contributors		*xiii*
Acknowledgements		*xvii*

1 Introduction: Fashion and the Practice of History
   A Political Legacy 1
   Beverly Lemire

Part One   Fashion Practice in Early Modern Europe

2 Middlemen and the Creation of a 'Fashion Revolution':
   The Experience of Antwerp in the Late Seventeenth and
   Eighteenth Centuries 21
   Ilja Van Damme

3 Fabricating the Domestic: The Material Culture of Textiles and
   the Social Life of the Home in Early Modern Europe 41
   Giorgio Riello

4 Luxury, Fashion and Peasantry: The Introduction of New
   Commodities in Rural Catalan, 1670–1790 67
   Belén Moreno Claverías

**Part Two   The Politics and Practice of Fashion in the
   Long Nineteenth Century**

5 Fashion Sprayed and Displayed: The Market for Perfumery in
   Nineteenth-century Paris 97
   Eugénie Briot

6 'Fashion has extended her influence to the cause of humanity':
   The Transatlantic Female Economy of the Boston Antislavery
   Bazaar 115
   Alice Taylor

| 7 | Silk and Sartorial Politics in the Sokoto Caliphate (Nigeria), 1804–1903
Colleen E. Kriger | 143 |

Part Three   Fashion Strategies, Global Practice

8	Designing, Producing and Enacting Nationalisms: Contemporary Amerindian Fashions in Canada *Cory Willmott*	167
9	Reclaiming Materials and Fashion-Work in the Urban Philippines *B. Lynne Milgram*	191
10	The City, Clothing Consumption, and the Search for 'the Latest' in Colonial and Postcolonial Zambia *Karen Tranberg Hansen*	215

Bibliography 235
Index 273

The History of Retailing and Consumption
General Editor's Preface

It is increasingly recognised that retail systems and changes in the patterns of consumption play crucial roles in the development and societal structure of economies. Such recognition has led to renewed interest in the changing nature of retail distribution and the rise of consumer society from a wide range of academic disciplines. The aim of this multidisciplinary series is to provide a forum of publications that explore the history of retailing and consumption.

Gareth Shaw, University of Exeter, UK

List of Figures, Maps and Tables

Figures

3.1	Value of textiles in 15 Swedish households compared to the value of furniture, 1673–1753 (in daler)	48
3.2	Value of textiles in 15 Swedish households compared to the total assets, 1673–1753	52
3.3	Selected furniture in Kent, 1600–1750	54

Maps

4.1	The town of Vilafranca del Penedés	69
7.1	The Sokoto Caliphate, now northern Nigeria	144

Tables

4.1	The presence of some 'superfluous' consumption in the Penedés, 1670–90 to 1770–90 (in %)	78
4.2	Structure of the auction of the personal property belonging to the farmer Pau Ferrer (1783)	80
4.3	Peasant consumption of certain items in the Penedés, broken down into different ownership categories 1770–90	81
4.4	The value of the purchases made by men and women at public auctions (in %). Vilafranca del Penedés (1770–90)	87

List of Illustrations

2.1	A 'tour à la mode' around 1650	24
2.2	The 'tapissierspand' was erected in the years 1550–54 to accommodate the thriving trade in tapestries	26
3.1	House of a Chinese official, part of ten drawings illustrating the interior of the house of a Chinese official at Canton. Opaque watercolour, c. 1800–1805. © All Rights Reserved. The British Library Board. Licence Number: UNIWAR03	45
3.2	A Cottage Interior: An Old Woman Preparing Tea, by William Redmore Bigg. Oil on canvas, 1793. Photo © Victoria and Albert Museum, London, 199–1885	46
3.3	Scene in a Bedchamber. Oil on canvas, c. 1695–1704. Photo © Victoria and Albert Museum, London, P.25–1976	50
3.4.	A Lady, attributed to Gilbert Jackson. Oil on canvas, c. 1625–34. Photo © Victoria and Albert Museum, London, 565–1882. Bequeathed by John Jones	55
3.5	Turkish carpet, possibly produced in Turkey or Egypt, c. 1550. Photo © Victoria and Albert Museum, London, 151–1883	56
3.6	Interior with Ladies by a Linen Cupboard by Pieter de Hooch, 1663. Oil on canvas, 72 x 77.5 cm. © Rijksmuseum, Amsterdam	64
6.1	Silk Antislavery Reticule, c. 1827. Photo © Victoria & Albert Museum, London, T.20–1951	122
6.2	Antislavery Potholder, nd, Chicago History Museum	123
6.3	Boston Antislavery Bazaar Pamphlet and Needlebook, 1855. Series 1, no. 9323, American Antiquarian Society	126
7.1	Sokoto Caliphate robe with white silk embroidery on magenta silk narrow strip cloth (barage). Ethnology Department, British Museum, accession # 1920.2-11.1. Photograph by the author. Courtesy of theTrustees of the British Museum, UK	153
7.2	Unfinished robe made of indigo and white cotton narrow strip cloth (sak'i or zabo). Staatliches Museum für Völkerkunde, Munich, accession # 15-26-56. Photograph by S. Autrum-Mulzer. Courtesy of the Staatliches Museum für Völkerkunde, Munich, Germany	156
7.3	British missionaries wearing Sokoto Caliphate robes, c. 1891. Source: C.H. Robinson 1900	160

8.1	Ron Everett Green's formline motifs on evening ensemble worn by Amerindian professional model at Aboriginal Voices Festival in Toronto, 1999 (Photo by Cory Willmott)	174
8.2	Tammy Beauvais, Dene Fur Clouds and D'Arcy Moses designs at Fashion-Nation, international annual trade show at Toronto, 2004 (Photo by and courtesy of Jessie Silverstein)	175
8.3	Flapper Southwestern Blanket Coats by Powers Fashions of Minneapolis, 1925 (Courtesy of Minnesota Historical Society, Loc# GT1.4i r8 Neg# 8463-A)	178
8.4	Fred Picard dress at Museum of Modern Art show in New York City, 1940: Creating a high end fashion market (Courtesy of National Archives and Records Administration, Photo # 75-CL-1R-3)	179
8.5	Design by Rifat Ozbek, Spring/Summer 1992 (Photo by Cory Willmott; courtesy of Victoria and Albert Museum, Catalogue # T.99 to 101–2001)	180
8.6	Turtle Concepts tuxedo vests modelled by Amerindian youths at Canadian Aboriginal Festival (CANAB) at Toronto, 1999 (Photo by Cory Willmott)	181
9.1	Two carrying bags made from recycled plastic juice drink containers. Photograph by B.L. Milgram, Manila, Philippines, 2007	200
9.2	Artisans working in the sewing section of the Artisan Multipurpose Cooperative. Photograph by B.L. Milgram, Manila, Philippines, 2007	203
9.3	A sewer-designer from the Artisan Multipurpose Cooperative. Photograph by B.L. Milgram, Manila, Philippines, 2008	205
9.4	Women working in the Artisan Multipurpose Cooperative. Photograph by B.L. Milgram, Manila, Philippines, 2008	208
9.5	The showroom at the Artisan Multipurpose Cooperative. Photograph by B.L. Milgram, Manila, Philippines, 2008	210
10.1	Fashion sign. Photograph by Karen Tranberg Hansen, 2004	224
10.2	Salaula market. Photograph by Karen Tranberg Hansen, 1992	227
10.3	Chitenge outfits. Photograph by Karen Tranberg Hansen, 2006	228

Notes on Contributors

Eugénie Briot is a Doctor in History of Technology at the Centre d'Histoire des Techniques et de l'Environnement (C.D.H.T.E.) of the Conservatoire National des Arts et Métiers (C.N.A.M., Paris) and an Assistant Professor at the Université Paris-Est Marne-la-Vallée. She has a specific interest in the problems arising from the luxury goods industries, especially as far as the link they maintain with their heritage and history. Her PhD research was devoted to the nineteenth-century French perfumery.

Karen Tranberg Hansen is Professor of Anthropology at Northwestern University. Her books include: *Distant Companions: Servants and Employers in Zambia 1900–1985* (Cornell 1989), *Keeping House in Lusaka* (Columbia 1997), the edited book *African Encounters with Domesticity* (Rutgers 1992), the co-edited book (with Mariken Vaa), *Reconsidering Informality: Perspectives from Urban Africa* (Nordic Africa Institute 2004), and *Salaula: The World of Secondhand Clothing and Zambia* (Chicago, 2000). Her interest in the dressed body culminated in an article in the *Annual Reviews of Anthropology* (2004), entitled 'The World in Dress: Anthropological Perspectives on Clothing, Fashion, and Culture'. Her recent research was part of a collaborative, multi-year project that was conducted in three rapidly growing cities: Recife in Brazil, Hanoi in Vietnam, and Lusaka in Zambia, *Youth and the City in the Global South* (Indiana 2008). She is working with colleagues on a book about dress, performance and popular culture in Africa.

Colleen E. Kriger is Professor of History at the University of North Carolina, Greensboro, USA, where she has been a faculty member since 1993. She focuses her research on artisans, skilled labour and commodity currencies in pre-colonial (pre-twentieth-century) African history. She has published articles in *Journal of African History*, *African Economic History*, *History in Africa* and *Textile History*. Her most recent publications are *Cloth in West African History* (2006) and 'Guinea Cloth' in *The Spinning World: A Global History of Cotton Textiles, 1200–1850* (2009).

Beverly Lemire is Professor of History and Henry Marshall Tory Chair in the Department of History & Classics and the Department of Human Ecology, University of Alberta, Canada. Books include *Fashion's Favourite: The Cotton Trade and the Consumer in Britain, 1660–1800* (1991), *Dress, Culture and Commerce: the English Clothing Trade before the Factory* (1997), and most recently *The Business of Everyday Life: Gender, Practice and Social Politics in England, c. 1600–1900* (2005). She recently published, with Giorgio Riello, 'East and West: Textiles and Fashion in Early Modern Europe', *Journal of Social*

History 41/4 (2008). She is currently investigating the practice of fashion in various European social communities and has a particular interest in the impact of global trade on new fashion forms between 1600 and 1820.

B. Lynne Milgram is professor of anthropology, in the Faculty of Liberal Studies at the Ontario College of Art & Design. Her research in the Philippines analyses the cultural politics of social change with regard to women's informal sector work in crafts, street vending and the secondhand clothing industry. This research is published in edited volumes and in journals. Milgram has co-edited the books: *Economics and Morality: Anthropological Approaches* (with K. Browne, 2009); *Material Choices: Refashioning Bast Fiber Textiles in Asia and the Pacific* (with R. Hamilton, 2007); *Artisans and Cooperatives: Developing Alternative Trade for the Global Economy* (with K. Grimes, 2000).

Belén Moreno Claverías received her Doctor of History (2002) from the European University Institute (Florence) and she was a postdoctoral researcher (2003–2004) at the Ecole des Hautes Etudes en Sciences Sociales (Paris). At the present, and since 2004, she is a professor of Economic History at the Universidad Autónoma de Madrid (Spain). She has worked on the consumption patterns in preindustrial Catalonia, especially on the introduction of new objects in the rural areas and the rise of social inequality between 1670 and 1790. In relation to this line of research, she has also investigated the social differentiation among the peasants taking into account other indicators, apart from consumption, such as the ways to access land and the different agrarian contracts that existed in the eighteenth century. She has several publications about both subjects (see Bibliography).

Giorgio Riello is Associate Professor in Global History and Culture at the Department of History of the University of Warwick. He has written on early modern textiles, dress and fashion in Europe and Asia. He is the author of *A Foot in the Past: Consumers, Producers and Footwear in the Long Eighteenth Century* (Oxford, 2006) and has co-edited *The Spinning World: A Global History of Cotton Textiles, 1200–1850* (Oxford, 2009) and *How India Clothed the World: The World of South Asian Textiles, 1500–1850* (Brill, 2009). He is currently writing a monograph entitled *Global Cotton: The Asian Fabric that Made Europe Rich*.

Alice Taylor is a Social Science & Humanities Research Council of Canada Postdoctoral Fellow in History at the University of Toronto. Her research focuses on abolitionism, children, consumerism and material culture in Anglo-America. She is currently preparing a manuscript for publication *Consuming Freedom: Women, Children and the Transatlantic Abolitionist Marketplace, 1780–1865* and has embarked on two new research projects about juvenile abolitionism and the Free Produce Movement. Taylor has presented her research widely and has published in the *New England Quarterly*, the Routledge *Fashion History Reader* (forthcoming) and the *Encyclopedia of the Material Culture of American Slave*

Life (forthcoming). She received the New England Consortium Fellowship and the Greenfield Fellowship in African American History at the Library Company of Philadelphia.

Ilja Van Damme is a member of the Centre for Urban History at the University of Antwerp, Belgium, where he currently holds a postdoctoral fellowship from the Fund for Scientific Research Flanders (FWO), Belgium. He has written and presented research on such diverse topics as consumption preferences, fashion and taste, advertising and shopping. Currently he is conducting research on the urban history of the eighteenth and nineteenth centuries. In particular he is analysing the rise of an antiquarian culture in Bruges.

Cory Willmott is an Assistant Professor in the Department of Anthropology at Southern Illinois University Edwardsville. Her work focuses on clothing and textiles among Great Lakes Algonquians and Han Chinese in cross-cultural and historical perspective. Recent publications have dealt with topics ranging from fur trade clothing and textiles 'From Stroud to Strouds' in *Textile History* (2005) and 'Dressing for the Homeward Journey' with Kevin Brownlee, in Carolyn Podruchny and Laura Peers (eds), *Gathering Places: Essays on Aboriginal and Fur Trade Histories* (2010), to an ethnography of Amerindian participation in the garment industry 'Aboriginal Labour and the Garment Industry in Winnipeg' with Raymond Wiest, in John Loxley et al. (eds), *Doing Economic Development* and the representation of Amerindian peoples in museum exhibits: 'Visitors Voices' in *Material Culture Review* (2008).

Acknowledgements

This collection developed out of a panel at the International Economic History Congress, Helsinki, 2006, on the theme of 'Fashion, Material Culture and Economic Life: Perspectives Across Time, Place and Politics'. The majority of participants from that session are represented in this volume. However, several key additional chapters have been added, expanding the range of methodological and chronological approaches to this topic, from a variety of geographic perspectives. I thank my panel co-organizer, Laurence Fontaine, who served as discussant in Helsinki and provided cogent and insightful remarks. I also thank the audience at this event for their rigorous and lively questions and comments. The wide-ranging discussions that ensued confirm the significance of this thematic approach. Thanks also go to the panellists and contributors to this volume for their commitment to this project. I am particularly grateful to Lynne Milgram for her timely conversations on this subject and to Karen Tranberg Hansen, Giorgio Riello, Maxine Berg, Ilja Van Damme, Cory Willmott, Bartholomé Yun and Alice Taylor for extensive discussions on the wider issues raised by the close study of fashion's force through time and place. I have also benefited from the insights provided by all the contributors to this volume. Continuing thanks also goes to the University of Alberta for their support of my research agenda and to my colleagues in the Department of Human Ecology; special thanks are extended to Arlene Oak. I have benefited from the time we have spent discussing fashion and the practice of material culture.

Chapter One

Introduction
Fashion and the Practice of History: A Political Legacy

Beverly Lemire

This interdisciplinary volume contributes to a wider comparative assessment of fashion, a multi-faceted phenomenon, expressed in various cultural forms. Fashion as a catalyst of material change, as a visible sign of distinction, has a complex past and an equally dynamic and contentious present. Though fashion's impact is not restricted to dress, the ebb and flow of clothing styles have historically been the most controversial of all the practices in virtually every cultural community. Political economies and cultural discourses of fashion present equally fertile dynamics, having shaped industries, defined communities and sparked conflicts. Yet, the study of fashion is still not comfortably situated within all precincts of the academy. This omission is illustrated, for example, in a recent volume on global history;[1] the absence of 'fashion' in the subject index reflects the still partial recognition of this pivotal topic, despite the fact that the themes addressed in this text, like the global trade in sugar or the industrialization of textile production, were themselves shaped by the social and cultural forces of fashion in various regions of the world. Scrutinized and problematized in some academic quarters, fashion is ignored and disdained in others reflecting the historic discomfort with this subject area in much of the academy. Gaps in scholarship proliferate as a result. At the same time issues surrounding expressions of fashion have frequently been highly politicized. Gender, institutional and imperial politics were among the dynamics that shaped the scholarly reception of this subject, leading to its acceptance (or rejection). However the tide is turning and the intricate cultural and economic forces underlying this phenomenon are more broadly recognized. The chapters included here reflect this new scholarly trajectory reclaiming fashion from the margins, exploring its cultural, economic and social force across time and place. Fashion has shaped markets, defined material priorities and brought profit or loss to its mediators; the fashion for one commodity over another defined

---

[1] Neither 'fashion' nor 'consumerism' was indexed as subjects in this recent survey of world history, the volume written by two of its preeminent exponents. J.R. McNeill and William H. McNeill, *The Human Web: A Bird's Eye View of World History* (New York, 2003), pp. 341, 342.

consumer markets. These and other topics are explored in this collection. Before introducing these findings, however, it is useful to consider the history of the study of fashion more generally and reflect on its variable position within the academy. My focus will be on the English-language tradition of this scholarship with most specific examples arising from Britain and America.

The Study of Fashion

For much of the twentieth century fashion hovered uneasily within the precincts of the modern academy, largely excluded from serious consideration, much like a well-dressed young woman at an inter-war tutorial, too often ignored when there were high-minded conversations among 'serious' men. The ephemeral essence of fashion and its implied frivolousness allowed many to rationalize this disregard. Consumption may indeed be 'the sole end and purpose of all production', as Adam Smith averred.[2] However, the role of fashion in shaping and expressing consumer drives garnered scant attention among academicians for generations. At odds with the major intellectual trajectories of Marxists and liberals, dominant through much of the century, neither camp ascribed importance to this phenomenon, while some were actively hostile to any close analysis of this subject. Clothing, as the most evident manifestation of fashion's force, was similarly neglected within academic circles. This broad disregard or antipathy was of long standing, rooted in the anti-luxury stance found in many religious traditions, which included clear gender biases towards women as the apparent agents of temporal desires. Amanda Vickery observes that: '[s]ocial commentators and moralists have long associated men with the spiritual [or intellectual] world and women with the material. Reputedly man's inferior in reason and public virtue, women have been relentlessly derided for their petty materialism and love of ostentation ... an allied tradition of socialist analysis imbued with a similar Puritanism, has habitually contrasted the cultures of production and consumption.'[3] Thus, irrespective of religious or political creed, there was a deeply held consensus on the triviality of the shifting material forms that were reflections of fashion, a view that was mirrored in twentieth-century scholarly communities.[4] This outlook may in fact explain the persistence of

---

[2] Adam Smith, *An Inquiry into the nature and causes of the wealth of nations...* (1776, London, 1852), p. 274.

[3] Amanda Vickery, 'Women and the world of goods: a Lancashire consumer and her possessions, 1751–81', in John Brewer and Roy Porter (eds), *Consumption and the World of Goods* (London, 1993), p. 274. With some exceptions, my comments on the treatment of fashion scholarship will address primarily the discipline of history and in that respect mostly that of British and western historiography.

[4] Antonia Finnane identifies this antipathy in mid-twentieth-century China, writing that: 'In China, the political climate in the Maoist era was unfavourable to research into fashion and costume history. ... In 1964 the eminent Shen Congwen embarked on an

Thorstein Veblen's interpretation of fashionable consumer practice in the late nineteenth-century American society in which he lived; the explanatory term he coined was 'conspicuous consumption' and he proposed simple emulation as the driving force behind the most evident consumer practices, offering a particular gendered interpretation of a process that he viewed in largely negative terms.[5] His analysis fit easily with the established analytical traditions, as they existed. Yet, despite the long and varied cultural aversion towards the study of fashion, occasional individuals or networks of scholars sought to unravel the puzzling and variable features of its origins, affected communities and political contexts. A contemporary of Veblen, Caroline Foley opined in her 1893 article that the 'study of the consumer … is once more occupying the attention of economic science in England' in a way that was 'more disinterested and genuine than in the past'.[6] The social scientist Georg Simmel approached this subject at the turn of the twentieth century from much the same perspective as Veblen, though offering several additional points on the question. Among other things Simmel observed that fashion was to be found more typically in what he termed 'higher civilizations', where the 'foreignness' of objects added to their attraction, rather than detracting – Simmel defined fashion as purely western and did not suppose it would arise elsewhere.[7] The physical changes evident in turn of the century Europe and America doubtless sparked these contemporary assessments. There was, at that same time, a small but important series of studies published by Johns Hopkins University Press. Across the first three decades of the twentieth century historians began to unravel the legislative and cultural interactions of sumptuary legislation enacted from England through Central Europe.[8] Sumptuary acts and decrees mirrored innovations in style and social self-fashioning. Thus this handful of volumes denotes truly pioneering efforts from at least one sector of the English language academy to understand this phenomenon, an intellectual endeavour that did not reach full fruition and found few followers during that era. A full

---

archival research project on clothing of the imperial era, but the project ground to a halt in the Cultural Revolution. Shen was sent down to the countryside to raise pigs and many of his research notes were destroyed.' *Changing Clothes in China: Fashion, History, Nation* (New York, 2008), p. 3.

[5] Thorstein Veblen, *The Theory of the Leisure Class: an economic study of institutions* (1899, reprinted New York, 1919).

[6] Caroline Foley, 'Fashion', *The Economic Journal*, 3/11 (1893): p. 458.

[7] Georg Simmel, 'Fashion', *International Quarterly*, 10 (1904): p. 136.

[8] Kent Roberts Greenfield, *Sumptuary Law in Nürmberg: a Study in Paternal Government* (Baltimore, 1918); Frances Elizabeth Baldwin, *Sumptuary Legislation and Personal Regulation in England* (Baltimore, 1926) and John Martin Vincent, *Costume and Conduct in the Laws of Basel, Bern and Zurich 1370–1800* (Baltimore, 1935) – the questions arising from fashion and its genesis were apparently being driven by Kent Greenfield of Johns Hopkins University. See, also, Wilfrid Hooper, 'The Tudor Sumptuary Laws', *English Historical Review*, 30 (1915): pp. 433–49.

generation later, in the 1960s there was a further brief flurry of interest in the topic of fashion in business history, where authors promoted the importance of this factor in assessing the development of markets over time.[9] But few university scholars rushed to engage in this research.

In fact, for much of the twentieth century, with these exceptions, the greatest extent of fashion research was undertaken in entirely different institutional venues, by museum curators and curatorial staff, many of whom were trained in the art history tradition, or were inspired by nationalist antiquarianism in the acquisition and study of collections of dress. Museums began establishing collections of textiles and dress from the later 1800s and built their holdings through the twentieth century. Most of these foundational collections were acquired by major museums from a predominantly male cohort of collectors;[10] these objects were then catalogued and placed within a narrative framework by an initially male curatorial staff. Their priorities were typically to assemble and catalogue according to aesthetics criteria of quality and/or nationalistic priorities; these privileged a French silk gown over worn linen shifts for example, or the English-made silk brocade suit rather than a middle-ranked woman's apparel. Cataloguing and collecting concerns were founded on clear aesthetic priorities, which became the basis of clothing analysis. Emulation figured as the driving force of fashion, typically originating in metropoles like Paris and arriving in dilute forms in provincial circles or ranks below the court aristocracy. Curators sought to construct their collections, filling in national narratives with key exemplary pieces. Indeed, the current curator of Colonial Williamsburg, Linda Baumgarten, acknowledges that the survival of garments in museum collections in general 'favors the beautiful and the unusual', while 'art museum's holdings may be limited to high style and designer examples'.[11] Publications produced from these institutions often focused on the cut, structure and fabric composition of garments, along with the shifts in form over time and celebrated elite dress and the social environs of its use.[12] Literary sources, diaries and paper from prominent

---

[9] Dwight E. Robinson, 'The Importance of Fashions in Taste to Business History: An Introductory Essay', *Business History Review*, 37/1/2 (1963): pp. 5–36; Herman Freudenberger, 'Fashion, Sumptuary Laws, and Business', *Business History Review*, 37/1/2 (1963): pp. 37–48; and Herbert Blumer, 'Fashion: From Class Differentiation to Collective Selection', *Sociological Quarterly*, 10/3 (1969): pp. 275–91.

[10] For a discussion of the significance of male collectors and their roles in establishing the collections in major London museums see Julia Petrov, '"The habit of their age": English genre painters, dress collecting, and museums, 1910–1914', *Journal of the History of Collections*, 20/2 (2008): pp. 237–51.

[11] Linda Baumgarten, *What Clothes Reveal: The Language of Clothing in Colonial and Federal America* (New Haven, CT, 2002) p. 2.

[12] The plethora of articles from the early twentieth century in *The Burlington Magazine*, or *The Metropolitan Museum of Art Bulletin*, for example, reflects these preoccupations. Examples include, Frances Morris, 'An Elizabethan Embroidery', *The Metropolitan Museum*

families were scoured for mention of apparel. And works by specialists like Cecil Willett and Phillis Cunnington, whose private collection became the basis for the Platt Hall Gallery of Costume in Manchester, produced shelves of books dating the characteristics of garments specific to time, place and rank. These antiquarian labours were undoubtedly important and provided a foundation from which later scholars could build. Unfortunately, the preoccupations encouraged by this style of work allowed for little or no engagement with scholarly concerns of the day, as for example, the early studies on women's history, the interest in cross-cultural contact through trade, or the growth of the *Annales* school of history in France.[13] Prolific authors, C. Willett and Phillis Cunnington began the *Handbook of English Costume* series in 1952 with the medieval era and proceeded to produce annotated catalogues on the components of dress through succeeding centuries, while also assessing occupational apparel. Some of their volumes are similar in structure to the systematic empirical enumerations of insects or plants; while other volumes included more thematic treatments.[14] Court fashions and the exquisite aesthetics of European elites likewise inspired other authors of the same generation like François Boucher. This work helped define the connoisseurship priorities among curators. Few considered these topics in university settings.[15] For all their enthusiasm and insights, the travails of these authors and the increasing number of female curators at work in post-war museums were largely ignored by academicians and had little if any impact on university courses or research priorities. Their work was

---

of *Art Bulletin*, 18/10 (1923): pp. 228–30; F.M. Kelly 'The Iconography of Costume', *The Burlington Magazine*, 64/375 (June 1934): pp. 278–84.

[13] These examples reflect only several of the major historical/social science developments of the early to mid-twentieth century, none of which are reflected in writings on fashion typical of this period. For a discussion of the academic dynamism surrounding these intellectual developments see, for example: Maxine Berg, *A Woman in History: Eileen Power 1889–1940* (Cambridge, 1996) – Power lectured widely on trans-national questions, so this was a far from isolated intellectual dynamic. She was also one of a number of female scholars to produce histories of women, as for example, Alice Clark, *Working Life of Women in the Seventeenth Century* (London, 1919) or Ivy Pinchbeck, *Women Workers and the Industrial Revolution* (London, 1930). Also, A.O. Hill and B.H. Hill, 'Marc Bloch and Comparative History', *American Historical Review*, 85/4 (1980): pp. 828–57.

[14] C. Willett and Phillis Cunnington, *Handbook of English Mediaeval Costume* (London, 1952) and *Handbook of English Costume in the Sixteenth Century* (London, 1954), *Handbook of English Costume in the Seventeenth Century* (London, 1955), *Handbook of English Costume in the Eighteenth Century* (London, 1957). These volumes were reprinted throughout the 1960s and 1970s; unfortunately there are as yet no entries on either author in the *Oxford Dictionary of National Biography*. Colonial American dress was explored with the same general priorities. See Alice Morse Earle, *Costume in Colonial Times* (New York, 1924).

[15] François Boucher, *20,000 Years of Fashion: the history of costume and adornment* (New York, 1967, new edition 1987); originally, *Histoire du costume en Occident, de l'antiquié à nos jours* (Paris, 1965).

judged to be of little interest in academic disciplines. The focus of those working with collections was very different from that found in universities. Moreover, in the third quarter of the twentieth century, few historians accepted that fashion was a legitimate topic worthy of serious study. They were not alone in this view. Anthropologists of the mid-twentieth century were also reticent to turn their attention to popular or fashionable dress (historical or contemporary).[16]

The neglect of the study of fashion within the discipline of history was less a benign response than a reflection of resistance to ideas, issues or communities outside established academic traditions. As the 1970s dawned, this topic of research was virtually absent in economic and social history, one of the most dynamic fields in the discipline at that time. Joan Thirsk, a historian of early modern England, challenged her colleagues to think more widely on subjects of economic and social change. In 1973, she noted the now glaring gap in scholarship and identified the cause, writing that:

> Fashion is accorded a lowly place by economic historians when they account for the rise of the clothing industries and the changing direction of their trade. They prefer to look for sterner economic explanations, such as the debasement of the coinage, war, new customs tariffs, and occasionally bad (or good) craftsmanship. Thus they turn their back on the evidence of contemporaries, and on the evidence of their own eyes in the modern world.[17]

Thirsk's comments reflect a frustration with the contemporary academic consensus and she went on to offer an example of what scholarship in this field could be, with a lively and discerning study of the role of fashion in the spread of new styles of hosiery in late Elizabethan London. Her's was a rather lonely initiative at this stage. University-based scholars were generally unwilling to engage with this issue, especially as related to dress, except in its most disembodied, aggregate form such as in the production levels of textiles, volumes of cloth traded, organization of labour, or the mechanics of production. Library shelves are filled with scholarly output of this sort, where considerations of the market stopped at questions of taste or avoid altogether considerations of the cultural dynamics of style. Moreover,

---

[16] Karen Tranberg Hansen summarizes recent research in dress in the field of anthropology, tacitly acknowledging the long hiatus before this aspect of material life was addressed in this discipline. Karen Tranberg Hansen, 'The World in Dress: Anthropological Perspectives on Clothing, Fashion, and Culture', *Annual Review of Anthropology*, 33 (2004): pp. 369–92.

[17] Joan Thirsk, 'The Fantastical Folly of Fashion: the English Stocking Knitting Industry, 1500–1700', in N.B. Harte and K.G. Ponting (eds), *Textile History and Economic History: Essays in Honour of Miss Julia de Lacy Mann* (Manchester, 1973), p. 50. Thirsk was among the earliest to write on the subject of popular consumerism in early modern England, a further example of her insightful perspective. *Economic Policy and Projects: the Development of a Consumer Society in Early Modern England* (Oxford, 1978).

there was very little formal collaboration between universities and museums, the site where most fashion research was being conducted. New academic programmes were developing on the history of dress; however, in many instances these were based in Departments of Home Economics or in other sections of the university without the academic authority of long-established fields. At least one author has characterized former academicians, dismissive of these initiatives, as dominated by a pervasive misogyny that gave little value to the material connoisseurship of curators or the knowledge developing in other precincts. Lou Taylor argues that: 'much of this academic criticism [of dress studies] came from male staff of "old" universities and was directed at a field still largely in the hands of women or gay men mostly in museum-based jobs or in "new" universities'.[18] Thus, within the UK universities, a major sector of the economy and a vital facet of human experience remained largely unexamined.

Change was underway, however. In England, one of the new mediating forces was the Pasold Research Fund. Established by the successful textile and clothing industrialist, Eric Pasold, this body was set in motion in the late 1960s and the initial Director, Ken Ponting, began to forge new links between museums and universities, with a focus on the history of textiles and dress. The beginnings of a fruitful interdisciplinary exchange were launched.[19] Negley Harte, who succeeded as Director, also advocated a closer collaboration of those working in the field, a process that was very much in its infancy. Harte acknowledged at the time that: 'The work of scholars approaching the history of dress from the point of view of the history of art or the history of material culture ... has not been integrated into economic or social history.' He likewise noted that the study of fashion was too commonly 'isolated from the rest of history'. However, Harte was also scathing about what he saw as the deficiencies of 'dress-studies' programmes; yet despite his comments, there can be no doubt about the efforts expended to bridge an academic chasm. Recognition was growing that these barriers needed to be addressed.[20] Further Pasold-funded conferences followed on a routine basis through the 1980s and 1990s, setting an example of inter-institutional collaboration that others

---

[18] Lou Taylor, *The Study of Dress History* (Manchester, 2002), p. 64.

[19] David Jenkins, 'Textile History: 40 Years On', *Textile History*, 39/1 (2008): pp. 10–11; and D.C. Coleman, 'Ken Ponting: An Appreciation', *Textile History*, 14/2 (1983): pp. 108–13.

[20] Negley Harte, 'Foreward', in 'Fabrics and Fashions: Studies in the economic and Social History of Dress'. Special Issue, *Textile History*, 22/2 (1991): p. 150. This special issue arose from a conference in 1985, the 1980s being the gestation period for these comments. In France there were evidently similar chasms between those who undertook curatorial or art history-based costume study and the wider historical profession. The noted French historian, Daniel Roche, remarked on the twentieth-century labours of costume historians that with '[a] few recent examples apart, it is a history which has not yet discovered how to respond to the questions which professionals ... have been asking for fifty years.' Daniel Roche, *The Culture of Clothing: dress and fashion in the ancien régime* (Cambridge, 1994), p. 5.

followed. A sea change was taking place on several fronts, with a growing focus on the elements of everyday material life.

One of the significant transformative forces was the new scholarship on women's history, followed by gender history. As is widely known, research on women's experience and practice gained momentum from the 1970s and claimed respectable academic status in the succeeding decades, while at the same time the past and present understanding of women from all social classes became the subject of intensive study and new interpretations. Within this context, women's pivotal roles as makers of fashion, agents of fashion, and subjects of fashion received fresh scrutiny. Particular attention was focused on their selection, management and repair of textiles, adoption of new forms of sociability such as tea drinking and their agency in shops and shopping. The shifting material context of daily life was scrutinized more extensively than ever before, a development not without contradictions and contentions. As Vickery asserts, 'much [early] feminist scholarship has displayed equal suspicion of the world of commodities, viewing fashion in particularly negative terms as emblematic of woman's decorative dependence, the gilding on the patriarchal cage'.[21] Yet the importance of possessions in the evolution of society could not be gainsaid. The interrogation of masculine social, political and material forms followed suit, with similarly important contributions to the understanding of material flows and their meanings. Close assessments of communities of various ethnicities, religions and social class revealed further complex processes of material self-definition, animating the understanding of fashion.[22] Interdisciplinary cross-pollination was encouraged by the spreading interdisciplinary influence of anthropologists like Marcel Mauss whose focus was re-oriented towards western society, as well as by anthropologists like Mary Douglas who re-examined western material practices anew. A new generation of scholars like Grant McCracken and Daniel Miller refocused attention on the circulation of goods; while French theorists like Pierre Bourdieu and Roland Barthe added new dimensions to the cultural engagement with objects in contemporary culture, devising theories later applied to previous time periods.[23]

---

[21] Vickery, 'Women and the world of goods', p. 274.

[22] For examples of new patterns of research see: Didier Gondola, 'Dream and Drama: The Search for Elegance among Congolese Youth', *African Studies Review*, 42/1 (1999): pp. 23–48; Margot Finn, 'Men's Things: Masculine Possession in the Consumer Revolution', *Social History*, 25/2 (2000): pp. 133–55; Sophie White, '"Wearing three or four handkerchiefs around his collar, and elsewhere about him": Constructions of Masculinity and Ethnicity in French Colonial New Orleans', *Gender & History*, 15/3 (2003) 528–49; Peter McNeil and Giorgio Riello, 'The Art and Science of Walking: Gender, Space and the Fashionable Body in the Long Eighteenth Century', *Fashion Theory*, 9/2 (2005): pp. 175–204.

[23] Marcel Mauss, *The Gift: Forms and Functions of Exchange in Archaic Societies*, translated by Ian Cunnison, (London, 1954) original French edition 1925; Mary Douglas and Baron Isherwood, *The World of Goods: Towards an Anthropology of Consumption* (New York, 1979) and for a collection of previously published essays Douglas, *Thought*

Simultaneously, from the 1970s onwards, quantitative historians began the painstaking exercise of measuring the goods owned across time and place in various Atlantic world communities – quantitative and qualitative analyses facilitated judicious comparisons. The assessment of probate inventories from the seventeenth through the eighteenth centuries enabled the possibility of large-scale comparisons of material life across a cross-section of people. Gender, social and regional distinctions could now be measured, at least in part, opening new research agendas. The works that ensued posed questions about the selection and meanings attached to the changing array of goods in the early modern era. In the United States the focus on material culture studies was driven in part by unique museum/academic alliances, epitomized by the scholars based in Colonial Williamsburg, the Winterthur Museum and Hagley Museum and Library programmes, which focused on the study of America's complex colonial past, employing both material and archival resources.[24] More researchers grasped the cultural power embedded in articles traded or created, bought, gifted or bequeathed and their studies garnered growing accolades and attention. These initiatives were paralleled by other ground-breaking assessments of material change. In England, Joan Thirsk's 1978 volume revealed the growing early modern production and trade in niceties and small fashionable accoutrements, a process she dated from the later sixteenth century and termed 'The Development of a Consumer Society in Early Modern England'.[25] The cheap lace, ribbons, combs, buttons, tobacco

---

Styles: Critical Essays on Good Taste (London, 1996); Grant McCracken, *Culture and Consumption: New Approaches to the Symbolic Character of Consumer Goods and Activities* (Bloomington, IN, 1987); Daniel Miller, *Material Culture and Mass Consumption* (Oxford, 1987); Pierre Bourdieu, *Distinction: a social critique of the judgement of taste* translated by Richard Nice (French edition 1979, Cambridge MA, 1984); Roland Barthes, *The Fashion System*, translated by Matthew Ward and William Howard (New York, 1983).

[24] In the use of probate inventories see, for example, Lorna Weatherill, *Consumer Behaviour and Material Culture in Britain 1660–1760* (London, 1988); Micheline Bauland, Anton J. Schuurman and Paul Servais (eds), *Inventaires Après-Decès et Ventes de Meubles: Apports à une histoire de la vie économique et quotidienne (XIVe–XIXe siècle)* (Louvain-la Veuve, 1988); Carole Shammas, *The Pre-Industrial Consumer in England and America* (New York, 1990); Cary Carson, Ronald Hoffman and Peter J. Albert (eds), *Of consuming interests: the style of life in the eighteenth century* (Charlottesville, 1994) and especially Lois Green Carr and Lorena S. Walsh 'Changing Lifestyles and Consumer Behavior in the Colonial Chesapeake', in Carson, Hoffman and Albert, *Of consuming interests*, pp. 59–166. The launch of the *Winterthur Portfolio* in 1964 marks the singular development of material culture studies in the US. For a discussion of the methodologies involved see, for example, Jules Prown, 'Mind into Matter: An Introduction to Material Culture Theory and Method', *Winterthur Portfolio*, 17/1 (1982): pp. 1–19 and for a more recent discussion of this field see Ann Smart Martin, *Buying into the World of Goods: Early Consumers in Backcountry Virginia* (Baltimore, 2008), pp. xi–xii.

[25] Joan Thirsk, *Economic Policy and Projects: The Development of a Consumer Society in Early Modern England* (Oxford, 1978). Careful attention to issues of dress did

pipes and hand-mirrors circulating in early modern England represented important new facets of production in this region of Europe. The demand for these goods also signalled novel social priorities and inaugurated new cultural practices across the labouring and middling folk. Thirsk points to the spread of these and other products as marking qualitative societal changes. Through the dynamic of these revisionist approaches, explanations of the onset of industrialization were revised, taking account of the power of popular vogues and the complex patterns of fashion. With the 1982 publication of *The Birth of a Consumer Society* Neil McKendrick, John Brewer and J.H. Plumb laid claim to the 'Commercialization of Fashion' in eighteenth-century Britain. A corner had been turned and the stuff of everyday life was assiduously dissected in an increasing range of communities in an effort to gauge the elements involved and dynamic processes of change.[26]

As one century ended and another began, the subject of fashion was no longer a marginal area of research within the academy – the intermittent trickle of studies was now a steady flow, with most of the attention directed at Europe and the American colonies.[27] Given the size and numbers of universities in North America, not to mention those of western Europe, this momentum is hardly surprising. But the concentrated examination of consumerism and fashion, and the focus on the Atlantic world, produced a significant interpretative imbalance at a time when scholarly research was also flourishing on non-western regions of the world and when global geo-politics was also in flux. This is a necessarily abbreviated account. Yet it is essential to acknowledge the issues that arose as a result of the initial geographic focus on the study of fashion.

One of the major contributors to the shifting scholarship on early modern life was the critically important scholar, Fernand Braudel. Braudel was a noted

---

not immediately take hold among historians, however. Some years later Margaret Spufford observed that: 'The social historian does not normally look at histories of costume with a serious analytical eye.' *The Great Reclothing of Rural England: Petty Chapmen and their Wares in the Seventeenth Century* (London, 1984), p. 98.

[26] For another example, E.L. Jones, 'The Fashion Manipulators: Consumer Tastes and British Industries, 1660–1800', in L.P. Cain and P.J. Uselding (eds), *Business Enterprise and Economic Change* (Kent, Ohio, 1973). Neil McKendrick, John Brewer and J.H. Plumb, *The Birth of a Consumer Society: the Commercialization of Eighteenth-Century England* (London, 1982); see also, Daniel Roche, *La Culture des apparences* (1989) translated as *The culture of clothing*; Beverly Lemire, *Fashion's Favourite: the Cotton Trade and the Consumer in Britain 1669–1800* (Oxford, 1991); and the myriad of articles in John Brewer and Roy Porter (eds), *Consumption and the World of Goods* (London, 1993).

[27] Fashion is defined here as antithetical to a reverence for material tradition; rather it reflects 'a love of change for its own sake, the need for novelty; [and] more technically ... the organic play impulses' shaping individuals and groups in complex ways. D.E. Allen, 'Fashion as a Social Process', *Textile History*, 22/2 (1991): p. 349. In his study of fashion, consumption and sumptuary legislation in various Western and Asian societies, Hunt emphasizes fashion's role as privileging change over tradition. Alan Hunt, *Governance of the Consuming Passions: A History of Sumptuary Law* (Basingstoke, 1996), p. 44.

historian of the *Annales* school of French history which emphasized long-term examinations of daily life. Braudel produced a magisterial three-volume work, *Civilization and Capitalism*, a comparative investigation of the rise of western capitalism from 1500 to 1800. Published in 1979 in French, the first English-language translation appeared in 1981 and had an immediate and long-term impact on research priorities. In this, Braudel justified the study of what he termed the 'material economy' and he included several significant sections on fashion. Braudel posed the critical question: 'Is fashion in fact such a trifling thing? Or is it, as I prefer to think, rather an indication of deeper phenomena – of the energies, possibilities, demands and *joie de vivre* of a given society, economy and civilization?'[28] He championed a rigorous examination of this subject challenging the casual disparagement still typical in many intellectual circles; his work inspired subsequent generations of researchers.[29] In this respect Braudel contributed significantly to the changing attitude towards this facet of human culture, politics and economy. However, Braudel's assertions on fashion also buttressed existing preconceptions. His vision of fashion was fundamentally Eurocentric; likewise, he envisaged fashion as flourishing solely within the highest social realms. Braudel hypothesized a material world that 'stood still' within Europe, with the exception of the elites, claiming as well that the desire for fashion was alien to the great centres of Eurasian civilization in China, Japan, India and Turkey.[30] He had held these views for some years and they remained unchanged in his later life.[31] He offered as proof of the absence of fashion outside Europe statements made by early modern European visitors to non-European regions at the time when these travellers were beginning to articulate a European exceptionalism. Braudel likewise reflected the deep-seated Hegelian perspective that permeated the western academy, which placed ancient non-western civilizations 'outside the domain of history'.[32] On this basis, Braudel, a specialist in French and Mediterranean history, claimed fashion for Europe and Europe alone. Furthermore, he insisted that the exemplars of fashion were only to be found within the courts, among the aristocracy and comparable elites; he recognized no 'street styles' in the early modern cities despite the flow of cheap and novel commodities that flowed through these cities. Nor did he suppose there was a robust self-fashioning among the bourgeois ranks except with those styles that trickled down from the court in dilute form to be mimicked by social inferiors.

---

[28] Fernand Braudel, *Civilization & Capitalism 15th–18th Century: The Structure of Everyday Life*, translated from the French by Siân Reynolds, (New York, 1985), p. 323.

[29] For example, Roche, *Culture of Clothing*. In this context Roche observes that: 'the history of material culture and the history of social behaviour are directly linked, as Fernand Braudel has shown.' (4).

[30] Braudel, *Structure of Everyday Life*, pp. 312–13.

[31] Fernand Braudel, *Capitalism and Material Life, 1400-1800*, translated by Miriam Kochan, (New York, 1973), p. 231.

[32] Finnane, *Changing Clothes*, p. 7. She further develops this critique in the first chapter of this book.

His declarations carried immense authority. His viewpoint was a common one throughout much of the post-war academy to the 1970s and 1980s. Given the dominance of western scholarship in the burgeoning field of consumerism and fashion and the wealth of publications that had accumulated over decades, it is perhaps not surprising that fashion was assumed by many to be a creature of Europe, only later 'exported' to other regions of the world with the development of regional, modern economies.[33] The list of those who unthinkingly subscribed to this doctrine is long and includes many who are otherwise thoughtful when considering other elements of the fashion question. French sociologist, Gilles Lipovetsky, certainly reflects the Eurocentric treatise, insisting that fashion 'took hold in the modern West and nowhere else'.[34] This view stubbornly persists. It is an often-unexamined assumption that remains comfortably ensconced in contemporary scholarship. More recently, two prominent academics in the field of fashion studies, Linda Welters and Abby Lillethun, explicitly insisted on this point in the introduction to their new *Fashion Reader*, writing that 'Fashion was born in Europe and it developed there', excluding the possibility of other points of origin.[35] Lipovetsky rightly decries the fact that even in the late 1980s, at the time of writing his volume, 'the question of fashion is not a fashionable one among intellectuals'.[36] But it is equally disturbing that those considering this topic should blithely claim fashion for Europe and Europe's ruling orders alone in human history, taking into account none of the recent scholarship arising from other world regions, interrogating other economies and societies.[37]

These claims raise significant problems for historians of the west. In the first instance, as Peter Burke writes: '[h]istorians of Europe will never be able to say what is specifically western unless they look outside the west'.[38] If, for example, fashion was employed as a political sign or politicizing force in the west, does this mean that it was not used for comparable purposes elsewhere before the twentieth century? In this regard, one of our authors in this collection makes

---

[33] With slight caveats, this is pretty much the picture painted by Peter Stearns in his introduction to the study of world consumerism. Peter N. Stearns, *Consumerism in World History: The Global Transformation of Desire* (New York, 2001), p. i.

[34] Gilles Lipovetsky, *The Empire of Fashion: Dressing Modern Democracy* translated by Catherine Porter (Princeton, 1994), p. 15. For a similar viewpoint see also, Anne Hollander, *Sex and Suits: The Evolution of Modern Dress* (New York, 1994), pp. 17–18.

[35] Linda Welters and Abby Lillethun (eds), *The Fashion Reader* (Oxford and New York, 2007), p. xx.

[36] Lipovetsky, *Empire of Fashion*, p. 3.

[37] This remains a contentious subject. A similar conclusion about Europe's singular role in the origins of fashion was recently presented by Marco Belfanti. 'Was fashion a European invention?', *Journal of Global History*, 3 (2008): pp. 419–43.

[38] Peter Burke, '*Res et verba*: conspicuous consumption in the early modern world', in John Brewer and Roy Porter (eds), *Consumption and the World of Goods* (London, 1993), p. 148.

plain the specific features of politicized fashions in nineteenth-century Islamic West Africa. Several years ago Sandra Niessen offered her critical assessment on the way in which the study of fashion had developed. Niessen notes that fashion history was founded on the precepts of western art history, which originally supposed a singular artistic tradition in the west and nowhere else. And while this perspective has long since been discarded among art historians themselves, the structural legacy of this perspective persisted in the study of fashion. Sandra Niessen observes: 'The definition of fashion was designed and assigned within the crucible of social Darwinism by those who *could*. In addition, descriptions of the system of dress found in the West were used as the [narrow] definition of fashion.'[39] Just as recent generation of art historians recast the once insular western interpretation of art,[40] many of the western-centred and class-based assumptions iterated with respect to fashion are being challenged. Niessen demands more careful comparative assessments of fashion, especially with respect to the history of apparel, to confront assumptions that have remained persistently in place for too long. The time is ripe to revise the claims advanced so uncritically, bringing western experiences in conversation with Asian, African and American. This volume contributes to the wider dialogue now underway, one that spans social class, ethnicities and regions. And, indeed, the necessity of this broader range of comparisons has never been more compelling.

Jack Goody is another of the scholars to question the unthinking assumptions of western exceptionalism entrenched in many disciplines. Over his lengthy career Goody has sought to determine what indeed was unique in the western experience and what was symptomatic of broader social or economic changes, symptoms shared by various parts of Eurasia, Africa or the Americas. He has written recently that 'with regard to the claim that fashion was uniquely European, Braudel was quite wrong'.[41] Goody insists that 'the use of clothing for distinguishing status and of laws to protect that, the role of fashion, while these vary, they are not unique to one culture in Eurasia but are found in all the major urbanized societies'.[42] However, some definitions of fashion can, when constructed around particular western examples, by their very specificity exclude other societies and clothing systems from consideration. Antonia Finnane critiques one theorist on precisely this point, noting that 'when fashion is defined very narrowly on the basis of particular empirical details as "a particular sort of society", the possibility of any other

---

[39] Sandra Niessen, 'Re-Orienting Fashion Theory', in Linda Welters and Abby Lillethun (eds), *The Fashion Reader* (Oxford and New York, 2007), pp. 106–7.

[40] See, for example, Ruth B. Phillips, *Trading Identities: The Souvenir in Native North American Art from the Northeast, 1700–1900* (Washington, 1998); Rosamund E. Mack, *Bazaar to Piazza: Islamic Trade and Italian Art 1300–1600* (Berkeley, 2002); Deborah Cherry and Janice Helland (eds), *Local/Global: Women Artists in the Nineteenth Century* (Aldershot, UK, 2006).

[41] Jack Goody, *The Theft of History* (Cambridge, 2007), p. 265.

[42] Goody, *Theft of History*, p. 265.

clothing culture being described as [having] "fashion" is by definition excluded'.[43] It behoves scholars to question general assertions on which intellectual edifices have been built.[44] The specificities of time and place must be more carefully addressed, with variations and commonalities mapped, in all societies, among a range of social groups, over a variety of time periods and including an array of commodities and their uses. This wider project requires collective effort.

Significant advances in scholarship are taking place. Fashion is increasingly recognized as a powerful, variable force shaping economies, cultures and societies; and this phenomenon is now the focus of many individual and collective investigations.[45] This topic is also an ingredient in an increasing number of projects; subtly mutable, with sometimes contradictory features, and closely connected to political and economic change, the better we understanding fashion's force the more fully we can explain past and present societies.[46] But it would be simple-minded to assume that so deep-seated a resistance to the study of fashion would be readily over-turned. It is somewhat ironic to find evidence of this resistance among modern French historians. Mary Lynn Stewart begins her recent monograph with the statement that: '[t]his book challenges the notion that fashion, including *haute couture*, is a trivial or marginal subject for serious historians'. She goes on to observe that 'Biographies of famous designers and studies of new styles have made little impression on twentieth-century economic, social, or gender history. Even the fine cultural history of *haute couture* by fashion historian Valerie Steel has barely infiltrated the new cultural history.'[47] The study of opponents of fashion is itself a worthy academic topic – indeed, anti-fashion has been in evidence since the birth of this social force. But denying the rich kaleidoscope effects of

---

[43] Finnane, *Changing Clothes*, p. 9. She also notes the unease with the Braudelian claims evinced by other scholars like Ruth Barnes and Joanne Eicher, at a time when there was little in the way of non-Western scholarship on dress and fashion.

[44] Craig Clunas, 'Modernity Global and Local: Consumption and the Rise of the West', *American Historical Review*, 104/5 (1999): pp. 1497–511.

[45] The establishment of the Centre for Fashion Studies at the University of Stockholm in 2006 is further indication of the growing dynamism in this field, likewise the adoption of the theme of fashion study by organizations such as the European Business History Association for their 2009 conference.

[46] For examples of the recent and diverse expressions of fashion scholarship see: Irene V. Guenther, 'Nazi "Chic"? German Politics and Women's Fashions, 1915–1945', *Fashion Theory*, 1/1 (1997): pp. 29–58; Laura Fair, 'Dressing Up: Clothing, Class and Gender in Post-Abolition Zanzibar', *Journal of African History*, 39/1 (1998): pp. 63–94; Jennifer Jones, *Sexing La Mode: Gender, Fashion and Commercial Culture in Old Regime France* (Oxford and New York, 2004); Hyung Gu Lynn, 'Fashioning Modernity: Changing Meanings of Clothing in Colonial Korea', *Journal of International and Area Studies*, 11/3 (2005): pp. 75–93; the special issue 'Cultures of Clothing in Later Medieval and Early Modern Europe', *Journal of Medieval and Early Modern Studies*, 39/3 (2009).

[47] Mary Lynn Stewart, *Dressing Modern Frenchwomen: Marketing Haute Couture, 1919–1939* (Baltimore, 2008), p. xi.

this phenomenon, for moral or political reasons, is a very different proposition than a wilful academic blindness to the power of this extraordinary process in human endeavours.

Further research is essential; comparisons and contrasts are indispensable, particularly those that bring various regions of the world into dialogue. What will ultimately emerge is a clearer recognition of the many and various material and social forms, some of which stretch the boundaries of fashion as currently described. Fashion has been part of the lexicon of protest; it is a feature of economic development and a vehicle of cultural expression. Businesses have failed through neglect of the mechanics of popular fashion and social movements have crafted dynamic fashions for political ends. Unpacking these complex human facets is a vital part of contemporary scholarship. The contributors to this volume make a contribution to this on-going venture.

This Volume

I have given particular attention above to the evolution of scholarship in fashion and to recent implicit debates surrounding fashion's western and non-western features. In the western intellectual tradition Asia was routinely cited as the antithesis of Europe, presented, as Antonia Finnane notes 'in binary opposition to Europe – as lacking in fashion among many other things'.[48] That said, this collection is not devoted to a comparative assessment of the fashion practices of Europe and Asia, worthy though that project may be. The concept of 'Asia' represented an intellectual marker at various times for all non-western societies whether or not they had that geographic locale. This collection includes studies from various parts of the world and various communities. Those chapters based in Europe approach the subject from a range of original perspectives. The complementary and contrasting themes explored by the authors break down the dichotomies of western/non-western scholarship, illustrating some commonalities, as well as regional and chronological distinctions. We must embrace a wider range in our readings (geographically and chronologically) in order to find the sites of difference and commonality. As Craig Clunas observes: 'The point is not that we need less work ... we need if anything much more.'[49] Thematic and regional specializations are necessary to advance knowledge. But it is equally important to put regions once seen as exotically unique in dialogue with more familiar zones, which in themselves reflect heterogeneous experiences. This inclusive assemblage breaks down knowledge barriers and demands that scholars more comfortable with particular areas or time periods adopt a more inclusive posture. The contributors here figure in this critical dynamic. Collectively, the authors present new insights, examining less-typical forces and forms of the fashion

[48] Finnane, *Changing Clothes*, p. 10.
[49] Clunas, 'Modernity Global and Local', p. 1507.

process; the combined impetus of these contributors signals the new patterns of scholarship.

How did fashion as a cultural force shape various societies? In what ways did fashion affect political agendas? What were the mechanics of the spread or restraint of fashion? These are some of the questions that underpin this volume, at the cusp of cultural, social and economic interactions. This collection engages with the complex history and present-day practice of fashion from a cross-cultural perspective. Fashion as Alan Hunt observed puts 'some conscious valuation on change' in material expressions of both individuals and groups; and while it is reasonable to distinguish between 'change' and 'fashion', the social elements that manipulate and privilege change through expressions of style suggest the sometimes problematic intersections that can arise.[50] The topics extend widely from early modern European domestic décor to abolitionist fancy work, from French perfumes to northern Nigerian robes and Philippine fashion accessories created from recycled containers. The values assigned particular items and the contexts in which they were supplied or constrained carry important information, offering revelations about fashion practice in a global context. Moving from a close examination of the middlemen in early modern Antwerp, the constraints on fashions in rural Spain, the political fashioning of First Nations designers in North America and the search for 'the Latest' in post-colonial Zambia provides important insights into fashion's force.

The debate persists with respect to the points of origin of fashion; but there can be no doubt of its multifaceted forms and directions, both in historical and contemporary periods. Commercial vigour based on trade, as well as urban dynamism appear to be essential requisites, where change and distinction (however contentious) featured in the selection of possessions and diffusion of styles. Additional histories of fashion may be found in commercial cities along major trade routes in the classical or medieval periods; certainly the nineteenth- and twentieth-century studies of fashion make clear its varied nature in many locales. Fashion takes many forms and it is not a unitary force. Nor should it be understood as simply the formalized expression of modern industry and media, driven by seasonal imperatives.[51] Fashion's history and practice arises from an amalgam of stimuli specific to time and place, a catalyst essential in the consumer process, shaping the range of materials desired, bought, used, remade and resold. The renewed academic focus on fashion promises critical contributions to the understanding of continuity and change in human society.

Early European disputes surrounding fashion are the starting point of the volume. Debates flowed across Europe arising from a deep-seated antipathy towards *la mode* and its challenge to the structural hierarchies of dress, as well

---

[50] Hunt, *Governance of the Consuming Passions*, p. 44.

[51] In this respect, the use of theories such as those of Roland Barthes, based on twentieth-century fashion media and industrial capacity, must be used with caution. Barthes, *The Fashion System*.

as vested interests among commercial communities. Fashion is commonly associated with flourishing trade. But there are other faces to this phenomenon. Ilja Van Damme focuses on a formerly dynamic trading city at its ebb. Antwerp lost its standing as an urban commercial powerhouse during the seventeenth and eighteenth centuries; and for many in Antwerp fashion seemed a threat, as local commentators bemoaned the craze for all things French. However, even as Flemish styles declined, along with prominent Flemish trades, retailers flourished serving local bourgeois with French-inspired styles, driving the retail sector. But as Giorgio Riello makes clear, not all patterns of consumption followed a similar chronology and not all styles are crafted for the body. The creation of a fashionable European home and the role of textiles in this process had a very different context and time-line. Beds and bedding, for example, were uniquely expensive investments throughout early modern Europe and were imbued with social expectations in ways different from clothing; the formulating of new styles of bedding took unique shapes in various parts of the continent. The trajectories of fashion are diverse and rural setting cannot be overlooked in the equation. Belén Moreno Claverías explores the spread of stylish goods within eighteenth-century Catalan society and shows the importance of cultural norms, as well as legal prescription, in the diffusion of newly fashionable wares. Her findings offer an important alternative vantage point to the well-studied urban centres of Europe. The meanings of goods are explored in a number of contexts, but no commodity was more ephemeral or more challenging for fashion marketing than scent. Eugénie Briot brings another new perspective with the selling of scent in nineteenth-century Paris and the creation of fashionable outlets for perfume, framed by explicit gender and class prescriptions. Politics and gender figure in several very distinct histories of fashion, illuminating the complexity of material politics. Alice Taylor and Colleen Kriger offer further unique examinations of the variability of nineteenth-century fashion politics: Taylor introduces the political dynamic of American anti-slavery bazaars, managed and directed by abolitionist women; Kriger introduces the new forms of male dress sanctioned in post-*jihad* northern Nigeria and adopted by generations of Muslim men. In both instances fashion was deployed for political ends, within particular regional circumstances and with distinctively different urban and trade contexts.

In the third and final section of this volume, three authors consider the interaction of fashion and community from perspectives that resonate with previously introduced themes. Economic decisions necessarily complicate fashion agendas and the particularity of place is a common thread running through all chapters in this section. Cory Willmott examines the nature of fashion production among indigenous peoples of North America, with particular attention to Canadian First Nations designers. Politics and fashion are intertwined in unique practices of self-representation that also aim to turn a profit. Lynne Milgram introduces another instance of effective political fashions, through a present-day Manila cooperative that produces fashion handbags from recycled plastic juice containers. The nationalist associations of the fruit imagery printed on the juice packets figure centrally in the cachet of the accessories. Milgram tracks the intersection of style and politics, showing the unexpected ways in which women reconfigured materials and opportunities in a global economy. Politics and fashion intersect in intriguing ways. In the final chapter, Karen Tranberg Hansen examines the ways in which the priorities and concerns of Zambian consumers reshaped the clothing markets in that Central African country. The style preferences of ordinary Zambians were given material expression through garments ordered from catalogues or bought from local secondhand dealers, but in all instances these items were selected or modified to fit distinct Zambian tastes. The power of regional communities to shape local and even international markets is one of the telling findings of recent scholarship.[52]

As these last authors make clear, the force of fashion interacts with and is shaped by the community within which it arises, as well as through the intersection of external economic, social and political trends. Changing sensibilities have profound consequences for economic practice; equally, political culture, social cohesion and aesthetic expressions combined to colour the time period and shape behaviours in distinctive ways. The cultural turn of recent decades has yielded an intense inter-disciplinary focus on material culture and has produced a wealth of studies exploring the acquisition and use of goods in many societies, as well as the contentious nature of certain patterns of fashion consumption or consuming populations.[53] We can now better gauge standards of living as well as the symbolic meanings of everyday and exceptional commodities. Building on the work of past and present generations of scholars, this collection challenges old geographic and cultural dichotomies. It further problematizes issues of social rank, region, ethnicity and gender in articulations of fashion. The debates reflected in this volume will continue at a greater pace in the years ahead.

---

[52] For another example of this phenomenon see, Jeremy Prestholdt, 'On the Global Repercussions of East African Consumerism', *American Historical Review*, 109/3 (2004): pp. 755–81.

[53] *Fashion Theory: the Journal of Dress, Body and Culture* was launched in 1997, marking the now respectable study of fashion in this and other contexts. The recent historiographic trend, which recognized the importance of shifting patterns of consumption, has transformed the scholarly landscape. Several influential and recent examples include: Ann Rosalind Jones and Peter Stallybrass, *Renaissance Clothing and the Materials of Memory* (Cambridge, 2000); Timothy Brook, *The confusions of pleasure: commerce and culture in Ming China* (Berkeley, 1998); S.A.M. Adshead, *Material Culture in Europe and China, 1400–1800: the rise of consumerism* (New York, 1997); Karen Tranberg Hansen, *Salaula: The World of Secondhand Clothing and Zambia* (Chicago, 2000); Jean Allman (ed.), *Fashioning Africa: Power and the Politics of Dress* (Bloomington, IN, 2004); Robert Ross, *Clothing: A Global History. Or, the Imperialists' New Clothes* (Cambridge, 2008).

PART ONE
Fashion Practice in Early Modern Europe

Chapter Two
Middlemen and the Creation of a 'Fashion Revolution': The Experience of Antwerp in the Late Seventeenth and Eighteenth Centuries

Ilja Van Damme

At the end of the seventeenth century, a period ravaged by political and economic turmoil, Pieter Cardon published a curious treatise in the Southern Netherlands. Clearly written from a mercantilist stance, the author vigorously attacked all the trappings he held responsible for the 'ruin and poverty of the Spanish Netherlands'.[1] In his opinion, only severe protectionism, strategies of import-substitution and product innovation could lift the country out of the doldrums. However, the self-indulgence and 'blind vanity' of contemporary consumers would be hard to overcome. To prove this point, Cardon analyses the sales practices of an Antwerp textile trader. Unsuccessful at selling his homemade silks of the highest quality, even at rock bottom prices, the retailer sets up an intriguing deal with a fellow merchant of Cambrai, in northern France. This last trader sold the Antwerp silks at double the price in France, and sent the lesser textiles back to the Antwerp merchant, but now with the label '*fabriqué à Paris*' ['made in Paris'] attached to them. And behold! The same products that were not wanted 'because of the name of the city of Antwerp', were now eagerly bought by 'all the principal ladies in town'. And everybody, unwilling to follow this 'new, French fashion', was mocked as a 'hypocrite and a fool, not knowing what fashion was'.[2]

---

[1] [Pieter Cardon], *Den oorspronck van de ruïne en armoede der Spaensche Nederlanden alsmede de aenwijsingen der hulpmiddelen om de selve landen wederom te herstellen ende in de selve te doen herleven den afgestorven koophandel, schipvaert, landtbouw, 't maecken van manufacturen ende alderhande soorten van handtwercken, tot een algemeyne welvaeren van de ingesetenen van de selve landen* (Liège, 1699). All quotations were taken from this second, revised edition (originally printed in 1691, but identically reprinted in Liège in 1699 by Geraert Cho(d)kier). The original, anonymous edition dates back from 1686 and can still be found in Municipal Archive Antwerp (MAA), *Pamphlets*, nr. 531/2.

[2] [Cardon], *Den oorspronck van de ruïne en armoede*, pp. 17–18: '*al degene die dese nieuwe Parijsche mode niet naer en volgden, wirden uyt-gemaeckt voor hypocryten oft slechthoofden en als niet wetende wat de mode was*'.

This amusing anecdote neatly illustrates the growing 'tyranny' of French fashions in the Antwerp society at the end of the seventeenth century, a phenomenon that persisted through most of the eighteenth century as well. Moreover, it introduces some of the themes and questions I will discuss in this chapter. After all, Cardon not only signals fashion as a reality to be reckoned with, he gives a partial explanation of its power and origins as well. Neither the quality of the inland production nor the cheap prices could convince consumers to buy what they bought. Already in the seventeenth century, the wealthy customers of a provincial town – which Antwerp had become at this time – were 'frenzied' to follow the current fashions. However, in struggling to be '*à la mode*', consumers were evidently fooled by the manipulations of cunning retailers and merchants. According to the same author, these tradesmen were at the root of all evils because they had encouraged the infatuation of their countrymen for the 'cursed' French imports.

Is this a cogent interpretation of fashion? Were buyers of fashionable clothing, furniture, and other shopping goods mere puppets, passively following each and every commercial nod from France? And what about the assumed power of the tradesmen and retailers? Were they indeed responsible for the increasing fashion-awareness of Antwerp society? To answer these broad questions, I will first provide more empirical findings regarding the advent of French fashions in the Southern Netherlands, particularly in Antwerp.[3] This will be explained as an encompassing process, not only with regard to fashionable material culture but also to society as a whole. A wider, more colourful and diverse urban, 'consumerism' was taking shape in seventeenth- and eighteenth-century Antwerp.[4] It was not so much fashion that was new in this period, as was its increased pace and pervasiveness in general – a trend that has been dubbed, rather portentously, the 'fashion revolution'.[5]

---

[3] In older literature the existence of fashion changes in this period is hinted at, but never fully explored. Read for example, Herman Van der Wee, 'Industrial dynamics and the process of urbanization and de-urbanization in the Low Countries from the Late Middle Ages to the eighteenth century. A synthesis', in Herman Van der Wee (ed.), *The rise and decline of urban industries in Italy and in the Low Countries (late Middle Ages–Early Modern Times)* (Leuven, 1988), pp. 360–62.

[4] Read Bruno Blondé, 'Tableware and changing consumer patterns. Dynamics of material culture in Antwerp, 17th–18th centuries', in Johan Veeckman (ed.), *Majolica and glass. From Italy to Antwerp and beyond. The transfer of technology in the 16th–early 17th century* (Antwerp, 2002), pp. 295–311; Bruno Blondé, 'Cities in decline and the dawn of a consumer society: Antwerp in the 17th–18th centuries', in Bruno Blondé, Eugénie Briot, Natacha Coquery and Laura Van Aert (eds), *Retailers and consumer changes in Early Modern Europe. England, France, Italy and the Low Countries* (Tours, 2005), pp. 37–52; Bruno Blondé and Ilja Van Damme, 'Retail growth and consumer changes in a declining urban economy: Antwerp (1650–1750)', *Economic History Review*, 63 (2010), early view via http://www3.interscience.wiley.com/journal/118509292/home.

[5] Read Neil McKendrick, John Brewer and John Harold Plumb, *The birth of a consumer society. The commercialization of eighteenth-century England* (London, 1982), p. 42.

Second, the role of tradesmen and retailers in 'creating' or influencing the fashion-cycles will be analysed. My argument here points to the importance of these economic actors, though not in the way described in Cardon's treatise, or as several historical interpretations have suggested. Retailers were not puppet masters but important 'middlemen', mediating between changes in demand and supply. Thus, the growing fashion sensitivity of the consumers and the increasing complexity of the material culture reinforced the power of middlemen of different kinds. In fact, 'traditional' interactions between a retailer and his customers – reinforcing strong, long-lasting, personal ties – hampered crude manipulations.[6] Finally, the goal of this chapter is to reassess the all too evident polarizations in our thinking about fashion. The fashion-phenomenon was, in some sense at least, a subtle process of negotiation between consumers and retailers, apt at adjusting the expectations of the one and reconciling the interests of the other.[7]

The Embarrassment of Fashions: Antwerp c. 1660–1800

At the end of the eighteenth century, an English visitor to the Southern Netherlands confirmed that 'the forms and fashions of the French in familiar life, their courtesy and style of society, their taste for shew and ornament, their amusements and entertainments, are imitated here'.[8] There can be no doubt, however, that already in the second half of the seventeenth century Antwerp and the Southern Netherlands as a whole – previously the showpiece of the Counter-Reformation under the tutelage of Spain and the Catholic Church – were transformed into epigones of French culture. That culture reached its apotheosis during the reign of Louis XIV, just as the Spanish Habsburg Empire was rapidly disintegrating.[9] France emerged as the shining example of civilisation, elegance, the last word in fashion and style.

Margaret Cavendish, the famous Duchess of Newcastle, in exile in Antwerp at that time, remarked: 'all those that had sufficient means, and could go to the price,

---

[6] This argument is extensively analysed in Ilja Van Damme, *Verleiden en verkopen. Antwerpse kleinhandelaars en hun klanten in tijden van crisis (ca. 1648–ca. 1748)* (Amsterdam: 2007).

[7] Similar remarks are to be found in John Styles, 'Product innovation in Early Modern London', *Past & Present*, 168 (2000): pp. 124–69; and Adri Albert de la Bruhèze and Onno de Wit, 'De productie van consumptie. De bemiddeling van productie en consumptie en de ontwikkeling van de consumptiesamenleving in Nederland in de twintigste eeuw', *Tijdschrift voor Sociale Geschiedenis*, 28 (2002): pp. 257–72.

[8] John Shaw, *Sketches of the history of the Austrian Netherlands* (London, 1786), p. 225.

[9] For the political background, read, for example, Jonathan I. Israel, *Conflicts of empires. Spain, the Low Countries and the struggle for world supremacy, 1585–1713* (London and Rio Grande, 1997), pp. 305–18.

kept coaches, and went the Tour for their own pleasure'.[10] However, this *Tour* or *Tour-à-la-mode* was widely criticized as being a contemporary manifestation of 'idleness, conceit and frivolity'.[11] The Jesuit Adrianus Poirters condemned this parade of decorated carriages and the flaunting of finery as an ostentatious pageant aimed at seduction and other worldly 'sins' (Illustration 2.1). Fashionable consumers were, indeed, warned against the threat of damnation by catholic preachers in this

Source: Adrianus Poirters, Het masker van de wereldt afgetrocken (Antwerp, 1646).

Illustration 2.1   A 'tour à la mode' around 1650: coaches and carriages drove slowly next to each other in opposite direction and with curtains open, so as to see each other and be seen

---

[10] Margaret Cavendish, *The life of William Cavendish, Duke of Newcastle*, ed. C.H. Firth, (London, 1886), p. 51. For further reading, see Ilja Van Damme, 'A city in transition. Antwerp after 1648', in Ben Van Beneden and Nora De Poorter (eds), *Royalist refugees. William and Margaret Cavendish in the Rubens house 1648–1660* (Antwerp, 2006), pp. 55–62. For further discussion on the luxurious habits adopted by English ex-patriots see Linda Levy Peck, *Consuming Splendor: Society and Culture in Seventeenth-Century England* (Cambridge, 2005).

[11] Adrianus Poirters, *Het masker van de wereldt afgetrocken* (Antwerp, 1646), pp. 43–4.

period;[12] but they were not inclined to follow the advice of the good shepherds. In the second half of the seventeenth century French immigrants were increasingly sought after as domestic servants, private tutors or simply connoisseurs of French *savoir-faire*. It was not by chance that the first dance instructor listed as a burgher of Antwerp in 1681 was an émigré from Paris.[13] Similarly, the Bergeyck family engaged French horticulturists to lay out and maintain their gardens. The count of Bergeyck was a prominent political figure in the Hapsburg administration of the Southern Netherlands and at the same time was an unabashed Francophile. Among domestic staff, appointments were secured on the basis of their knowledge of all things French – French cuisine, hairstyling and fashion. And styles were given French names like *La Roche*, *Notté* or *Triqué* as an indicator of their elegance, sophistication and stylishness.[14] For the same reasons, Antwerp's *à-la-mode* shops, which mushroomed from the 1660s on, were given French names with associations to Paris and all things French, names like *Au magasin de Paris*, *Au miroirs de Paris*, *Au petit Paris* or *Dans le royaume de France*.[15] As to entertainment, French theatre companies were welcomed with open arms in late seventeenth-century Antwerp. Their impact was immediately evident: between 1690 and 1744 French comedies and operas were the most popular events in Antwerp's flourishing entertainment scene[16] (Illustration 2.2).

The appropriation of French and other 'foreign' usages was not confined to language, customs and etiquette, but applied to material goods as well. Clothing underwent a remarkable change. The sober and severe Spanish style of dressing in the Southern Netherlands, notable for the extensive use of black, was swapped for the gaiety and colourfulness of French inspired clothing.[17] Lighter fabrics, *indiennes* (such as batiste or muslin), and mixed-cottons (like *siamoises*) increasingly replaced heavy woollens and silks. *Marchands de mode*

[12] Read Ilja Van Damme, 'Zotte verwaandheid. Over Franse verleiding en Zuid-Nederlands onbehagen, 1650–1750', in Raf de Bont and Tom Verschaffel (eds), *Het verderf van Parijs* (Leuven, 2004), pp. 187–203.

[13] See the unpublished database compiled by Bruno Blondé, Laura Van Aert and Ilja Van Damme, based on François Melis, *Poortersboeken* (Antwerp, 1977).

[14] For those and other examples, see Koen De Vlieger-De Wilde, *Adellijke levensstijl. Dienstpersoneel, consumptie en materiële leefwereld van Jan van Brouchoven en Livina de Beer, graaf en gravin van Bergeyck (ca. 1685–1740)* (Brussels, 2005), pp. 55–9, 75–82.

[15] Marie Coppens, '"Au magasin de Paris". Une boutique de mode à Anvers dans la première moitié du XVIIIe siècle', *Belgisch Tijdschrift voor Oudheidkunde en Kunstgeschiedenis*, 52 (1983), p. 103.

[16] See, for example, Alfons K.L. Thijs, *Van geuzenstad tot katholiek bolwerk. Antwerpen en de contrareformatie* (Turnhout, 1990), pp. 161-185; and Carolien Luypaers, *'Le goût pour les spectacles est tellement devenu à la mode'. Spektakelcultuur in het achttiende-eeuwse Antwerpen* (Unpublished Master-dissertation, Catholic University of Leuven, 2001).

[17] Harald Deceulaer, *Pluriforme patronen en een verschillende snit. Sociaal-economische, institutionele en culturele transformaties in de kledingsector in Antwerpen, Brussel en Gent, 1585–1800* (Amsterdam, 2001), pp. 159–202 and 233–56.

Source: Reconstruction by Timothy De Paepe.

Illustration 2.2 The 'tapissierspand' was erected in the years 1550–54 to accommodate the thriving trade in tapestries. In the seventeenth-century it fell into disuse, and the building was eventually redecorated into a theatre and opera house in the eighteenth century, when the fashion for French opera was at its height

retailed typical fashionable 'populuxe' items like fans, pipes and snuffboxes.[18] And after the introduction of the periwig by, among others, French immigrants in the 1670–80s, a corporation of periwig-makers was quickly assembled. In 1738 the city of Antwerp counted 50 master-*perruquiers*, with 30 journeymen and 20 apprentices, all dedicated to meeting the demand for wigs.[19] French styles affected many facets of local material culture. French building schemes and architectural decorations became widespread in the Southern Netherlands, especially after the Revocation of the Edict of Nantes in 1685; these political events led to an influx of Huguenot artisans in the Low Countries, including the famous architect, designer and engraver Daniel Marot.[20] In the interior of the homes, the once-fashionable tapestries were gradually replaced by wallpaper; silver and pewter tableware was recast in more 'modern' designs or rejected in favour of trendy, initially imported, alternatives such as porcelain or glass.[21] French inspired rush-bottomed chairs increasingly replaced Spanish-styled chairs made of oak and leather. The type of chimney cloths used in Antwerp homes also changed significantly between 1680 and 1730: cotton, which had hitherto been rare, ultimately took up 70 per cent of the market and remained popular throughout the eighteenth century.[22] The growing popularity of hot beverages such as tea, coffee and hot chocolate, which was becoming a general trend throughout Europe, also encouraged an increase of related utensils in Antwerp households. Around 1730, tea tables and sugar-spoons, for example, figured prominently in the homes of rich and modest families alike.[23] The origins of many of these commodities lay outside Europe and were the fruits

---

[18] The term 'populuxe' is used in the same meaning as Cissie Fairchilds, 'The production and marketing of populuxe goods in eighteenth-century Paris', in John Brewer and Roy Porter (eds), *Consumption and the world of goods* (London and New York, 1993), pp. 228–9.

[19] MAA, *Guilds & Corporations*, nr. 4006: archives concerning the governmental research of corporations of 1738. See also Fernand Smekens, 'Ambachtswezen en "nieuwe nijverheid"', in *Antwerpen in de 18de eeuw* (Antwerp, 1952), pp. 65, 79.

[20] Linda Meganck, 'Architectuur als décor voor het sociale leven in de 18de eeuw', in Jaak Van Schoor, Christel Stalpaert and Bram Van Oostveldt (eds), *Performing arts in the Austrian 18th century: new directions in historical and methodological research* (Ghent, 1999), pp. 9–10.

[21] Blondé, 'Tableware and changing consumer patterns', pp. 295–311; and Blondé, 'Cities in decline', pp. 37–52.

[22] For a more comprehensive treatment of this example and numerous others, see Van Damme, *Verleiden en verkopen*, pp. 187–228. Cotton became everywhere in the eighteenth century an overnight success; see Beverly Lemire, *Fashion's Favorite: the Cotton Trade and the Consumer in Britain, 1660–1800* (Oxford, 1991).

[23] Read also Bruno Blondé and Hilde Greefs, '"Werk aan de winkel", De Antwerpse meerseniers: aspecten van de kleinhandel en het verbruik in de 17de en 18de eeuw', *Bijdragen tot de Geschiedenis: De lokroep van het bedrijf. Handelaars, ondernemers en hun samenleving van de zestiende tot de twintigste eeuw. Liber amicorum Roland Baetens*, 84 (2001), pp. 216–20.

of colonial and Asian trade; but the rage for these commodities in France, as well as elsewhere in Europe, increased the taste for these goods in Antwerp society.[24]

In light of these changes in material culture, the decline of Antwerp's urban export industry from the last quarter of the seventeenth century onwards comes as no surprise.[25] The reasons for this process of de-industrialization have long been sought in purely political circumstances, such as the persistent wars and the harsher mercantilist climate that ensued during that period.[26] There can be no doubt that Colbert's protectionist tariffs of 1667–68 delivered a severe blow to Antwerp's textile and luxury goods industries like the diamond, silk and tapestry industries, as well as other locally made crafts. The weakened Brussels central government was in no position to forge a strong protectionist response. After the peace treaties of Münster (1648) and the Pyrenees (1659), Spain withdrew its military, financial and diplomatic backing from their catholic stronghold in the North. In addition, particular tendencies within the Southern Netherlands blocked any pro-industrial measures in favour of a pro-commercial course.[27]

But at the same time, demand-side issues also had a part in this complex tale of regional industrial decay and an expanding fashion markets.[28] Of course the widening 'crisis' in industry and in the war-ridden countryside led to a substantial fall in the purchasing power of certain income groups.[29] However, to the wealthy,

---

[24] For a discussion of the spread of Asian commodities in Europe see: Maxine Berg, *Luxury & Pleasure in Eighteenth-Century Britain* (Oxford, 2005) chapter 2, 'Goods from the East', pp. 46–84.

[25] Alfons K.L. Thijs, 'De nijverheid', in *Antwerpen in de XVIIde eeuw* (Antwerp, 1989), pp. 141–7; and more specifically, John Everaert, 'Een "nobele besogne" in verval. De kwijnende trafiek in kunst en edelstenen tussen Vlaanderen en Spanje (1650–1685)', in Hugo Soly and René Vermeir (eds), *Beleid en bestuur in de Nederlanden. Liber amicorum Prof. Dr. M. Baelde* (Ghent, 1993), pp. 183–8.

[26] See, for example, S. Despretz-Van de Casteele, 'Het protectionisme in de Zuidelijke Nederlanden gedurende de tweede helft der 17de eeuw', *Tijdschrift voor Geschiedenis*, 78 (1965), pp. 294–317; and Reginald De Schrijver, 'Oorlog en vrede voor de Zuidelijke Nederlanden 1678–1700', in *Algemene Geschiedenis der Nederlanden*, v. 8, (Haarlem, 1979), pp. 308–19.

[27] See extensively Ilja Van Damme, 'Het vertrek van Mercurius. Historiografische en hypothetische verkenningen van het economisch wedervaren van Antwerpen in de tweede helft van de zeventiende eeuw'.

[28] Read more in general Bruno Blondé and Ilja Van Damme, 'Low Countries: Southern Netherlands between 1585 and 1830', in Joel Mokyr (ed.), *The Oxford encyclopedia of economic history*, v. 3, (Oxford: 2003), pp. 392–4.

[29] See Alfons K.L. Thijs, 'Structural changes in the Antwerp industry from the fifteenth to eighteenth century', in Van der Wee (ed.), *The rise and decline of urban industries*, pp. 207–12; Alfons K.L. Thijs, 'Antwerp's luxury industries: the pursuit of profit and artistic sensitivity', in Jan Van der Stock (ed.), *Antwerp, story of a metropolis, 16th and 17th century* (Ghent, 1993), pp. 105–13.

fashion-conscious buyers of tapestries, paintings or richly decorated writing desks, money did not matter nearly as much as taste and style.[30] And it was precisely in this area that things started to change after 1648. Slowly but surely, both local and foreign consumers demonstrated a preference for new style French fashions and products. This shift in the demands of wealthy clients severely undermined the competitiveness of goods from Antwerp. Moreover, it undoubtedly contributed to the demise of the city's industrial sector. The demand for the baroque, 'Counter-Reformationist' pomp and splendour, at which Antwerp had excelled, gave way to a taste for the French late baroque and classicist styles; once a trend-setter in the days of Rubens and Van Dyck, Antwerp became a mere follower of fashion. These changes were especially apparent in the textile sector of the city. In the period 1640–69, no less than 134 sellers of silk and 43 sellers of silk sheets were active in the city; in the period between 1670 and 1699 these numbers dropped to 61 and 12 respectively.[31] Employment in the trimming and silk weaving-mills plummeted from 4800 labourers in 1650 to a meagre 290 in 1738. Workers in fur also complained in 1661, how 'in these calamitous times the wearing of furs and other related goods is going out of use because of the French fashions'.[32] The use of furs in clothing, like tapestries for the home, was no longer in style.

Small wonder that the Cardon treatise became a real bestseller. The author cashed in on the general prevailing unrest and anxiety about French fashions in this region and linked this phenomenon to the cunning tactics of commercial manipulators said to be at the root of this fashion trend. Cardon's argument was one that was widely shared across the social spectrum, leading to sometimes violent outbreaks. In the years 1701–1702, for instance, *à-la-mode* shops and warehouses were ransacked and 'Indian cloth and cottons' burned.[33] Again in the year 1718 frustrated labourers in the silk industry assaulted the houses and shops of Antwerp merchants: Austrian army troops had to intervene to restore peace in the streets.[34]

---

[30] The same remark can be found in Bruno Blondé, 'Art and economy in seventeenth- and eighteenth-century Antwerp: a view from the demand side', in Simonetta Cavaciocchi (ed.), *Economia e arte secc. XIII–XVIII* (Firenze, 2002), p. 384; and in Bruno Blondé, 'Indicatoren van het luxeverbruik? Paardenbezit en conspicuous consumption te Antwerpen (zeventiende-achttiende eeuw)', *Bijdragen tot de Geschiedenis*, 84 (2001): pp. 497–512.

[31] Alfons K.L. Thijs, *De zijdenijverheid te Antwerpen in de zeventiende eeuw* (Antwerp, 1969), pp. 9, 96.

[32] MAA, *Lawsuit Supplements*, nr. 6732, Rescriptie voor de cremers ende meerseniers deser stadt rescribenten tegens de dekens van het peltiers ambacht supplianten (not dated [1661]): '*desen calamiteusen tijt waerinne door de Fransche modes, dracht van faillen ende anderssints (...) is geraeckt in ongebruijck*'.

[33] See MAA, *Chamber of Privileges*, nr. 788, f. 207 (19 march 1702): '*indiaensche stoffen ende cattoenen goederen*'.

[34] Read Bruno Blondé and Ilja Van Damme, '11 augustus 1723. Indische Compagnie trekt naar de beurs', in Gustaaf Asaert (ed.), *De 25 dagen van Antwerpen* (Amsterdam, 2006), p. 287. The same anxieties were at work in England, more or less at the same time.

From a structural viewpoint, however, the arrival of French fashions was only one element in a shifting socio-economic landscape. Two things become apparent when contemporary statements about fashion are closely analysed. First, the velocity of fashion-cycles increased at a quickening pace. As the Jesuit R.P.F. Gallore remarked in almost modern terms:

> Today, there is such a flood of fashions, that no military state, person of position & profession can avoid being shipwreck (...) Almost every year, & sometimes even faster, one can see the world changing, like the seasons (...) fashions just go through a perpetual circle; a fashion of fifty years ago is beginning to return; old fashions become new & new fashions are already aging....[35]

Second, the authority of fashion infiltrated more and more layers of Antwerp society. Catholic preachers agitated most especially against this mixing and blurring of the social ranks, a complaint that arose in many societies. The spread of fashion-consciousness among a widening affluent middle-class led to the common complaint that 'it becomes hard to distinguish between the daughters of ordinary citizens and those of the nobility'.[36] For the first time in the seventeenth century a new sumptuary law was introduced in the Southern Netherlands on 26 January 1679 in an effort to control these forces. Typically, it was to no avail.[37]

To summarize: the late seventeenth- and eighteenth-century consumer pattern was becoming increasingly fashion-sensitive.[38] This is as apparent for

---

See U. Priestley, 'The marketing of Norwich stuffs, c. 1660–1730', *Textile History*, 22 (1991): p. 204.

[35] *Sentiments de monseigneur Jean Joseph Languet eve'que de Soissons, et de quelques autres Savants & Pieux écrivains de la compagnie de Jésus, sur le faux bonheur & la vanité des plaisirs mondains, spécialement des bals, des comédies et autres amusements dangereux nouvellement recueillis par Jean Baptiste Vermeersch, curé de S. Michel à Gant*, (Ghent, 1738), pp. 191, 194–5: '*Il y a aujourd'huy, comme une espèce d'inondation de ces Modes, où il n'y a guerres d'état, qualité & de profession, qui ne fasse naufrage (...) De sorte que presque toutes les années & quelquefois encore plus souvent, l'on voit le monde changer, comme les saisons (...) les modes ne sont ainsi que faire un cercle perpétuel; ce que l'on a vu il y a cinquante ans, commence après de revenir; ce qui était vieux, devient nouveau, & ce qui est nouveau, commence aussitôt à vieillir.*'

[36] The quotation dates from 1712 and is cited in Katelijne Rotsaert, *Tussen Eva en Maria. De vrouw volgens de predikanten van de 17de en 18de eeuw* (Aartrijke, 1992), pp. 91–2: '*dat men qualijck meer onderkennen en kan de Dochters van gemeense Borgers tusschen den Edeldom*'.

[37] Rotsaert, *Tussen Eva en Maria*, p. 94. Concerning the history and meaning of sumptuary laws, read the excellent Alan Hunt, *Governance of the consuming passions. A history of sumptuary law* (Bastingstoke, 1996), pp. 17–22.

[38] The growing dependence on fashion in this period was also attested for England, France, Italy and the Dutch Republic. Read, for instance, the special issue on clothing and fashion in *Textile History*, 22:2 (1991); Maxine Berg, 'French fancy and cool Britannia: the

the historian today as it was for the people living in those days. The Antwerp probate inventories, for instance, reveal a keen and growing fashion-sensitivity in the objects listed in these documents. The rare incidences referring to the quality of goods in the eighteenth century were no longer confined to descriptions such as '*good*' and '*bad*', but included words such as '*fashionable*' and '*new*' as well.[39] Even newspapers frequently advertised products as being '*French*', '*new*' or '*à la mode*', indicating the importance ascribed to these more precise descriptive terms.[40] Fashion and design also affected the price of objects on more and more occasions as well.[41]

As has already been noted the Antwerp retailers, too, were eager to sell the growing range of consumer products. Membership of the Antwerp Retailers guild [the *meerseniers*], which included all persons engaged in commercial activities, was continuously growing in relative numbers, in striking contrast with the de-urbanization of the town in the first half of the eighteenth century.[42] In 1700, at the height of the economic and political crisis of Antwerp, the corporation still counted 2291 members.[43] For a population of about 70,000 inhabitants, this amounted to a retail-ratio of approximately 1 to 31: that is, each individual retailer thus supplied 31 local consumers with his wares. In assessing the importance of these figures,

---

fashion markets of Early Modern Europe', in Simonetta Cavaciocchi (ed.), *Fiere e mercati nella integrazione delle economie Europee secc. XIII–XVIII*, (Firenze, 2001), pp. 519–56; C.H. Crowston, 'The queen and her "minister of fashion": gender, credit and politics in pre-revolutionary France', *Gender & History*, 14 (2002): pp. 96–116; Laurence Fontaine, 'The circulation of luxury goods in eighteenth-century Paris: social redistribution and an alternative currency', in Maxine Berg and Elizabeth Eger (eds), *Luxury in the eighteenth century. Debates, desires and delectable goods* (Basingstoke, 2003), pp. 89–102; and Bibi Panhuysen, *Maatwerk. Kleermakers, naaisters, oudkleerkopers en de gilden (1500–1800)* (Amsterdam, 2000), pp. 91–107.

[39] Unpublished probate inventory database from Bruno Blondé, research professor, Centre for Urban History, University of Antwerp.

[40] Based on my unpublished analysis of the *Gazette van Antwerpen* for the years 1700–1705, 1723–27 and 1743–47.

[41] The same remarks were made by Helen Clifford, 'A commerce with things: the value of precious metalwork in Early Modern England', in Maxine Berg and Helen Clifford (eds), *Consumers and luxury. Consumer culture in Europe 1650–1850* (Manchester, 1999), pp. 165–6; and Harm Nijboer, 'Fashion and the Early Modern consumer evolution. A theoretical exploration and some evidence from seventeenth century Leeuwarden', in Blondé, Briot, Coquery and Van Aert (eds), *Retailers and consumer changes*, pp. 21–36.

[42] In 1550 the Antwerp population still accounted for 27 per cent of the aggregate population of Antwerp, Amsterdam, Paris and London. By 1700 this percentage had fallen back to scarcely 5 per cent. See Jan De Vries, *European Urbanization, 1500–1800* (London, 1984), appendix 1.

[43] Laura Van Aert and Ilja Van Damme, 'Retail dynamics of a city in crisis: the mercer guild in pre-industrial Antwerp (c. 1648–c. 1748)', in Blondé, Briot, Coquery and Van Aert (eds), *Retailers and consumer changes*, p. 147.

one has to bear in mind that the guild of secondhand dealers, non-corporate retailers, peddlers, ambulant market traders and the like were not even included in these statistics.[44] This relative growth of retailers in Antwerp, especially in a period of economic turmoil, was probably less a reflection of survival strategies than it was an answer to a blossoming consumer society. In any case, it is striking to notice how shopkeepers, peddlers, and the like appropriate the distribution of all kinds of new and fashionable goods.[45] Indeed, historical literature has been apt in pointing out the importance of commercial infrastructures, organizations and practices that made possible the distribution, marketing and selling of a growing consumer output.[46] But which role exactly did the retailers play when interacting with consumers' demand? Were the large numbers of retailers and tradesmen in Antwerp responsible for the increasing fashion-awareness of people? Did they manipulate the increasing velocity of fashion cycles and facilitate the pervasiveness of fashion in the Antwerp society?

Manipulators or Middlemen? Commercial Agents and the Tyranny of Fashion

Sociological explanations of fashion in particular, and the appearance of new consumer patterns in general, usually lead to the famous and long established Veblen-Simmel theses.[47] Intelligent and sophisticated as these were, however, their mutual jargon of 'emulation' and 'differentiation' describes the mechanisms of fashion at work, but always needs historical contextualization.[48] Status competition and processes of trickle-down, upward or sideways, makes the dynamism of fashion changes and fashion cycles intelligible, but leaves contingencies in the

---

[44] The enormous density of mercers in Antwerp was surprisingly enough comparable to the London retail-ratio of 30 persons per shop in 1759, a period of incomparable economic growth and urbanization in England. See Hoh-Cheung Mui and Lorna H. Mui, *Shops and shopkeeping in eighteenth-century England* (Kingston, 1989), pp. 37–41.

[45] Van Aert and Van Damme, 'Retail dynamics of a city in crisis', pp. 153–67.

[46] See, amongst others, Cissie Fairchilds, 'Consumption in Early Modern Europe. A review article', *Comparative Studies in Society and History*, 35 (1993): pp. 850–58; Pieter N. Stearns, 'Stages of consumerism: recent work on the issues of periodization', *Journal of Modern History*, 69 (1997): pp. 102–17; Pieter Musgrave, *The Early Modern European Economy* (Basingstoke, 1999), pp. 59–85.

[47] Read as an introduction, for instance, D.E. Allen, 'Fashion as a social process', *Textile History*, 22 (1991): pp. 347–58.

[48] See Thorstein Veblen, *The theory of the leisure class: an economic study of institutions* (London, 1970); Georg Simmel, 'Fashion', *American Journal of Sociology*, 62 (1957): pp. 541–9 [originally *Die Mode*, 1904]. For an overview, read Peter Corrigan, *The sociology of consumption* (London, 1997), pp. 161–76; Steven Miles, *Consumerism as a way of life* (London, 1998), pp. 90–106; Tim Edwards, *Contradictions of consumption: concepts, practices and politics in consumer society* (Buckingham, 2000), pp. 149–64.

pace of the fashion phenomenon and its diffusion through society unexplained.[49] One popular argument links the growing pervasiveness of fashion to a widening social mobility during this period.[50] As the possibility of wealth accumulation and leisure time increased, more and more people abandoned old customs and conventions. A strict hierarchy of clothing, for instance, also receded with the more open context of cities. Thus, new material expressions through consumption and perpetual fashion changes became the norm, establishing social differences in the seventeenth and eighteenth centuries. As more and more people had the means and time to redefine themselves materially, these processes accelerated social differentiation through new goods and new fashions, a practice some described as aping one's betters.

Several historians have pointed out that precisely in the late seventeenth and eighteenth centuries, these processes of 'chase-and-flight' – in which a small group of trendsetters tried to distinguish itself from imitating behaviour – were further stimulated by a growing commercialization of the market.[51] Neil McKendrick in particular makes a passionate plea for the existence of a so-called 'fashion revolution'. The growing fashion-sensitivity of eighteenth-century consumers needed, to use the authors words, 'careful guidance and skilful exploitation' by commercial entrepreneurs.[52] To show that 'men and women increasingly had to wear what commerce dictated', McKendrick analyses commercial innovations of this period, such as fashion dolls, fashion prints, fashion magazines and fashion advertisements.[53] Unquestionably, many of these marketing techniques were new and innovative, but they were not as decisive in the selling of styles in general, nor were they as successful in generating fashions as McKendrick suggests. Even today, the presumed manipulative and ever-refined force of advertising is in serious doubt.[54] Assuming that men and women 'had to raise or lower their hems and their heels at the dictates of the cloth manufacturers and the shoe sellers',

---

[49] For a similar critique on the Veblen-Simmel model, read Colin Campbell, 'The desire for the new. Its nature and social location as presented in theories of fashion and modern consumerism', in Daniel Miller (ed.), *Consumption. Critical concepts in the social sciences* (4 vols, London and New York, 2001), vol. 1, pp. 247–50.

[50] Read, for example, W.E. Minchinton, 'Convention, fashion and consumption: aspects of British experience since 1750', in H. Baudet and M. Bogucka (eds), *Types of consumption, traditional and modern* (Budapest, 1982), p. 37.

[51] The term 'chase-and-flight' was coined by Grant McCraken, *Culture and consumption: new approaches to the symbolic character of consumer goods* (Bloomington, 1988), p. 94.

[52] McKendrick, 'The commercialization of fashion', p. 42.

[53] McKendrick, 'The commercialization of fashion', p. 40 (quotation) and pp. 41–99.

[54] A good introduction can be found in Clemens Wischerman, 'Placing advertising in the modern cultural history of the city', in Clemens Wischerman and Elliott Shore (eds), *Advertising and the European city: historical perspectives* (Aldershot, 2000), pp. 1–31.

is, indeed, subscribing to the existence of a passive and obedient consumer.[55] In this scenario, tradesmen and retailers functioned as 'materialistic' agents plotting against a wholly innocent, submissive customer who accepts 'commodities' and 'fashions' proposed to him unthinkingly.[56] However, Colin Campbell, amongst others, has argued convincingly that consumer desires, passions, and mentalities need to have altered before fashion dealers could become successful.[57]

Keeping Campbell's analysis in mind, it seems more likely that changing consumer preferences also had a hand in the Antwerp fashion dynamic.[58] No longer did consumers necessarily prefer high quality and long lasting luxury products (such as silks, tapestries or oak and leather furniture). Rather, new and fashionable products were eagerly sought in keeping with the sensibilities of the time.[59] For example, customers of the *Au magasin de Paris*, a self-consciously titled fashion shop in Antwerp, continuously asked the retailer, Madame Hoffinger, '*ce qu'il y a de plus nouveau et de plus galant*' ['what is the newest and most elegant'].[60] And whether buying or restyling, customers wanted their choices to reflect the appropriate mode. A certain widow Van Bommel, living in Bergen-Op-Zoom, asked the shop 'to patch my bonnets according to the latest fashion'.[61] The power of consumer demand was even discussed among the highest levels of society. Financial counsellors, for instance, advised the Austrian government in Brussels to withdraw their support for the tapestry industries in the second half

---

[55] McKendrick, 'The commercialization of fashion', pp. 40–41.

[56] A similar remark can be found in K. Pomeranz, *The great divergence. China, Europe, and the making of the modern world economy* (Princeton, 2000), p. 128.

[57] Colin Campbell, *The romanthic ethic and the spirit of modern consumerism* (Oxford, 1987); Gilles Lipovetsky, *L'empire de l'éphemère. La mode et son destin dans les sociétés modernes* (Paris, 1987); Chandra Mukerji, *From graven images: patterns of modern materialism* (New York, 1983); M. Bianchi (ed.), *The active consumer. Novelty and surprise in consumer choice* (London: 1998).

[58] See, for instance, Ilja Van Damme, 'Changing consumer preferences and evolutions in retailing. Buying and selling consumer durables in Antwerp (c. 1648–c. 1748)', in Bruno Blondé, Peter Stabel, Jon Stobart and Ilja Van Damme (eds), *Buyers and sellers. Retail circuits and practices in medieval and early modern Europe* (Turnhout, 2006), pp. 199–223; Bruno Blondé and Veerle De Laet, 'Owning paintings and changes in consumer preferences in the Low Countries, seventeenth-eighteenth centuries', in Neil De Marchi and Hans J. Van Miegroet (eds), *Mapping markets for paintings in Europe, 1450–1750* (Turnhout, 2006), pp. 69–84.

[59] The same is attested for England and France. Read, for instance, T. Kusamitsu, 'Novelty, give us novelty: London agents and northern manufacturers', in Maxine Berg (ed.), *Markets and manufacture in early industrial Europe* (London, 1991), pp. 114–38.

[60] Cited in Coppens, '"Au magasin de Paris", p. 93 with more examples there.

[61] MAA, *IB*, nr. 2363: letter of P.V. Uffele, widow Van Bommel, Bergen-Op-Zoom (dated: 21 August 1750): '*[mijn mutsen] na de nieuwste mode wilt opmaken.*'

of the eighteenth century because customers increasingly preferred wallpapers.[62] Consumer demand focused on novelty and fashion, and, thus, shoppers wanted cheaper, more easily replaceable, lighter and less durable products.

New production techniques and the substitution of expensive raw materials with cheaper ones resulted in declining prices that further stimulated changing consumer preferences.[63] Indeed, fashion became intrinsically linked to processes of product innovation and diversification; Maxine Berg emphasizes that 'a theory of fashion must relate to a theory of product innovation'.[64] In Antwerp, too, newness and fashion were introduced more rapidly and familiar commodities came in ever-larger quantities and variations. By experimenting with colours and patterns, forms, shapes, material and quality of products, it became possible to induce small changes in familiar products, and, thus, to introduce 'novelties' on a regular base.[65] These evolutions gradually changed the role of tradesmen and retailers, but not in the way McKendrick envisioned. Instead of puppeteers, commercial men of all sorts became important 'middlemen', mediating between changes in demand and supply.

The increasing diversification and complexity of urban material culture translated itself into an added transaction cost for the customer.[66] A fondness for novelties and wish to be *à la mode*, made the process of shopping and deciding even more troublesome than before. With the range of choice constantly widening, consumer stress rose at an even pace and a conscientious shopper came to rely

---

[62] As mentioned in Ingrid De Meuter, 'De wandtapijtindustrie te Brussel ten tijde van het Oostenrijks bewind. De bestellingen geplaatst door keizerin Maria-Theresia', in *De Oostenrijkse Nederlanden, het Prinsbisdom Luik en het Graafschap Loon in de 18de eeuw. Bijdragen over cultuur, politiek en economie* (Hasselt, 1989), p. 89.

[63] See also Carole Shammas, *The pre-industrial consumer in England and America* (Oxford, 1990), pp. 76–118; Carole Shammas, 'The decline of textile prices in England and British America prior to industrialisation', *Economic History Review*, 48 (1994): pp. 483–507; Pomeranz, *The great divergence*, pp. 152–4; and Mark Overton, 'Prices from probate inventories', in Tom Arkell, Nesta Evans and Nigel Goose (eds), *When death do us part: understanding and interpreting the probate records of Early Modern England* (Oxford, 2000), pp. 120–42.

[64] Berg, 'French fancy and cool Britannia', p. 522. Read more about this theme in Maxine Berg, 'Product innovation in core consumer industries in eighteenth-century Britain', in Maxine Berg and Kristine Bruland (eds), *Technological revolutions in Europe. Historical perspectives* (Cheltenham, 1998), pp. 138–57; Maxine Berg, 'From imitation to invention: creating commodities in eighteenth-century Britain', *Economic History Review*, 55 (2002): pp. 1–30.

[65] This was also attested for England, see David Corner, 'The tyranny of fashion: the case of the felt-hatting trade in the late seventeenth and eighteenth centuries', *Textile History*, 22 (1991): p. 154.

[66] The same remark can be found in Jan De Vries, 'The industrious revolution and economic growth, 1650–1830', in Paul A. Davids and Mark Thomas (eds), *The economic future in historical perspective* (Oxford, 2003), pp. 61–2.

on the advice and information of a knowledgeable 'middleman'. Commercial entrepreneurs stood in a privileged position to claim this function. They could make new fashions and novelties comprehensible and attractive, explain the use or meaning of new products, or formulate and reformulate a proper product definition. In serving consumers, 'middlemen' informed, advised and selected the goods that fulfilled individual demand; working with the producers, they translated consumer desires, or subcontracted craftsmen to produce the requisite goods, craftsmen who formerly would probably have negotiated independently with the customer. In England, the so-called 'upholder'-type traders worked as such middlemen, for domestic consumption at least.[67] According to an English manual of 1757, the upholder was the man 'upon whose judgement I rely in the choice of goods; and I suppose he has judgement not only in the materials, but taste in the fashions and styles of workmanship'.[68] The most successful of these became real 'arbiters of taste', powerful enough to influence the course and articulations of fashions themselves. The *marchands merciers* of the illustrious fashion streets of Paris, the Rue Saint Honoré and Rue Richelieu, were renowned for their inventiveness in creating fashion cycles.[69] By constantly being informed and knowledgeable about the widening material culture, they had invaluable advice on the most satisfying pursuit on offer, or could even set a fashion change successfully in motion.[70] New products were imported, or existing ones transformed (with the help of subcontracted craftsmen) into a new 'craze' or *fureur*.[71] Typically, fashions were launched at the time of popular plays (*à la Figaro*), after famous discoveries (*à la Montgolfière*), to celebrate a military victory (*à la Belle-Poule*), and so on, just to keep the wheels of commerce spinning.

---

[67] Read Matthew Craske, 'Plan and control: design and the competitive spirit in early and mid-eighteenth-century England', *Journal of Design History*, 12 (1999): pp. 208–11; and more in general Clive Edwards, 'The upholsterer and the retailing of domestic furnishings 1600–1800', in Blondé, Briot, Coquery, Van Aert (eds), *Retailers and consumer changes*, pp. 60–66.

[68] R. Campbell, *The complete London tradesman* (London, 1757), p. 169, as cited in M. Craske and M. Berg, 'Art and industry. The making of modern luxury in eighteenth-century Britain', in Cavaciocchi (ed.), *Economia e arte*, p. 832.

[69] As analysed extensively by Carolyn Sargentson, *Merchants and luxury markets. The marchands merciers of eighteenth-century Paris* (London, 1996), pp. 41–142; and Carolyn Sargentson, 'The manufacture and marketing of luxury goods: the marchands merciers of late 17th- and 18th-century Paris', in Robert Fox and Anthony Turner (eds), *Luxury trades and consumerism in Ancien Régime Paris. Studies in the history of the skilled workforce* (Aldershot, 1998), pp. 104–37.

[70] A business strategy that has been called 'eonomies of scope'. See Neil De Marchi and Hans J. Van Miegroet, 'Transforming the Paris art market, 1718–1750', in De Marchi and Van Miegroet (eds), *Mapping markets*, pp. 388–91.

[71] Read also Paul Verlet, 'Le commerce des objets d'art et les marchands merciers à Paris au XVIIIe siècle', *Annales. Economies. Sociétés. Civilisations*, 13 (1958): pp. 10–29.

In the Southern Netherlands, too, certain fashion-changes originated or were set into motion by distinguished fashion dealers. An almanac produced in Gent, dated 1712, spoke for instance, of 'strange fashions and forms *(...) à la Berger, à la Manier, à la Crispet, à la Garcet, à la Bisard, à la Gaillard*'.[72] These names referred to famous fashion dealers and fashion 'makers', known by the literate audiences of those days. Of course, not every 'middleman' was that powerful or influential in playing on the fashion-sensitivity of the elite or would be stylish consumers. But on a lower, less exclusive level, the same logic was at work. Consumers were all too happy to be advised and informed by a trustworthy retailer. Indeed, for some, the troublesome process of choosing the right attire oneself was too onerous and a customer of the *Au magasin de Paris* relied on Madame Hoffinger. She was instructed by one customer with the comments that: 'you have seen me and as a result you know I do not suffer under too much facial paint and what is necessary for a dark type such as me, the dress (…) should be *à la mode*, thus I let it under your complete directions'.[73] In order to keep up-to-date, the shopkeepers themselves, in this case the Hoffinger family, were informed on a regular basis by at least one fashion-connoisseur based in Paris. In his letters to the Hoffingers he talked about '*la dernière mode*', about what was most beautiful and new, and should be considered '*bon goût*', good taste.[74] The samples of cloth, materials or patterns he included in his letters were used in the shop and shown to the customers and sometimes real attire, bonnets or *coiffures* were brought over from Paris to be used as models. Customers could try them on, and, if suited, order them right away. By introducing changes and novelties in the familiar context of a shop, these customers were probably less hesitant to follow the latest fashions.

Conclusion

Changing consumer preferences and the growing complexity of the material culture in late seventeenth- and eighteenth-century Antwerp certainly reinforced the strategic importance of the retailer in 'creating' or influencing fashion cycles.

---

[72] Cited in M. Deneckere, 'Histoire de la langue française dans les Flandres (1770–1823)', *Handelingen der Maatschappij voor Geschiedenis en Oudheidkunde te Gent*, 6 (1952), p. 203: '*vreemde modens en fatsoen (...) à la Berger, à la Manier, à la Crispet, à la Garcet, à la Bisard, à la Gaillard*'.

[73] As cited in Coppens, "Au magasin de Paris", pp. 93–4: '*vous m'avez vue et par conséquent vous savez que je ne pêche pas par trop de blancheur et ce qu'il faut pour une noiraude de mon espèce, la robe (...) il faut la faire à la mode enfin que je vous en laisse entièrement la direction*'.

[74] MAA, *Chamber of Insolvent Inventories*, nr. 2363: letter of J. Sollier to Hoffinger (dated: Paris, the 24 October 1742). For similar remarks, read the letters dated on 26 and 30 October 1742 and 28 March 1743.

Most of them, however, were neither impostors nor cunning manipulators. Not all consumers had identical material aspirations and the shopkeeper had to take into account the desires, actions and intelligence of contemporary customers. Deceitful interactions with customers or the sharp maximization of profit were ultimately an inefficient business strategy for the retailer. Relations among buyers and sellers thrived on the basis of long-lasting ties, often of an informal kind.[75] Customers were willing to hand over at least a part of the decision-making process to a 'middleman' – and increasingly so when the proliferation of fashions made shopping more complex. But this reliance on a retailer would persist only when the trustworthy reputation of the trader in question was beyond doubt. By giving good advice and information about the current fashions and new products, by being knowledgeable about changes in the material culture, by listening to the preferences of customers and trying to find a suitable response, retailers could forge strong, personal bonds with their clients. The so-called 'traditional' commercial practices, such as price-negotiation and credit-payments, were not only an economic necessity, but underlined the structural importance of trust, reputation and reciprocity between buyers and sellers.[76] By continually expanding their services, and by contracting (or subcontracting) craftsmen of all sorts, certain middlemen, such as the *marchands merciers* of Paris, could become real arbiters of taste, personally setting the wheels of fashion in motion. But then again, they themselves profited from the widening appeal of all things French.

There was an element of truth in Pieter Cardon's assignment of blame to retailers for the growing tyranny of French fashions in his time, given the extensive interactions of consumers and tradesmen, day in and day out. However, Cardon was mistaken in assuming this relationship to be one dimensional and asymmetrical, with the retailers hovering almighty above their clients. Retailers had to listen, as well as instruct, meeting the needs of a wide range of customers. In analysing such an elusive and volatile phenomenon as fashion, no single explanation will suffice to explain its dynamism. Certainly retailers were not the source of this phenomenon, even if they benefited from its vitality. The goal of this chapter was to better grasp the role of tradesmen and retailers in relation to the growing fashion-sensitivity in Antwerp, from the late seventeenth century onwards. If there was such a thing as a

---

[75] Also read Bruno Blondé, Peter Stabel, Jon Stobart and Ilja Van Damme, 'Retail circuits and practices in medieval and early modern Europe: an introduction', in Blondé, Stabel, Stobart and Van Damme (eds), *Buyers and sellers*, pp. 19–20.

[76] Read in the first place Craig Muldrew, *The economy of obligation: the culture of credit and social relations in Early Modern England* (New York, 2001); Craig Muldrew, 'Hard food for Midas: cash and its social value in Early Modern England', *Social History*, 18 (1993): pp. 163–83. For Antwerp, the importance of credit as an instrument of trust, is analysed by Bart Willems, *Leven op de pof: krediet bij de Antwerpse middenstand in de achttiende eeuw* (Amsterdam, 2009) [this is the published version of the previously unpublished PhD-version].

'fashion-revolution', it was a gradual and a negotiated process, and not inflicted by a powerful force outside the consumer. Its dawn was structurally interwoven with, and as complex as, the mechanisms of our own consumer society.

Chapter Three

Fabricating the Domestic: The Material Culture of Textiles and the Social Life of the Home in Early Modern Europe[1]

Giorgio Riello

Textiles have long been at the centre of interest among historians, be they economic, social, cultural and, more recently, material. However, the historical and methodological understanding of textiles has been heavily influenced by dress. The way in which men and women clothe their bodies and engage with the so-called 'culture of appearances' informs the wider theoretical categories into which textiles are inscribed. This is particularly true for the concept of *fashion*, as the ever-changing material base of dress, decoration and adornment and an overarching idea of cultural and social change. If fashion is the guiding concept of the relationship between textiles and the personal sartorial choices made by individuals in their daily lives, what conceptual/historical categories can we adopt for the study of the vast range of textiles that were produced to decorate but also organize and govern our domestic life?

Until recently fashion scholars have been very cautious about mingling with textiles, as if materiality would encroach on the tapestries of academic weaving. One can observe a shift away from the very materiality of textiles towards approaches that emphasize instead the conceptual value of fashion. However, not all interest or knowledge on textiles has been lost. Thanks to the cumulative expertise, much of which has arisen from museum-based research, we now know a great deal about so-called 'flat textiles', their design, their technical aspects, from spinning down to finishing, passing through weaving, knitting, calendaring, and printing. Such knowledge is object-based, comparative and increasingly cross-cultural.[2] The material form of fabrics is thus an essential component – practical and methodological – for the enhancement of the historical study of textiles.

---

[1] I would like to thank Glenn Adamson, Richard Butler, Hannah Greig, Peter McNeil and Lilian Pérez for their comments and criticism.

[2] See for instance, Natalie Rothstein and Santina M. Levey, 'Furnishings, *c.* 1500–1780', in David Jenkins (ed.), *The Cambridge History of Western Textiles* (2 vols, Cambridge, 2003), vol. 1, pp. 631–58. Research has been done also on specific artifacts. See for instance

This chapter attempts to reflect on the relationship between textiles and domestic interiors by starting from the material culture of the artefacts. It does so by raising some basic questions about textiles and the formation of domesticity, the transformation of a house into a home and the specific notion of a domestic environment created by textiles. It argues that textiles for furnishing and domestic decoration should not be seen as passive remnants of the past, but should be used instead to unlock historical meanings and practices that historical research based on documentary evidence can only approach tangentially.

The Material Culture of Textiles

The Englishman John Garland, a private tutor living in thirteenth-century France, underlined what a fashionable gentleman's house had to include:

> a decent table, a clean cloth, hemmed towels, high tripods, strong trestles, firebrands, fuel logs, stakes, bars, benches, armchairs, wooden frames and chairs made to fold, quilts, bolsters, and cushions.[3]

Garland's list was not an inventory, but a wish list, containing the *desiderata* of a comfortable gentlemen's house, defined not so much by bricks and mortar, but by furniture and textiles that would shape the desired cultural environment. He pointed out that textiles were a necessity for comfortable living and a *necessaire* for respectable social life. It is an uncontroversial fact that textiles represented a major sector in early modern Europe: their production accounted for a substantial share of the economy and their consumption – in the shape of clothing and domestic textiles – was second only to food in early modern household budgets.[4]

However during the early modern period, textiles – and domestic textiles in particular – evolved from relatively scarce and costly commodities to become increasingly common in European households among all but the very poor. There are several indicators of such a trend, although the quantitative evidence on the increasing importance of domestic textiles is fragmentary. Figures on total textile production can be conjectured from export and demographic trends, but it is difficult to estimate with precision the percentage of textiles employed for domestic use and furnishing. Even Gregory King, to whom we owe probably the

---

on Marseilles quilts: Clare Rose, 'The Manufacture and Sale of "Marseilles" Quilting in Eighteenth-Century London', *CIETA Bulletin*, 76 (1999): pp. 104–11; on Scotch carpets: Vanessa Habib, 'Scotch Carpets in the Eighteenth and Early Nineteenth Centuries', *Textile History*, 28/2 (1997): pp. 161–75.

[3] Quoted in John E. Crowley, *The Invention of Comfort: Sensibilities and Design in Early Modern Britain and Early America* (Baltimore, 2001), p. 6.

[4] Carole Shammas, *The Pre-industrial Consumer in England and America* (Oxford, 1990), p. 64.

most thorough examination of the sartorial economics of late seventeenth-century England, reveals little about the consumption of textiles that were not transformed into dress.[5]

Faced with these difficulties, historians have made ingenious use of other sources, literal and functional, and have reconstructed the material culture of homes and the material life of households from the sixteenth to the early nineteenth century. Inventories, in particular, have been employed fruitfully to quantify different typologies of domestic artefacts, across time and space.[6] The work of Lorna Weatherill, Carole Shammas and more recently the University of Exeter project co-ordinated by Mark Overton, has provided exceptional quantitative data on trends that underpin the historical study of consumer preferences and practices.[7] In different ways, they have identified an increasing availability of textiles in the home, paired with a rising number of commodities. Textiles were used to upholster chairs, cover tables and floors, and decorate walls, in the pursuit of a comfortable space in which to live.

The long history of the achievement of comfort has been central in explaining textiles – especially upholstery – in the material life of the home. The idea of comfort emerged during the seventeenth and eighteenth centuries to identify the relationship between the body and material environment and was initially an extension of the more traditional meaning of comfort as a moral and emotional state.[8] We must recognize that this is a very precise attribution of meaning to textiles – a governing concept that does not necessarily appreciate textiles for their

---

[5] Negley Harte, 'The Economics of Clothing in the Late Seventeenth Century', *Textile History*, 12/2 (1991): p. 288.

[6] But inventories are not the panacea of historians. Although abundant, they require labour–intensive exercises of transcription and computerization. They also systematically disregard clothing, rendering the measurement of the proportion between clothes and other textiles impossible to quantify. The fact that they do not offer any indication of the rationales of consumers' sensibly limits their value. See Giorgio Riello, '"Things Seen and Unseen": Inventories and the Representation of the Domestic Interior in Early Modern Europe' (Unpublished paper, V&A/RCA conference on Inventories in Renaissance and Early Modern Europe, May 2004).

[7] Carole Shammas, 'The Domestic Environment in Early Modern England and America', *Journal of Social History*, 14/1 (1980): pp. 3–24; Lorna Weatherill, 'Consumer Behaviour and Social Status in England, 1660–1750', *Continuity and Change*, 1/1 (1986): pp. 191–216; Shammas, *Pre-industrial Consumer*; Stana Nenadic, 'Middle-Rank Consumers and Domestic Culture in Edinburgh and Glasgow, 1720–1840', *Past and Present*, 145 (1994): pp. 122–56; Lorna Weatherill, *Consumer Behaviour and Material Culture in Britain, 1660–1760* (Oxford, 1996); Mark Overton, Jane Whittle, Darron Dean and Andrew Hann, *Production and Consumption in English Households, 1600–1750* (London and New York, 2004).

[8] John E. Crowley, 'The Sensibility of Comfort', *American Historical Review*, 104/3 (1999): p. 751. See also Crowley, *Invention of Comfort* and the book review by Patrick Griffin, 'The Pursuit of Comfort: the Modern and the Material in the Early Modern British Atlantic World', *Reviews in American History*, 30 (2002): pp. 365–72.

intrinsic qualities (colours, design, texture, etc.) and extrinsic meaning (social, cultural and economic attributions). The association between textiles and comfort, vital to so much literature and often borrowed from the realm of furniture, is thus not considered thoroughly in this paper. Rather I relate domestic textiles to four broad ideas explaining how rising levels of material possession were sought, and what role domestic textiles played in the 'fashioning' of early modern material culture. I will refer first to the nature of textiles and the specific European notion of permanence. This will be followed by a discussion of textiles as signifiers of wealth and status and their part in the language of taste and innovation. And I will conclude by referring to the artefacts themselves and their 'social life'.

On Permanence and Transition

The conceptual and practical division between domestic textiles and clothing textiles extends well beyond the realm of quantification. One of the issues that encroach upon the understanding of fabrics is their nature within the wider world of goods available to people through the ages. Is the use of textiles in Europe part of a specific way of understanding materiality? If so, does this provide a key on how to read textiles in the context of a medieval, early modern or modern home? S.A.M. Adshead suggests that European material culture was organized around principles that were different from those adopted in China (Illustrations 3.1 and 3.2). Ming and early Qing people distinguished between dress and shelter in a less radical way than did Europeans.[9] Adshead notes that in Asia, dress and shelter were part of a continuum between body and space and the life cycle of both belonged to one temporal unit. In contrast, in Europe, at least since the early Christian period, a distinction between dress and shelter was made in terms of durability. Dress was characterized by a comparatively short life-span, whilst shelter, in the form of buildings, made of stone, bricks or marble was characterized by relative permanence. Adshead concludes that in Europe, while buildings were seen as part of the 'kingdom of the perdurable' and contextualized in the *longue durée*, dress was seen as a manifestation of the ephemeral and part of the *événementel*.

Such a distinction became more marked in the early modern period when wooden houses were replaced by brick and stone buildings making the house, in the words of Fernand Braudel, 'an enduring thing… [and] perpetual witness to the slowness of civilizations, of cultures bent on preserving, maintaining and repeating'.[10] Braudel contrasts this with the claim that several Asian populations continued to use 'poor building materials' (wood, earth and fabric) as in the case of

---

[9] S.A.M. Adshead, *Material Culture in Europe and China, 1400–1800* (Basingstoke, 1997), p. 104.

[10] Fernand Braudel, *Capitalism and Material Life, 1400–1800* (Glasgow, 1974), p. 192.

In Chinese houses the wooden structure is complemented by the use of textiles and soft furnishing.

Illustration 3.1 House of a Chinese official, part of ten drawings illustrating the interior of the house of a Chinese official at Canton. Opaque watercolour, c. 1800–1805. © All Rights Reserved. The British Library Board. Licence Number: UNIWAR03

Although this late eighteenth-century English interior represents a much lower class type of domestic space, one can see the structural function of stone and plaster and in this case the relative absence of textiles.

Illustration 3.2   A Cottage Interior: An Old Woman Preparing Tea, by William Redmore Bigg. Oil on canvas, 1793. Photo © Victoria and Albert Museum, London, 199–1885

the mud-houses in central Asia, or the tents used by nomads and Mughal princes.[11] This should not be taken as a sign of inferiority compared with the stone buildings of Europe. The use of wood in Japan or China allowed for better insulated and lighter spaces. The tents used by the wealthy in India were admired by European travellers for the rich colours and design printed on calico.[12] What both Braudel and Adshead underline instead is the different ways in which material culture was understood at the opposite ends of Eurasia.

[11]   Braudel, *Capitalism and Material Life*, pp. 194–7.

[12]   See for instance François Pyrard, *The Voyage of François Pyrard of Laval to the East Indies, the Maldives, the Moluccas and Brazil* (London, 1887–88), p. 222. Pyrand describes a wooden house that 'within is hung with cotton or silk cloths of all colours, and of the finest and richest description available'. Pyrand, *Voyage*, p. 146.

Domestic textiles and furniture provide an intermediate category in between the durable and the transient, less structural than buildings, but linked to wider chronologies than clothing. Such a distinction is not recent and explains the very structure of inventories, documents that exclude both the transient (including clothing) and the durable (the so-called fixtures). This categorization has arrived to us in the broad division between 'real estate' (*immobilier* in French, *beni immobili* in Italian) and 'movable goods' (from which the Italian *mobile*, to signify a piece of furniture).[13] Since the later Middle Ages, domestic textiles have thus been seen in European culture as the connection between the short and long period, as well as between the individual dimension of clothing and the collective notion of a house. Rather than using the vocabulary and rules of fashion, as applied to textiles used in clothing, domestic textiles – though still shaped by elements of fashion and style – developed a rather more 'permanent' life, connected to the structuring of a household, its inner working, its continuity over time and its self image as a collective 'body'.[14]

A corollary of this European idiosyncrasy is the association between textiles and furniture. Part of the story of domestic textiles in early modern Europe relates to their complementarity with tables, chairs and beds. Textiles acted as facilitators in the use of new as well as old types of furniture and at the same time acquired from furniture a sense of permanence that was not necessarily inherent in their actual materiality.[15] But we must remember that this association, natural to Europeans, was not part of the way in which the domestic was structured and organized in other continents or other ethnic groups. In the Ottoman Empire, for instance, the complementarity between textiles and furniture never became common practice. The French observer Thévenot commented upon the fact that in late seventeenth-century Istanbul, '*quand il est heure de manger, les Turcs étendent à terre une nappe de maroquin, qu'ils appelent sofra*' ['when it is time to eat, the Turk spreads a Moroccan cloth on the floor, which they call a *sofra*'].[16] In Turkey, textiles had much more of a structural function and the absence of wooden furniture was made up with carpets, rugs, and cushions.[17]

---

[13] Adshead, *Material Culture*, pp. 102–3.

[14] Some of these points are developed by Whitney Walton with reference to nineteenth-century furniture. See Whitney Walton, '"Life is Nothing Without Furniture": Consumer Practices of the Parisian Bourgeoisie 1814–1870', *Proceeding of the Annual Meeting of the Western Society for French History*, 17 (1990): pp. 278–85.

[15] Kristen B. Neuschel, 'Noble Households in the Sixteenth Century: Material Settings and Human Communities', *French Historical Studies*, 15/4 (1988): pp. 602–3.

[16] Thévenot, *L'Empire du Grand turc, vu par un sujet de Louis XIV*, ed. F. Billacois (Paris, 1965), p. 92. Cit. in Jean–Paul Pascual, 'Meubles et objets domestiques quotidiens des intérieurs damascains du XVIIIe siècle', *Revue du Monde Musulman et de la Méditerranée*, 55–6 (1990): p. 200.

[17] A similar use of carpets and cushions on platforms for sitting, slightly raised from the floor, persisted in Spanish homes into the early modern era, as a result of Moorish

In contrast the common European trajectory of use for domestic furnishing was intertwined intrinsically with the *mobilier*. This is a point illustrated clearly in the quantitative analysis of inventories of Swedish households for the period 1673–1753.[18] This data shows a direct correlation between the value of textiles in a house and the value of furnishing (Figure 3.1).

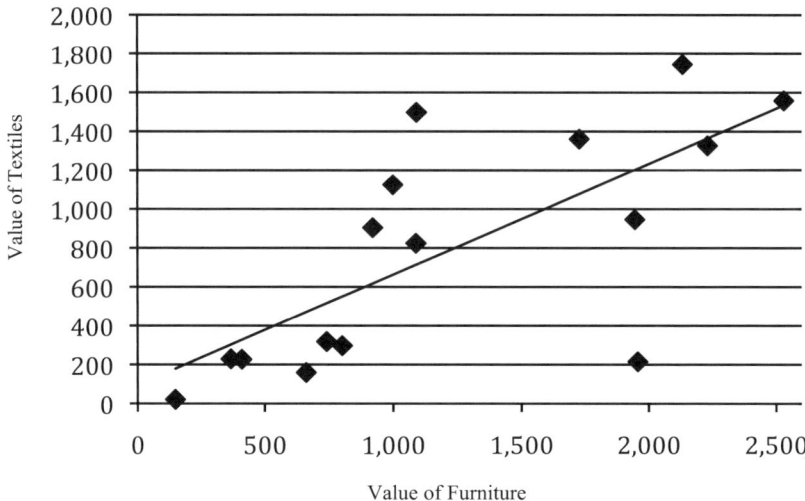

Source: Gudrun Andersson 'A Mirror of Oneself: Possessions and the Manifestation of Status among a Local Swedish Elite, 1650–1770', *Cultural and Social History*, 3/1 (2006), p. 26.

Figure 3.1   Value of textiles in 15 Swedish households compared to the value of furniture, 1673–1753 (in daler)

Rather than being in competition, or acting as substitutes, furnishing and textiles went hand-in-hand. New types of furniture in early modern Europe were closely linked with rising standards of material comfort. The expansion of textiles and clothing in the second half of the eighteenth century, for instance, induced the appearance of new pieces of furniture for storing textiles such as the chest of drawers and the wardrobe.[19] But textiles were central also to new social practices, such as the consumption of new drinks like tea, coffee and chocolate in the

---

influence. This example is a reminder of the sometimes variable relationships with domestic textiles even within Europe.

[18] Gudrun Andersson, 'A Mirror of Oneself: Possessions and the Manifestation of Status among a Local Swedish Elite, 1650–1770', *Cultural and Social History*, 3/1 (2006): pp. 21–44.

[19] Hester C. Dibbits, 'Between Society and Family Values: The Linen Cupboard in Early–Modern Households', in Anton Schuurman and Pieter Spierenburg (eds), *Private*

eighteenth century. Thus we find Benjamin Franklin explaining in his epistolary correspondence to his wife in 1758, how in London diaper tablecloths 'are to be spread on the Tea Table, for nobody breakfasts here on the naked Table, but on the Cloth set a large Tea Board with the Cups'.[20] Such new social practices needed material props both in terms of furniture and domestic textiles. Eighteenth-century conversation pieces capture the sense of material refinement that is in equal measures constructed by furniture, furnishing and domestic fabrics.

It is thus not surprising that the bed – the bedrock of the house, the site of conjugal bliss and the marital space of a couple, the place of birth and death – was not just the most prized piece of furniture, but also the most important space for textile use and display.[21] From the Middle Ages to at least the late seventeenth century, beds and bedding represented the most important item of expenditure in a house (Illustration 3.3).[22] Several layers of textiles that might include quilts, coverlets, counterpoints, sheets and pillows, completed the bed. Heavy bed curtains provided protection from the cold and a refuge for intimacy. William Harrison's 1577 *Description of England* reported on the spreading use of feather beds down the social scale, replacing the traditional flock beds employed for generations.[23] By the early seventeenth century it was not unknown even for relatively poor labourers to own several linen sheets. Robert Tettrington of Bedfordshire, who died in the late 1610s, owned five pairs of harden and two pairs of flaxen sheets valued at 26s. 8d. out of total assets worth just £4 17s.[24] Bedding also comprised the majority of household textiles in early eighteenth-century Chester County, Pennsylvania, with only 18 per cent of all textile items being for the table and 71 per cent for the bed.[25] The bed was central in the life of poor and rich alike. It was one of the most treasured belongings as confirmed by the fact that beds were

---

Domain, Public Inquiry: Families and Life–Styles in the Netherlands and Europe, 1550 to the Present (Hilversum, 1996), p. 138.

[20] Quoted in Brenda Collins, 'Matters Material and Luxurious – Eighteenth and Early Nineteenth–Century Irish Linen Consumption', in Jacqueline Hill and Colm Lennon (eds), *Luxury and Austerity: Papers Read before the 23rd Irish Conference of Historians* (Dublin, 1999), p. 114.

[21] Margaret Ponsonby, *Stories from Home: English Domestic Interiors, 1750–1850* (Aldershot, 2007), p. 111. See also Clive Edwards, *Turning houses into Homes: A History of the Retailing and Consumption of Domestic Furnishings* (Aldershot, 2005), pp. 18–19.

[22] Already in the thirteenth century a desirable bed included a feather mattress, under which there was a support in straw. T. Hudson Turner, *Some Account of Domestic Architecture in England from Richard II to Henry VIII* (2 vols, Oxford, 1859), vol. 2, p. 100.

[23] William Harrison, *Description of England*, ed. Georges Edelen (Ithaca, 1968), pp. 200–201.

[24] Anne Buck, 'Clothing and Textiles in Bedfordshire Inventories, 1617–1620', *Costume*, 34 (2000): p. 32.

[25] Adrienne D. Hood, *The Weaver's Craft. Cloth, Commerce, and Industry in Early Pennsylvania* (Philadelphia, 2003), p. 126.

The painting shows a bedroom interior with red furniture, including a four-poster bed with the curtains drawn in one corner.

Illustration 3.3   Scene in a Bedchamber. Oil on canvas, c. 1695–1704. Photo © Victoria and Albert Museum, London, P.25-1976

bequeathed to loyal servants or as charitable gifts to hospitals and institutions.[26] It was not uncommon for eighteenth-century French households to invest from 25 to 40 per cent of their wealth in beds.[27]

Already in the 1400s the canopy, curtains, headboard, bedspread and wall hangings formed a matched ensemble for the wealthy: this was the birth of the *chambre*.[28] The bed and its textile 'apparel' was at the same time the great cradle that provided a sense of protection from the cold, a site of intimacy and the conveyor of a sense of wealth and worth. Annik Pardailhé-Galabrun gives voice to the detailed descriptions of pillows, valances, curtains and bedposts, in a range of cottons, canvas, serge, taffeta, brocatelle, damask, satin and, more rarely, silks. The architecture of the bed varied from the *bâtard* bed to the more prestigious

---

[26] Annik Pardailhé–Galabrun, *The Birth of Intimacy: Privacy and Domestic Life in Early Modern Paris* (Philadelphia, 1988), p. 74. For Britain see: Francis W. Steer, *Farm and Cottage Inventories of Mid-Essex, 1635–1749* (Colchester, 1950), pp. 17–20.

[27] Pardailhé–Galabrun, *Birth of Intimacy*, p. 79. Daniel Roche, for instance, suggests that linen sheets became not only more frequent, but also longer, exceeding six metres in length in mid–eighteenth–century France. Daniel Roche, *A History of Everyday Things. The Birth of Consumption in France, 1600–1800* (Cambridge, 2000), pp. 183–4.

[28] Cit. in Georges Duby (ed.), *A History of Private Life. Vol. II. Revelations of the Medieval World* (5 vols, Cambridge, MA and London, 1988), pp. 494–5.

à l'impériale and *en tombeau*; the bed was as much aimed at securing physical comfort as it was the showcase of a wide array of textiles.[29] As John Crowley has observed, until the technological revolution in furniture in the early nineteenth century, novelty in beds was about textile display, rather than improvements in mattresses and bedsteads – a reflection of the new fashioning of domestic space in a process spread over generations.[30]

Wealth, Status and Display

This brief synthesis of the European history of beds and bedding illustrates how textiles were at the same time the result of increasing material sophistication and shapers of cultural and social well-being.[31] The economic and cultural values of these fabrics, although belonging to two separate conceptual spheres, overlapped considerably, especially in the conveyance of notions of status and in the visual arena of display. Domestic textiles were used as a sign of wealth as evidenced by their high elasticity compared to income (Figure 3.2).[32] This was true up to high levels of wealth when other more conspicuous articles, such as silver, paintings and other artistic products, replaced textiles as signs of social standing.[33] However, for most people, the accumulation of textiles remained a function of their income. The setting up of a household implied in all probability a consistent initial outlay that continued over time both in terms of the acquisition of additional (non-essential) items and frequent repairs. Textiles were a social priority as they provided colour, but also warmth, privacy, decoration and, above all, status.[34]

Adrienne Hood provides an illuminating view of the role of textiles (both as apparel and domestic fabrics) in creating and in consuming the wealth of relatively prosperous households in late seventeenth-century rural Pennsylvania. She calculates that a family of six would need 45 yards of cloth each year just to replace a minimal amount of worn fabrics. While petticoats, shifts, cloaks, breeches, shirts, waistcoats and coats needed a relatively small amount of cloth (2 to 4 yards) with occasional larger amounts for great coats (5 yards) and gowns (7 yards), textiles for the home could be produced either by using very small lengths (less than a yard for a napkins, a tablecloth or a towel) or conspicuous

---

[29] Pardailhé–Galabrun, *Birth of Intimacy*, pp. 75–9.
[30] Crowley, *Invention of Comfort*, p. 7.
[31] Dibbits, 'Between Society and Family Values', p. 130.
[32] Here I use total value as a proxy of income. *See Andersson, 'A Mirror of Oneself'*.
[33] See for instance the splendid catalogue of the Exhibition *At Home*, held at the Victoria and Albert Museum in 2006. Marta Ajmar-Wollheim and Flora Dennis (eds), *At Home in Renaissance Italy* (London, 2006). For a methodological analysis see also: Marta Ajmar-Wollheim, Flora Dennis, and Ann Matchette (eds), *Approaching the Italian Renaissance Interior: Sources, Methodologies, Debates* (Malden, MA, 2007).
[34] Edwards, *Turning Houses into Homes*, p. 14.

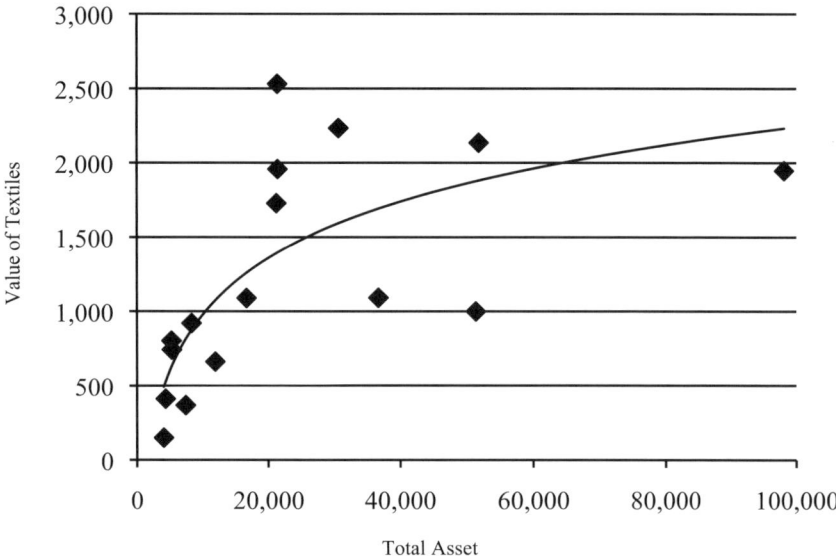

Source: Gudrun Andersson 'A Mirror of Oneself: Possessions and the Manifestation of Status among a Local Swedish Elite, 1650–1770', *Cultural and Social History*, 3/1 (2006), p. 26.

Figure 3.2　Value of textiles in 15 Swedish households compared to the total assets, 1673–1753

quantities of cloth as in the case of sheets and blankets (6 yards) or bed ticks (10 yards). Bed furniture could require an enormous amount of fabric: 50 yards for a set of bed curtains, valences, covers and window curtains.[35] The considerable initial investment in domestic textiles and their continuous upkeep channelled wealth into a more permanent and material form.

Even as we focus on the patterns of accumulation, it is important to note that early modern houses would appear very bare to our modern eyes. In recent decades historians have identified a 'consumer revolution' in seventeenth- and eighteenth-century England, Continental Europe and Colonial America. An unprecedented expansion in the supply, retail and final consumption of a variety of consumer goods transformed the material appearance of dwellings from the top of the social ladder down to the poorer sorts. Historians have analysed the influence of new and exotic materials and commodities, and the excitement inspired by petty luxuries and populuxe goods.[36] However, there is a risk in over-emphasizing abundance.

---

[35] Adrienne Hood, 'The Material World of Cloth: Production and Use in Eighteenth-Century Rural Pennsylvania', *William and Mary Quarterly*, 53/1 (1996): pp. 48–50.

[36] Cissie Fairchilds, 'The Production and Marketing of Populuxe Goods in Eighteenth-Century Paris', in John Brewer and Roy Porter (eds), *Consumption and the World of Goods*

This was a long-lasting process rather than an immediate achievement, secured over the course of many generations. Nearly two decades ago, Lorna Weatherill emphasized the relatively low starting point in the material well-being of late seventeenth- to mid-eighteenth-century people. Floors were mostly uncovered, curtains were largely absent, as were wall hangings and cushions. If in the upper social strata such objects were relatively common before 1675, they still had to find their way into the houses of the majority of people by 1730.[37]

The low starting point makes the growing use of domestic textiles appear particularly intense; however, a further problem remains in that the increasing availability of specific items was often counterbalanced by the disappearance of other forms of material culture. The data collected by Mark Overton and his team for the county of Kent in England during the period 1600–1750 indicates how over 150 years the median number of items of furniture doubled, rising from 12 to 24 items per household (Figure 3.3).[38] Feather beds became on average more common. By contrast, and as part of the increasing association between furniture and textiles, carpets and cushions declined and increasingly were replaced by upholstered furniture[39] (Illustration 3.4). The connection between upholstering and furniture started in the mid 1600s and continued for around three centuries until the interwar period, thus validating the aphorism about the 'rise of soft furnishing in hard times'.[40] Other commodities such as coverlets and quilts also multiplied during the seventeenth and eighteenth centuries; but their surge was accompanied by the disappearance of other established forms of decorative and practical textiles such as bed rugs.[41] Likewise, during the seventeenth century, especially in North-western Europe, it was not uncommon to replace traditional linen tablecloths with more sophisticated and fashionable Turkish rugs (Illustration 3.5).[42]

(London and New York, 1993), pp. 228–48; Maxine Berg, 'New Commodities, Luxuries and Their Consumers in Eighteenth-Century England', in Maxine Berg and Helen Clifford (eds), *Consumers and Luxury: Consumer Culture in Europe, 1650–1850* (Manchester, 1999), pp. 63–85. For a general survey of debates see: Maxine Berg, *Luxury and Pleasure in Eighteenth-Century Britain* (Oxford, 2005). Linda Levy Peck presents a more conservative view for the seventeenth century in Linda Levy Peck, *Consuming Splendor: Society and Culture in Seventeenth-Century England* (Cambridge, 2005).

[37] Weatherill, *Consumer Behaviour*, p. 8.
[38] Overton, et al., *Production and Consumption*, pp. 91, 95.
[39] Overton, et al., *Production and Consumption*. Their use still remained widespread for all of the seventeenth century. Rothstein and Levey, 'Furninshings', p. 631.
[40] On early seventeenth-century upholstered furniture see Ralph Edwards, *A History of the English Chair* (London, 1951).
[41] Hood, 'Material World of Cloth', p. 62.
[42] As in La Fontaine's fable: '*Sur un tapis de Turquie / Le couvert se trouva mis.* On a rug in Turkey made / The host's table has been laid'. Cit. Pardailhé-Galabrun, *Birth of Intimacy*, p. 97.

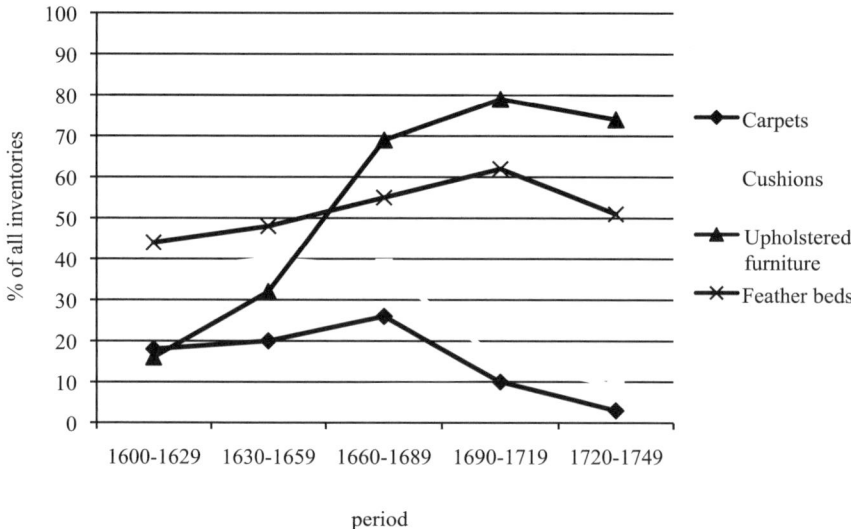

Source: Mark Overton, Jane Whittle, Darron Dean and Andrew Hann, *Production and Consumption in English Households, 1600–1750* (London and New York, 2004), pp. 91–5.

Figure 3.3   Selected furniture in Kent, 1600–1750

Figures are limited when we consider qualitative changes over time. Many textile historians have underlined that an increasing variety of choice, innovation in texture and colours, in weave and material effects that characterized both domestic and bodily textiles during the early modern period. Silk, and even more so the new draperies and later cottons, brought reduced prices, modified products and changed the average life of domestic textiles; they also produced new uses and inspired novel practical and conceptual associations between space, people and cloth. And such variety augmented choice among people of different means. The use of tapestries and other wall coverings, for instance, was popular in seventeenth and eighteenth-century Paris, with more than three-quarters of inventories describing such items.[43] The most common of such tapestries, worth just 10 *livres* per *aune* [1.15 m], was the so-called 'Bergamo', as it was originally

---

[43]   In England, painted cloth became common in the sixteenth century. More than a third of the inventories examined by Anne Buck for early seventeenth-century Bedfordshire mention painted cloths, especially in 'lodging chambers'. They were probably rough decorative textiles made of coarse linen, Osnabrucks and brown hemp roles, and painted with large strokes of green, red and brown. Very few of them survive. Buck, 'Clothing and Textiles', p. 33; Margaret Spufford, *The Great Reclothing of Rural England: Petty Chapmen and Their Wares in the Seventeenth Century* (Oxford, 1984), p. 112; Nicholas Mander, 'Painted Cloths: History, Craftsmen and Techniques', *Textile History*, 28/2 (1997): pp. 119–48.

This lady, probably a noblewoman, is standing next to an upholstered chair. This would have been a new item of furnishing still to be found only in wealthy households in the first half of the seventeenth century.

Illustration 3.4. A Lady, attributed to Gilbert Jackson. Oil on canvas, c. 1625–34. Photo © Victoria and Albert Museum, London, 565–1882. Bequeathed by John Jones

produced in the eponymous Northern Italian town, but as early as the 1620s it was imitated successfully in Lyons. Middle-class Parisian consumers preferred instead Auvergne tapestries, a more expensive type in such demand as to command royal protection from the 1660s. At the top of the social ladder, the rich could afford Flemish tapestries worth from 60 to 100 *livres* per *aune*.[44] In the eighteenth century, this segmentation of the market was altered by the introduction of new materials, both textiles and non-textiles.[45] Wallpaper and wood panelling were of course new options that transcended textiles, and were possible thanks to new standards

---

[44] Pardailhé-Galabrun, *Birth of Intimacy*, pp. 147–9.
[45] Braudel, *Capitalism and Material Life*, pp. 213–14.

Turkish 'rugs' or 'carpets' used to cover tables are often represented in sixteenth- and seventeenth-century paintings of Dutch interiors.

Illustration 3.5   Turkish carpet, possibly produced in Turkey or Egypt, c. 1550. Photo © Victoria and Albert Museum, London, 151–1883

of warmth and lower levels of damp than in previous centuries.[46] But the strong French tradition in textile wall decoration – still visible in the preservation of floral textile design on wallpaper in many French dwellings – meant a new engagement with velvets, *brocatelles*, *siamois*, silk moiré and printed cottons.[47]

Quantitative increases and the extension of choice and variety conceal profound differences between commodities and consumers. Floor coverings, in the shape of floor-cloths, for instance, became common only in the second half of the eighteenth century, achieving popularity only with the introduction of linoleum in the 1860s.[48] In many other cases the adoption of specific textiles was influenced by cultural and

---

[46]   Christine Velut, 'Between Invention and Production: The Role of Design in the Manufacture of Wallpaper in France and England at the Turn of the Nineteenth Century', *Journal of Design History*, 17/1 (2004): pp. 55–69. For their success in the nineteenth century see: Helen C. Long, *The Edwardian House. The Middle-Class Home in Britain 1880–1914* (Manchester, 1993), pp. 154–7.

[47]   Pardailhé-Galabrun, *Birth of Intimacy*, pp. 140–51.

[48]   Clive D. Edwards, 'Floorcloth and Linoleum: Aspects of the History of Oil-coated Materials for Floors', *Textile History*, 27/2 (1996): pp. 148–71; Sophie Sarin, 'The Floorcloth and Other Floor Coverings in the London Domestic Interior 1700–1800', *Journal of Design History*, 18/2 (2005): pp. 133–45.

social preferences: what one might call the '*mentalité* of materiality'.[49] Objects act as the articulation of personal and social identities, and were used to pursue strategies of cultural, social and economic advancement. They were, at the same time, tokens of belonging to specific social groups that share collective values, principles and ideas. Maxine Berg's research on wills, for instance, confirms the importance of linen as an item of value. Her comparative analysis of men's and women's wills in eighteenth-century Birmingham and Sheffield shows how linen was amongst the most common personal belonging left by testators. But women, much more than men, invested linen with personal meaning, and often collected in the course of their lives items to be passed down to future generations at their death.[50]

Regional practices and geographic peculiarities were profoundly influential in shaping patterns of consumption. Focusing on window curtains, Lorna Weatherill chartered a correlation between increasing material prosperity and the construction of new ideas such as the concept of privacy. But the use of curtains was as much a function of new ideas and principles as of specific circumstances or access to markets. Thus curtains were used by just 6 per cent of rural households in late-seventeenth- and early eighteenth-century England, compared to 15 per cent in urban households and by a very high 43 per cent in London dwellings.[51] There were also profound differences from place to place. In the first half of the seventeenth century, for example, upholstered furniture was already widespread among Kentish gentlemen, as well as middle-class retailers, and a century later all classes of all incomes possessed at least one item of upholstered furniture. Kent, situated in the southeast of England, in proximity to London and with a number of major ports, was well positioned amidst the flow of commodities and was a relatively wealthy region. On the other hand, upholstered furniture remained limited in the remote southwestern county of Cornwall, showing even a regression between the end of the seventeenth and the mid-eighteenth century.[52]

---

[49] On this perspective see: Dominique Poulot, 'Une nouvelle histoire de la culture matérielle?', *Revue d'Histoire Moderne et Contemporaine*, 44/2 (1997): pp. 344–57.

[50] Maxine Berg, 'Women's Consumption and the Industrial Classes in Eighteenth-Century England', *Journal of Social History*, 30/2 (1996): pp. 420, 424, and 426. In Birmingham women were 50 per cent more likely than men to bequeath linen in their wills. In Sheffield such difference was 90 per cent. Berg, 'Women's Consumption', p. 420.

[51] Weatherill, 'Consumer Behaviour', pp. 201–2. See also Margaret Ponsonby, 'Towards an Interpretation of Textiles in the Provincial Domestic Interior: Three Homes in the West Midlands, 1780–1848', *Textile History*, 38/2 (2007): pp. 165–78.

[52] Overton, et al., *Production and Consumption*, p. 191.

The Meaning of Textiles

Agency, together with meaning, becomes a central issue in the analysis of early modern material culture and domestic textiles in particular.[53] If income and the relationship with furniture seem to explain a great deal about the quantitative presence of textiles in early modern households, the same cannot be said about the shifting significance attributed by people to textiles. The study of materiality – what is now developing as the discipline of the history of material culture – moves the focus of analysis from people to things and people's relationship with things.[54] By doing so, it presents fresh views on the relevance of human agency, beyond the classic economic cliché of the individual consumer maximizing his or her own utility. In this context, reliance on inventories, for instance, can be misleading.[55] Inventories provide guidance and hard evidence on structural changes over time, but forget the vast number of people with little or no choice on the matter of their physical and material belongings. And those excluded are not just people '*sans feu, sans lieu, sans aveu*' ['without heat, without position, without acknowledgement'], as defined in sixteenth-century France.[56]

According to John Styles, inventories exclude also the great number of people who lived in rented accommodation and benefited from the use of furnishings and textiles that they possessed, but did not own. The nuclear family, in legal possession of its material belonging and possibly of the house it inhabited, was perhaps the most common social structure, but was surely not the only one. Styles's recent research is in line with what historians have gathered from inventories and other sources. In London in the mid-eighteenth century, sheets and blankets were the items most commonly stolen from lodging, easy to carry away, but also clearly omnipresent. Pillows, bolsters, bed and window curtains, valances, testers and head cloths followed in the list. However, this research proposes a different interpretation of their meaning. Their personal and material value and the connection between textiles and other objects that is less concerned with choice

---

[53] On the methodological issues related to material culture see Richard Grassby, 'Material Culture and Cultural History', *Journal of Interdisciplinary History*, 35/4 (2005): pp. 591–603; Leora Auslander, 'Beyond Words', *American Historical Review*, 110/4 (2006): pp. 1015–44.

[54] See for instance Karen Harvey (ed.), *History and Material Culture* (London, 2009).

[55] See Giorgio Riello, 'Geography and Environment', in James Marten and Elizabeth Foyster (eds), *A Cultural History of Childhood and Family. Vol. 4: The Age of Enlightenment (1650–1800)* (Oxford, forthcoming, 2010).

[56] Joël Cornette, 'La révolution des objets: le Paris des inventaires apres décès (XVIIe–XVIIIe siècles)', *Revue d'Histoire Moderne et Contemporaine*, 36 (1989): p. 480. See also Jean Queniart, 'L'utilisation des inventaires en histoire socio-culturelle', in Bernard Vogler (ed.), *Les actes notariés. Sources de l'histoire sociale XVIe–XIXe siècles. Actes du colloque de Strasbourg (mars 1978)* (Strasbourg, 1979), pp. 242–3.

and more a factor of people's shifting fortunes, material compromise, and transient economic and social situation in life.[57]

The concept of agency is particularly appropriate for the study of domestic textiles. Historically, fashion with all its apparent folly, irrational characterization and bodily appearance, has been regarded as dominated by women, and shaped by female desires and angst. Domestic textiles propose a different interpretation. Shifting from the public arena of fashion, to the private arena of the home, the acquisition of these goods posits a rather more cautious view of consumption shaped by collective needs that transcend the individual. Again, women are central, but this time as shapers and shakers as well as custodians of materiality. The maternal and uxorial figure is thus not just a character in the construction of house, home and household, but the nexus between ideas, expectations and anticipations of familial life and the actual physical forms that these assume over time, be it either historical time, the time of a lifecycle or the seasons of a year. Women, through their work on embroidery, shell-work and general needlecraft, were instrumental in shaping the physicality of domestic textiles, but also in influencing the overall ideas that such textiles conveyed within domestic settings.[58] Ladies produced large pieces of needlework that an upholsterer could then use for coverings of seats and chairs.[59] Historians of textiles, design and botany have long analysed the complex process of transposition between nature and artefact, identifying sources for inspiration and learning for textiles from prints and paintings, botanical samples and herbals. The language of flora was a shared idiom through which exteriors and interiors, natural and artefactual were connected. The *Female Spectator* of 1745 instructed its readers on the 'Beauty and Fragrancy' of the rose, the jasmine, the orange-flower or the auricola and remarked upon the fact that 'When deprived of the originals by the cold Blasts of Winter, we have them copied in Painting, Japanning and in Embroidery'.[60]

Women were expected to be knowledgeable about the techniques of production of domestic textiles, their up-keep and the best way to make them fully part of a house. By the mid-eighteenth century this combination was framed into a tacit code

---

[57] John Styles, 'Lodging at the Old Bailey: Lodgings and their Furnishings in Eighteenth-Century London', in John Styles and Amanda Vickery (eds), *Gender, Taste and Material Culture in Britain and North America, 1700–1830* (New Haven and London, 2006), pp. 61–80. See Also John Styles, *The Dress of the People: Everyday Fashion in Eighteenth-Century England* (New Haven and London, 2007).

[58] Amanda Vickery, *Behind Closed Doors: At Home in Georgian England* (London and New Haven, 2009), pp. 233-4. See also Ruth Geuter, 'Reconstructing the Context of Seventeenth-Century English Figurative Embroideries', in Moira Donald and Linda Hurcombe (eds), *Gender and Material Culture in Historical Perspective* (London, 2001), pp. 97–111.

[59] Ponsonby, *Stories from Home*, p. 80.

[60] Quoted in Peter McNeil, 'Everlasting: The Flowers in Fashion and Textiles', in *Everlasting: The Flowers in Fashion and Textiles* (Victoria, Australia, 2005), p. 17.

of 'harmonization of design influences'. If only the wealthy could afford room sets, authored by the latest designer, an increasing share of consumers conceived tastefulness in terms of integration between textiles and other forms of material culture, with hybrid elements of style added to rooms. In 1750, for instance, the well-to-do lady Mary Delany explained in a letter to her sister the importance of 'putting up blue and white linen and blue and white paper hangings'.[61] Cotton textiles were central in such a transformation. Their modest price, bright colours and bold patterns allowed decoration on a scale hitherto unknown. And as observed by Beverly Lemire, their success across Europe started in the sixteenth century in domestic settings providing for panelling and screens, cushions and other textile hangings, thus eventually slipping onto the bodies of fashion-conscious consumers a century later.[62] The invention of copper plates in the mid-eighteenth century furthered the process of integration of textiles into the visual and design appearance of other realms of domestic material culture. Increasingly textiles were fashioned in lighter colours with vast expanses of whites on which blues and reds told stories of battles, fables, of ancient ruins and pleasant country scenes.[63]

I have examined elsewhere the relationship between such a syntactic shift in the language of textiles and eighteenth-century European technological innovations in printing and dyeing.[64] Here, let me observe only how the success of *toiles* was not limited to their multifarious semiotic nature. Increasingly they fell into line with a specific European aesthetic idea of domestic design based on the organic association between textiles, porcelain, furniture, and other realms of material culture. I would like to suggest that textiles experienced profound transformations in terms of their making and meaning as part of an overall re-configuration of materiality in its quantity, character, nature and economic and cultural value. In some cases such co-ordinations are still with us. The aesthetic association between the vitreous paleness of chinaware and the whiteness of diaper tablecloth, for instance, has been reinforced by the fossilization of social practices over the last two centuries. This of course was true for the top of the social hierarchy whose houses were the result of concerted efforts between haberdashers, designers and clients, particularly since the eighteenth century. But it was also true for the more modest interiors, where the rising figure of the modern consumer was keen to invest money, time and attention to create a *comfortable* environment, and such comfort was increasingly psychological rather than physical.

---

[61] Quoted in Collins, 'Matters Material and Luxurious', p. 112.

[62] Beverly Lemire, 'Domesticating the Exotic: Floral Culture and the East India Calico Trade with England, c. 1600–1800', *Textile: The Journal of Cloth and Culture*, 1/1 (2003): pp. 65–85.

[63] Beverly Lemire and Giorgio Riello, 'East and West: Textiles and Fashion in Eurasia in the Early Modern Period', *Journal of Social History*, 41/4 (2008): pp. 887–916.

[64] Giorgio Riello, 'Asian Knowledge and the Development of Calico Printing in Europe in the Seventeenth and Eighteenth Centuries', *Journal of Global History*, 5 (2010).

The Life of Textiles

One of the problems in analysing domestic textiles and their change over time is the act of imbuing them with a certain degree of 'independence', thus supporting an explanation of their existence – and at time numerical incidence – simply by conferring shifting cultural meanings upon them. This is a wider problem that affects many parts of the 'world of goods' as it has been defined by Brewer and Porter and later developed by a long string of consumer historians. Economic historians have sorted out this problem by anchoring their explanations to straightforward aggregate or individual value. Appadurai, insisted 20 years ago that the simple process of economic commodification was not sufficient to explain things; he suggested contextualizing materiality within a social life that was as much human as material.[65] Thus the meaning of a certain object does not explain its existence. Rather this existence is the result of an interactive process between objects and people in which 'meaning' is a temporary agreement in the continuous process of negotiation between the parts. Such interaction and negotiation is defined as a 'social life'.

This explanation about the very existence of things is necessary in order to highlight a grey area in the study of domestic textiles. The history of architecture and interior decoration has given scant attention to textiles. The classic books on the history of Tudor, Georgian or Victorian interiors – with rare exceptions – hardly refer to textiles. When authors of such books take textiles into consideration at all, the roles they ascribe are superficial, decorative at most, the final touch to structural elements. Thus, the Georgian interior is created through the use of fireplaces, tiles, marbles, statues, architectural elements, doors and window frames.[66] The fact that the historical study of interiors is based on sources about their construction prevents us from seeing how textiles shaped the subsequent life of such interiors. Their re-styling and updating relied upon new upholstering or fashionable wall coverings to refresh the appearance of a house at a fraction of the original construction cost.

Textiles are relevant in the daily life of a house or household, through cycles of use and replacement in time. Textiles could hardly achieve patina, but often blended into interiors that were 'homely' and 'cosy', rather than fashionable.[67] As Margaret Ponsonby observes 'The habit of "recycling" furniture and furnishings meant that items were retained in the home long after fashion had changed'.[68]

---

[65] Arjun Appadurai (ed.), *The Social life of Things: Commodities in Cultural Perspective* (Cambridge, 1986), see in particular the editor's introduction.

[66] Hannah Greig and Giorgio Riello, 'Eighteenth-Century Interiors – Redesigning the Georgian: Introduction', *Journal of Design History*, 20/4 (2007): pp. 273–89.

[67] On the concept of patina see: Grant D. McCracken, *Culture and Consumption: New Approaches to the Symbolic Character of Consumer Goods and Activities* (Bloomington, 1988).

[68] Ponsonby, *Stories from Home*, p. 80.

What I would define as the 'social life of textiles' was connected not just with time but also to space. The space of a home is the physical 'condition' in which textiles are located, but at the same time is also a practical concept that is influenced by textiles. Lena Orlin, for instance, shows how in the sixteenth century a simple linen sheet could be used to divide spaces and thus create intimacy, in a world in which physical separation was not necessarily constructed by a wall.[69] From the seventeenth century, textiles were also used in ways that reinforced the architectural specialization of space.[70] Their presence or absence, and also their purpose and physical and design qualities created hierarchies in the functional division of a house into discrete spaces of activity.[71] The relationship between material culture and space is now a focus of research of a new generation of historical geographers. So far, however, their interest has been directed mostly towards geographies of urban and rural space,[72] leaving the connection between the spatial and the artefactual under-studied. How peculiar, for instance, is the European mix between horizontal (a carpet), vertical (a tapestry) and self-standing (upholstered furniture) – all dimensions of textiles? And what is their relationship in time in the evolution of furnishings?[73]

These are just a few of the questions that future research on the fashioning of material culture will have to address. Let me just highlight here how instrumental textiles were in the connection between space and time in a household. The very action of storing and preserving coverlets, stuffs, and even more so linen, was central to the domestic ritual of medieval and early modern life. Textiles had to

[69] Lena Cowen Orlin, 'Walls and their Chinks in Early Modern England' (Paper presented at the Workshop 'Putting Objects in Their Places', Shakespeare Institute, Stratford, 18 June 2005.

[70] Ursula Priestley and Penelope J. Corfield, 'Rooms and Room Use in Norwich Housing, 1580–1730', *Post-Medieval Archaeology*, 16 (1982): pp. 93–123; Frank E. Brown, 'Continuity and Change in the Urban House: Developments in Domestic Space Organisation in Seventeenth-Century London', *Comparative Studies in Society and History*, 28/3 (1986): pp. 558–90. See also Adrian B. Evans, 'Consumption and the Exotic in Early Modern England: A Socio-Material Investigation of the Retail, Domestic Ownership and Use of Exotic Goods in Suffolk and Bristol' (Unpublished Ph.D. thesis, University of Bristol, 2001).

[71] See for instance Mimi Hellman, 'Furniture, Sociability, and the Work of Leisure in Eighteenth-Century France', *Eighteenth-Century Studies*, 32/4 (1999): pp. 415–45.

[72] See in particular Miles Ogborn, *Spaces of Modernity: London's Geographies, 1680–1780* (New York and London, 1998); Carl B. Estabrook, *Urbane and Rustic England: Cultural Ties and Social Spheres in the Provinces 1660–1780* (Manchester, 1998); Jane Rendell, *The Pursuit of Pleasure: Gender, Space and Architecture in Regency London* (London, 2002); Miles Ogborn and Charles W.J. Withers (eds), *Georgian Geographies: Essays on Space, Place and Landscape in the Eighteenth Century* (Manchester and New York, 2004). For a summary of literature see: Miles Ogborn, 'Georgian Geographies?' *Journal of Historical Geography*, 24/2 (1998): pp. 218–23.

[73] This is one of the interpretations of Chinese furniture. See Sarah Handler, *Austere Luminosity of Chinese Classic Furniture* (Berkeley, 2001), p. 22.

last as long as possible. In the mid-seventeenth century an English yellow canvas was said to resist 11 or 12 years of constant use compared to the more pleasant but also more fragile German linen lasting just five or six years.[74] Use was an engagement that required constant care and attention. This was firstly seasonal as 'vermin gather when the cold weather of autumn and winter growth milder and be born in the summer'.[75] The *Boke of Nurture*, written between 1460 and 1470, also explains that the domestic task of the mistress of a house included the maintenance of textiles as she must 'brusche them clenly and ... never wollyn cloth ne furre passé a sevenyght to be unbrosshen and skakyn'.[76] Periodical 'little laundries' were as important as the annual or seasonal 'big streamings' in a culture increasingly attentive to cleanliness.[77]

Georges Vigarello proposed that linen acquired an intrinsic connection with a culture of cleanliness in early modern Europe.[78] This was a notion of cleanliness based on textiles touching the body rather than on ablutions involving the body itself. Physical comfort was related firstly to the body and from there to the bed where white sheets, nightcaps and nightgowns were progressively seen as necessary tools of health and comfort. Such health, hygienic and sanitary connotations made linen the most popular textile for clothing as well as domestic use until the late-eighteenth century.[79] The replacement of woollen hangings by linens and, later, cottons provided not only lighter materials and colours but also a dramatic drop in the bugs and vermin that had, for centuries, infested beds and pillows, bolsters and bed curtains. Linen's identification with cleanliness and purity was thus shifted from the bed into the realm of polite social interaction, serving as a material base for the omnipresent napkins and tablecloths.

---

[74] Spufford, *Great Reclothing*, p. 111.

[75] John Russell, 'Boke of Nurture', in F.J. Furnivall (ed.), *Early English Meals and Manners: John Russell's Boke of Nurture* (London, 1868), p. 64.

[76] Russell, 'Boke of Nurture', p. 64.

[77] Roche, *History of Everyday Things*, p. 160.

[78] Georges Vigarello, *Concepts of Cleanliness: Changing Attitudes in France since the Middle Ages* (Cambridge, 1988). See also Douglas Biow, *The Culture of Cleanliness in Renaissance Italy* (Ithaca and London, 2006).

[79] Veronika Sekules, 'Spinning Yarns: Clean Linen and Domestic Values in Late Medieval French Culture', in Anne L. McClanan and Karen Rosoff Encarnación (eds), *The Material Culture of Sex, Procreation, and Marriage in Premodern Europe* (Basingstoke, 2001), pp. 79–91. My estimates for mid-eighteenth-century England suggest that linen accounted for 55–57 per cent of all textiles for value. However, due to their low price per yard compared to woollens and silks, hemp and flax fabrics were probably around 70–73 per cent of all domestic textiles and clothing. Their use comprised sheets, bedding, window hangings, table cloths and napkins, as well as towels and kitchen cloth. Giorgio Riello, 'The Ecology of Textiles in Early Modern Europe: Possibilities and Potentials' (Unpublished paper presented at the GEHN Conference on 'A Global History of Cotton Textiles', University of Padua, 17–19 November 2005) (http://www.lse.ac.uk/collections/economicHistory/GEHN/GEHNPaduaConferencePapers.htm).

Linen, perhaps more than any other textile became central in the life of European households until the twentieth century. It conveyed notions of wealth and established precise gender relationships in the management of a household. The investigation of the seventeenth-century linen chests shows how linen was inscribed within relationships between gender, space and textiles in the Dutch Republic. Gender relationships in seventeenth-century Dutch households were mediated through the symbolic and practical functioning of linen chests.[80] The chest was a microcosm that represented the wider household and was used as the *inner sanctum* of privacy and family memories, thus conveying notions of worth and worthiness that were consciously deposited in female hands (Illustration 3.6). Women were measured

This painting shows the importance of managing the safe keeping of linen. The mistress of the house is busy checking the household linen with the help of a maid.

Illustration 3.6   Interior with Ladies by a Linen Cupboard by Pieter de Hooch, 1663. Oil on canvas, 72 x 77.5 cm. © Rijksmueum, Amsterdam

---

[80] Rachel Fuller, 'Out of Sight, Out of Mind? The Meaning of the Linnenkast in the Material and Conceptual Landscape of the Seventeenth-Century Dutch Republic' (Unpublished MA Thesis, V&A/RCA History of Design Programme, 2004).

by their performance as good housewives and their conduct was compared with the abundant moralistic and prescriptive literature on housekeeping.[81] But the linen chests worked also as a token of display: they were often placed in visible positions in the house, and richly decorated, they transmitted to visitors and guests a clear sense of lineage, patina and wealth, by suggesting, rather than showing, its content. Textiles in this case functioned as a spatial marker of status through a conceptual and metaphorical reference. Women as the key holders, controlled not only the right of access to the textile treasures inside a chest, but functioned also as guarantors to the genuine existence of a content worthy of praise and admiration.[82]

Conclusion

This chapter situates textiles within the physical and conceptual *milieu* of early modern European domestic spaces. It has done so firstly by considering the recent theoretical and historical research carried out in the broad field of the history of material culture and by raising a series of questions on how textiles interacted with other realms of materiality. Historians have suggested a rise in the physical presence of textiles, especially in the seventeenth and eighteenth centuries. But what was the outcome of such a material shift? Textiles can assume as wide a range of meaning as the uses for which they are employed. In this sense, they connect different chronologies and different ideas of spatiality in the life of a house. Some of these meanings are peculiarly European and are born out of a specific way of organizing material life. Others have changed in time and fostered the continuous re-invention of what textiles are and what textiles mean, refashioning the home in the process.

---

[81] See for instance for the Netherlands, Simon Schama, *The Embarrassment of Riches: An Interpretation of Dutch Culture in the Golden Age* (London, 1987), pp. 375–97.

[82] See for instance Dibbits, 'Between Society and Family Values'. On table linen, see Pardailhé-Galabrun, *Birth of Intimacy*, pp. 96–7.

Chapter Four

Luxury, Fashion and Peasantry: The Introduction of New Commodities in Rural Catalan, 1670–1790

Belén Moreno Claverías

To be a peasant in pre-industrial Catalonia, one not only had to live *off* the land and *in* the country, one also had to seem like a peasant. In a society that found itself halfway between the old and the new regimes, the codes that served to identify the distinguishing features of certain social groups were still unequivocal. A peasant – *pagès* in Catalan – came across unmistakably as a peasant, regardless of income. There is clearly a link between consumption habits and belonging to a specific group; but what was the cause and effect relationship between these two variables? In other words, was it class that determined consumption or was it consumption that determined class?[1]

This issue arose at a time when the dividing lines between different social strata were becoming blurred or, at least, more permeable. Stratified society was breaking down, partly due to the development of the market economy. Money began to acquire more importance than birth when it came to determining an individual's position on the social ladder, and some social sectors took advantage to climb up a few rungs. This was the case, for example, with certain craftsmen or merchants whose new-found wealth enabled them to rub shoulders with members of high society, to dress and eat like them, all of which was absolutely essential if they wanted their offspring to secure marriages with members of social classes superior to their own. It was in these processes of social climbing that the role of consumption as an indicator of wealth and family status manifested itself most explicitly.

This is also the period in which the 'consumer revolution' made its presence felt in certain parts of Europe. McKendrick suggests that eighteenth-century England was witness to the first 'consumption revolution', comparable only, in his opinion, with the Neolithic Revolution in terms of the far-reaching social changes it produced. However, it was not the desire to consume that was new in the eighteenth century, since this desire is as old as mankind itself, but rather 'the ability to do so which was new', which led to the creation of a new structure of demand in

---

[1] Moreno Claverías, Belén, *Consum i condicions de vida a la Catalunya Moderna. El Penedès, 1670–1790* (Vilafranca del Penedès: Andana, 2007).

English society. For this author, the 'consumption revolution' was 'the necessary analogue to the industrial revolution, the necessary convulsion on the demand side of the equation to match the convulsion on the supply side'.[2] In order to investigate this process, he adopted two ideas from the field of social sciences: the notion of 'conspicuous consumption' developed by Veblen in 1899 and Simmel's 'trickle-down' concept in 1904.[3] From this point of view, the consumption revolution of the eighteenth century was a status contest between the different social sectors, in which fashionable consumer goods became the best tool for social climbing. Since the investigations of McKendrick, Porter and Brewer, numerous monographs have analysed changes in consumption patterns in Europe and the United States. Most of them, however, refer to consumption patterns in urban areas, whereas rural regions have aroused far less interest.[4] What was happening in the country while people in the big cities 'were going mad' about luxury and fashion? Were peasants in some way involved in the development of the supply of manufactured products and in the changes in demand? What was their relationship with this expansion of luxury and fashion?

In order to find out, over 800 post-mortem inventories for the period 1670 to 1790 have been analysed, 56 per cent of which belong to people classed as 'peasants' in the notarial documents. The geographic sphere of analysis is el Penedés, a region of Catalonia which stretches inland from the coast, to the south of the city of Barcelona, although a sample from the Catalan capital has been assessed in order to observe the differences between urban and rural consumption (see Map 4.1).

Why use post-mortem inventories for an historical account of consumption? Because in spite of their limitations, they are still the most suitable source of information for analysing the relationship between families and the objects they acquire. The inventory is a list of the personal property, real estate and rent that constituted a family's assets when the head of the family died. The commissioner for oaths, or the copying clerk, would go to the home of the deceased and note down the characteristics of the objects, such as their material, colour and condition, as they were found in each part of the house. Rooms, wardrobes, trunks, and drawers would be opened in order to note everything and the exact location of each item. The final part of the document describes the real estate, rent and credits (the deceased's investments in livestock, business activities and credit instruments). The post-mortem inventory is the key that lets us into the homes of the past.

---

[2] N. McKendrick, J. Brewer, J. H. Plumb, *The Birth of a Consumer Society* (London, 1982) p. 9.

[3] D. Poulot,'Une nouvelle histoire de la culture matérielle?', *Revue d'Histoire Moderne et Contemporaine*, 44/2 (1997): pp. 344–57.

[4] A recent exception, that compares rural and urban material resources is: Mark Overton, Jane Whittle, Darron Dean and Andrew Hann, *Production and Consumption in English Households, 1600-1750* (London, 2004).

Source: Independently produced. Property of the Author.

Map 4.1   The town of Vilafranca del Penedés

However, the whole population was not represented in the same way, as drawing up inventories was not a widespread practice. By comparing the annual number of adult deaths in Vilafranca del Penedés (from the parish records) with the number of inventories drawn up in the same town, it is possible to calculate, with a fair degree of accuracy, the proportion of cases in which this document was drawn up. This proportion is about 9 per cent both between 1670 and 1690 and between 1770 and 1790, increasing to around 15 per cent if only the inventories of men's assets are taken into account.[5] This small percentage suggests that an inventory was only drawn

---

[5] For the 1670–1990 period we have located the inventories of 13.7 per cent of deceased men and 2.4 per cent of deceased women, or in other words, of 8.7 per cent of adults, both men and women. For the 1770-1790 period, we have located the inventories of 8.9 per cent of the deceased adults in Vilafranca; exactly 15.1 per cent of the men and 2.5 per cent of the women.

up when it was felt that a family conflict might complicate what should otherwise be the 'natural' way of doing things in matters of inheritance and succession.[6]

Unlike many other places,[7] the Catalan inventories belong to individuals or families from all social groups, excluding those who neither owned nor rented a house. This inclusion of the poorest social sectors is one of the strengths of this source in Catalonia, another being that the socio-professional position of the head of the family always appears. However, while the inventories of poor and very poor families are relatively plentiful, it is true that wealthy families are better represented than others.[8]

---

[6] I have dealt with this matter in B. Moreno Claverías, 'Pautas de consumo en el Penedés del siglo XVII. Una propuesta metodológica a partir de inventarios sin valoraciones monetarias', *Revista de Historia Económica*, 20 (2003): pp. 207–45.

[7] For example, Weatherill, who works with British inventories, points out that: 'The inventories give their best results for the middle ranks, from the lesser gentry down to the lesser yeomen. They are extremely rare for labourers.' *Consumer Behaviour and Material Culture in Britain 1660-1760* (London, Routledge) p. 3. For her part, Shammas, who also works with American inventories, states that: 'The estates of affluent people more frequently went through probate than the estates of poor householders; consequently they are over-represented in the inventory samples.' *The Pre-industrial Consumer in England and America* (Oxford, 1990) p. 19. Daumard, and other authors make similar points. A. Daumard, 'Structures sociales et classement socioprofessionel. L'apport des archives notariales au XVIIIe et XIXe siècle', *Revue Historique*, 227/1 (1962): p. 162.

[8] Moreno Claverías, 'Pautas de consumo y diferenciación social en la Cataluña preindustrial'. Regarding the use of post-mortem inventories for the analysis of consumption trends, see: M. Baulant, 'Typologie des inventaires après décès', in Van der Woude y A. Schuurman (eds), *Probate inventories. A new source for the historical study of wealth, material culture and agricultural development* (Utrecht, 1980) pp. 33–42; and 'Nécessité de vivre et besoin de paraître. Les inventaires et la vie quotidienne', in M. Baulant, A.J. Schuurman, P. Servais (eds), *Inventaires après-décès et ventes de meubles* (Louvain-la-Neuve, 1988) pp. 9–14 ; B. Bennassar, 'Los inventarios post-mortem y la historia de las mentalidades', *II Coloquio de Metodología Histórica Aplicada*, vol. 2 (Santiago de Compostela, 1984); L. Castañeda , 'Ensayo metodológico sobre los inventarios post-mortem en el análisis de los niveles de vida material: el ejemplo de Barcelona entre 1790–1794', *Primer Congrés d'Història Moderna de Catalunya*, vol. I, Barcelona, pp. 757–69 (1984); A. Van der Woude and A. Schuurman, *Probate inventories. A new source for the historical study of wealth, material culture and agricultural development* (Utrecht, 1980); P. Goubert, 'Intérêt et utilisation historique des papiers de succesions: inventaires aprés décès, partages, comptes de tutelle', *Revue d'Histoire Contemporaine*, 1/1 (1954) : pp. 22–38; X. Lencina Perez, 'Los inventarios post-mortem en el estudio de la cultura material y el consumo. Propuesta metodologica. Barcelona, siglo XVII', in J. Torras and B. Yun (eds), *Consumo, condiciones de vida y comercialización. Cataluña y Castilla, siglos XVII–XIX*, (Junta de Castilla y León, 1999) pp. 41–59; N. Pellegrin and J. Péret, 'Meubles et vêtements dans les inventaires après décès poitevins au XVIIIe siècle: une source et ses problèmes', in J. Goy and J.P. Wallot (eds), *Évolution et Éclatement du Monde Rural* (Paris-Montréal, 1986) pp. 469–73; A.J. Schuurman, 'Probate inventory Research: Opportunities and Drawbacks',

Elsewhere I have enumerated the advantages and limitations of this source in Catalonia. One of its main limitations is that in Catalan inventories, unlike those of other areas, there are no monetary valuations of the personal property and real estate. This is due to the Catalan system of inheritance, although a more accurate term in this case would be 'succession': the first-born son succeeded his father in the possession of assets that ideally were passed on in their entirety through generations.[9] Therefore, there was no point in valuing assets that did not have to be divided among the inheritors. The inventory only had to accurately reflect everything that was to be transferred.

Thus, we have no option but to take the family's possessions – especially the real estate, the rent and the objects of value – as indicators of its economic situation, even though it is not possible to quantify these.[10] The inventories are also 'snapshots' taken at a given moment and, as such, are structurally weak when it comes to showing flows.[11] Even so, there is no better source for finding out what type of objects these families possessed and what use they made of them, what their preferences were according to a wide range of variables (patrimonial wealth, profession, place of residence or the owner's sex) and how these preferences evolved as time went by. To add further quality to this analysis of consumption patterns in this Catalan agrarian area, some complementary sources have also been used – wills, public auctions, marriage settlements, parish records, account books and engagement books.

Luxury, Fashion and Peasantry

How can we distinguish between luxury and necessity? This distinction can be made from two different perspectives: the economic and the sociological. For the former, luxury would be defined by the income elasticity of demand for

---

in M. Baulant, A.J. Schuurman, P. Servais (eds), *Inventaires après-décès et ventes de meubles* (Louvain-la-Neuve, 1988) pp. 19–28 ; P. Servais, 'Inventaires et ventes de meubles: apports a l'histoire économique', in M. Baulant, A.J. Schuurman, P. Servais (eds), *Inventaires après-décès et ventes de meubles* (Lauvain-la-Neuve, 1988) pp. 29–35 ; M. Spufford, 'The limitations of the probate inventory', in J. Chartres and D. Hey (eds), *English rural society, 1500-1800* (Cambridge, 1990) pp. 139–75.

[9] A. Barrera, *Casa, herencia y familia en la Cataluña rural* (Madrid, 1990), p. 24.

[10] As A. Eiras Roel maintains, although it is true that 'the eloquent external signs' (debts, bonds, promissory notes, stocks of grain and merchant goods, jewels, silver objects, valuable clothing) of the assets do not evaluate the fortune in figures, they do convey the differences of possession and position that are their consequence'. A. Eiras Roel, 'La documentación de protocolos notariales en la reciente historiografía modernista', *Estudis Històrics i Documents dels Arxius de Protocols*, vol. 7 (Barcelona, 1980): p. 15.

[11] Jan De Vries, 'Between purchasing power and the world of goods: understanding the household economy in early modern Europe' in John Brewer and Roy Porter (eds), *Consumption and the world of goods* (London, 1993).

goods. A good would be a luxury good if its income elasticity were greater than one, and it would be a necessity if this ratio were less than one. According to classical economists such as Ricardo and Marx, basic necessities are historically determined and depend, mainly, on the level of technological development and on labour power. For this reason, what used to be considered 'superfluous' may now be considered 'necessary'.

The sociological perspective, on the other hand, is relevant for a society in which the position of individuals basically depends on extra-economic criteria, such as birth, race or sex. In pre-industrial societies, birth determined the social class or rank of all members. From this point of view, we could use Sombart's definition of luxury as 'any extravagance that goes beyond the necessary', bearing in mind that 'the necessary' will be delimited by the parameters of the social group to which an individual belonged.[12]

Neither perspective would be adequate for analysing the consumption trends in a society that is halfway between a stratified society and a fully developed market society. This was a period of transition in which the market economy gradually arose, first in the cities and eventually, after quite some time, in the country. For this reason it can be said that two worlds coexisted during this period, a 'traditional' one in which the distinguishing signs were birth and rank, and a 'modern' one in which consumption was the clearest indicator of individual wealth.

But what is the purpose of luxury? Do refined and expensive goods indicate each individual's position on the social ladder? Luxury certainly has the ability to signify rank and communicate the social position of families.[13] As Thorstein Veblen pointed out in 1899, 'it is taken for granted that in order that consumption may effectively improve the consumer's good reputation, superfluous things have to be consumed. In order to create a good reputation, this consumption has to be extravagant. It cannot derive any merit from the consumption of what it strictly necessary for surviving, unless in comparison with those who are so poor that they cannot even afford to spend what it takes to acquire this minimum necessary for survival.'[14]

In the eighteenth century, Europe witnessed an unprecedented demand for luxurious and fashionable articles, intensifying intellectual debates among those in favour of these new consumption habits and those who objected.[15] The latter

---

[12] W. Sombart, *Lujo y capitalismo* (Madrid, 1979).

[13] M. Douglas and B. Isherwood, *The World of Goods: Towards an Anthropology of Consumption* (London, 1979), p. 112.

[14] T. Veblen, *The Theory of the Leisure Classes: an Economic Study of Institutions* (1899) translated, *Teoría de la clase ociosa* (Barcelona, 1988), p. 9.

[15] The history of luxury has a very extensive bibliography. Among others, the following authors have emphasized the importance of cities in creating new consumption habits: M. García and B. Yun, 'Pautas de consumo, estilos de vida y cambio político en las ciudades castellanas a fines del Antiguo Régimen', in J.I. Fortea Pérez (ed.), *Imágenes de la diversidad. El mundo urbano en la Corona de Castilla (s.XVI–XVIII)* (Santander, 1997)

felt that luxury was the cause of ruin and corruption, that it undercut traditional hierarchies and practice and that, given its capacity to alter established habits and hierarchies, it jeopardized the stable order of society. Luxury was 'depraved' because it offended Christian morality and because it blurred the necessary dividing lines between classes.[16] These commentators opposed the spread of luxury, demanding that the authorities take the appropriate actions, applying sumptuary laws, for example, laws that had been enacted continually by nearly all the Spanish monarchs of the early modern age. One of the many exponents of this argument in Spain was Don Melchor de Macanaz, who in 1724 urged Philip V: 'to decree that each individual dress according to his class, so that his clothes indicate his profession, and so that neither nobles are confused with commoners, nor high-ranking persons with the middle ranks'.[17] On the other hand, the 'apologists of luxury' argued that luxury was a vitally important factor for the creation of wealth, since it intensified domestic trade and boosted the productive sectors. From the moral and political point of view, many of those in favour of luxury believed it was a 'useful vice': it was a factor of moral corruption, but at the same time it was absolutely inevitable and necessary.[18]

The consumption of luxuries and fashionable goods is typically examined within the context of large cities and allied with the development of urban life. From the theoretical point of view, Veblen emphasized the connection between both variables, noting that 'consumption is a more important element in city life than in country life'.[19] His theory of emulation can only be explained in relation to the dynamic of urban societies. Furthermore, Veblen has had a considerable

---

pp. 245–82; Veblen, *Teoría de la clase ociosa*; Neil McKendrick, et al., *The Birth of a Consumer Society: the Commercialisation of Eighteenth-Century England* (London, 1982); Weatherill, *Consumer Behaviour*; P. Malanima, *Il lusso dei contadini. Consumi e industrie nelle campagne toscane del sei e settecento* (Bologna, 1990); D. Roche, *La culture des apparences. Une histoire du vêtement (XIIIe–XVIIIe siècle)* (Paris, 1989). Some works on luxury in Old Regime Europe include: M. Berg and H. Clifford (eds), *Consumers and luxury: Consumer Culture in Europe 1650–1850* (Manchester, 1999); M. Berg, *Luxury and pleasure in eighteenth century Britain* (Oxford, 2005); R. Fox and A. Turner (eds), *Luxury, trades and consumerism in ancien regime Paris* (Aldershot, UK, 1998); C. Sargentson, *Merchants and luxury markets: the marchands merciers of eighteenth-century Paris* (London, 1996); Ch. J. Berry, *The Idea of Luxury: a conceptual and historical investigation* (Cambridge, 1994); N. Coquery, *L'hôtel aristocratique: le marché du luxe à Paris au XVIIIe siècle* (Paris, 1998); Philippe Perrot, *Le luxe. Une richese entre faste et confort. XVIIIe–XIXe siècle* (París, 1995).

[16] F. Díez, 'La apología ilustrada del lujo en España. Sobre la configuración del *hombre* consumidor', *Historia Social*, n. 37 (2000), p. 9.

[17] In J. Sempere and Guarinos, *Historia del lujo y de las leyes suntuarias en España*, vol. 2 (Madrid, 1788), pp. 160-64.

[18] F. Díez, *Utilidad, deseo y virtud. La formación de la idea moderna del trabajo*,(Barcelona, 2001), p. 126.

[19] Veblen, *Teoría de la clase ociosa*, p. 90.

influence on a number of authors: both Neil McKendrick and Daniel Roche speak of the supremacy of London and Paris as the epicentres of consumption in the eighteenth century. It was in the capitals that fashions spread most rapidly, not only because of the physical proximity of people, but also because the city was the place where the new means of promoting products through newspapers and prints were first introduced, and where shop windows began to be used to display fashionable products to the public.[20] There is also another reason that connects changes in consumption habits to the level of urbanization: the usefulness of luxury in cities is accentuated by anonymity. In a large population centre, individuals denoted their social position by consuming *visible* goods, to enable all to discern their status. In a small community it was easy to know who is who. Therefore, the *visible* consumption of luxury goods would have less importance in a village than in a city. What is the point of acquiring new and refined products when there is nothing to prove what is not already known? In small agrarian towns, family wealth can be expressed by other means, such as the accumulation of cattle or traditional objects, accumulation which Sombart calls 'quantitative luxury'.[21]

Much has been written about the dramatic rise in demand for luxury and fashionable commodities in large European capitals, although other smaller cities experienced the same phenomenon. The development of foreign trade facilitated the changes in demand in many population centres, especially if they had a nearby port. According to one contemporary observer, the citizens of Barcelona (a city of 120,000 to 130,000 inhabitants by 1800), 'are increasingly adulterated with luxury, greater dealings, foreign fashions, the progress of trade, the love of comfort and liberty, and the neglect of time-honoured seclusion and seriousness'.[22] The baron of Maldá, an impoverished nobleman living in eighteenth-century Barcelona, wrote disconsolately that: 'nowadays, luxury and fashion, most of which comes from French actresses, has altered in many men and women the good order of the purity of customs and class distinction as far as clothing is concerned (…). Luxury has driven many men and women mad, as it seeks to put craftsmen on an equal footing with merchants, and the latter on a par with honest citizens [gentlemen].'[23] The growing demand for stylish goods and services coincided with the increase

---

[20] Roche, *La culture des apparences*, pp. 481–2.

[21] W. Sombart makes a distinction between 'qualitative luxury' and 'quantitative luxury'. He states that quantitative luxury is synonymous with 'extravagance', such as, for example, 'having one hundred servants when one will do' or 'using three matches to light a cigarette'. Qualitative luxury, on the other hand, is 'the consumption of a better class of goods', and he adds that 'luxury, considered in its qualitative aspect, gives rise to the *luxury object*, which is a refined good (i.e. a valuable object)'. Sombart, *Lujo y capitalismo*, pp. 63–4.

[22] F. de Zamora, *Diario de los viajes hechos en Cataluña* (Barcelona, 1973), pp. 463–4.

[23] R. d'Amat, Baró de Maldà, *Viles i ciutats de Catalunya. A cargo de Margarida Aritzeta* (Barcelona, 1994), p. 86.

in supply, with the consequent proliferation of shops and businesses capable of satisfying and intensifying these new needs.[24]

But if this is what was happening in the city of Barcelona, what was going on in the rural areas around the capital? Zamora, he who claimed that the citizens of Barcelona were being 'adulterated' by luxury and foreign fashions, also claimed that 'customs in the villages and homes of peasant farmers are innocent, simple and natural'.[25] In other words, he not only differentiated between rural consumers and their urban counterparts, but also introduced a moral evaluation as far as consumption was concerned.

Fashion and luxury were closely linked by the fact that new consumer products were often regarded, to begin with, as luxuries. For example, chocolate was a fashionable extravagance when first consumed in early modern Europe by elites; but it gradually became a mass consumption product. The same could also be said of many other objects such as watches, shoe buckles, certain articles of clothing and various household items such as mirrors, paintings, curtains and clocks. However, although fashion and luxury are in some ways related, they are different concepts. Luxury is a permanent designation based on rarity and expenditure, but fashion is ephemeral. Keeping up with the latest fashions implies enjoying a certain degree of luxury (fashion has to be paid for); but it could actually be cheaper to be *à la mode* than ostentatious. In other words, fashion, both now and in the past, can reach a larger proportion of the population than luxury. And that is what is assumed to have occurred in eighteenth-century Europe. The development of manufacturing and transport multiplied the quantity of goods on the market, some of which were no more than low-priced imitations of certain fashionable, luxury goods consumed by the upper classes.

As Maxine Berg maintains, the demand for new manufactured products in the eighteenth century was determined, to some extent, by fashion, which spread more easily thanks to the development of international trade. Manufacturers made some of these luxury goods with expensive materials for the wealthiest consumers, and once they became fashionable, they made them with cheaper materials for the rest of the population, taking it for granted that the lower classes would imitate them as soon as they discovered the innovation.[26] But were there peasants among these lower classes with an interest in fashion? Or were just the urban lower classes so affected?

Up until now, the studies carried out for various places in Europe and North America have insisted on linking the expansion of luxury with urban consumption

---

[24] 'There are some watchmaker's shops that are constantly expanding because nearly everyone carries a pocket watch; there are ironmonger's, cap maker's, dressmaker's, hairdresser's and chocolate maker's that are growing every day (...); due to the great consumption of chocolate, there is now a chocolate maker's guild.' R. d'Amat, Baró de Maldà, *Viles i ciutats de Catalunya*, p. 87.

[25] De Zamora, *Diario de los viajes hechos en Cataluña*, p. 463.

[26] Maxine Berg (ed.), *Mercados y manufacturas en Europa* (Barcelona, 1995), pp. 29–39.

habits. The few studies devoted to rural areas seem to agree on the negligible significance of luxury and fashionable products in peasant economies. For example, and without leaving Spain, Fernando Ramos has confirmed that, between 1750 and 1840, Castilian families continued to spend most of their available income on satisfying basic needs (food, housing, clothing), leaving only a small proportion of the family budget for segments of the demand relating to cultural or luxury goods.[27] For his part, Paolo Malanima – who has studied consumption in pre-industrial Tuscany – argues that the expansion of fashion was basically an urban phenomenon, because it was in the city where individuals observed and compared themselves with one another. Gestures, behaviours and new objects were the instruments used in the processes of emulation and social competition.[28] In the country, although consumption habits gradually changed, the emphasis was on permanence rather than on change. Fashion would have far less influence in the country than in the city. In this respect, Malanima points out that, reduced to the bare essentials, the Tuscan peasant's wardrobe, even in the nineteenth century, still consisted of shirt, trousers and any kind of jacket to wrap up in during the coldest months, given that 'for the vast majority of the inhabitants of Old Regime Europe, variations in clothing had no influence whatsoever'.[29] Does this mean that Tuscan peasants did not alter their consumption habits in the slightest? Not at all, but the changes were moderate. Luxury, virtually unknown in eighteenth-century rural Tuscany, gradually began to enter the homes of those peasants who possessed sufficient land and capital. During the course of this century, peasants as a whole began to consume more – especially textile goods – and, therefore, turned to the market on a more frequent basis. This transformation would open up a gap in the subsistence economy into which monetary relations penetrated, eventually leading to a profound change in the economic behaviour of the traditional peasant family.[30] However, as in the Catalan case, these families were far from experiencing a 'consumption revolution' such as the one that was taking place in the major European cities. Furthermore, the vast majority felt it was necessary to guard against fashion, since it could soon lead to 'household ruin'.[31]

---

[27] F.C. Ramos Palencia, 'Una primera aproximación al consumo en el mundo rural castellano a través de los inventarios post-mortem: Palencia, 1750–1840', in J. Torras and B. Yun (eds), *Consumo, Condiciones de vida y Comercialización. Cataluña y Castilla, siglos XVII–XIX*, (Junta de Castilla y León, 1999), p. 120.

[28] P. Malanima, *Economia preindustriale* (Milan, 1995), pp. 541–2.

[29] P. Malanima, *Il lusso dei contadini. Consumi e industrie nelle campagne toscane del sei e settecento* (Bologna, 1990), pp. 24–5.

[30] Malanima, *Il lusso dei contadini*, pp. 8–9.

[31] A. Parés i Puntals, *Tots els refranys catalans* (Barcelona, 1999), p. 271.

'Superfluous' Consumption in Rural Areas from 1670 to 1790: Change and Permanence

On comparing the Catalan inventories of the late eighteenth century with those drawn up one hundred years earlier, we find that houses contained very few genuinely new objects: religious prints, chocolate pots, coffee pots and a few other items. With regard to another area of Catalonia, el Prat, it has been pointed out that, in the eighteenth century, the 'major domestic conquests are chocolate pots, wineskins with a long spout, clocks, glassware and silk, while the individual fork and spoon were also becoming widespread'.[32] Indeed, these products were spreading, albeit slowly. For example, at the end of the eighteenth century, there were still very few houses in el Penedés with glass windows; these were only to be found in the living rooms of priests, jurists and wealthy merchants. The vast majority of the population protected themselves from the cold and the heat with wooden shutters. Clocks and watches were also quite rare in rural areas at the end of the century.

There were two main changes in consumption patterns between 1670 and 1790, as revealed by the inventories: (1) The supply of traditional products increased in terms of materials, colours and forms (which was clearly the case with textile goods, among which cotton clothing began to spread, as opposed to those of wool and linen). (2) Certain household goods listed in some of the 1670–90 inventories (such as cutlery, chairs, wardrobes, curtains) began to appear more frequently. However, both of these phenomena emerged more slowly and to a lesser extent in peasant households than in the homes of liberal professionals, merchants, priests and craftsmen. Table 4.1 shows the presence of consumption indicators in the two periods under consideration, broken down into three large socio-professional groups.

It would seem that peasants were less inclined than other social groups to possess certain types of things, such as curtains, forks, chairs, wardrobes, books and mirrors. Perhaps the relative isolation of their homes and, therefore, the difficulty of being seen, meant that curtains were not as necessary as they were for craftsmen and the middle classes. Yet the peasants who lived in the town's narrow streets did not have curtains either. As for forks, it is well known that people in rural areas continued to eat with their hands long after this habit had died out in cities, where courtesy and fear of infectious diseases helped spread the use of cutlery. Norbert Elias, on the other hand, maintained that the increasing use of the fork in particular, had little to do with hygiene and instead stemmed from the desire, among the upper classes, to avoid making disagreeable impressions, such as getting one's fingers greasy, considered unseemly and 'uncivilized'.[33]

Chairs were not very common objects in eighteenth century peasant households either, since benches could seat three or four people at the same time. Wardrobes

---

[32] J. Codina, *Delta del Llobregat. La gent del fang (El Prat; 965–1965)* (Barcelona, 1966).

[33] Norbert Elias, *El proceso de la civilización* (México, 1989), pp. 168–70.

Table 4.1 The presence of some 'superfluous' consumption in the Penedés, 1670–90 to 1770–90 (in %)

	Peasants		Craftsmen		Liberal professionals and merchants	
	17th C	18th C	17th C	18th C	17th C	18th C
Table napkins	49	60	60	63	88	83
Curtains	2	11	9	27	69	79
Cotton textiles	7	28	19	36	49	83
Spoons	23	74	45	62	59	76
Forks	7	31	19	40	37	76
Devotional *objets d'art*	20	44	60	59	81	72
Chairs	11	27	31	62	72	100
Wardrobes	3	12	16	21	23	62
Chocolate pots	0	24	0	33	0	69
Books	3	7	5	9	31	55
Silver objects	55	32	64	36	81	76
Mirrors	4	11	6	23	35	72

Source: Produced with 400 inventories found in the Arxiu Històric Comarcal de Vilafranca del Penedés (hereafter AHCVP) for 1670–90 and 1770–90.

were also rare; clothes were usually kept in trunks or, in the case of the less disadvantaged, chests of drawers. Books were practically non-existent in these homes, even if their owners possessed many hectares of land. However, there was a significant increase in the possession of table linen, cotton textiles, spoons, devotional *objets d'art* and chocolate pots. In addition, peasants tended to decorate their homes with devotional prints, paintings and sculptures more frequently than a century earlier. And they also consumed more chocolate. By comparing the inventories of farmers' possessions in two different periods we discover the decreasing presence of only one type of item: articles made of silver and gold. By about 1700 there is evidence of a significant peasant tendency to accumulate precious metals which at that time was possibly the best means of overcoming the occasional cash-flow crisis; but this tendency diminished sharply during the following century. How should we interpret this? Is it a sign of a process of relative impoverishment, or is it simply the consequence of a greater tendency to consume other 'superfluous' goods?

Peasants usually invested in producer goods; farm equipment, wine barrels, presses, while pack and draught animals were usually the most valuable movable property. As Veblen maintains, this fact not only has an economic explanation, but is also related to the most effective means of social promotion. The more land, ploughs, heads of cattle and savings (in currency or in gold and silver objects) a peasant possessed, the better his reputation. In relation to consumer goods, however, peasant families had a clear predilection for household textiles like blankets, bedspreads, tablecloths, towels, serviettes and, especially, sheets, both in 1670–90 and in 1770–90. As Malanima has pointed out, the quantity of sheets could be 'one of the best indirect elements for valuing a family's fortune'.[34] Some inventories show a clear 'stockpile', with over 40 sheets per family. Is this perhaps the 'quantitative luxury' that Sombart refers to? It certainly confirms the importance of the bed as a focus of domestic consumption, as Riello discusses in this collection. On the other hand, the peasant farmers seem to show a certain indifference towards articles of clothing, irrespective of income levels. The clothing of a wealthy peasant was of better quality than that of a poor peasant, but the garments were more or less the same: trousers, stockings, shirt, waistcoat and knee-length cloak. No peasant, however, wore a dress coat, that article of men's clothing so fashionable in the eighteenth century. These coats were almost certain to be found in the trunks and wardrobes of a commissioner for oaths, doctor, successful craftsman or merchant; but we will not find one in a peasant's house however rich he was.[35] Cravats and tailcoats were similarly absent.

The analysis of auctions – the public sale of a person's belongings, normally to pay off their debts after death – gives us a clearer idea of the structure of these families' movable property assets. For example, all the personal property of the farmer Pau Ferrer (who had nine hectares of land for cereal and vines) was sold for a total of 320 pounds in 1783, with the details shown in Table 4.2.[36]

The peasant property auctions analysed confirm that producer goods and household textiles head the list of family expenditures; whereas furniture, household implements and clothes occupy more discreet positions. This is exactly the opposite of what occurred in the auctions of property belonging to craftsmen, merchants and liberal professionals. The fact that it is possible to detect some specifically 'peasant' consumption habits does not mean that there are no significant differences within this social group. These differences depended mainly on the different disposal of land and capital, which in turn necessarily affected consumption. Table 4.3 shows the peasant consumption of certain items, broken down into different ownership categories in 1770–90.

Peasants with large properties were able to accumulate certain types of goods and benefit from the increased supply brought about by the development of

---

[34] Malanima, *Il lusso dei contadini*, p. 18.

[35] During the eighteenth century, the dress coat became a mark of distinction of certain liberal professionals. The Catalan collection of proverbs makes some references to the symbolic characteristics of this item of clothing. For example, '*metge de gran casaca, poca saviesa i molta butxaca*' ['the doctor who wears a capacious dress coat has little wisdom and big pockets', i.e. a lot of money]. Parés i Puntals, *Tots els refranys catalans*, p. 304.

[36] AHCVP, APN, J. Mullol, P-XVIII-132-1, f. 134.

Table 4.2 Structure of the auction of the personal property belonging to the farmer Pau Ferrer (1783)

Commodity	Value in pounds	% value out of the total amount
Producer goods: farming equipment, wineskin bottles and pack and draught animals (one ox)	100.1	31.3
Textile household goods	93.6	29.2
Production reserve (wheat, wine and barley)	36.4	11.4
Furniture	27.5	8.6
Kitchen and table utensils	20.7	6.5
Clothes	19.5	6.1
Silver objects	14.8	4.6
Devotional *objets d'art*	4.2	1.3
Others	3.2	1.0
Total	**320**	**100**

Source: AHCVP, APN, J. Mullol, P-XVIII-132-1, f. 134

manufacturing and transport. This period also saw an extraordinary rise in the number of street traders, whose wares – many of which were 'popular luxury' or 'populux' products[37] – managed to find their way into the most isolated rural house. This could explain the presence of an increasing number of religious prints on the walls of farmers' homes as the eighteenth century progressed, as well as the increase in cotton clothing, muslins, handkerchiefs or caps. However, we must ask ourselves why other items that pedlars had to offer are absent – books, mirrors, spectacles, maps, watches, shoe buckles, bureaus, quills, braids, forks or tobacco boxes.[38] All these commodities were increasingly abundant in the middle-class houses of Vilafranca, the small capital of the Penedés region, but there is no trace of them in peasant homes, regardless of their location or their sources of income.

---

[37] Cissie Fairchilds uses the word 'populuxe' to refer to cheap imitations of luxury products. For example, the watches worn by a small proportion of the lower classes were always made of silver, as opposed to the gold in the case of the middle classes and the urban aristocracy. The dress coats, traditionally upper and middle class items of clothing, were made of cheaper and lower-quality fabrics. 'Determinants of Consumption Patterns in Eighteenth-Century France', *XI International Economic History Congress. Material Culture: Consumption, Life-style, Standard of Living 1500–1900* (Milan, 1994), pp. 50–70.

[38] Fontaine, *Histoire du colportage en Europe*; and Fontaine and Schlumbohm, *Household strategies for survival*.

Table 4.3   Peasant consumption of certain items in the Penedés, broken down into different ownership categories, 1770–90

	Average number of sheets (units)	Average number of table napkins (units)	Average number of shirts (units)	Inventories with silver objects (%)	Inventories with jewels (%)	Inventories with objets d'art (%)
Labourers	8.6	10.2	5.9	7.1	4.8	14.3
Small and medium proprietors	15.3	12.0	7.5	28.2	15.5	46.5
Large proprietors	32.5	41.4	9.8	57.2	50.0	64.3
Total	**19.4**	**24.2**	**7.8**	**32**	**24.9**	**44.4**

Source: 169 inventories of farmers found in the AHCVP, 1770–90.

This suggests that among peasants there was a certain tendency towards austerity and a certain rejection of 'frivolities'.

The mode of rural consumption, if such a term may be used to describe the consumption patterns of farmers, has a number of common characteristics. These characteristics were still recognizable in the final decades of the eighteenth century. According to David Hiler and Laurence Wiedmer, they included a certain liking for the permanence and solidity of objects. In their homes, therefore, we find relatively few objects made of porcelain, glass or fragile types of wood. As well, there was an emphasis on usefulness, which meant there was less room for luxury objects than in the homes of craftsmen or the middle classes. And, finally, there was a rejection of cultural changes that required the adoption of new appearances associated with urban consumption habits. For a peasant, therefore, it was easier to do without certain personal accessories like watches, ties, hats and gloves and it did not seem necessary to 'dress' the house, so chairs, windows and walls were not covered.[39] However, this does not alter the fact that peasant homes did become more permeable to the new commodities, a process that began first in the peasant houses located in or near an important city.

In fact, peasant consumption was distinctly more diversified in areas near medium-size or large cities than in isolated hamlets and farms.[40] Peasants

---

[39] D. Hiler and L. Wiedmer, 'Le rat de ville et le rat des champs. Une approche comparative des intérieurs ruraux et urbains à Genève dans la seconde partie du XVIIIe siècle', in M. Baulant (ed.), *Inventaires apres-décès et ventes de meubles. Actes du séminaire tenu dans le cadre du 9ème Congrès International d'Histoire Economique de Berne (1986)* (Louvain-la Neuve, 1988), pp. 146–7.

[40] Belen Moreno Claverías, 'Révolution de la Consommation Paysanne? Modes de Consommation et Differentiation Sociale de la paysannerie catalane, 1670–1790', *Histoire*

who lived in or near the city of Barcelona at the end of the eighteenth century consumed more chocolate, possessed more table linen, curtains, devotional *objets d'art*, mirrors and clocks than farmers living in el Penedés. As far as clothing is concerned, they were more likely to use underwear, and cotton clothes were, in relative terms, more important than in the country. Access to novelty and luxury was directly proportional to the degree of urbanization of each population centre, to the importance of its manufacturing and commercial activities and, therefore, to the extent of its inhabitants' relations with the domestic and foreign markets. Yet although fashionable and luxury goods were to be found more frequently in the homes of farmers living in or near an important city than in hamlets and villages, they still had not spread to the degree found among urban social sectors.[41]

Peasant Women and the World of Objects

A number of theories emerged at the end of the eighteenth century to explain the attraction that women supposedly felt towards inessential novelties, which made them potential consumers of these objects to a greater extent than men.[42]

---

et Mesure, 21/1/2 (2006): pp. 141–83.

[41] Daniel Roche has also detected a more diversified consumption among peasants on the outskirts of Paris in comparison with those who lived in rural areas further away from the city. Nevertheless, he also emphasizes that this peasant consumption was a long way behind in comparison with the changes that were taking place in urban sectors. '*Dans les campagnes, la conquête du linge précède celle des vêtements et des goûts changeants qui imposent les modes urbaines. On perçoit ce retard tout près de Paris, dans le Vexin français ou dans les grandes fermes (...) La durée et la solidité des vêtements son encore très fortes (...) Les hommes ont l'essentiel, de moindre valeur qu'à Paris et d'une moins grande diversité (...). Dans les campagnes les valeurs de la stabilité, identifiée au solide et à l'usage réitéré des vêtements, ne disparaissent pas, ni le réemploi, ni les reprises et les raccommodages qui confèrent aux habits paysans leur aspect spécifique. Le goût par les toiles rustiques et les tissus solides peut trahir une habitude qui n'est pas dictée par la seule imitation des grands et des riches et par les disponibilités financières.*' D. Roche, *Histoire des choses banales. Naissance de la consommation XVIIe-XIXe siècle* (Paris, 1997), pp. 233–4.

[42] For example, J.J. Rousseau emphasized women's capacity to rapidly absorb the visual world around them. Women would excel in anything that requires the senses, whereas men would excel in activities that require intellect. Female sensory capacities would make women highly susceptible to pleasant and frivolous objects and, therefore, more likely to consume these objects than men. Jennifer Jones, '*Coquettes* and *Grisettes*. Women Buying and Selling in Ancien Régime Paris' in Victoria De Grazia and Ellen Furlough (eds), *The Sex of Things. Gender and Consumption in Historical Perspective* (Berkeley, 1996) pp. 35–6. See also Paul Hoffmann, *La femme dans la pensée des lumières* (Strasbourg, 1977); G.J. Barker-Benfield, *The culture of sensibility. Sex and society in Eighteenth-century Britain* (Chicago, 1992); John Styles and Amanda Vickery (eds), *Gender, Taste, and Material Culture in Britain and North America, 1700–1830* (London, 2006) and Elizabeth Kowaleski-Wallace, *Consuming Subjects: Women, Shopping, and Business in the Eighteenth Century* (New York, 1997).

However, it is important to bear in mind that most of the theorists who detected the existence of this 'eminently female' manner of consuming based their theories on the observation of a small group of women: those belonging to the upper classes in important cities such as Paris and London. Little is known about the consumption habits of the majority of women, who were poor and lived in rural areas. The main aim of this section is to analyse this issue in the context of pre-industrial Penedés, paying special attention to the effects of the legal system as it applied to the Catalan family and to the influence that the age and marital status of women had on their possession and use of goods.[43]

The nominal separation of spheres (public-male and private-female) and roles according to gender meant that women were burdened with many of the responsibilities relating to family consumption. In the nineteenth century, with the development of middle-class consumption based on the 'feminized' world of the home, women would be responsible for incorporating, maintaining and transmitting the new signs of identity. Their duties included showing the family's social position, its style and tastes in comparison with other middle-class families, and differentiating its class with respect to the aristocracy and the working classes.[44] According to Veblen, the *raison d'être* of leisure-class women was to consume and display what the men produced. The clothes they wore were the tangible proof of their husband's purchasing power.[45] For Sombart, however, women not only reflected their husbands' wealth, but were also very active and dominant consumers as far as family comfort was concerned. According to this author, the courtesans and aristocratic women living in major cities were responsible for the uncommon increase in luxury in the eighteenth century, which would be a necessary stimulus for the development of capitalism. In this hypothetical process, men appear to be passive subjects whose basic function was to pay for female whims. 'The triumph of women' as regards fashion and luxury would be limitless.[46]

Although the theories put forward by Veblen and Sombart have been refined and qualified over the years, they retained considerable influence on subsequent studies of consumption, material culture, the separation of the public and private spheres, and the creation of the meaning of 'the domestic'. However, many experts who base their work on these theories forget that Veblen referred exclusively to 'ladies of the leisure class' and that when Sombart spoke of 'women' he was

---

[43] I have dealt with these aspects in B. Moreno Claverías, 'Mito y realidad de la 'feminización del consumo' en la Europa Moderna: Las pautas de consumo de las mujeres en el Penedés preindustrial' ['Myth and reality of the 'feminization of consumption' in Modern Europe: the consumption habits of women in pre-industrial Penedés'], *Arenal*, 11/1 (2004): pp. 119–52.

[44] De Grazia and Furlough, *Sex of Things*, pp. 18–19.

[45] Veblen, *Teoría de la clase ociosa*, p. 58.

[46] Sombart, *Lujo y capitalismo*, pp. 103, 105. In contrast, see Margot Finn's discussion of men's roles as consumers. 'Men's Things: Masculine Possession in the Consumer Revolution', *Social History*, 25/ 2 (2000): pp. 133–55.

referring specifically to the wives and, above all, the mistresses of kings, aristocrats, wealthy financiers and high-ranking officials living in Europe's capital cities. They said nothing or very little about the vast majority of women. Oddly enough, this 'absence' has continued to be a defining feature of studies about the history of female consumption. According to Roche, for example, women were the indisputable protagonists of the new weakness for ostentatious objects that took Paris by storm in the eighteenth century. In all social categories, it was the women who were allegedly responsible for spreading the taste for new objects and the new values of superfluous consumption.[47] However, in spite of this propensity to consume new artefacts, the same author verifies that the economic value of the male and female clothing of the Parisian working classes, that is, the majority of the city's inhabitants, was very similar, with a slight advantage for the male wardrobe.[48]

In keeping with Sombart, Amanda Vickery emphasizes that women, in their housekeeping role, attached family and private meanings to personal belongings. The fact that women were prevented from possessing significant landed property and from practising a profession would result in them concentrating on 'personal and household artefacts to create a world of meanings and ultimately to transmit her history'.[49] The author reaches these conclusions by studying the diaries kept by a Lancashire 'gentlewoman' from 1762 to 1781, and she maintains that post-mortem inventories are not useful for perceiving this kind of thing. Lorna Weatherill analysed the consumption patterns of English men and women from 1660 to 1740 using probate inventories and she detects some differences in their consumption attitudes. Whereas men owned more books and watches than women, the latter (especially widows) possessed more gold and silver objects, table linen and textile household goods, glassware, mirrors and paintings. However, the author concludes that the gender contrasts were too subtle to suggest the existence of a distinct female material subculture and it was evident that status, wealth and occupation were more influential than gender alone.[50]

I reached the same conclusion on examining the Catalan inventories corresponding to women and men, where the objects belonging to the wife are specified.[51] Yet if, as Vickery maintains, women's consumption was confined to the private sphere (small, personal objects, often with a sentimental value), the first thing that needs to be pointed out is that the post-mortem inventories tell

---

[47] Roche, *La culture des apparences*, p. 480.

[48] The average value of a man's wardrobe was 17 pounds, as opposed to 15 pounds in the case of women. Roche, *La culture des apparences*, p. 100.

[49] Amanda Vickery, 'Women and the world of goods: a Lancashire consumer and her possessions', in John Brewer and Roy Porter (eds), *Consumption and the world of goods* (London, 1993), p. 294.

[50] Lorna Weatherill, 'A Possession of One's Own: Women and Consumer Behaviour in England, 1660–1740', *Journal of British Studies*, 25/2 (1986): p. 151.

[51] We have 60 inventories for women between 1670 and 1690, to which we must add the 132 inventories for men in which the wife's belongings are recorded separately.

us virtually nothing about their existence. Complementary sources are critical supplements for this period, such as public auctions.

Were women in rural areas mainly responsible for the expansion of fashion in their communities? The analysis of the 1670–1790 inventories of women from el Penedés suggests that they displayed limited consumption of the frivolities which some suggest they felt naturally attracted to. If anything, these inventories are more modest than those of the men belonging to same social classes, and evidence of both luxury and fashion are less frequent. In order to understand women's relationship with the possession and management of personal and landed property, it is essential to mention Catalan civil law, which determined what women could and could not do. The family economic system in force at the time was that of the separation of estates or division of marital property: each spouse owned and was entitled to enjoy their own property, that which they possessed before marrying and that which they acquired during the course of their marriage. In practice, however, this was mitigated by the dowry, which is why some jurists prefer to call it the *dowry system*.

The dowry, which was the form taken by the daughter's share of an estate, consisted of the bride's trousseau and a sum of money in cash, and very rarely included real estate. These items were fundamental for the survival of women, especially in a hereditary system characterized by indivisibility. In fact, management of the family assets passed from the head of the family to the first-born son (*hereu*), and only when there was no direct male descendant (son, brother, nephew, grandson) did the eldest daughter become the heiress (*pubilla*). In spite of the fact that the contents of the dowry were the only property that women were going to have during their entire life, the husband was in charge of administering them as soon as the marriage had taken place. The fact that women could not touch the monetary part of their dowry without the express consent of the husband made it very difficult for wives to spend money at their own discretion. Married women also needed the husband's express authorization for any significant financial operation.

Marital status had a decisive influence on women during the different stages of their life, and, in this respect, consumption was no exception. By marrying, a woman saw her social status grow regardless of the person she married. While they were single, women prepared themselves for this change of status, saving as much as they could, making their trousseau and giving the impression of being 'modest', not given to superfluous spending, behaviour required of any aspiring bride, especially among peasants.[52] Once married, not only were they able to show off what they had jealously guarded in their trunks, but they also became an expression of the husband's status. In 1789, a learned gentleman from el Penedés remarked that there was no difference in men's outward appearance according to

---

[52] In this respect, see the eighteenth-century diary of the Catalan peasant Sebastià Casanovas, who repeatedly insists that austerity and dressing simply were two indispensable virtues in peasant women. S. Casanovas i Canut, *El manuscrit de Palau-Saverdera: Memòries d'un pagès empordanès del segle XVIII* (Anglada, 1986).

marital status; whereas among women the differences were clear: 'married women wear better gold and silver earrings than single women, and they dress better'.[53] Certain items of jewellery formed part of a woman's dowry and others were gifts from their husband. In reality, however, what the husband actually gave his wife was his 'right to use' or enjoy.[54]

Married women actually had less autonomy than widows and single women who were under the protection of a father or brother. Moreover, married women's contribution to the family economy did not actually result in their being considered economic agents. What did they do with the income from their work? The majority of post-mortem inventories suggest that the consumption of basic items, ensuring family survival, likely reduced to a minimum possible spending from women's and children's wages on whims. A detailed examination of the auctions and the purchaser of each item of property gives a clearer idea of the types of purchases made by men and women; an analysis was made of 20 public auctions held in Vilafranca between 1770 and 1790.

First, most of the purchases were made by men, and women bought the cheapest items. Whereas the average amount paid for the objects bought by women was less than one pound, the items bought by men fetched an average price of 4.5 pounds. In fact, 88 per cent of the more expensive purchases of five pounds or more were made by men. Second, the items most commonly purchased by women were, in this order: household textiles (especially table linen and sheets), clothes (particularly men's shirts), kitchen utensils and religious prints. The items most frequently bought by men also included household textiles (especially sheets), clothes (particularly men's shirts), farm equipment, kitchen utensils, furniture and devotional *objets d'art*. The majority of men also usually bought their wife's clothes.[55] The third point is that of the majority of the auctioned luxury goods, most of which came from priests' homes, were purchased by men, typically learned gentlemen and businessmen of the local middle-class. These men purchased the majority of window curtains, bed draperies, mirrors, bureaus, rugs, display cabinets, easy chairs and other quality pieces of furniture, as well as books and

---

[53] Manuel Barba i Roca, *El corregiment i partit de Vilafranca del Penedès a l'últim terç del segle XVIII* (Vilafranca del Penedès, 1991), p. 82.

[54] Something similar occurred in Renaissance Florence in relation to clothing. The husband 'dressed' his wife to his liking on the occasion of their wedding, although the clothes continued to belong to her. Raffaella Sarti, *Vita di casa. Abitare, mangiare, vestire nell'Europa moderna* [*Europe at Home: Family and Material Culture 1500–1800*] (Rome and Bari, 1999), pp. 251–2.

[55] There are numerous proverbs and sayings that advise a husband to control his wife's purchases or to make them himself. This opinion was very widespread among peasant families until quite recently. See Barrera, *Casa, herencia y familia*. Sebastià Casanovas, the Gerona *pagès* who left behind some diaries in the eighteenth century, advised men not to let their wives buy their own clothes and shoes, to which he attributed 'many household misfortunes'. Casanovas i Canut, *El manuscrit de Palau-Saverdera*, p. 39.

silver and gold objects. Table 4.4 shows the most commonly sold goods and the part of their value paid by men and women respectively.

Table 4.4 The value of the purchases made by men and women at public auctions (in %). Vilafranca del Penedés (1770–90)

Commodities	Value of the goods bought by men (in %)	Value of the goods bought by women (in %)
Men's shirts	60.2	39.8
Other articles of men's clothing	71.0	29.0
Women's shirts	62.8	37.2
Other articles of women's clothing	62.9	37.1
Sheets, table napkins, tablecloths, towels, dishcloths	55.3	44.7
Blankets, bedspreads, curtains	71.3	28.7
Kitchen utensils	62.4	37.6
Religious prints	58,2	41,8
Paintings and sculptures	89.4	10.6
Books	100	0
Silver and gold objects	93.2	6.8
Luxury furniture (mirrors, small ornamental mirrors, bureaus, display cabinets, rugs, easy chairs)	95.3	4.7
Draught animals	100	0
Farm equipment	87.3	12.7
Wine barrels	85.2	14.8
Total	**76.6**	**23.4**

Source: 20 public auctions held between 1770 and 1790 in Vilafranca del Penedés. AHCVP.

In short, the objects many contemporaries regarded as 'frivolities' were bought at the public auctions mainly by men. Were they perhaps gifts for their wives? Some inventories suggest otherwise, since they are recorded among the goods 'belonging to' to the husband.[56] The fact that women had such narrow scope for

---

[56] For example, the inventory of a commissioner for oaths who died in 1778 states that 'the easy chair, the green silk curtains and the mirror with gold frame belonged to the

making deals, selling, buying and managing the family income must even have affected the type of goods they were able to purchase at a public auction, even if these goods were of little value.[57] Likewise, these men clearly had a taste for the niceties found in the consumer market, even if second-hand.

One might assume that the only women who were able to dispose of income at their own discretion were the *pubilles*, the female heiresses appointed in the absence of a male heir. Husbands of these wealthy women did what the vast majority of women were obliged to do: they left their family home to settle in their spouses' homes. However, marriage automatically entitled the husband to administer his wife's properties, credit instruments, personal belongings and cash. In other words, not even these rich and property-owning women were able to give free rein to their supposed 'natural' propensity for superfluous consumption. Their inventories describe austere ancestral homes, with no curtains in the windows, few art objects, no carpets, no mirrors. In fact, it is impossible to distinguish the interior of a farmhouse according to the gender of its owner.

Theoretically the relative freedom enjoyed by widows, especially those with no young children to maintain, could result in 'individual' rather than 'family' consumption strategies and, therefore, more scope for purchasing things that appealed to 'feminine tastes'. However, for the vast majority of widows this relative autonomy was limited by the poverty they faced. All the research relating to the situation of widows confirms a process of impoverishment, which would be more or less acute depending on factors such as the age at which a woman became a widow, whether or not she had children, the status of the deceased husband, the type of relations she maintained with the heir and the economic value of the dowry.[58] The principal resources that enabled women to get on in life included the options like marrying for the second time, pawning objects, selling property, small

---

deceased, who had purchased them at a public auction last year'. AHCVP, APN, Francesc Llorens, P-XVIII-81-1.

[57] In the opinion of Shammas, 'the master, whether father or employer, bore the primary responsibility for ordering goods for the early modern household. Wives might actually do the marketing for food and choose some of the durables, but, as they had no legal control over the money needed to pay for purchases, the ultimate authority over these requisitions rested with the husband'. Shammas, *The Pre-industrial Consumer*, p. 210.

[58] See, for example, L. Tilly and J.W. Scott, *Women, Work and Family* (New York, 1978); Leonore Davidoff and Catherine Hall, *Family Fortunes: Men and women of the English middle class 1780-1850* (Chicago, 1987); Barbara Diefendorf, 'Women and property in *ancien régime* France. Theory and practice in Dauphiné and Paris', in John Brewer and Susan Staves (eds), *Early Modern Conceptions of Property* (London, 1995); A. Fauve-Chamoux, 'Vedove di città e vedove di campagna nella Francia preindustriale: Aggregato domestico, trasmissione e strategie familiari di sopravvivenza', *Quaderni Storici*, 98, (1998): pp. 301–32; M. Nash (ed.), *Més enllà del silenci: les dones a la història de Catalunya* (Barcelona, 1988); Olwen Hufton, *The prospect before her. A History of Women in Western Europe. vol.I, 1500-1800* (2 vols, London, 1995); M. Carbonell, *Sobreviure a Barcelona. Dones, pobresa i assistència al segle XVIII*, Vic (1997).

businesses and resorting to aid institutions. These narrow alternatives highlight how difficult it was for widows to consume the superfluous objects traditionally associated with 'feminine tastes'.

The gradual impoverishment of widows can easily be verified through the public auctions at which their property was sold. Take, for example, the case of Rosa Fuster, the widow of a furrier from 1763 to 1778, the year in which she died at the age of 78.[59] During these 15 years of widowhood she had lost practically all her own belongings while managing to hold on to her husband's. The total value of his personal property amounted to 61 pounds, whereas hers was sold for just seven pounds. In other words, everything this woman owned at the time of her death was worth nearly nine times less than her husband's property, even though he had died 15 years earlier.

The differences in the material culture of women were shaped by the status of their fathers and husbands. However, the differences between the living conditions of some women and others seem to stem more from the different prevailing consumption strategies in their family or the social group they belonged to, than from the greater or lesser extent to which they were allowed to manage important sources of income. Fauve-Chamoux has observed that the widows of the wealthiest families in pre-industrial France were no more fortunate than those of poor families.[60] However, they did consume more than other women.

In the case of el Penedés, this phenomenon can be verified by analysing the inventories of some widows of liberal professionals, rich merchants or noblemen. Indeed, these women consumed more than peasant women or craftswomen, but less than their husbands. The case of Orosia Nin, who died in 1773, is fairly illustrative of this point. This woman did not live in a hamlet or on a farm, but in Vilafranca del Penedés, the capital of el Penedés (with about 4,000 inhabitants at the end of eighteenth century). And neither was she a peasant, but instead the daughter and wife of doctors of laws who occupied public posts in the municipal government. Orosia inherited her parents' estate and brought a dowry of 4,000 pounds to her marriage.[61] She owned two houses in Vilafranca, a bread-baking oven, nearly 100 hectares of land and 10 leaseholds with a total value of 1,153 pounds. The house where she lived with her husband and children consisted of nine bedrooms (including one 'for the maids'), three living rooms, kitchen, dining room, study, drawing room, cloakroom, kneading trough, cellar, porches, balcony and *'necessária'*. This was one of the few 'bathrooms' that have been discovered in the inventories of this period. This woman's consumption was ostentatious, as is evidenced by her 34 sheets (some made of linen and cloth), her 50 books inherited from her father, her 43 devotional *objets d'art*, her 40 silver items of

---

[59] AHCVP, APN, J. Mullol, P-XVIII-131-1, s/n.

[60] Fauve-Chamoux, 'Vedove di città e vedove di campagna nella Francia preindustriale', p. 324.

[61] The marriage settlement was drawn up in 1764. AHCVP, APN, Joan Rovira, P-XVIII-63-1, f. 62.

cutlery, trays and candelabras and her 19 articles of gold and precious stone, including some diamond and ruby earrings 'made in the fashionable style'. She also owned desks, display cabinets, easy chairs, mirrors, screens and numerous lighting elements. Some of the items found in her house were virtually unknown as household items in this period, including one of the very few coffee pots among all the inventories analysed, while other luxury items such as 24 glasses, 'six saucers, two *mancerinas*[62] and six china chocolate cups' also filled her cupboards. This woman was a great consumer right up until her death. In her will she requested the celebration of 400 charity masses, each one at a cost of six *sueldos*, and that four *dineros* be given to the poor on the day of her death.[63]

What determined Orosia's taste, lifestyle and consumption habits: the fact that she was a woman or her social origin? There is no better way of finding out than to compare her inventory with that of her husband, who died three years later. The inventory of Esteve Ravella – whose property is clearly separated from his wife's – includes more 'superfluous' and 'fashionable' objects than Orosia's.[64] For his personal use, he had 40 linen and cloth shirts, as compared with the 16 owned by his wife; he possessed 88 silver objects (twice as many as his wife), half of which were for everyday use at the dining table, plus a not inconsiderable number of clothing accessories such as buttons, garter clasps, along with a bow tie and footwear, and, of course, a sword. Esteve owned more jewels than Orosia (27 as opposed to 19), and his inventory included more household textiles: 50 sheets (Orosia possessed 34), 142 serviettes (she owned 84) and 34 tablecloths (she had 15). He also had more pieces of cutlery, glassware and crockery, including a 'pocket chocolate box' – a real luxury at that time in a rural area such as this. He also owned 300 books, six times more than his wife. The only items that his wife possessed in greater quantity were devotional *objets d'art*: she owned 43, whereas he had 31.

Therefore, it is no coincidence that the inventories used to illustrate 'feminine' consumption correspond to upper-class women who lived in urban or semi-urban environments at the end of the eighteenth century. They had more access to the new products that were inundating the markets and shops. It is worth asking ourselves, however, whether this consumption should be gendered 'feminine' or simply 'middle class'. Descriptions of the appearances of Catalan men and women from the end of the eighteenth century by the baron of Maldá, suggest that these varied enormously not only according to wealth, but also according to rank'. His account indicates that wealthy peasant women dressed differently from craftswomen and middle-class women. Obviously, rich peasant women dressed better than poor women belonging to the same 'rank', but their distinguishing signs differed from those of the bourgeois world. Only the 'first and second rank', that is, the aristocracy and the middle-classes, used virtually the same distinguishing signs. What Maldá regarded as the dreadful expansion of luxury and fashion was

---

[62] Saucer with an attached chocolate cup holder.
[63] The will: AHCVP, APN, Joan Rovira, P-XVIII-63-2, f. 112.
[64] AHCVP, APN, Joan Rovira, P-XVIII-64-1, f. 12.

still not far-reaching enough for a peasant woman or a craftswoman to pass for an aristocrat or a bourgeois, no matter how well-off they were.

Furthermore, it should not be forgotten that women, regardless of whether or not they had possessions, could do no more than reproduce the cultural model in which they found themselves immersed. Their decisions in the domestic sphere favoured their sons for reasons relating purely to family strategy. One of these complementary sources is an account book kept by Francesca Nin, a widow belonging to the middle-class elite of Vilafranca, in which she carefully made a note year after year of the sums spent on buying clothes and shoes for her and her children from 1718 to 1734.[65] She had two children: a girl, Josefa, and a boy, Francesc, the *hereu*, who was studying law at the University of Cervera. From 1718 to 1727, Francesca bought eight items of clothing for herself, at a total cost of 5.4 pounds. Six articles of clothing were ordered for her daughter, for which the tailor was paid 5 pounds, and 16 were purchased for her son at a cost 22.4 pounds. Between 1727 and 1730 the mother purchased seven pairs of shoes for herself (at a total cost of 4.5 pounds), 11 pairs for Josefa (for which she paid 6.9 pounds) and 14 for Francesc (for a total of 13 pounds). In other words, Francesca spent four times as much on her son's clothes and twice as much on his shoes than on her daughter. This woman, who had internalized her 'housekeeping' duties and fully realized the importance of her children's appearance, was simply fulfilling her responsibility for ensuring the social promotion of the heir. Thus, for women with family responsibilities, the family's consumption needs were much more important than their own. The culture of individuality, the vindication of the individual over the family that took place in cities throughout the eighteenth century and especially during the following century, was still alien to the rural sphere – even among the rich, educated elites. Therefore, consumption-related behaviour obeyed family rather than individual logics.

Conclusion

Fashionable luxuries, and popular fashions, spread throughout rural areas at a much slower rate than in the cities. At the time, many members of the middle class attributed this delay to the conservatism and blind resistance to change of the peasant classes. After all, this reluctance to acquire certain consumer goods directly undermined the potential profits of their businesses. Peasant consumption habits were judged and misjudged without considering the economic and social logic behind them. However, analysis of peasant consumption habits suggests that they were absolutely rational given the institutional, cultural and economic

---

[65] This account book is entitled 'Llibreta de las sabatas y roba se ha feta per compte de la Sra. Francisca Nin, viuda, comensant en lo any 1727', and can be found in the AHCVP, in the 'Documents pendents de classificar' section.

environment in which peasant farmers lived their lives. But this environment was also in flux.

Peasant consumption did not remain fixed during the eighteenth century. It is true that there were no 'revolutionary' changes, but new objects did appear and, above all, the variety of common objects increased thanks to a much wider breadth of materials, colours, forms and prices. Consumption of certain items grew – textiles and recently popularized objects such as cutlery and chocolate pots illustrate this trend, perhaps at the expense of items that fell into decline. The new artefacts and new forms of consumption had different characteristics and spread at different rates. This was due not only to the limits of supply, the degree of accessibility to new products, and distribution problems, but also to the existence of 'different demands', diverse tastes, and the multiple values and uses attached to the same objects by different communities. The examination of peasant household interiors – male or female, rich or poor –suggests that, where applicable, it is social class that determines consumption. In other words, consumption in agrarian sectors seems to be influenced more by the origin, profession and social position of the individuals than by income levels. In contrast, among craftsmen and the middle classes there seems to be a close link between income levels and consumption, which would explain a greater propensity to acquire new and high-quality products. For these social groups the wealth they could show off was more important than their social origin.

The affect of gender on consumption habits was equally complex; the majority of women could not easily become independent economic agents, nor act as self-governing consumers. The learned discourse, which attributed to the 'feminine nature' an unhealthy propensity to consume superfluous products, and which would inform so many studies about the emerging consumer society, is not borne out by the available sources. The vast majority of women, poor and living in rural areas, were not able to embellish themselves and their homes with the new objects that upper-class women found in the shops of Paris and London. The Catalan legal framework explicitly delimited what women could and could not do, and managing income at their discretion was not among the duties they were permitted to perform. The fact that women were mainly responsible for managing family consumption, especially the consumption of perishable goods, does not necessarily imply that that they were allowed to dispose of the family resources with total freedom, let alone squander them. A predilection for superfluous and fashionable objects was more a feature of 'bourgeois' consumption than of 'feminine' consumption. So much so that what contemporaries called 'frivolities' (perfumes, mirrors, silk products, wigs, watches, canapés, display cases, etc.) were equally abundant in the inventories of bourgeois fathers, brothers or husbands.

Only those who were no longer peasant farmers regarded the consumption of luxury and fashionable goods as a viable and effective way to ensure social promotion. The rest, even though they enjoyed more comforts as time went by, continued to have other priorities more in keeping with their environment: for example, acquiring more land and cattle. These espoused other values, such as saving, pragmatism and austerity. These characteristics of peasant identity, many of which stemmed from pure economic logic, were disparaged by certain social sectors with vested interests in the manufacture and trading of consumer goods. Their irritated voices simply dismissed peasants as coarse, uncouth and lacking in the sensitivity required to delight in beautiful things. But over this century Catalan peasants chose how and what they would add to their households, adopting some new styles, even as they rejected others.

PART TWO
The Politics and Practice of Fashion in the Long Nineteenth Century

Chapter Five

Fashion Sprayed and Displayed: The Market for Perfumery in Nineteenth-century Paris

Eugénie Briot

A toute heure du jour les passants apercevaient cette jeune ouvrière, assise dans un vieux fauteuil de velours rouge, le cou penché sur un métier à broder, travaillant avec ardeur. Sa mère avait un tambour vert sur les genoux et s'occupait à faire du tulle. [...] Un rentier se disait après avoir examiné la maison avec l'oeil d'un propriétaire : – Que deviendront ces deux femmes si la broderie vient à n'être plus de mode?[1]

Honoré de Balzac, *Une double famille* [*A second home*], 1830

Fashion is one of the driving forces of economic life: Honoré de Balzac noted this when evoking the threat to the work and livelihood of his two poor needlewomen following the Restoration, and Daniel Roche analysed this phenomenon in *La culture des apparences* [*The Culture of Clothing*][2] in the case of *ancien régime* Paris. As far as clothing is concerned, Daniel Roche stresses the 'necessity, with a view to survive, to maintain the flood of new clothes, and, to win, to accelerate the rhythms of their renewal'.[3] Alchemy perfumers of the nineteenth century applied themselves to arousing the desire of their clients through fashion, at a time of considerable disruptions to their trade. In numerous respects the end of the

---

[1] Honoré de Balzac, 'Une double famille', *La Comédie humaine. Œuvres complètes de M. de Balzac* (12 vols, Paris, 1842), vol. 1, pp. 252–3. 'At any hour of the day the passer-by could see the young needlewoman seated in an old, red velvet chair, bending over an embroidery frame, stitching indefatigably. Her mother had a green hoop on her knee, and busied herself with making tulle. [...] A house-owner, after studying the house with the eye of a valuer, would have said, "What will become of those two women if embroidery should go out of fashion?"'.

[2] Daniel Roche, *La culture des apparences: une histoire du vêtement XVIIe–XVIIIe siècle* (Paris, 1989). English edition: *The Culture of Clothing: Dress and Fashion in the Ancien Régime* (Cambridge, 1996). On the material construction of appearances, see also: Philippe Perrot, *Le corps féminin: le travail des apparences XVIIIe–XIXe siècle* (Paris, 1984); and on cosmetics: Catherine Lanoë, *La poudre et le fard: une histoire des cosmétiques de la Renaissance aux Lumières* (Paris, 2009).

[3] Roche, *La culture des apparences*, p. 48. 'nécessité pour survivre d'entretenir le flux des habits neufs, et pour gagner, d'accélérer les rythmes de leur renouvellement'.

nineteenth century showed notable changes in the history of olfaction, odours and perfumery, from an economic as well as a cultural point of view.

The work undertaken by Alain Corbin at the beginning of the 1980s has produced a precise understanding of the social imagination and behaviours related to olfaction over time. Corbin studied the several different networks of images linked to the sense of smell in *Le Miasme et la jonquille*[4] [*The Foul and the Fragrant*] and assesses the steps of the slow deodorizing process that lead to the relative olfactory silence of our present environment, with the main rupture arising at the end of the eighteenth century. Through his study Corbin highlights a major evolution of sensibilities with a significant drop in the olfactory tolerance point, which caused people to shy away from the heavy odours of filth and musk and move toward the refined exhalations of pure light smells such as daffodil. The Pastorian revolution of the end of the 1800s,[5] which led to the identification of pathological agents and the disengagement of the foul (odour) from infection (the germ), defined a major new shift in the history of olfactory sensibilities and had major consequences on the practices and politics of hygiene, as analysed by Georges Vigarello, Julia Csergo, as well as Alain Corbin.[6] From this point on, a putrid smell no longer indicated noxiousness, and hygiene exceeded mere visible cleanliness as well as the absence of smell. On the basis of these major works, I will focus on the only positive, creative manifestation of this history of smell: perfume.

The history of smell and of the social imagination of odour do not take the exact place of the history of perfumery, just as the history of perfumery does not replicate the history of olfactory fashions. Social imagination, built on a cultural and scientific background, governs the history of smell; whereas taste constructed by social norms governs fashion. Beneath the great history of representations established by Alain Corbin, a history of olfactory tastes appears feasible, expressed by the olfactory choices the perfumery of a time offered to its consumers and by the reception these scents received. It is at this intersecting point – the act of production and of its reception – at the meeting of creative processes and of consumptive choices that the olfactory fashions of a time arise. What I intend to do here is not to redraw the history of the fashions of nineteenth-century perfumery, but to highlight its main processes and to emphasize its links to the economic vitality of this sector.

From an economic point of view the nineteenth century was a crucial time in the evolution of the perfumery market. It was an age of transition that turned perfumery products from luxury items to broadly distributed and more widely

---

[4] Alain Corbin, *Le Miasme et la jonquille: l'odorat et l'imaginaire social XVIIIe-XIXe siècles* (Paris, 1982), p. 336. English edition: *The Foul and the Fragrant: Odour and the Social Imagination* (London, 1994).

[5] Louis Pasteur (1822–95), a French microbiologist, made major breakthroughs in the identification of the causes of various diseases, advancing the germ theory of disease.

[6] On the history of the practices of hygiene in the nineteenth century see: Georges Vigarello, *Le Propre et le sale: l'hygiène du corps depuis le Moyen âge* (Paris, 1985) and Julia Csergo, *Liberté, égalité, propreté: la morale de l'hygiène au XIXe siècle* (Paris, 1988).

diffused commodities. Perfumery products include all fragrant toiletries: alcoholic extracts, toilet waters and vinegars (meant to perfume the water used to wash oneself), eaux de Cologne (whose use was often therapeutically prescribed as well as hygienic), lotions, hair oils and pomades, rice powders, fragrant wardrobe sachets, and soaps – these last items represented a very massive part of the industry products.[7] In 1810, the perfumery trade in France represented a little less than 2 million francs.[8] By 1900 production of these assorted products had risen in value to 80 million francs.[9] It is during the decade from 1880–90 that production developed in particular, rising from 45 million francs in 1878 to 70–75 million in 1889.[10] The reports of the Universal Exhibitions underline the obvious reasons that led to the dramatic growth of this sector. In the first instance, this development intersects with the analyses of historians of hygiene: as early as in 1855 the reporter commented on the 'almost general use'[11] of the products necessary for toilet care, of 'perfumes, whose use tends to spread wider and wider, as the progresses of an affluent lifestyle and the habit of a better hygiene bring into the masses more delicacy into senses'.[12] And when the time arrived to assess the state of the industry at the end of the century, the reporter of the Universal Exhibition of 1900 expressed exactly the same opinion, stressing the democratization of perfumery products: 'The sphere of activity [of perfumery] is all the more extensive than the

---

[7] In a characteristically convoluted style the reporter of the 1855 Universal Exhibition in Paris underlined the common product forms: 'L'état dans lequel les parfums s'introduisent plus ordinairement dans nos habitudes domestiques, c'est celui de savon parfumé, genre de produit dans lequel la substance détersive dont l'emploi est devenu nécessaire se trouve ainsi associée à l'arôme que nous préférons' ['The state under which perfumes most ordinarily enter our domestic habits is the one of a fragrant soap, a type of product in which the detergent substance whose use has become necessary finds itself associated with our favourite smell'], *Rapports du jury mixte international publiés sous la dir. de S.A.I. le Prince Napoléon, président de la commission impériale* (Paris, 1856), p. 533.

[8] Charles-Louis Barreswil, 'La parfumerie en 1862', in Charles Laboulaye (ed.), *Annales du Conservatoire Impérial des Arts et Métiers* (Paris, 1863), 1st series, vol. 4, p. 273.

[9] Alfred Picard, 'Industrie chimique. Industries diverses. Economie sociale', in *Exposition universelle internationale de 1900 à Paris. Le bilan d'un siècle (1801-1900)* (6 vols, Paris, 1906), vol. 5, p. 115. The figures Alfred Picard gives for the production of perfumery products are: 12 million francs in 1836, 18 million in 1856, 26 million in 1866, 45 million in 1878, 70 to 75 million in 1889 and 80 million in 1900.

[10] At the same time the population of Paris, being the very first consumer of these products, grew considerably as well (from 547,000 inhabitants in 1801 to about four million in 1901), but to an infinitely lesser extent, just like the French population (from 28.25 million in 1801 to 38.96 million in 1901).

[11] 'emploi presque général'.

[12] *Rapports du jury mixte international*, p. 532. 'ces parfums, dont l'usage tend à se répandre de plus en plus, à mesure que les progrès de l'aisance et l'habitude d'une plus grande propreté amènent dans les masses plus de délicatesse dans les sens'.

development of well-being and of an affluent lifestyle, the improvement of processes and the drop of the prices imparted a great expansion to consumption.'[13] The works of Alain Corbin, Julia Csergo and Georges Vigarello, as noted above, reveal the complex political, economic, and cultural processes that underpinned this dramatic evolution within nineteenth-century society. New hygienic practices were, if not yet global, becoming a more regular and routine part of daily life. However, even though the shift of sensibilities and the progress of hygiene in the development of the perfume industry were critically important, these were not sufficient to account for the widespread consumption of scented products. Like clothing, perfumes were part of a cultural communication, as described by Daniel Roche:

> The social and cultural function of clothes cannot be understood other than in terms of communicability. It is thus important to analyse the effects caused by the one who is seen on the one who sees just as for any kind of discourse where the one who comes first is not the one who utters the speech but the one who listens to it.[14]

Thus, perfume offers an excellent opportunity to position the person who wears it into the normalized social field of his/her time. On this account, like any other element of women's costume, perfume consumption was a fashion fact and its uses reflect on the priorities of the time and the ethos of its consumers. It is also essential to note that the nineteenth-century perfumery market was fundamentally a women's market. Although sources are lacking to provide researchers with precise data on the division between men's and women's perfumery, very few perfumes in the 1800s are explicitly dedicated to men, and men's consumption of perfumery products (except for soap) was generally restricted to eau de Cologne, for hygiene or even therapeutic purposes and scented oils for the hair. In the olfactory field as well as in the sartorial one women are delegated the principal role as representatives of fashion.

Perfume is a unique fashion product. Practically, from an economic point of view, perfume is a commodity whose life by its very nature is relatively short: perfume is consumed, perfume spoils with time, and as a consequence perfume has to be renewed. As such, perfume can be bought or received as a present but cannot live a second life by being transferred or transformed. Perfume has no secondhand market, unlike so many other fashion artefacts. Thus, perfume represents a product

---

[13] Picard, 'Industrie chimique. Industries diverses. Economie sociale', p. 116. 'Le champ d'action [de la parfumerie] est d'autant plus étendu que le développement du bien-être et de l'aisance, l'amélioration des procédés et l'abaissement des prix ont imprimé un vif essor à la consommation.'

[14] Roche, *La culture des apparences*, p. 488. 'La fonction sociale et culturelle du vêtement ne peut se comprendre qu'en termes de communicabilité. Il importe donc d'analyser les effets produits par celui qui est vu sur celui qui voit comme pour tout ordre de discours où qui est premier n'est pas le sujet qui profère la parole mais celui qui l'écoute.'

of pure consumption, in the sense that its very use wastes it away in a short time. Therefore the succession of fashions in perfumery might theoretically be subjected to a weaker inertia than other fashion products. Nonetheless, from a social point of view, the nineteenth-century diffusion of perfumery fashions is problematic in several respects. From an economic point of view, perfume consumption could be related to the consumption of short-lived products such as food items for instance; these products are rarely considered as fashions, and their prices are market driven and largely related to their production costs. Indeed, from a social point of view the consumption of perfume might well be related to more culturally informed immaterial goods, since the symbolic value of the product goes far beyond the intrinsic value of its material use.

Studying fashion facts we can assess problems at the intersection of social and economic history. In the case of perfumery, how can this fashion phenomenon be related to the economic development of the industry in the nineteenth century? Focusing on the Parisian market – then the largest in Europe – this study will examine the way fashion and industrial concerns interacted to shape the social olfactory landscape of the time. I will explore these problems through three main trajectories. The first deals with the specificities of perfumery with regard to fashion in nineteenth-century Parisian society; the second investigates three different cases of synthetic raw materials for perfumery and their relation to fashion phenomena; and the last tackles the subject of the fashioning and marketing of perfume products in the general context of industrialization and the decrease in production costs.

A Problematic Diffusion of Olfactory Fashions

As a first point, obvious though it may seem, I would like to insist on the specificities of perfumery with respect to the fashion context of nineteenth-century Parisian society. Understood as a manifestation of collective taste, fashion emerges from the tension between imitation and distinction, the two main forces whose roles were first described by Georg Simmel in 1904.[15] Simmel underlined two tendencies in this phenomenon: the first one consists of the propensity for an individual to merge with his or her own social group; the second inclination is the move to separate from one's cohort, even while staying inside of it, the individual trying to do better and better, or become differentiated from other members of his/her own group. The collective dimension of fashion is basic to this dynamic. The norm within this collective element mediates the social olfactory field between approved perfumes and prohibited perfumes, between chic ones and vulgar ones. As a first principle and in its most refined form of expression, taste and more especially good taste was typically shaped by the most expressive and influential members of a social group. In nineteenth-century Parisian high society only good taste could govern preferences and choices, and this expression of taste likewise

---

[15] Georg Simmel, 'Fashion', *International Quarterly*, 10 (1904): pp. 130–55.

shaped purchase and use. Good taste was defined by codes of distinction, conveyed by such powerful prescriptive agents such as manuals of manners or the women's press; both published forms had grown considerably over the century, with wider and wider distribution.[16] If not as prolix on the topic of scent as was the case for sartorial fashion, both sorts of publications took a passionate interest in perfume and sought to dictate its correct uses, denouncing its misuses. In this way scent was consecrated as a social sign of distinction.

Although such mechanisms were not peculiar to olfactory fashions, specific processes nevertheless distinguished olfactory styles from vogue in dress. As a first and fundamentally distinctive feature, unique in comparison to other dress-related trades, the business of perfumery had to compensate for the absence of visual imagery in its products. Indeed, more than any other commodity, perfume's visuality was constructed from start to finish. As such, perfume offers a problematic case for the theory of conspicuous consumption put forward by Thornstein Veblen.[17] Paradoxically, in the Veblenesque quest for distinction by consumers, there are no visible signposts in the selection of perfume. Materiality is manifested through olfactory senses alone. Utterly superfluous and notoriously frivolous, perfume remains intrinsically fleeting, evanescent – elusive. In contrast to any other element of a woman's costume such as clothes, make-up and jewellery, in contrast to decorative furniture, which delight the sense of sight first, the quest for distinction in perfume is only revealed through transient smells, fleetingly and only within a close proximity to the anointed body. To spread, olfactory fashions cannot rely on the direct visual observation, or distant ocular demonstrations of consumption. Compare scent to colour; the latter can become fashionable when elegant people wear it *en masse* and manufacturers advertise the shade in shop windows and brochures. Olfactory choices will become known solely within the physical boundaries of intimacy. An elegant woman will always remain olfactorily silent to the vast majority of people removed from her immediate path. Even more problematic: this elegant woman would rarely know anything but what the perfumer decided to say to her about the intrinsic quality of the content of the bottle of scent she bought. There were very few people who would ever be able to identify, on mere olfactory criteria, the nature or the quality of the raw materials used to compose it, to distinguish the finest essences from products of more common quality, to estimate, in a word, the financial or fashionable value of the eddy of scent left in her wake as she moved through society.

This material ambiguity was all the more significant in the nineteenth century since a strong emphasis on discretion governed the rules of etiquette. Even if the

---

[16] *La Mode illustrée* counts 40,000 subscribers in 1866, *Le Moniteur de la mode* 200,000 in 1890, and *Le Petit écho de la mode*, more popular, of a more modest price (it was sold for 0.10 francs in 1913 whereas *Le Moniteur de la mode* cost 0.50 francs), 210,000 right from its beginnings in 1893. Evelyne Sullerot, *La Presse féminine* (Paris, 1963), p. 11.

[17] Thorstein Veblen, *The Theory of the Leisure Class* (New York, 1899).

argument of hygiene helped diffuse the practice of perfume use, there were also powerful advocates for moderation and discernment in the choice and amount of fragrance employed, advice intended to guide readers in the soundest taste. One guide for young women insisted on only 'A hint of a very light and very decent scent can be tolerated, [...] provided that it should remain nothing but a hint'.[18] Another author advised readers in 1892: 'Do not perfume yourself excessively, for it may seriously distress your neighbours. [...] For both good taste and to avoid bothering other people a unique and soft scent is recommended.'[19] These injunctions to observe an olfactory discretion tended to grow over the course of the century, going so far as to exclude heavier perfumes, if not all scents. Authors of these rules were unequivocal in their warnings:

> A good-mannered woman does not wear any perfume. She leaves them to women of easy virtue, for whom they are the exclusive prerogative. Sprays of lavender, white lily-of-the-valley from gardens, violet petals, roses and lilies are the only scents to perfume the items of linen of a well-kept house.[20]

> Not only is the use of perfume for the young lady ill-considered coquettishness, it is unseemly coquettishness. Apart from a few drops of Eau de Cologne that will accompany your morning ablutions, and a hint of violet or of iris that will freshen the contact of your lingerie, you should never use any perfume.[21]

Moral arguments were marshalled to justify the banishing of heady perfumes, particularly a use of scent likely to contravene the approved reserve prescribed for women in polite society. Failure to accede to these regulations carried its own punishment:

---

[18] M. Maryan and G. Béal, *Le Fond et la forme: le savoir-vivre pour les jeunes filles* (Paris, 1896), p. 108. ['Un soupçon d'odeur très légère et très comme il faut peut être toléré [...] à la condition de rester un soupcon'.]

[19] Baronne Staffe, *Règles du savoir-vivre dans la société moderne* (Paris, 1892), p. 334. ['Ne vous parfumez par à outrance, car cela peut incommoder sérieusement vos voisins. [...] Le bon goût et le désir de ne causer aucune gêne à autrui sont d'accord pour prescrire une senteur unique et douce'.]

[20] Ermance Dufaux de la Jonchère, *Le savoir-vivre dans la vie ordinaire et dans les cérémonies civiles et religieuses* (Paris, 1883), p. 66. ['Une femme bien élevée ne porte sur elle aucun parfum. Elle les abandonne à la femme de moeurs faciles, dont ils sont l'apanage exclusif. Les gerbes de lavande, les bouquets du blanc muguet des jardins, les pétales de violettes, de roses et de lis, parfument seuls le linge d'une maison bien tenue.']

[21] Comtesse de Gencé, *Code mondain de la jeune fille* (Paris, 1909), pp. 95–6. ['L'usage des parfums n'est pas seulement pour la jeune fille une coquetterie maladroite, c'est une coquetterie désobligeante. [...] A part les quelques gouttes d'eau de Cologne qui agrémenteront vos ablutions matinales, le soupçon de violette ou d'iris qui rendra plus frais le contact de votre lingerie, vous ne devrez donc jamais employer de parfum.']

Little indulgence is shown, within the polite society, toward women that use perfumes indiscriminantly. [An elegant woman] remains within the limits of good breeding by *concealing* [her favourite perfume] from the people in her entourage. People of our acquaintance must not suspect us of wanting to broadcast our perfume. That would be of a kind of vanity that would quickly earn a bad reputation, or, at least, very deserved criticism.[22]

Nineteenth-century Olfactory Fashions

Olfactory volume figured as one of the principal elements in the social olfactory field of nineteenth-century Paris. The fragrance milieu was further structured by a classification of socially permitted odours, subdivided between fashionable perfumes and more common or even vulgar ones. The olfactory norm of the time accepted only a relatively small range of aromas. Eau de Cologne and lavender water held an unquestionable supremacy as the two main olfactory constants of the time; they reflected an ideal discretion and their hygienic authority was never in dispute. Only within the strict limits of this norm, defined by good taste, could fashions flourish every now and then. Throughout the century fashionable variations arose exclusively among floral essences, shaped in part by the gendered logic of floral symbolism;[23] the choice of the principal raw material determined the distinction of the product. The very fleetingness of these products, from Veblen's angle of conspicuous consumption, make them all the more efficient agents of distinction because they are intrinsically and totally wasteful – perfume, once sprayed, gradually evaporates into nothing at all. This olfactory ephemerality was ineluctably tied to issues of refinement. Consider, in contrast the characteristics of musk, and more generally raw materials of an animal origin, all of which are very strongly fragrant and long lasting. These powerful scents were antithetical to good taste, the very incarnations of vulgarity and impropriety.[24] And this offensiveness was ascribed to such perfumes whatever the rank of the person who wore it, however elevated the social position; though of irreproachable stature,

---

[22] Comtesse de Gencé, *Le cabinet de toilette d'une honnête femme* (Paris, 1909), pp. 418–19. ['On montre généralement peu d'indulgence, dans la société polie, pour les femmes qui usent immodérément des parfums. [...] [Une femme élégante] ne restera toujours dans les limites de la bonne éducation qu'en *dissimulant* [son parfum de prédilection] aux personnes de son entourage. Il ne faut pas que les gens qui nous connaissent puissent nous soupçonner de l'intention de faire valoir notre parfum. Ce serait une forme de vanité qui nous vaudrait vite une mauvaise réputation, ou, tout au moins, des critiques très méritées.']

[23] On this theme, see Corbin, *Le miasme et la jonquille*, p. 218.

[24] 'Retenez que les parfums les plus fins ne sont pas les plus pénétrants, tandis que ces derniers sont souvent les plus banals' ['Remember that the finest perfumes aren't the most penetrating ones, whereas the latter are often the most common ones'], the comtesse de Gencé says in 1909: Gencé, *Le cabinet de toilette d'une honnête femme* p. 415.

the perfume chosen by Queen Victoria at the time of her official visit to Paris in 1855 contained a 'distasteful hint of musk'[25] that *Le Messager des modes* did not hesitate to denounce. On this subject all the authorities effectively agreed to condemn this scent:

> [Women] should above all distrust concentrated essences, said to be triple, rich in musk and amber, which produce the most subtle and pervasive exhalations: the snake is hidden under the flowers![26]

There, too, as much as the actual composition of the product, the cultural symbols linked to the raw materials themselves defined its reception within the marketplace. And for the very reason musk was decried, violet was revered. Violet scents had an extraordinary vogue throughout the second half of the nineteenth century, a phenomenon for which there is no other explanation but the strength of the symbolism this flower engenders. Other perfumes playing on the same olfactory discretion certainly aroused a similar craze and others also enjoyed shorter-lived fads. But at a time when a perfume was most closely associated with its principal ingredient, violet benefited from the symbolic force of the flower itself, synonymous with the ideals of modesty expressed in the language of flowers – an idiom women of the time mastered perfectly – and a floral conceit that did not infringe in any way on the reserve that above all else exemplified feminity, whether aristocratic or middle-class. The manuals of manners raised a unanimous cry: 'Iris, violet are to be recommended.'[27]

The humble violet was indisputably triumphant in perfume markets in the second half of the nineteenth century. In 1860, in its fashion columns *Le Bon ton* listed a few violet-scented cosmetics before adding: 'What else could I mention? La Reine des Abeilles is so rich in wonderful products. To perfume the handkerchiefs of Chapron, please take: les Violettes d'Italie. There are a thousand other superior extracts, but this one is above all fashionable.'[28] Again, in 1896 *La Mode illustrée* made a similar claim with the same conviction: 'At the moment the favourite perfume for the handkerchief is violet. [...] We will applaud this choice:

---

[25] Corbin, *Le miasme et la jonquille*, p. 323, n. 126.

[26] Ernest Monin, *Le Trésor médical de la femme* (Paris, 1906), p. 286. ['[Les femmes] devraient surtout se méfier des essences concentrées, dites triples, riches en musc et en ambre, qui dégagent abondamment les effluves les plus subtils et les plus pénétrants : le serpent est caché sous les fleurs!']

[27] Baronne Staffe, *Règles du savoir-vivre*, p. 334. ['L'iris, la violette sont à recommander'.] Iris and violet are of very close olfactory nature.

[28] *Le Bon ton*, 26/2 (1 July 1860). ['Que citerai-je encore ? La Reine des Abeilles est si riche en merveilleux produits. Pour parfumer les mouchoirs de Chapron, vous prendrez : les Violettes d'Italie. Il y a mille autres extraits supérieurs, mais celui-ci est surtout à la mode'.]

violet, infinitely finer, sweeter, more distinguished, is well the perfume that suits respectable ladies.'[29]

This preference began some time earlier in the century and persisted over decades. During the whole of 1860, of 17 total mentions of perfumes in the fashion reviews of *Le Petit messager des modes*, 30 per cent concern the scent of violet, 18 per cent lavender water and 18 per cent Eau de Cologne. In 1870, violet still represented 25 per cent of all perfume commentaries, beside ylang-ylang, which represents 25 per cent as well. At the same time a perfume house such as *A la reine des abeilles* (whose perfumer is named Violet), was the most often mentioned in *Le Petit messager des modes*. Fully 75 per cent of passages on perfumery referred to this house in 1860 and 33 per cent in 1870, suggesting that there was a monetary connection and that these articles were paid for by perfume houses. This particular business offered between 60 and 70 different perfumes in its catalogue,[30] just like many perfume houses. But here too a large place was reserved for violet. Around 1880, Houbigant's *Violette idéale* devised the most extensive range of products in the catalogue, the essence being available in six different strengths, toilet water in five, as well as in the form of a lotion, brilliantine, oil, soap and rice powder. The end of the century was consecrated to the reign of violet when, in 1893, Tiemann and Kruger, at the end of lengthy research on this subject, succeeded in synthesizing ionon, which smells of both violet and iris. They obtained this compound from the citral extracted of the essential oil of lemongrass. This quest for a synthetic substitute reveals the intense economic interest in a fashionable scent such as violet. Significantly enough, *La Nature*, the journal of the Academy of Science, echoed this discovery in its pages.[31] Just as an artificial source for mauve and violet colours had been discovered in the 1850s for one of the nineteenth-century's most popular shades, now a synthetic source for violet scent had been uncovered. In France, Tiemann's French patents for the synthesis of ionon were bought by the Société De Laire, with which Roger & Gallet, then among the most powerful perfume houses in the world, negotiated exclusive rights to ionons, in return for buying minimum annual quantities of this compound. In 1910, there were five lines of violet-perfumed products that co-exist in the catalogues of Roger & Gallet: *Violette de Parme* (created in 1880), *Violette ambrée* (1890), *Vera Violetta* (1892), *Violette merveilleuse* (1905) and *Violette Rubra* (1910). In 1905

---

[29] *La Mode illustrée*, 37/24, (Sunday 14 June 1896): p. 191. ['En ce moment le parfum préféré pour le mouchoir est la violette. [...] Applaudissons ce choix : la violette, infiniment plus fine, plus douce, plus distinguée, est bien le parfum qui convient aux femmes comme il faut'.]

[30] A la reine des abeilles (Paris), *Catalogue général de la fabrication des savons et parfums de Violet* (Paris, 1865), p. 44.

[31] 'Académie des sciences – séance du 25 octobre 1893', *La Nature*, 2 (1893): p. 351.

the *Vera Violetta* range included 31 references to 16 different products, testimony to the continuing power of this scent.[32]

In 1952, Ernest Beaux, the perfumer who in the 1920s created Chanel N°5, claimed: 'It is on chemists that we must rely to find new compounds thanks to which original olfactory notes could develop. Yes, as far as Perfume is concerned, the future is above all in the hands of chemistry.'[33] It seems, however, that right from the beginning of the history of synthetic perfumery artificial compounds were to play a major part in the development of the industry. The case of piperonal, with the scent of heliotrope, was characteristic of this. The synthesis of piperonal did not result from research specifically undertaken with this in mind. Synthesized in 1869 by Fittig and Mielk, piperonal is produced industrially from 1874 and reached a significant output by 1886. Entirely new in perfumery,[34] the scent of heliotrope appeared in perfumers' catalogues at the very beginning of the 1880s: in 1878 it was presented in the Guerlain catalogue[35] in the form of soap ('sapoceti') whereas the 1882 catalogue[36] opened with a full-page engraving of a bottle of white heliotrope extract. Between 1879 and 1899, the price of one kilogram of piperonal fell dramatically, from 3,790 francs to 37.5 francs. In this case, the synthesis of a potentially fashionable fragrance, derived from industrial techniques, produced notable profits for its manufacturer. This windfall took place before the drop in price brought the new heliotrope scent within the reach of a larger market, the social diffusion of this fragrance reflecting its great success. Both economic and social factors interacted to explain and generate the fashion for heliotrope.

In the same way, both economic and social factors interacted to sustain the longevity of the vogue for violet, a huge success that must not mask the gradual loss of prestige linked to its social diffusion. Prince Charles Egon of Furstenberg ordered three little jars of *Pommade de l'Impératrice* scented with *Violette de*

---

[32] *Roger & Gallet: parfumeurs et créateurs, 1806-1989, Exposition du Musée municipal de Bernay 3 juin–3 septembre 1989* (Bernay, 1987), pp. 49–50.

[33] ['C'est sur les chimistes qu'il faudra compter pour trouver des corps nouveaux grâce auxquels pourraient éclore des notes originales. Oui, pour le Parfum, l'avenir est surtout entre les mains de la Chimie.']

[34] ['Dans le domaine des parfums, un cas plus intéressant encore peut se présenter. C'est lorsque le produit chimique apporte une note nouvelle que le parfumeur ne possédait pas encore: il en est ainsi pour l'héliotropine, le terpinéol, l'aldéhyde phénylacétique'] 'In the field of perfumery, an even more interesting case can occur when an artificial product brings a new olfactory note that perfumers didn't have before: it is thus for piperonal, terpineol, phenylacétic acid', Septimus Piesse, *Chimie des parfums et fabrication des essences* (Paris, 1903), p. 192.

[35] Guerlain, *Prix-courant de Guerlain, Parfumeur breveté (S.G.D.G.), 15 rue de la Paix* (Paris, Imprimerie de T. Jeunet, 1878, p. 13. Guerlain Archives.

[36] Guerlain, *Prix-courant de Guerlain, Parfumeur breveté (S.G.D.G.), 15 rue de la Paix, Paris*, 1882, p. 5. Guerlain Archives.

Parme from Pierre-François-Pascal Guerlain on 2 October 1861.[37] But this scent did not remain an elite commodity for every long. In 1867, violet had become the preferred perfume of Thérèse Raquin, one of Emile Zola's characters who ran a haberdasher's shop at the Passage du Pont-Neuf and whose husband worked as an employee in the railway administration.[38] In February 1869 Octave Mouret put a silver fountain of violet water in the middle of his department store, *Au Bonheur des dames*, on the day of the linen sale he organized – this scent was now synonymous with the bourgeoisie.[39] By 1880, violet had become *Nana*'s perfume, in Zola's classic tale of a prostitute's reign in the fashionable demi-monde.[40] Thus violet perfume went through various cultural associations over time, as well as permeating various social ranks. Its diffusion was facilitated by both the drop in production costs and in price, its fashion kept alive by the tendency to imitation described by Georg Simmel, its reception among consumers sustained by the complexities within the cultural matrix through which it diffused.

Technical and industrial factors played major roles in the development and persistence of perfumery fashions. Other fashions, more or less lasting, more or less powerful, remained through a decade or two of the century, mostly due to the discoveries of chemically synthetic substances. These fragrances included ylang-ylang in the 1870s[41] to heliotrope, as I observed above, in the 1880s, from the white olfactory notes of lily-of-the-valley and lilac in the 1890s[42] to carnation in the very last years of the century.[43] However, I must emphasize the fact that the success of a scent was first conditioned by its inscription within the social olfactory field of tolerable smells. The synthesis of musk by Baur in 1888, should it have been the result of an effective quest, did not result in a fashion for musk-based perfumes, despite the drop in its production costs. Musk was used widely, for it was necessary to compound perfumes; but musk under no circumstances became a fashionable scent. There was an essential ambiguity in its use that had to be hidden at all times from consumers of perfume, as this contemporary explained:

> Colours are not debatable, and so, neither are perfumes. It is fashionable today to say that you do not like musk, Piesse says. My great experience allows me to say that the taste of the public for this scent is as big as perfumers can wish. Any perfume that will contain some musk will always be the one that the public

---

[37] Guerlain Archives.
[38] Emile Zola, *Thérèse* (Paris, 1868), pp. 77, 118.
[39] Emile Zola, *Au Bonheur des dames* (1883, reprinted Paris, 1984), p. 455.
[40] Emile Zola, *Nana* (1880, Paris, 1994), pp. 413, 416, 447.
[41] The scent of ylang-ylang is not due to a new chemical synthesis but to the distillation of a newly exploited plant from Manila and the Philippines.
[42] Conditioned by the synthesis of terpineol.
[43] The synthesis of isoeugénol by Tiemann was made in 1890.

prefers, as long as the merchant is sure to tell the buyer that there isn't any. What Piesse says is true.[44]

What counted in the final analysis was what was said about perfume and its content, as perfumers themselves concurred. Of course the ingredients were not unimportant. But their symbolic power, the distinction they conveyed, whether it was because they were different or because they were new, eclipsed the olfactory criteria or even the argument of effectiveness. The choice of nut oil by César Birotteau, Honoré de Balzac's character of a perfumer, to compound his *Essence Comagène* (a men's hair oil), was carefully considered and part of a strategy intended to 'sink' *Macassar Oil*, the perfumer's great rival and sworn enemy. But when the scientific authority of whom he requires the advice, the great chemist Vauquelin, assured him that absolutely no oil, Macassar, nut or whatever, can make hair grow, César Birotteau confirms his choice to his assistant Popinot all the same:

> 'What a great man! what a glance, what penetration!' said Birotteau. [...] 'Yes! nothing can make the hair grow; Macassar, you lie! Popinot, our fortune is made. Let's go to the manufactory tomorrow morning at seven o'clock; the nuts will be coming, and we will press out some oil. It is all very well for him to say that any oil is good; [but] we should be lost if the public knew it. If there weren't a little bit of scent and the name of a nut for our oil, how could we sell it for three or four francs the four ounces!'[45]

Marketing Perfumes, Fashioning Scents

Thus, paradoxical as it may seem, because of perfume's intrinsic fleetingness, because of the taste of nineteenth-century Parisian society for the most delicate

---

[44] 'Le musc en parfumerie', *La Parfumerie*, 2/25 (12 August 1888). ['On ne discute pas des couleurs, il en est de même des parfums. C'est une mode aujourd'hui de dire qu'on n'aime pas le musc, dit Piesse. Ma grande expérience me permet de dire que le goût du public pour cette odeur est aussi grand que peuvent le désirer les parfumeurs. Les parfums quelconques qui en contiennent sont toujours ceux que le public préfère, tant que le marchand à soin d'assurer à l'acheteur qu'il n'y en a point. Ce que dit Piesse est vrai.']

[45] Honoré de Balzac, 'Histoire de la grandeur et de la décadence de César Birotteau', *La Comédie humaine. Œuvres complètes de M. de Balzac*, vol. 10, (12 vols, Paris, 1844), pp. 278, *The Rise and Fall of César Birotteau*. ['– Ce grand homme! quel regard et quelle pénétration! dit Birotteau. [...] Ah! rien ne peut faire pousser les cheveux, Macassar, tu mens! Popinot, nous tenons une fortune. Ainsi, demain, à sept heures, soyons à la fabrique, les noisettes viendront et nous ferons de l'huile, car il a beau dire que toute huile est bonne, nous serions perdus si le public le savait. S'il n'entrait pas dans notre huile un peu de noisette et de parfum, sous quel prétexte pourrions-nous la vendre trois ou quatre francs les quatre onces!']

perfumes and its demand for the utmost discretion in their use – which all work towards restricting, from an olfactory point of view, the social circulation of perfumes and their fashions – the fashioning process remained somewhat removed from the fragrance itself. In the case of perfume, the function of visual communications described by Daniel Roche about clothes was not effective in the olfactory context, as an agent of diffusion. Indeed, most properties of the perfume were accounted for, and even constructed, by the discourse of which it was a part, whether this was expressed by consumers themselves or by the prescriptions of the women's press or of the manuals of manners. All of these components formulated a judgement of taste and value, praising or disparaging a product to structure its reputation. This reputation was also expressed by the very system of signs that directly surrounded the perfume itself: its name, its bottle, its label, its advertisements, the boutiques in which it was sold – all contributed to embody the product, to convey an image to which the product was linked. This commercial rhetoric was the only way to associate perfume to elements of a visible and expressible nature. Here was the real arena where a fashioning process was consciously employed. Here was the real field in which nineteenth-century perfumers displayed their marketing skills and their struggle for sales. This endeavour was exemplified in the scene devised by Honoré de Balzac, as his character César Birotteau was thinking of a new *Essence Comagène*:

> The perfumer, lost in his computations, was meditating as he went along the Rue Saint-Honore on his duel with Macassar Oil. He was reflecting about his labels and the shape of his bottles, worked out the structure of the corks, the color of the advertising placards. And yet people say there is no poetry in commerce! Newton did not make more calculations for his famous binomial than Birotteau made for his Comagene Essence, – for by this time the Oil had become an Essence again, he went from one description to the other but didn't perceive their actual value. His head spun with his computations, and he took this activity of an unclear thought for the substantial work of real talent.[46]

With the improvements in colour printing and in glass bottle production, the attention paid to the material appearance of perfume products became all the more decisive in the sales of these products and examples could be cited at length. The

---

[46] Balzac, *The Rise and Fall of César Birotteau*. 'Histoire de la grandeur et de la décadence', pp. 266. ['Le parfumeur, perdu dans ses combinaisons, méditait en allant le long de la rue Saint-Honoré sur son duel avec l'Huile de Macassar, il raisonnait ses étiquettes, la forme de ses bouteilles, calculait la contexture du bouchon, la couleur des affiches. Et l'on dit qu'il n'y a pas de poésie dans le commerce! Newton ne fit pas plus de calculs pour son célèbre binôme que Birotteau n'en faisait pour l'Essence Comagène, car l'Huile redevint Essence, il allait d'une expression à l'autre sans en connaître la valeur. Toutes les combinaisons se pressaient dans sa tête, et il prenait cette activité dans le vide pour la substantielle action du talent.']

label for instance was often a highly delicate and ornate one. L.T. Piver's labels in particular are engraved by Alexandre Brongniard Fils, the director of the Sèvres manufactory of porcelain or by his pupils.[47] Likewise, in the perfumers' catalogues each perfume was offered with packaging of several different bottle sizes, up to about 20 for some products. The *Eau de Cologne rectifiée N°18* of the catalogue of the perfumer Violet in 1865 was offered to customers with a choice of 18 different forms of packaging.[48] The price of the bottle itself determined the final cost of the product.[49]

Whether symbolic or formulated, the discourse surrounding this fashioned product came first. The care brought to the presentation, to the promotion and to the distribution of the product aimed to construct its symbolic value and its desirability in the consumers' eyes. In a general context, with the drop in production costs due to the fall of the price of raw materials and to the industrialization of the sector, it was all the more essential to associate perfumery with the concept of luxury.[50] What the product lost in intrinsic value had to be gained in symbolic value. The introduction of perfumery in such new distribution centres as department stores, with much more attractive prices than in perfumers' boutiques, further encouraged perfumers to emphasize these strategies of distinction. The same perfume, the Lubin toilet water for instance, offered at 1.85 francs at the Galeries Saint-Martin department store, was sold for 2.25 francs in the Lubin boutique of the rue Royale.[51] The margins perfumers saved for themselves on their perfumes were important enough to make such differences possible. César Birotteau indeed rejoiced at the comfortable margin that the particularly cheap bottles discovered by his assistant Popinot for his *Huile céphalique* would provide him: 'Four sous!' said Birotteau. 'Do you know that we could use oil at three francs, and make a profit of thirty sous, and give twenty sous discount to retailers?'[52] César Birotteau thus saves himself a

---

[47] Jacqueline Robert-André, 'A la Reine des fleurs', *La Tribune Piver*, 5/1 (1960): p. 9.

[48] A la reine des abeilles (Paris), *Catalogue général de la fabrication des savons et parfums de Violet*, Paris, A la reine des abeilles, 1865, 44 pp.

[49] I will not develop these aspects of the marketing techniques of the perfumers of the nineteenth century, as they have been discussed elsewhere. On this subject see: Eugénie Briot, 'César Birotteau et ses pairs: poétiques et mercatique des parfumeurs dans le Paris du XIXᵉ siècle', in Bruno Blondé, Eugénie Briot, Natacha Coquery and Laura Van Aert (eds), *Retailers and consumer changes in Early Modern Europe. England, France, Italy and the Low Countries* (Tours, 2005), pp. 71–102.

[50] Mechanisation transforms the sector and Rosine L'heureux-Icard's analyses highlight a relative drop of the salaries between 1847 and 1892. Rosine L'heureux-Icard, 'Les parfumeurs entre 1860 et 1910 d'après les marques, dessins et modèles déposés à Paris', Thèse pour le diplôme d'archiviste-paléographe, Ecole Nationale des Chartes, 1994, p. 67.

[51] L'heureux-Icard, *Les parfumeurs entre 1860 et 1910*, p. 88.

[52] One 'sou' was equivalent to 0.05 francs. Balzac, 'Histoire de la grandeur et de la décadence', pp. 288. *The Rise and Fall of César Birotteau*. ['Quatre sous, sais-tu que nous pouvons mettre l'huile à trois francs et gagner trente sous en en laissant vingt à nos détaillants?']

margin of 1.50 francs on the wholesale price and of 2.50 francs on the retail price in his own boutique of the *Reine des Fleurs*.

On the one hand, the enticing surroundings of boutiques where customers received a deferential welcome from numerous salesmen or women, as in the newly built areas of the Opera in Paris, for instance, were part of the marketing. In the elegant engraving of the boutique of L.T. Piver, produced in 1863, no less than seven salesmen and women were depicted serving only four customers.[53] And a boutique such as the *Cherry Blossom*, located on the *boulevard des Italiens*, n° 12, included such picturesque display elements as a scene with rock, water, a mirror and greenery.[54] The women's press praised such boutiques in which perfumes were sold and these accolades formed part of the discourse of this sector and were an integral part of its image.

On the other hand, however, the price itself was also part of the image of the product and contributed to the desire for consumption in some sectors, as the Veblen effect postulated,[55] a fact addressed by a wholesale merchant from Grasse. He advised his clients very bluntly on this question. 'For many Perfumery merchants (those mostly in oils and pomades) with accessory articles, which makes the selling of other products easier, I encourage these gentlemen to keep to quite high prices (as high as their trade will allow).'[56] Thus, despite the growth in the production of perfumery and the drop in the cost of raw materials and in labour costs, prices seem to be sustained at the high end of the trade over the second half of the century. A perusal of the catalogues of the Coudray perfumery, between

---

[53] A. Hermant, 'Grandes industries françaises: la parfumerie, La Maison L.T. Piver', *Le Monde illustré* (1862), p. 251.

[54] The *Cherry blossom* boutique is the subject of an article of *La Construction moderne* in 1893: ['Quant au rocher, [...] il n'apparaît pas déplacé dans cette boutique sévère, car il produit une note gaie avec ses effets d'eau, ses glaces et ses points de verdure. La nuit, il présente un tout autre aspect, peut-être plus agréable avec ses effets de lumière électrique de diverses couleurs'] 'As to the rock, it doesn't seem out of place in this severe boutique, for it brings a lively note with its water effects, its mirrors and greenery points. At night it presents an entirely different aspect, maybe more pleasant, with its effects of electric light of various colours'. G. Hennequin, 'Boutique de parfumerie, à Paris, boulevard des Italiens', *La Construction moderne* (Paris, 1893), pp. 126–7.

[55] It is here referred to the notion of Veblen effect as described by Harvey Leibenstein:, Harvey Leibenstein, 'Bandwagon, snob, and Veblen effects in the theory of consumers' demand', *Quarterly Journal of Economics*, 64 (1950): pp. 183–207. On the question of the social desirability of luxury products see: Alain Quemin, 'Luxe, ostentation et distinction : Une lecture contemporaine de *La théorie de la classe de loisir* de Thorstein Veblen', in Olivier Assouly, (ed.), *Le luxe : Essais sur la fabrique de l'ostentation* (Paris, 2005), p. 142.

[56] François Rancé, *Prix courant des parfumeries de la fabrique de François Rancé* (Grasse, s.d., n.p). ['Chez beaucoup de Négocians la Parfumerie (principalement les pommades et huiles) n'étant qu'un article accessoire, qui facilite la vente d'autres marchandises, j'engage ces Messieurs à porter leurs demandes toujours à des prix assez élevés (autant cependant que leur commerce le leur permettra).']

1850 and 1876, shows for instance a remarkable stability in the prices during this period. In a general context of rising salaries, perfumery became a relatively more accessible product. Considering, however, that the average daily wage of a man in the department of the Seine rose to 6.15 francs in 1893,[57] it was still an expensive item. In this respect, perfumery products show a social diffusion more than a real democratization. And, as production costs fell, the sector strengthened its margins even further, thanks to the image of a luxury product it has patiently crafted.

Conclusion

Thus, at the turn of the twentieth century, perfumery represented the particular interests of a luxury commodity, more widely distributed, with a more and more powerful means of communication. The case of perfume raises questions concerning the fashioning of these products in significantly different terms than with clothing, since its intrinsic lack of image hindered the social diffusion of scents by purely olfactory means. Culturally defined fashions for specific scent tones set the parameters for perfumers working with a range of the raw materials including new artificial molecules such as ionon, piperonal, musk or other fragrant organic compounds. Over the late nineteenth century the production of perfumery became rapidly industrialized and the drop in the cost of perfume production tended to disconnect its intrinsic value from its price. However, a symbolic value was constructed through the emerging techniques of marketing and communication. What was observed by potential consumers was not the product itself, but its presentation through bottle and label designed to entice. In this respect, the end of the nineteenth century appears to be a crucial time in the evolution of the perfumery market, an age of transition combining unique conditions within the industry and the marketplace favourable, as I demonstrate, to the emergence of a distinct fashion process for perfumery. Emphasis shifted from the fragrance itself, which remained difficult to diffuse in the cultural context of the nineteenth century, to the display of the discourse that surrounded it. The very beginning of the twentieth century, however, soon found a way to resolve this intrinsic lack of image by linking perfumes to couture houses. This alliance, which was to emerge in the 1910s, strengthened after World War I and throughout the interwar years, with perfumes launched by such couturiers as Paul Poiret, Gabrielle Chanel, Jean Patou or Jeanne Lanvin. In their hands, under their names and among their models, perfume then became, in the full sense of the term, a modern fashion accessory.

---

[57] E. Levasseur, *Questions ouvrières et industrielles en France sous la troisième République* (Paris, 1907), p. 245, quoted by L'heureux-Icard Rosine, *Les parfumeurs entre 1860 et 1910*, p. 66.

Chapter Six

'Fashion has extended her influence to the cause of humanity': The Transatlantic Female Economy of the Boston Antislavery Bazaar

Alice Taylor

In December 1836, Anne and Lucia Weston kept logs of their work for the Boston Antislavery Bazaar.[1] The journals describe in vivid detail the whirlwind of activity preceding an antislavery fair; they talk of last minute committee meetings, hastily arranged sewing circles, of composing Antislavery mottos, decorating the fair hall and 'arrang[ing] the things which had come in, in great profusion'.[2] The sisters' journals discuss themes and practices that reverberate throughout private and public correspondence about the Boston Bazaar. Taken together these sources generate insights into organization of the Bazaar, as well as the quotidian duties of charity fair work. What emerges is a remarkable portrait of a female economy in which almost all participants – manufactures, managers, retailers, and consumers – were women.[3] The Boston Bazaar organizers established a transatlantic commercial network that harnessed the labour, resources and talent of women in the United States, Great Britain, and other parts of the world, to supply the annual sale with goods and services. 'Let it be remembered' Maria Weston Chapman declared in an advertisement for the 1844 Boston Bazaar, 'that this fair is mainly the product of female skill, toil, and generosity'.[4] What began in 1834 as a modest sale of

---

[1] Lucia Weston to Deborah Weston, 16 December 1836. Boston Public Library (BPL), Boston, Ms.A.9.2.8.89; Anne W. Weston to Deborah Weston, 21 December 1836. BPL, Ms. A. 9.2.8.79–80. The sisters wrote the journals in letter form and when the Fair was over, they sent them to their sister Deborah, who was in New Bedford, MA.

[2] Anne W. Weston to Deborah Weston, 21 December 1836, BPL, Ms. A. 9.2.8.79–80.

[3] The Bazaar was organized hierarchically with Maria Chapman and her sister Anne Warren Weston in the role of 'chief managers' and beneath them sat a 'fair committee' of roughly three dozen women who assisted in promoting and organizing the Bazaar. The 'managers' – as Chapman, Weston and the committee called themselves – supervised the American and British associations that supplied goods and services to the Boston Bazaar.

[4] *The Liberator*, 20 December 1844. Chapman went on to characterize men's role in the Bazaar as that of the consumer, in contrast to the prevailing ideology of the 'consuming

'useful' home-made articles had by the time it closed in 1857 raised over $65,000 for the Antislavery cause. It was also recognized by the Boston elite as 'the most fashionable shopping resort of the holidays'.[5]

Through this female economy, Boston Fair managers generated a vision of consumerism that applied the skills of household management and the virtues of benevolence to the commercial marketplace. 'Domesticity was the given of the women's fair', Beverly Gordon wrote in her study of American fundraising fairs, 'for it was what women had to work with'.[6] Boston Bazaar organizers promoted a liberal economic model that championed free labour capitalism, encouraged commercial competition, celebrated consumption and fostered an expanded role for women in the economy. But they did so largely within a framework of domestic charity rather than market capitalism.[7] The Boston women's reliance upon the tropes of domesticity and upon the virtues and the practices associated with female benevolence enabled them to create what historian Alison Kay has identified as 'their own feminized marketplace of ritualized retail and consumption'.[8] Through this feminized marketplace, abolitionist women engaged the wider world of Anglo-American business, politics, and culture.

This study examines the intersection of gender, charity and the marketplace at the Boston Antislavery Bazaar, with the objectives of uncovering the internal dynamics of the event and analysing the fair's relationship to the larger antebellum economy. I begin with a brief look at the cycle of activities to demonstrate that although the sale took place only once annually, the Bazaar was a year-round enterprise, built upon established practices and longstanding relationships. Woven into this discussion is an examination of the female associations and supply networks that supported the Boston Antislavery Fair. I conclude with an analysis

---

woman'. Chapman followed up her declaration that the women had nobly 'done their part' with a challenge for the men to do theirs. 'It is now for THE MEN to say whether they will do theirs, by becoming the prompt and liberal purchasers of the many beautiful and useful articles which will be spread before them.'

[5] *Report of the Twenty-First National Antislavery Bazaar* (Boston, 1855), p. 32. It was none other than Harriet Beecher Stowe, who christened the Bazaar the most fashionable shopping venue in Boston.

[6] Beverly Gordon, *Bazaars and Fair Ladies: The History of the American Fundraising Fair* (Knoxville, 1998), p. 5. In a subsection of her first chapter, 'Domesticity as a Fair Staple', Gordon offers a detailed discussion of the various ways in which American women used the tropes of domesticity in their fundraising fairs. Gordon does not look at Britain, but the same practices are seen in fundraising fairs held in the UK.

[7] *The Liberator*, 23 January 1846. 'The private parlor has given place to Faneuil Hall' *The Liberator* reported when the Bazaar, first held in a private home, moved into the historic and very pubic 'Cradle of Liberty', so named because of its role in the American Revolution.

[8] Alison C. Kay, 'Retailing, Respectability and the Independent Woman in Nineteenth-century London', in Robert Beachy, B. Craig and A. Owens (eds), *Women, Business and Finance in Nineteenth-Century Europe: Rethinking Separate Spheres* (Berg, 2006), p. 155.

of the debate over female charity bazaars in the mid-nineteenth century. Millions of women in the marketplace created anxiety and resentment in a number of quarters that translated into public attacks on charity bazaars. Boston Antislavery Fair managers formulated a defence of their right to engage in the commercial arena by assertively claiming their status as a successful and professionally run 'mart' that abided by the practices and precepts of the market economy.[9] The Boston Fair managers created a venue that combined the social and material world of middle class womanhood with contemporary commercial practices.

To contextualize its import as an economic and cultural institution within the Anglo-American antislavery movement, the Boston Antislavery Bazaar must be considered in relationship to the larger world of antebellum consumer activism.[10] 'Philanthropy in nineteenth-century America was a widespread phenomenon' historian Barbara Saez argues, 'which was manifest in the culture in diverse and complex ways'.[11] Charity bazaars were a significant part of the socio-economic

---

[9] Antebellum female reformers frequently drew upon maternal and domestic discourses to argue their right or more frequently their 'duty' to engage in public life. In this context, domesticity was, to borrow from Anna Clark's 'Critique of Chartism', 'a trope that performed specific political functions' within reformist language. Anna Clark, 'The Rhetoric of Chartist Domesticity: Gender, Language, and Class in the 1830s and 1840s', *The Journal of British Studies*, 31/1 (1992): p. 63. By evoking domesticity, reform women attempted to engage in public life without explicitly contravening prescribed gender norms. This manipulation of the dominant discourses of femininity and domesticity was not seamless, nor was it always effective. Female abolitionists who engaged in explicitly 'masculine' and 'political' acts, such as speaking publicly and petitioning Congress and Parliament were punished, rhetorically and physically, for their transgressions. The female reformers' argument that women's sphere of influence should be understood as conceptual rather than spatial was, nevertheless, a powerful means of creating room for female public voice(s) in antebellum America. See also, Julie Roy Jeffrey, *The Great Silent Army of Abolitionism: Ordinary Women in the Antislavery Movement*, (Chapel Hill, 1998); Clare Midgley, *Feminism and Empire: Women Activists in Imperial Britain, 1790–1865* (London and New York, 2007); Clare Midgley, *Women Against Slavery: The British Campaigns, 1780–1870* (London and New York, 1992); Jean Fagan Yellin, *Women and Sisters: The Antislavery Feminists in American Culture* (New Haven, CT, 1989).

[10] Benjamin Quarles, 'Sources of Abolitionist Income', *The Mississippi Valley Historical Review*, 32 (1945): pp. 71–4. Quarles has argued that while the Boston Bazaar was exceptional in size, scope and caliber, it was representative of antebellum charity fairs in terms of its organizational structure. 'Begun in 1834, by far the most successful of these organizations [charity fairs] was the Boston group', Quarles writes, 'which worked in the interests of the American [Antislavery] Society' (p. 71). While overshadowing the others in the scope of its activities, the Boston Bazaar was typical in *modus operandi*', organizing sewing circles, soliciting contributions in kind from merchants and manufacturers, advertising the event, organizing volunteers to decorate halls and serve as saleswomen, and publishing fair reports.

[11] Barbara Saez, 'The Discourse of Philanthropy in Nineteenth-Century America', *American Transcendental Quarterly*, 11/3 (1997): p. 163.

fabric of the Western world in the nineteenth century. Frank Prochaska estimates that over 1,000 charity bazaars were advertised annually in nineteenth-century British newspapers and that thousands more were advertised informally via community organizations and through word of mouth.[12] He calculates that the hundreds of thousands of British fairs raised 'tens of millions of pounds' for charity in the nineteenth-century.[13] Beverly Gordon describes American fundraising fairs as a 'major institution', a 'phenomenon' which 'collectively involved millions of people and raised many millions of dollars'.[14] Given the character and the scope of women's fundraising fairs, I hazard to call this pattern of commercial activism a movement rather than a phenomenon.[15] The term phenomenon implies that women's charity bazaars were both exceptional and that they appeared without cause or explanation. Prochaska and Gordon's work has demonstrated that charity bazaars were, in fact, more ordinary than extraordinary in the nineteenth century and I argue that the Boston fair managers were very much in step with antebellum Anglo-American trends in fundraising, entertainment, fashion, politics and commerce. Consequently, far from operating in a vacuum, women's charity bazaars were conspicuously, if not always comfortably, etched into the nineteenth-century Anglo-American cultural and economic landscape.

In terms of abolitionism, Deborah Van Broekhoven calculates that women's fundraising initiatives sustained organized antislavery activity in the 1840s and 1850s. In 1847, for example, the Boston Fair donated over half of the Massachusetts Antislavery Society's operating budget for that year and throughout the 1840s and 1850s, the Philadelphia Antislavery Fair underwrote one-third to one-half of the state society's budget.[16] The collective spirit of benevolent consumerism expressed in the charity bazaars of the antebellum period represented an unprecedented

---

[12] F.K. Prochaska, 'Charity Bazaars in Nineteenth Century England', *The Journal of British Studies*, 16/2 (1977): pp. 65–6. Published more than 30 years ago, Prochaska's work on English charity bazaars and on English charities remains an authority on the subject. See also: F.K. Prochaska, *Women and Philanthropy in Nineteenth-Century England* (Oxford, 1980).

[13] Prochaska, 'Charity Bazaars', p. 68.

[14] Gordon, *Bazaars and Fair Ladies*, p. xix.

[15] 'Movement n. 8A'. *Oxford English Dictionary*, 2nd ed., *OED Online*, Oxford University Press (accessed 20 October, 2009). Millions of female participants in charity bazaars constituted a 'movement' in the sense that they followed 'a course or series of actions and endeavours on the part of a group of people working towards a shared goal'. While the women involved in fairs held widely competing beliefs and objectives, they nevertheless subscribed to a strikingly similar operational template. In the same manner that reform societies followed customary patterns of organization – drafting constitutions, electing officers, passing resolutions, etc – charity fair organizers followed established guidelines for planning, organizing and conducting their sales. See Jeffrey, *The Great Silent Army* for a detailed discussion of the structure of American women's Antislavery societies.

[16] Deborah Van Broekhoven, '"Better than a Clay Club": The Organization of Antislavery Fairs, 1835–1860', *Slavery and Abolition*, 19/1 (1998): p. 31.

and unrivalled Anglo-American movement of female commercial activism and economic management.

Lucia and Anne Westons' journals offer a unique window into the activities preceding and during the Boston Antislavery Fair; however, they detail a fraction of the total work involved in staging an event as extravagant as the Boston Bazaar of the 1840s and 1850s. Preparations for the annual Christmas sale began in late January or early February when the Fair Committee declared its intention to hold another bazaar and ended twelve months later when the Committee issued its 'Fair Report' early in the New Year. Winter was far and away the most hectic season in the Boston Fair calendar; managers began in January and February to plan the upcoming Bazaar in the midst of tying up the loose ends for the sale that had just ended. Taking care of the economic and social obligations that accompanied the end of a Bazaar was an unenviable task; the managers had to settle outstanding accounts; ship articles purchased via mail order,[17] and write, publish and disseminate the 'Fair Report' to the 'friends' of the Bazaar in the US and abroad. In the spring, summer and fall, managers spread the word about the Bazaar. They advertised locally and internationally, issued regular updates to fair volunteers, and facilitated interest in the Bazaar through personal visits and private correspondence with local women and women overseas. These off-season activities were conducted with an eye towards creating and sustaining a foreign and domestic supply chain of buyers, manufacturers, middle(wo)men, retailers and consumers for the Boston Bazaar. Attractive and fashionable contributions were the foundation of the fair managers' agenda to make antislavery profitable and fashionable and the planning and politics of securing a steady supply of goods from foreign and domestic contributors was a year-round enterprise.

In the United States particularly, antislavery sewing circles were the most common means by which women supplied goods to the Boston Fair. Most women who sewed for the Bazaar had never depended on the needle for personal income, but they would nevertheless have been trained in the 'art' of plain and fancy needlework. Through sewing circles, women and girls became aware of their needles as social, economic, political and historical 'weapons'. Circles varied widely in their degree of formal organization and in their members' levels of commitment; some groups gathered regularly throughout the year, some met steadily in the five or six months prior to the fair and some circles sewed for more than one fair, dividing their resources across several different charitable events. Whatever their level of commitment or the

---

[17] An advertisement for the 1844 Bazaar informed readers that 'Such as cannot be present, can easily by letter employ some one of the Managers of the Fair, or some particular friend in the city, to make purchases for them to the amount of five, ten, or fifty dollars, according to their liberality of heart and pecuniary ability'. A 'donation book' was also placed in the Antislavery Offices, at 25 Cornhill Street, Boston, so that individuals could register orders with the managers that they would do their best to fill. See: *The Liberator*, 20 December 1844.

regularity with which they met, sewing circles were the most consistent means of ensuring steady material donations to the Bazaar.

Sewing circles performed a variety of functions outside of producing saleable commodities, however; they were 'parties' – 'working parties', 'reading parties, tea-parties, conversation parties – occasions of festivity, and means of social improvement' as well as manufacture. In this way, Boston Bazaar organizers hoped to broaden the appeal of sewing circles (and abolitionism), so that '[t]heir numbers may thus be multiplied and their benefits increased'.[18] They also hoped to combine work and fun with 'social improvement'. Educational aspects of sewing circles most often involved a female member reading antislavery literature aloud while other members 'sewed, knitted, braided, or pieced articles for an upcoming sale'.[19] Through these activities, sewing circles fostered tangible relationships between abolitionist women who relied on them both for regular fellowship in their communities and for a sense of a larger group identity.[20]

Sewing circles were also instrumental in teaching women to recognize the market value of their labour; women who sewed for antislavery bazaars took pride in their work and in the monetary worth of the articles they produced. In her journal, Anne Weston recorded the value of the goods she and other family members produced for the Boston Bazaar. 'Caroline has made 11 dollars worth of things for the fair and ... I gave only my 12 bags and wrote a piece of poetry in Ann Chapman's book, Lucia's sewing work gave $25.00 worth'.[21] These women celebrated market value as the antithesis of unfree labour; the dollar value assigned their stitchery was central to this project, where fashion, utility, and politics worked hand in hand. Sewing for benevolent and reform organizations functioned as both an extension of women's traditional domestic duties and as a public act that saw middle class or even elite females commercialize and politicize their craft.

---

[18] *The Liberator*, 4 December 1846.

[19] Van Broekhoven, 'Better than a Clay Club', p. 38.

[20] Pat Ferrero argues that quilting bees functioned as 'invaluable agents of cultural cohesion and group identity' for women and sewing circles operated similarly. Pat Ferrero, Elaine Hedges and Julie Silber, *Hearts and Hands: The Influence of Women and Quilts on American Society* (San Francisco, 1987), p. 48. Julie Roy Jeffrey describes sewing circles as a method of recruitment; once women were drawn in, then exposure to abolitionist talk and literature would reinforce their dedication to the cause. Deborah Van Broekhoven argues that sewing, not petitioning, was the most effective political weapon wielded by female abolitionists. Sewing for the slave brought women together, sustained their commitment to the cause and provided them with a regular forum for expressing their political views through the articles they produced. Jeffrey, *The Great Silent Army* and Deborah Van Broekhoven, *The Devotion of These Women: Rhode Island in the Antislavery Network* (Amherst, 2002).

[21] Anne W. Weston to Deborah Weston, 21 December 1836. BPL.Ms. A. 9.2.8.79–80.

Through their sewing 'for the slave', women became explicitly aware of the needle's political influence.[22] Pithy antislavery slogans and mottos appeared on an array of 'useful' and 'fancy' articles, though 'homely' domestic objects represented the vast majority of the 'marked' goods sold at fairs. Both categories of articles that were imprinted with abolitionist rhetoric were blatantly political, yet they operated differently, appealing to different audiences, circulating in different spaces and enjoying different relationships to their owners and their producers. Fancy silk purses, displayed publicly, openly identified their owners as abolitionists, whereas potholders and pincushions were designed for private use within the home. Less obviously, these articles also operated differently to their producers. Fancy objects were professionally stamped with abolitionist images and text. In 1837, female abolitionists in Boston, New York and Philadelphia commissioned 100 pieces of silk stamped 'from the plate representing a slave mother and her infant sitting under a tree'.[23] The plate was likely purchased or donated from British abolitionists who had earlier produced silk bags imprinted with the same image. Illustration 6.1 is an example of a British antislavery bag that was made from this plate. It was produced by the Female Society for Birmingham and it dates from around 1827.[24]

Female abolitionists cut out and assembled the stamped silk into fashionable purses and workbags such as those featured above, but they were removed from the actual process of 'marking' the objects. Conversely, the mottoes on 'utilitarian' articles, most of which related to sewing – pincushions, needle-books, workbags, and samplers – were hand sewn onto the objects by the women making them. Often the seamstresses were also the authors of the words that they embroidered on their articles. As the Boston Fair increased in popularity, women were pressured

---

[22] For more information on 'marked' objects at antislavery fairs see: Lee Chambers-Schiller's, '"A Good Work Among the People": The Political Culture of the Boston Antislavery Fair', in Jean Fagan Yellin and John C. Van Horne (eds), *The Abolitionist Sisterhood: Women's Political Culture in Antebellum America* (Ithaca, 1994), pp. 249–74; Andrea M. Atkin, '"When Pincushions Are Periodicals": Women's Work, Race, And Material Objects In Female Abolitionism', *American Transcendental Quarterly*, 11/2 (1997): pp. 93–113; and Julie Roy Jeffrey, '"Stranger, Buy … Lest Our Mission Fail': The Complex Culture of Women's Abolitionist Fairs', *American Nineteenth Century History*, 4/1 (2003): pp. 1–24.

[23] A series of letters exchanged between Anne Warren Weston and Juliana Tappan in 1837 detail the process of getting the silk stamped. Julia Tappan to Anne W. Weston 21 July 1837. BPL Ms.A.9.2.9.49; JT to AWW, 18 September 1837. BPL Ms.A.9.2.9.70; JT to AWW, 11 October 1837. BPL Ms.A.9.2.9.79.

[24] The antislavery reticule was made by the women of the Female Society for Birmingham. The bag measures 23.5 cm by 20 cm and is stamped with the image of a nursing slave mother sitting beneath a palm tree that was likely designed by Samuel Lines. The bags, filled with antislavery literature, were given as gifts and in the United States, were also sold at antislavery fairs. This image is from the Victoria & Albert Museum Digital Database: http://images.vam.ac.uk/objectid/O68954 (accessed 10 October 2009).

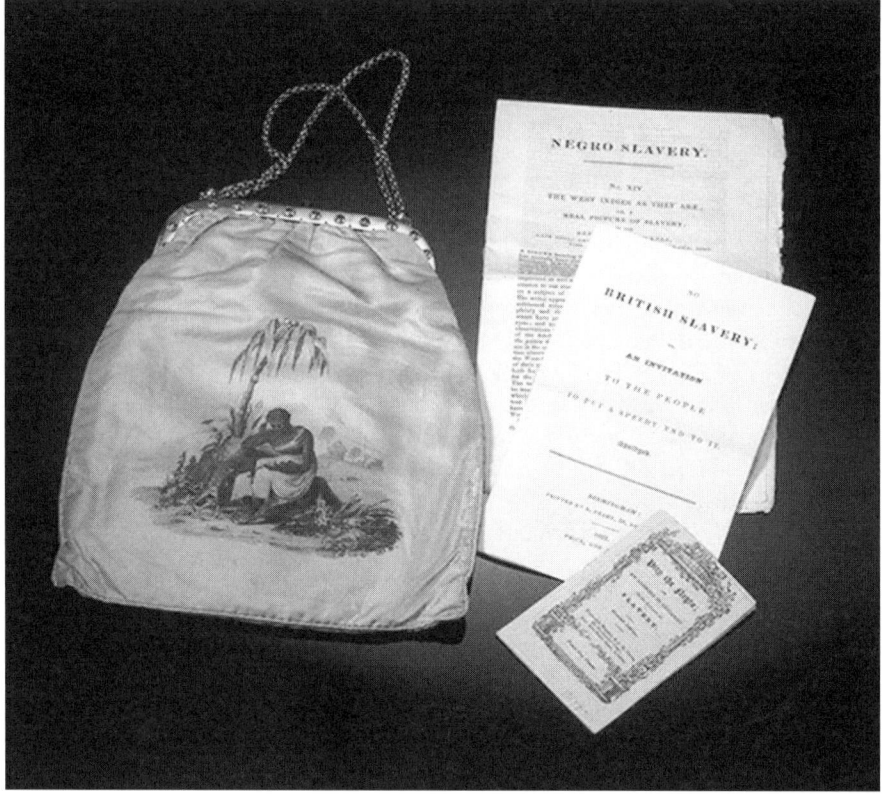

Illustration 6.1   Silk Antislavery Reticule, c. 1827. Photo © Victoria & Albert Museum, London, T.20–1951

to come up with clever new slogans. 'Many of the mottos on the articles offered for sale were original' boasted an advertisement, 'and strikingly appropriate'.[25]

The majority of these objects were crudely rendered in comparison to professionally manufactured articles. These wonderfully witty potholders depicting two slaves dancing to the slogan 'Any Holder but a Slave Holder' illustrates the difference in quality and formality between the two kinds of 'marked' objects that would have been available at the Boston Bazaar (Illustration 6.2).[26]

---

[25]   *The Liberator*, 28 December 1838.

[26]   http://www.digitalhistory.uh.edu/ahd/wps19b.html (accessed 10 October 2009). The potholders are in the Chicago Historical Society Collections. According to the Chicago Society records, the potholders were purchased at the Great North West Sanitary Fair but they are typical of the kinds of marked domestic objects that appeared at antislavery fairs. Beverly Gordon includes the smaller of the potholders featured here in *Bazaars and Fair Ladies* and she argues that the potholder likely originated at an antislavery fair. I agree

'Fashion has extended her influence to the cause of humanity' 123

Illustration 6.2   Antislavery Potholder, nd, Chicago History Museum

The potholders also demonstrate the blatantly political messages contained in domestic objects sold at antislavery Fairs. Other examples included quills labelled as 'Weapons for Abolitionists' and pen-wipers inscribed with the invocation that they be used to, 'Wipe out *the blot of Slavery*'.[27] Several scholars have argued that these objects functioned as political tracts 'by intruding on the everyday activities' of their owners, 'strategically deploy[ing] abolitionism via their character as innocuous homely objects'.[28]

Unlike the professionally manufactured articles, these hand-made items were less of an abolitionist emblem than a personal and political communication from woman to woman. There is a spirit of playfulness in the potholder that is missing with Gordon, particularly as women commonly recycled goods purchased at charity fairs, donating goods that they had purchased at an earlier fair to subsequent sales.

[27]   *The Liberator*, 2 January 1837.

[28]   Chambers-Schiller, 'A Good Work among the People', p. 261 and Atkin, 'When Pincushions Are Periodicals', p. 96.

from the professionally stamped bags. On the potholder the slaves are dancing, the relationship depicted is between a man and a woman not a distraught slave mother and her imperiled infant. Moreover, the potholder illustrates two slaves coming together rather than being torn apart. The message expressed in the silk workbags is one of vulnerability and need; it was intended to inspire feminine and even more particularly maternal sympathy that translated into 'work' for the slave. Of course the potholder was also intended to spark women's commitment to the antislavery cause, but its focus was on the potential of slave liberation rather than the harsh reality of slave's lives.

The slogan 'Any Holder but a Slave Holder' proposes that any option was preferable to remaining enslaved. It also transfers ownership of the 'slaves' to the object's 'holder' thereby tying her to the process of liberation – the slave's potential freedom was in her hands. This object operated along 'paradigmatic' principles. In semiotic terms, this is the idea of replacing one object for another within a line of signifiers. The object endeavors to replace slave holder, with a 'related' term, pot holder, illustrating that slaveholding is not fixed or unchangeable. It creates a new paradigmatic chain. It reveals that slave holding is not a natural fact but a cultural fact, and it can be displaced by something else. Replacing one object for another was how this object created meaning.[29]

However, the object also invokes a metonymic relationship; it places objects in relation to one another (i.e. the pot holder and the purchaser). By purchasing the potholder the buyers help to displace slave holding (with something domestic and unthreatening), but they also place that pot holder in relation to themselves, their identity, their bodies, and their homes. They have intimate contact with it by touching it and using it. This means that they actively partake in replacing slave holding (resignifying and rethinking it).[30] The power of this unpretentious domestic object was far greater than might be assumed. Through it, the women who produced it, purchased it or received it as a Christmas gift, were reminded that their actions – sewing, shopping and even cooking – were intimately bound to the larger project of slave emancipation.

In addition to commercializing and politicizing needlework, sewing for antislavery fairs encouraged women's awareness of the historic importance of needlework. The middle decades of the nineteenth century witnessed growing nostalgia for the needle at the time when middle-class women were increasingly removed from sewing for necessity. In the preface to *A History of Needlework*, the British 'authoress' juxtaposes the needle ('and its beautiful and useful creations') to 'its glittering antithesis' the sword, arguing that throughout history the needle had been employed as a weapon of production whereas the sword had been used only to sow 'destructi[on]'. The intention of the book is to give the needle its

---

[29] Lianne McTavish, e-mail message to author, 20 September 2007. See: Daniel Chandler, *Semiotics: The Basics* (London, 2004); Stuart Hall, (ed.), *Representation: Cultural Representations and Signifying Practices* (London, 1997).

[30] Lianne McTavish, e-mail message to author, 20 September 2007.

place in history: '[T]he time seems at length arrived, when the triumph of female ingenuity and industry, 'THE ART OF NEEDLEWORK', as opposed to the ART OF WAR, 'may be treated as a fitting subject of historical and social record.'[31]

The Boston Bazaar tapped into this trend, commissioning a reproduction of a needlebook presented to Queen Victoria by a Manchester needle maker at the Crystal Palace Exhibition.[32] The front of the needlebook, produced for the Bazaar in 1855, featured eleven specimens of 'NEEDLES IN THEIR PRINCIPLE STAGES' of manufacture (Illustration 6.3).

The needles are accompanied by text that provides a history and geography lesson on the needle, as well as detailed instructions on how the modern needle is made. The description is composed as a letter to a young girl who had never considered the time and energy expended in the production of her ordinary needles. 'I wonder if any little girl who may read this, ever thought how many people are all the time at work in making the things which they everyday use', the letter begins. 'What can be more common, and, you may think, more simple, than a needle? Yet, if you don't know it, I can tell you, that it takes a great many persons to make a needle; and it takes a great deal of time too. Let us take a peep into a needle factory.'[33] The narrator proceeds to guide the young girl around the factory, describing each step in the process of a needle's manufacture. The real needles affixed to the front of the book serve as material guides to the needle's evolution and testify to its historic and industrial progress.[34]

In spite of its venerable status, the needle to be sure had oppressive, as well as, liberating tendencies. Privately, Lucia Weston commented several times in her journal how exhausted she and others were from sewing for the Bazaar. 'We all spent the day working at the fair' she reported on Saturday 17 December 1836. The following Wednesday she was still hard at work for the sale, '[M]y fingers are nearly sewed off…' she confessed 'I will write no more now.'[35] Publicly,

---

[31] Mrs. Henry Owen, *The Illuminated Book of Needlework: Comprising Knitting, Netting, Crochet, and Embroidery, Proceeded by a History of Needlework, Including an Account of the Ancient Historical Tapestries*, ed., Countess of Wilton (London, 1847), pp. iii–iv.

[32] 'Needles in their principle stages, as presented to the Queen', 16 June 1851, manufactured by Abel Morrall, Studley Warwickshire, and 7 High Street, Manchester, late of class 6, no. 240, Great Exhibition, London. Prepared for the Boston Antislavery Bazaar, 1855 (Manchester, 1855). Archive of Americana Database, American Broadsides and Ephemera, Series 1, no. 9323 (accessed October 10, 2009). The original is in the American Antiquarian Society collections.

[33] 'Needles in their principle stages', p. 3.

[34] The needlebook also asserts that the 'the Art of Needle Making was introduced into London by a Spanish Negro in the year 1545', (p. 1) which earned him commemoration in the Needle Makers crest. For the Boston women, this acknowledgement of the needle's historic importance served the twofold purpose of demonstrating the instrument's centrality across time and culture, as well as illustrating that a black man contributed to the advancement of modern technology, supporting abolitionist's claims of 'negro' intelligence and industry.

[35] Lucia Weston to Deborah Weston, 16 December 1836. BPL Ms.A.9.2.8.89.

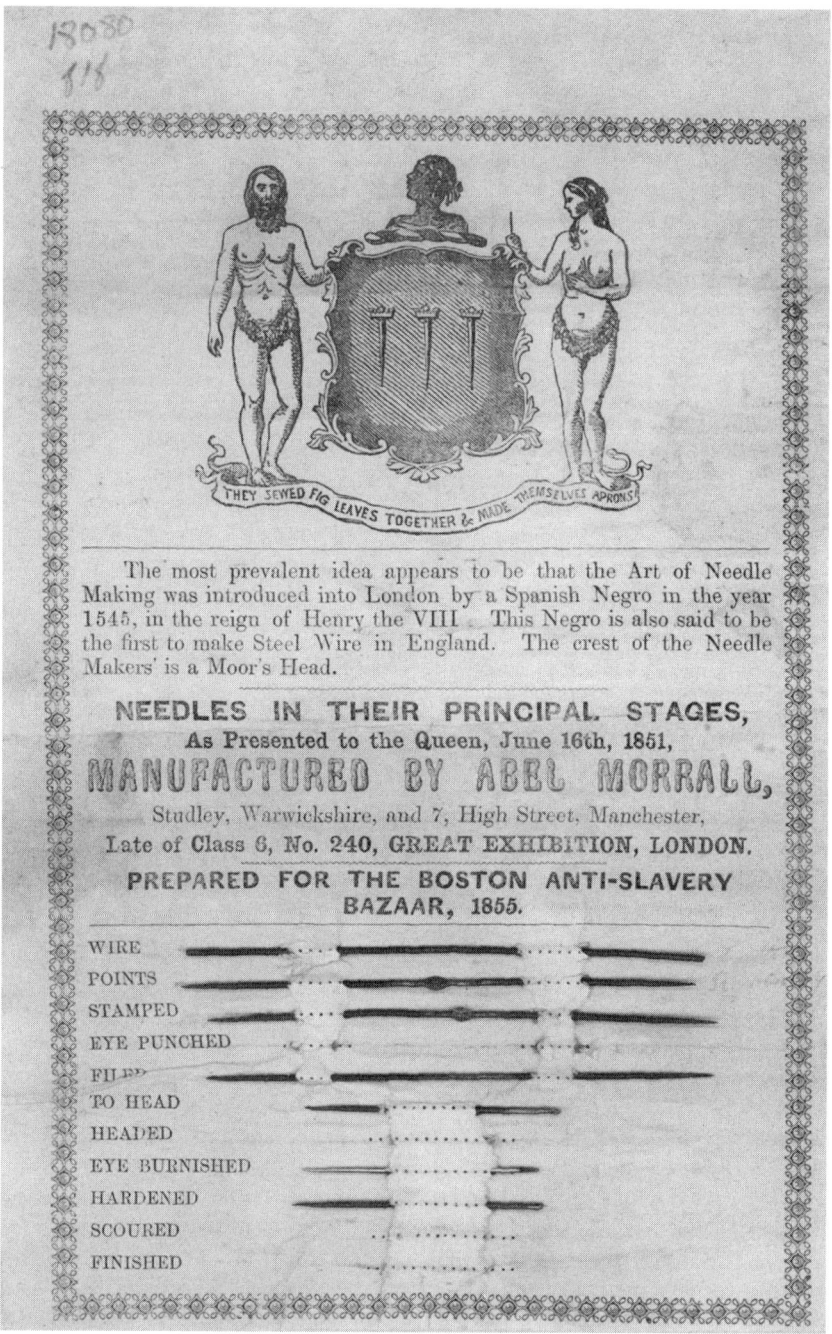

Illustration 6.3   Boston Antislavery Bazaar Pamphlet and Needlebook, 1855. Series 1, no. 9323, American Antiquarian Society

Maria Weston Chapman invoked the image of the needlewoman to generate a sense of collective 'toil' amongst those who sewed for the Bazaar. Chapman universalized and romanticized the sacrificial nature of abolitionist seamstresses in her 1843 Fair report:

> There is not a woman in our broad New England through, who has toiled at midnight by the feeble light of her well-saved lamp, to produce these exquisite works which you so much admire, who has not done it at a sacrifice of which you can form no idea, unless you have also been an abolitionist.[36]

In spite of the fact that the majority of sewing for fairs was done through the communal ritual of the sewing circle, Chapman chose to present the abolitionist needlewoman as a solitary figure, toiling long into the night, accompanied only by the light of her 'well-saved lamp'. Chapman characterized the hardships as well as the rewards of fair work through images of shared sacrifice, which she argued could not be comprehended by women who contributed to the Bazaar as spectators and purchasers only.[37]

When the Fair began, tremendous pride was shown in women's needlework. An advertisement for the 1843 sale proudly asserted that, '[t]here was ingenuity manifested in many of the little needlebooks … ingenuity, which may be called genius'.[38] Over time, however, the bond between the Boston managers and their

---

[36] Maria Weston Chapman, *The Liberator*, 12 January 1844.

[37] The needle, and more particularly the needlewoman, had tremendous iconic importance in the nineteenth century. The image of the needlewoman appeared in Art, fiction and prescriptive literature as a powerful signifier of women's sacrifice of social, economic and, at times, moral position. This notion of sacrifice was taken up by abolitionist writers. Antislavery rhetoric offered clear recognition and celebration of the needlewoman's sacrifice, although care was taken to stress that the abolitionist needlewoman did not sacrifice her families' interests but rather her own comfort, pleasure and social ties. For a discussion of the practice and cultural meanings of needlework see: T.J. Edelstein, 'They Sang the "Song of the Shirt": The Visual Iconography of the Seamstress', *Victorian Studies*, 23 (1980): pp. 183–210; Rozsika Parker, *The Subversive Stitch: Embroidery and the Making of the Feminine* (London,, 1996); Christine Stansell, *City of Women: Sex and Class in New York, 1789-1860* (Urbana, 1987); Wendy Gamber, *The Female Economy: The Millinery and Dressmaking Trades, 1860–1930* (Urbana, 1997); Anne D. Wallace, '"Nor in Fading Silks Compose": Sewing, Walking and Poetic Labor in Aurora Lee', *English Literary History*, 64/1 (Spring, 1997): pp. 223–56; Barbara Burman (ed.), *The Culture of Sewing: Gender, Consumption, and Home Dressmaking* (Oxford, 1999); Sarah A. Gordon, '"Boundless Possibilities": Home Sewing and the Meanings of Women's Domestic Work in the United States, 1890–1930', *Journal of Women's History*, 16/2 (2004): pp. 68–91; Beth Harris (ed.), *Famine And Fashion: Needlewomen In The Nineteenth Century* (Hampshire, 2005); Mary C. Beaudry, *Findings: The Material Culture of Needlework and Sewing* (New Haven, 2006).

[38] *The Liberator*, 20 January 1843. Surely one of the most ingenious, as well as most blatantly political, articles ever produced by women for the Bazaar was a pair of shoes

female sewing circles began to break down. The 1840s and 1850s brought increased public demand on Bazaar organizers to provide them with rare and fashionable goods. As the event gained in reputation and prestige, 'marked' objects were increasingly replaced by 'unmarked' articles valued for their fashion and aesthetic beauty rather than their political importance as abolitionist tracts. By the end of the 1840s, the marked objects were all but eclipsed by professionally manufactured goods that were largely imported from Europe and Great Britain.

This change was indicative of a broader shift in the managers' priorities away from creating new abolitionists through organized work for the Bazaar toward attracting wealthy customers and selling expensive goods. Increasing competition from merchants and from other fancy fairs forced the Boston managers to constantly expand and improve their inventory in order to remain commercially viable. The competition between the Bazaar and local merchants was fierce with each group vying to make the claim that their merchandise 'could be found nowhere else' in Boston, New England, or even the United States. This contest reached a fever pitch when local merchants threatened to organize an effort to oust the women from Faneuil Hall in 1848. That fall, Anne Weston wrote to her sister Caroline explaining that 'the *fancy goods* dealers were opposed to our having it [Faneuil Hall] on the ground that we undersold them and injured their business and had thoughts of presenting a protest'.[39] The women prevailed in this instance and continued to hold the Bazaar in Faneuil Hall for several more years, but by the early 1850s they were forced to find new venues for their sale.

These economic and social pressures placed a considerable burden on Fair managers, but they also put pressure on 'ordinary' women to produce good quality, fashionable items to donate to the sale. For many American women the pressure became untenable. The majority of American donors to the Bazaar lived in small New England towns and villages. In the increasingly sophisticated Boston marketplace, these women could not compete with growing numbers of imported manufactured goods being sold at the Fair. Even when keeping in mind the deferential tone common to female writers of this period, the expressions of inadequacy are evident in letters written by rural donors to the Fair. Mary Gibbons registered dissatisfaction with her rural sewing circle's contributions to the 1844

---

made to 'fit' members of the 'Third Party and New Organization'. After 1840, the AASS competed with both the Liberty Party and the AFASS for membership and in the case of the Bazaar, for donations. The remarkable shoes sold at the Bazaar and described by Chapman were designed in such a way that the 'heel piece' was fit to the front, not the back of the shoe, 'so that the track shall deceive those on the trail of slavery into thinking that the wearer is advancing, while he is, in fact, on the retreat'. Chapman's audience would have been aware of the acrimony between the different factions of the American Antislavery movement and therefore would have understood that Chapman intended the shoes to be read as a material reminder that the other organizations were backward, deceitful and 'on the retreat'. See *The Liberator*, 12 January 1844.

[39] Anne W. Weston to Caroline Weston, 12 November 1848. BPL Ms.A.9.2.24.47.

Bazaar. 'It is with feelings of regret' Gibbons stated in the opening line of her letter to Maria Chapman, 'tho not unmingled with satisfaction, that we now make our little offering to the Fair. We regret that it is not more worthy both in quality and in quantity... .' The contributions made by the West Brookfield women were, as Gibbons herself noted, 'few and comparatively of little value': four cotton shirts, three pairs of white stockings, three pairs of coloured stockings, two black silk aprons and two needle books.[40]

By the early 1840s Fair advertisements and reports began appreciably to downplay 'useful' American goods in favour of showcasing 'ornamental' foreign articles. '[T]here will be a multitude of rare and beautiful foreign *petit objets*', promised a Fair advertisement in 1842, 'a very large selection of Wooden Mosaic or Tunbridge Ware ... carved work of Switzerland, Jewellery and Perfumery, Dioramas, Pieces of Tapestry.'[41] The contrast of these articles to Mary Gibbon's donations is stark. As the preference for fancy goods increased, many American women felt slighted by the indifference to their 'useful' contributions. An appeal to American women from Anne Weston, speaks of American women's growing alienation:

> The articles sent from abroad are so beautiful, in many instances so costly, that, to some extent, an unfavorable impression prevails that it is hardly worth while for the American ladies to give much time to the manufacture of articles in which they will very probably find themselves excelled. But this is quite a mistaken view. Local fashions prevail everywhere. The demand that these occasion no foreign work can supply.[42]

Despite Weston's protestations, by the mid-1840s, the Boston managers were less and less interested in supplying Boston with 'local fashions', which they often donated to antislavery fairs held in smaller, less sophisticated markets. In the context of the growing demand for fancy foreign goods, donations of labour and household produce became a more reliable means for New England women to contribute to the sale. After 1845, American women increasingly donated perishable food items that were then forwarded to professionals to turn 'into suitable forms for the benefit of the fair'.[43] Rural women also contributed the greenery used to

---

[40] Mary Gibbons to Maria Weston Chapman, 23 December 1844. Ms.A.9.2.20.130. While Gibbons was clearly unsatisfied with the 'quantity and quality' of her contributions, she nevertheless expressed 'satisfaction that we have anything to offer' given the 'bitter feelings', 'strong opposition' and 'silent contempt' that she and her fellow female abolitionists faced from their peers. The cash value of the donated goods was estimated at $13.25.

[41] *The Boston Press and Post*, 20 December 1842.

[42] *The Liberator*, 30 January 1852.

[43] Beginning in 1843, the fair committee regularly ran advertisements in the *Liberator* asking for 'the friends of the cause' to donate 'cream, eggs, sugar, butter, lard, fruit of all kinds; in short, every kind of provision'. The fair managers would then transport the items to William W. Marjoram, a Boston confectioner, who had a shop on Marshall Street.

decorate the fair halls, the cotton to cover tables and helped to set up and sell the goods once the fair was open.⁴⁴ The organizational mantra of the Bazaar was 'sell everything and buy nothing'; no articles were taken on commission and the fair managers relied heavily on the contributions and labour of rural women to furnish and decorate the hall.'⁴⁵ Fair reports extolled the frugality and resourcefulness of the Bazaar managers. Supplies that the managers themselves could not provide were often borrowed from friends or, later when the fair was more popular, from local merchants.⁴⁶ Organizers incurred significant savings through American donations of labour and raw materials. Maria Chapman calculated that volunteers at the 1845 Fair saved the committee $300 in expenditures.⁴⁷

American women who persisted in donating prepared articles did so knowing that their goods might not sell in the Boston market, but were reassured that their articles would be dispersed to smaller 'country' fairs. In a letter accompanying the Worcester donations in 1850, Lucy Earle confided to Anne Weston that she had 'hear[d]' that the Bazaar had 'a very fine display of foreign articles this year'. Earle wished Weston 'the best success at selling them' but requested that any Worcester contributions remaining after the sale be returned to her 'as there is a demand here for some of them if they don't sell in Boston'.⁴⁸ Earle's request demonstrates rural women's growing awareness of local economies, as well as a desire on the part of rural women to retain some control over their labour by placing restrictions on their donations. As women became more experienced in the business of organizing charity bazaars, they gained appreciation of market trends; goods that sold readily in urban centres did not necessarily appeal to the sensibilities or the financial means of smaller localities.

British women, most of whom were unfamiliar with the vagaries of the American market, received regular 'updates' from the Boston managers about what goods to

---

Marjoram would then take the raw ingredients and make them fancy treats for the desert table. See *The Liberator*, 15 December 1843; 5 December 1845; 18 December 1846.

⁴⁴ *The Liberator*, 12 December 1845. Fair circulars provided local women with detailed instructions about the fair decorations. The Liberator also included information about the kinds of materials the Fair managers desired, how much of each product they wanted and when the goods needed to be delivered to the Hall. 'The wreaths of running-pine (*several hundred yards* could be advantageously used in the execution of the plan already drawn), ought all to be in Boston on the preceding Friday, the 18th in order to allow Saturday and Monday for the work of preparation.' *The Liberator*, 13 November 1846.

⁴⁵ Caroline Weston to Samuel May, 24 October 1871. BPL Ms. B. 1.6.v.13 no. 94; see also Weston to May, 21 October 1871. BPL Ms. B. 1.6.v.13 no. 94.

⁴⁶ *The Liberator*, 19 January 1849. In return for their 'generous contributions', the company names and addresses of the donors were included in the Fair Reports. In her Bazaar Report of 1849, Anne Weston also advertised new products that were donated to the Bazaar. Whitaker's Miniature Solar Lamp, Cheever's Fire Kindling and Mrs. Cook's Chinese Polishing Iron were all mentioned in her report on the fifteenth Bazaar.

⁴⁷ *The Liberator*, 23 January 1846.

⁴⁸ L.H. Earle to A.W. Weston, 19 December 1850. BPL Ms.A.9.2.25.56.

send and where to send them. When British women wrote to Maria Chapman in the early 1840s, to inform her that they intended to 'aid' the Bangor Antislavery Fair *in addition* to the Boston Bazaar, Chapman formulated an economic case against it. 'Bangor is a small place in comparison with Boston', she related, 'and the *market* here is far surer and more extensive.' She assured the British women it would be more financially prudent to send their donations only to Boston. [T]here are more of the abolitionists in the first rank of society in Boston than elsewhere', Chapman explained, which 'enables us to get up our bazaars with far more success than in any other place.'[49]

Chapman framed her argument squarely in terms of market forces: 'If the articles are sent in any large quantity to Bangor, the probability is that they will not be disposed of.' Although no doubt partially motivated by self-interest, Chapman was nevertheless correct in her analysis of the market. Rural fair organizers welcomed small donations of foreign and luxury articles to attract customers, but they could not accommodate large shipments of extravagant and costly goods. As more female antislavery societies began holding their own fairs, a complex web of exchange developed to supply the demands of specific markets. By the late 1840s, the Boston organizers regularly furnished smaller and rural fairs with goods that 'remained unsold' in the more discriminating Boston marketplace. By the end of the 1840s, Maria Chapman estimated that nearly a quarter of the left-over Boston goods were disposed of at 'country fairs'.[50]

The dramatic rise in foreign contributions to the Bazaar in the 1840s and 1850s was partially a response to the Garrisonian campaign to mobilize British support for the American Antislavery Society (AASS) in the wake of the 'schism' of 1840 that split the American abolitionist movement into two distinct and often warring factions.[51] In the wake of the split, British women were forced to choose

---

[49] These statements by Chapman are from excerpts of letters that appear in the inelegantly titled publication 'Some particulars of the late Boston Antislavery Bazaar with a Sketch of the Antislavery Movement in the United States', prepared by Dublin's Hibernian Antislavery Society in 1842. The report is located in the Kroch Library Rare books and manuscripts at Cornell University, E441.M46. vol. 53 no.14. Hibernian Antislavery Society, (ed.), *Some Particulars of the late Boston Anti-slavery Bazaar: With a Sketch of the Antislavery Movement in the United States* (Dublin, 1842), pp. 10–11.

[50] Maria W. Chapman to Mary A. Estlin, 20 January 1847, Estlin Papers, as cited in Chambers-Schiller, '"A Good Work among the People"', pp. 255–6, n.21.

[51] By the late 1830s, the AASS was internally divided over issues related to women's rights, proslavery churches, and the role of government in society. 'Garrisonians' as the followers of William Lloyd Garrison's brand of abolitionism came to be called, believed that women should hold leadership positions within the AASS; that all ties should be cut with churches that did not renounce slavery from the pulpit; and that any institution that condoned slavery should not be supported. The Garrisonians were also proponents of universal reform, including temperance, pacifism, Chartism and a variety of other causes. Other abolitionists held more traditional views of women, religion, and government and were not opposed to abolishing slavery by political means or engaging in violent opposition

between William Lloyd Garrison's re-organized AASS and Lewis Tappan's newly founded American and Foreign Antislavery Society (AFASS). The majority of women, particularly those residing in Scotland and Ireland, aligned with Garrison. 'Garrisonians' actively courted British women; approximately 1,500 letters from American Garrisonians to and from female abolitionists in Britain demonstrate the intensity of the relationship between the two groups. Conversely, the AFASS largely corresponded with men in Britain.[52]

It was in this contentious atmosphere that the Boston fair managers sought to convince British women to donate to the Bazaar. Boston women issued their appeals for foreign donations through letters, circulars, advertisements, fair reports, travelling agents and personal appeals designed to convince British women that the Bazaar presented the most effective means of expressing their support for American abolitionism. And they were largely successful. Clare Midgley argues in her study of transatlantic antislavery that working on behalf of the Boston Bazaar provided British women with 'a channel for their [antislavery] energies'.[53] One of the more ingenious means of generating British support for the Boston Bazaar was through an appeal for donations that was inserted in the appendix to the Dublin edition of the *Narrative of the Life of Frederick Douglass*. Douglass became a celebrity in Ireland and Great Britain during his lecture tour in 1845–46 and women were particularly taken with him, making his plea for their support even more commanding:

> Contributions to the BOSTON ANTI-SLAVERY BAZAAR of any article of use or ornament, which will bear to be packed without injury, ladies' fancy work, or the products of manufactories, especially such works of taste or art as are not manufactured in the United States; in fine, any products of British taste or industry, as well as donations of money, will be appropriated in an effectual manner for the promotion of the cause.[54]

---

against slavery if necessary. They also believed that the focus of the AASS should be only on the abolition of slavery. By 1840, the two factions of the AASS had become so divided that the society split into two distinct and independent societies – the AASS and the BFASS. After a bitter struggle, Garrison retained control over a much-diminished AASS and Lewis Tappan emerged as the leader of the American and Foreign Antislavery Society, the evangelical wing of the American Antislavery movement. The BFASS focused their attentions on lobbying religious institutions to denounce slavery. For a discussion of the split's effect on female abolitionists in the United States and Great Britain see: Midgley, *Women Against Slavery*.

[52] Midgley, *Women Against Slavery*, p. 132. The vast majority of the 1,500 letters that Midgley cites are housed in the 'Weston Collection' at the Boston Public Library. A useful selection of these letters are included in Clare Taylor, *British and American Abolitionists: An Episode in Transatlantic Understanding* (Edinburgh, 1974).

[53] Midgley, *Women Against Slavery*, p. 134.

[54] Frederick Douglass, *Narrative by of the Life of Frederick Douglass An American Slave. Written Himself* (Dublin, 1845), pp. 124–5.

Douglass' appeal concluded with a list of more than two dozen women throughout Britain who had, 'consented to receive … contributions for the Annual Bazaar'. Several women were prominent British reformers and/or literary figures, including Harriet Martineau, Elizabeth Pease, Mary Carpenter and Ann Knight.[55] Publishing the names and addresses of British 'superintendents' who received goods for the Bazaar became a regular practice in the 1850s in the British and Irish antislavery newspapers the *Anti-slavery Reporter* and *The Anti-slavery Advocate*.

While Chapman and her managers celebrated the British donations, they acknowledged that the addition of hundreds, likely thousands, of contributions greatly increased the labour involved in staging the Bazaar. 'We never attempt to deny that these are *most fatiguing occasions*', Maria Chapman conceded, 'for the constant vigilance and activity required to do justice to this amount of property entrusted to us under such conditions, ought to draw deeply and to the utmost upon all the powers of brain and body.'[56] For managers, the foreign donations added yet another layer to the already massive infrastructure of the annual sale. By the mid-1840s, the logistics involved in getting the goods from the producers to the fair tables assumed the dimensions of a significant commercial endeavour; the scale and mercantile structure of the Boston Bazaar in the 1840s and 1850s was truly remarkable.

In a 'typical week' leading up to the Bazaar seven ships departed British ports carrying donations bound for Boston. Historian Benjamin Quarles estimated that after 1850, the Boston Bazaar annually received boxes from Edinburgh, London and Dublin, Glasgow, Newcastle, Leeds, Manchester, Cork, Perth, Liverpool, and Paris.[57] In 1857, the 'peak year' for British donations, Quarles determined that 'the bazaar received twenty-four cases from across the Atlantic; twenty of these came from the British Isles, two from Paris, one from Rome and one from Florence'.[58] The process of collecting articles from their manufacturers and preparing them for transport got underway in the early fall. Ideally goods would depart British and European ports in the first week of November, thereby ensuring the articles would reach Boston by early December. Managers wanted foreign donations to arrive in sufficient time to examine the contents of the boxes, adjust the prices to the market rate, and advertise accordingly. 'It is very important to us to receive our boxes in good season', Chapman informed her British donors, 'or we cannot do justice to their contents by examining and appraising them in the leisurely way that is so essential.'[59]

Organization of the foreign and American donations followed along similar lines, however, in the case of foreign goods, delays in communication and transportation, customs hassles and cultural difference, complicated the process

---

[55] Douglass, *Narrative by of the Life of Frederick Douglass*, pp. 124–5.
[56] *The Liberator*, 25 January 1856.
[57] Quarles, 'Sources of Abolitionist Income', p. 72.
[58] Quarles, 'Sources of Abolitionist Income', pp. 72–3.
[59] *The Liberator*, 26 January 1855.

considerably. Poor planning, rough seas, shipwrecks and even war interrupted the timely arrival of the foreign donations.[60] A series of letters and reports written by several individuals involved in the transportation of the 'Irish Boxes' to the 1841 Bazaar illuminates the process of moving goods across the Atlantic.[61] After collecting the Irish contributions from their donors, members of the Hibernian Antislavery Society in Dublin gathered to undertake the annual ritual of 'classifying, arranging and stowing away' the goods for their 'voyage across the great waters'. The Irish abolitionists reportedly 'took pleasure in the experience' of pricing and packing the goods, taking the opportunity to 'speculate' on the 'money they would make' and the 'pleasure they would bring' at the Boston Bazaar.[62] The goods were shipped to Liverpool, where they were loaded onto a steamer bound for Boston. The ship departed Liverpool on 4 December arriving in Boston on 19 December 1841, the day before the Boston Bazaar opened.

Although the boxes arrived before the Bazaar opened they did not clear customs until the following afternoon. Public anticipation for the foreign articles was so great that the managers unpacked a portion of the goods at the hall amidst 'throngs' of eager customers. Maria Chapman described the chaotic scene, apologizing to the Irish donors that she had been unable to record the prices brought by the articles because they vanished so quickly into the hands of eager customers:

> I am sorry I cannot tell you the prices that all the beautiful contributions brought. But they arrived in the midst of so busy a day of the fair, that 'an earthquake might have rolled unheededly away;' and it was important they should be got ready in an instant, to meet the tide of purchasers. So we put high prices on them, and *got* high prices for them.[63]

Opening up the foreign boxes in the midst of the sale became a popular and profitable part of the Bazaar. To generate excitement and heighten profits, managers advertised new shipments of goods that arrived while the Fair was underway. 'Fresh goods have arrived from China and others being expected from Paris', declared an advertisement published on New Year's Eve, 1846, 'The managers have decided on a GREAT REDUCTION OF PRICES; and to make room for the

---

[60] In her report on the twenty-first Bazaar, Anne Weston informed her readers that 'The boxes from Edinburgh, Glasgow, Perth, Milnthorp, London, Bury, Cork and Belfast' did not arrive 'in season'. 'They were detained at Liverpool', Weston explained, 'owing to the unexpected occupation of the Cunard steamers in the Government service for conveying troops to the Crimea – a circumstance entirely so unforeseen as to have precluded any previous arrangement.' *The Liberator*, 26 January 1855.

[61] The letters appear in: *Some particulars of the late Boston Antislavery Bazaar.*

[62] *Some particulars*, p. 4.

[63] *Some particulars*, p. 9.

new goods by placing in the centre of the hall all those articles that it would be a greater sacrifice to retain, than to dispose of at an EXTREMELY LOW RATE'.[64]

The practice of selling off inventory to accommodate fresh merchandise is further proof of the managers' remarkable business acumen. Organizers continued to stress the 'moral' and 'entertainment' value of the Bazaar, but profit and prestige were increasingly significant parts of their endeavour. In December 1844, Maria Chapman asserted that 'to those pining in hopeless captivity', declarations on the immorality of slavery or 'praise of the [Fair] spectacle' were worthless 'unless accompanied by substantial deeds'. In Chapman's opinion, the most effective means of supporting the slave was to spend liberally at the Bazaar. 'It is THE BUYERS' she proclaimed 'who are ... the most efficient and only practical friend of the slave.'[65] This remarkably forthright declaration clearly shows that while not the only priority, profit was a primary motivation for staging the Bazaar by the mid-1840s. Beverly Lemire demonstrates in her recent study of the *Business of Everyday Life* that by the middle of the nineteenth-century, women on both side of the Atlantic were deeply entrenched in 'quantitative culture' within the household.[66] Lemire argues that one of the ways in which this culture manifested itself was through women's attention to household profit – defined by money saved as well as money earned.[67]

Profit was front and centre in the minds of donors as well. Information about the price and popularity of goods donated to the Bazaar was crucially important to contributors. Like their formal commercial counterparts (shopkeepers and milliners), women in Great Britain and the United States demonstrated a desire to be regularly informed on issues of taste, fashion, and the vagaries of the market. Contributors wished to know what goods were 'saleable' in Boston, how much money certain goods sold for and whether or not they should send the same kinds of goods next year. 'Please as early as possible advise us how the articles sell', Catherine Paton wrote to Maria Chapman in a letter accompanying the Glasgow donations to the 1844 Bazaar, 'what are most suitable and what are not so suitable, on account of taste or duties, that we may as early as possible be apprised of what to make for next year that our means and labours may be as productive as can

---

[64] *The Boston Courier*, 31 December 1846.

[65] *The Liberator*, 20 December 1844.

[66] Beverly Lemire, *The Business of Everyday Life: Gender, Practice and Social Politics in England 1600–1900* (Manchester and New York, 2005), p. 187.

[67] Lemire, *Business of Everyday Life*, pp. 209–10. In Lemire's examples, household efficiency, achieved through application of management practices, was intended to be privately executed. 'The running of a respectable home' Lemire asserts, 'demanded no overt sign of exertion, for, in the looking-glass world of the Victorian household, domestic labour did not constitute toil, household management was an ephemeral act never brought to public notice…' Although Antislavery fairs applied the principles of domestic housekeeping to the management of the fair, they did so in a public manner, which openly flaunted the value of their labour.

be made.'[68] This communication reinforces the notion that working for the Bazaar encouraged women on both sides of the Atlantic to come to terms with and learn to celebrate the economic value of their labour. It also indicates that Fair managers understood not only the Boston and American markets but the British and European markets as well. Chapman and her managers kept abreast of British and Continental fashions through European publications and through trips abroad, developing a sense not only of what was fashionable in Europe but, as importantly, what European goods were most 'saleable' in the American market.

Through their experience organizing and managing the Bazaar, the Boston women became remarkably proficient 'businesswomen', a designation they wore proudly and defended strenuously. The history of women's role in and relationship to the market has been complex and uneven in its development. Women have largely been ignored by traditional business and economic historians, who focused their attention on big business and its leaders, both of which were male dominated categories.[69] More recently, however, growing numbers of historians have worked to bring the fields of business and women's history together, demonstrating that women were not only historically present in business, but that they were present in significant numbers, as retailers and managers, as well as labourers and consumers.[70] Recent work on women and business in the antebellum/Victorian

---

[68] Catherine Paton to Maria Weston Chapman, 30 November 1844. BPL Ms.A.9.2.20, p. 110.

[69] In Laura Cochrane's recent analysis of the holdings in Harvard's Baker Library's business manuscript collection she found that while many eighteenth- and nineteenth-century women engaged in the commercial marketplace as merchants and manufacturers, their presence had been largely overlooked by the historical record. '[B]ecause they mainly oversaw small or short-lived concerns' she concludes that women's 'enterprises did not fit into traditional understandings of successful business, either in their own time or later, when the field of business history developed in the twentieth century' (p. 465). Cochrane concludes that one result of this paradigmatic blind spot was that curators at business libraries focused their energies toward generating large collections of manuscripts relating to big business and important industrialists, thereby erasing women from the picture. In the British context, Alison Kay's examination of the sources used to study Victorian businesswomen similarly found that gendered biases inherent in the sources themselves have in many ways shaped modern analysis of British women's role(s) in the nineteenth-century market economy. Like Cochrane, Kay argues that because the majority of nineteenth-century women were either wage labourers or small retailers, they have been overlooked by traditional business histories. See: Laura Cochrane, 'From the Archives: Women's History in the Baker Library's Manuscript Collection', *The Business History Review*, 74/3 (2000): pp. 465–76; and Alison Kay, 'Revealing her assets: Liberating the Victorian businesswoman from the sources', *Business Archives: Sources and History*, 92 (2006): pp. 1–16.

[70] Historians have demonstrated that women were present in large numbers in the new industrial labour force of the antebellum Northeast, particularly in textiles, shoe-making and the garment industry. See for example, Thomas Dublin, *Women at Work: Transformations of Work and Community in Lowell Massachusetts, 1826–1860* (New

period has found that European and American women were very active in the retailing sector, owning and managing a significant number of small businesses.[71]

Demonstrating women's presence in the 'public' arena of business in nineteenth-century Britain and the United States is a vital exercise, but does it not, as Joan Scott argues in her analysis of gender in business 'allow us to raise new questions for business history?'[72] For Scott, the objectives of viewing business through a gendered lens are not only to document 'exclusion, resistance and agency'; but also to expose how gender (and other power relations) has organized and structured business and its history. The question then is not only how did charity bazaars, and more particularly antislavery bazaars, enable women to participate in the marketplace economy of the 1830s, 40s, and 50s; but also how did the presence of hundreds of thousands of women in the marketplace engage and influence the practice of business in this period?

York, 1979); Alice Kessler-Harris, *Out to Work: A History of Wage-Earning Women in the United States* (New York, 1982); Christine Stansell, *City of Women: Sex and Class in New York, 1789–1860* (New York, 1986); Susan Porter Benson, *Counter Cultures: Saleswomen, Managers, and Customers in American Department Stores, 1890–1940* (Urbana, 1988); Mary H. Blewett, *Men, Women and Work: Class, Gender and Protest in the New England Shoe Industry, 1780–1910* (Urbana, 1988); Claudia Goldin, *Understanding the Gender Gap: An Economic History of American Women* (New York, 1990); Jeanne Boydston *Home and Work: Housework, Wages and the Ideology of Labor in the Early Republic* (New York, 1994); and Thomas Dublin, *Transforming Women's Work: New England Lives in the Industrial Revolution* (Ithaca, 1994). On gendered construction of the consumer see: Charlotte Sussman, *Consuming Anxieties: Consumer Protest, Gender & British Slavery, 1713–1833* (Stanford, 2000); Jennifer Scanlon (ed.), *The Gender and Consumer Culture Reader* (London, 2000); Jennifer Scanlon, *Inarticulate Longings: The Ladies' Home Journal, Gender and the Promise of Consumer Culture* (New York, 1995); Victoria de Grazia and Ellen Furlough (eds), *The Sex of Things: Gender and Consumption in Historical Perspective* (Berkley, 1996); Elaine Abelson, *When Ladies Go a Thieving* (London, 1989); William R. Leach, 'Transformations in a Culture of Consumption: Women and Department Stores, 1890–1925', *Journal of American History*, 71/ 2(1984): pp. 319–42.

[71] For a historical look at female entrepreneurship and women's involvement in retailing and small business in Europe see: Beachy, *Women, Business*. In the American context see: Wendy Gamber, *Boardinghouses in Nineteenth-Century America* (Baltimore, 2007); Angel Kwolek-Folland, *Incorporating Women: A History of Women and Business in the United States* (New York, 1998); Susan Ingalls Lewis, 'Female Entrepreneurs in Albany, 1840–1885', *Business and Economic History*, 21(1992): pp. 65–73. See particularly, the 'Gender and Business History: Special Section', *Business History Review*, 72/2 (Summer 1998): pp. 185–249. This special edition includes, Philip Scranton, 'Introduction: Gender and Business History', 185–7; Wendy Gamber, 'A Gendered Enterprise: Placing Nineteenth-Century Businesswomen in History', pp. 188–217; Kathy Peiss, 'Vital Industry and Women's Ventures: Conceptualizing Gender in Twentieth-Century Business History', pp. 219–41 and Joan W. Scott, 'Comment: Conceptualizing Gender in American Business History', pp. 242–9.

[72] Scott, 'Conceptualizing Gender', p. 244.

Indeed, much of what is remarkable about the charity bazaar movement is not that women were engaging in the commercial arena, but rather that they were doing so in such incredibly large numbers and with so much organizational control and management of capital.[73] The presence of so many women in the marketplace had the effect of disrupting the masculine discourse of business by introducing a female commercial model that applied the skills and practices of domesticity to the marketplace. As Beverly Gordon rightly points out, '[a]lmost everything that made the fairs appealing, from flowers to perfume to music, was part of what women dealt with daily.'[74] In a period when prescriptive literature constructed the market and the home as 'separate spheres' this commodification of domesticity was seemingly 'a contradiction in terms'.[75] Women's charity fairs commercialized domesticity not only through the sale of household objects, but also through the public trading of domestic skills and practices. By linking consumption with charity, women's bazaars created a space for domesticity as a marketable commodity.

The blurring of business and household worlds generated considerable anxiety and anger across many sectors of society, which prompted widespread attacks on

---

[73] Though drawn from divergent classes, races, ages and value-systems, charity fair organizers shared common attitudes toward the marketplace. In spite of variances in their allegiances and convictions, fair managers collectively operated on the premise that the market could and *should* be used for benevolent purposes. Female supporters of fairs organized around the belief that women could respectably engage in commerce – as producers, managers, retailers, and as consumers – provided it was done in the name of a 'good cause'. Fair organizers' attitudes toward the market varied along class, religious, ethnic and racial lines, yet by virtue of selling their goods in a public mart, charity fair operators implicitly, if not explicitly, validated the positive potential of the market. For an excellent discussion of how class, religion and race shaped the market attitudes of members of the Boston Female Antislavery Society see 'The Boston Female Antislavery Society Fair' in Debra Gold Hansen, *Strained Sisterhood: Gender and Class in the Boston Female Antislavery Society* (Amherst, 1993), pp. 124–39.

[74] Gordon, *Bazaars and Fair Ladies*, pp. 5–6.

[75] Gordon, *Bazaars and Fair Ladies*, p. 5. Scholars have argued that America's obsession with domesticity was partly due to the manner in which the majority of Americans experienced the transition to a capitalist market economy in the early republic. For example, Jeanne Boydston argues that the 'peculiarly intense and sentimental character of American domesticity' is related to the fact that Americans filtered capitalism through the medium of the family unit and that the transition to capitalism 'coincided with a political revolution that emphasized the bourgeois family and male economic independence'. Jeanne Boydston, 'The Woman Who Wasn't There: Women's Market Labor and the Transition to Capitalism in the United States', *Journal of the Early Republic*, 16/2 (Summer,1996): pp. 198–9. See also: Carole Shammas, 'Early American Women and Control over Capital', in Ronald Hoffman and Peter J. Albert (eds), *Women in the Age of the American Revolution* (Charlottesville, 1989), pp. 140–47; Susan Branson, 'Women and the Family Economy in the Early Republic: The Case of Elizabeth Meredith', *Journal of the Early Republic*, 16/1 (1996): pp. 47–71; Gloria L. Main, 'Gender, Work and Wages in Colonial New England', *The William and Mary Quarterly*, 51/1 (1994): pp. 39–66.

women's fundraising fairs. Beverly Gordon has argued that, '[m]en often insisted on keeping women's fairs a thing apart', attempting to keep the 'world of work' separate from 'the seemingly frivolous women's institution built around what was 'not work' and 'not serious', i.e.; around women and their domestic interests'.[76] Damaging critiques of women's fancy fairs appeared in British and American newspapers, periodical literature, novels, poetry, music, cartoons and even high art from the 1830s onward. Although their chosen medium varied, opponents of female fundraising fairs were tediously consistent in their critique of the institution and its supporters. In both Britain and the United States, tropes of women's 'fancy fairs' or 'charity bazaars' construed the female marketplace as a dangerous site of illicit sexuality (women were selling themselves as well as their wares); as economically threatening to 'legitimate' businessmen; as robbing working class women of employment; as luring unsuspecting customers into spending beyond their means; and as vain amusements ('vanity fairs') run by gossipy socialites rather than serious reformers and legitimate businesswomen.[77]

It is the last critique that seems to have vexed the Boston Bazaar managers most. Because the majority of the organizers were well-to-do and because the sale catered to the taste and pocketbooks of elite Bostonians, the women were accused of sacrificing their abolitionist principles at the alter of materialism and social status. '[I]mputations have been cast upon those who act most prominently in conducting this [Boston] fair', stated an article in Frederick Douglass' *The North Star*. 'It is said they seek popularity and play into the hands of the Beacon street aristocracy.'[78] In response to these 'imputations' the managers attempted to formulate a distinct (and distinctive) identity for the Boston Bazaar that distanced that event from other women's fundraising efforts. Anne Weston addressed the issue of frivolousness and unprofessionalism head on in her report of the Twentieth National Bazaar. 'To the minds of most persons', Weston wrote, 'the mention of a Ladies' bazaar suggests ideas of a purely gay and festal character; of an occasion, where it is well if the gaiety and festivity do not degenerate into mere thoughtlessness and frivolity'. Weston readily acknowledged that other fundraising fairs did succumb to these tendencies, but emphatically rejected the notion that the Boston Bazaar in any way resembled the ordinary 'ladies' fancy fair. '[O]urs is grave work', she asserted, 'performed in any but a thoughtless and irresponsible spirit.'[79]

When city officials – likely reacting to pressure from male merchants and from competition from other fairs – 'shut out' the Boston Fair from Faneuil Hall in the early 1850s, the managers were forced to relocate to other venues, including Boston's Horticultural Hall. Anne Weston again vigorously asserted the difference

---

[76] Gordon, *Bazaars and Fair Ladies*, p. 6.

[77] See Beverly Gordon and Frank Prochaska for a discussion of the various criticisms that were leveled against women's charity bazaars.

[78] *The North Star*, 7 January 1848. The article proceeds to refute these accusations but it nevertheless makes clear that the Boston Bazaar was attacked on these grounds.

[79] 'Report of the Twentieth National Antislavery Bazaar' (Boston, 1854), p. 4.

between the Boston Fair and other charity bazaars, by refusing the conflation of the Fair with feminine trifles. When the organizing committee was forced to hold the Fair in the Horticultural Hall, Weston proclaimed the change in venue to be 'a great declension of dignity'. She asserted that the Fair was far better suited to Faneuil Hall, with its 'pictures of old heroes and associations of struggle and revolt and stormy revolution' than to the Horticultural Hall 'suggestive of nothing but fruits and flowers'.[80] Weston responded to local critics who claimed that Horticultural Hall befitted the frivolous nature of a fancy fair by arguing that the 'spirit in which we labour' and the commercial profitability of the Bazaar legitimated its claim to Faneuil Hall. To 'that class' who 'feel the latter instead of the former were our proper place', Weston declared, 'we shall not debate the question here'. In lieu of debate, Weston instead issued a public statement of the Bazaar's financial 'success' as proof of its claim on Faneuil Hall.[81]

Male critics' attempts to value and de-value work based on its relationship to traditionally gendered skills and sensibilities cut to the heart of the problem that the Boston Bazaar managers faced – how to legitimate the feminine marketplace. 'The results of the recent *Boston Antislavery Bazaar* have been very successful', Maria Weston Chapman declared in an article that appeared in the British abolitionist newspaper *The Anti-slavery Reporter* in April 1857:

> realizing 5200 dols., [dollars] an amount exceeding any before obtained by one sale....These results also indicate, that, commercially, the *Boston Bazaar* is a well-conducted enterprise; that *business* men and women are the managers; and that it has become an established mart, to which all purchasers find their way, because of the elegant assemblage of articles found there suited to their taste as Christmas purchases. It is not anti-slavery people alone who frequent the *Boston Antislavery Fair*: slaveholders and their friends resort there from year to year, and while they make their purchases, they receive many profitable lessons, and directly, though it may be unwillingly, help on the cause of freedom.[82]

This brief account (and accounting) of the twenty-second annual Boston Antislavery Bazaar stakes a series of commercial claims – professionalism, business acumen, retail success – for Fair managers and for the Boston Bazaar itself. Chapman did this is by offering up a public report of the fair proceeds, the success of which she contends is evidence that: (1) the sale is run according to the orderly values of market culture; (2) it is managed by *business* women and men, not socialites and dilettantes; and (3) it is an established commercial, not simply charitable enterprise. It is an established and widely recognized 'mart', demonstrably by the fact that even slaveholders could not resist purchasing their holiday gifts there.

---

[80] *The Liberator*, 28 January 1853.
[81] *The Liberator*, 28 January 1853.
[82] 'The Boston (U.S.) Bazaar' *The Anti-slavery Reporter*, 1 April 1857.

In formulating their defence of the Bazaar, Weston, Chapman and the other managers employed the precepts of classical liberalism as a shield against the criticism that women's charity fairs were all frivolous amusements that were poorly managed and sold inferior merchandise at greatly inflated prices.[83] The managers used the professional making of money, albeit for a good cause, undertaken in a commercially viable manner, as a claim to commercial respectability and legitimacy for women.[84] Accusations of frivolity and incompetence clearly offended Boston Fair management, but the fact that non-abolitionists purchased goods there and that Boston merchants treated them as serious rivals underscored the Bazaar's success as a commercial *and* a charitable enterprise. Boston Fair managers celebrated their commercial accomplishments, speaking frequently of their reputation, longevity, and, of course, their financial success. For a quarter of a decade, the Boston Antislavery Bazaar was the leader of a vast network of antislavery fairs that spread across the Northern United States and Great Britain. By the late 1850s, it was importing thousands of dollars of fancy European goods and earning between 5,000 and 6,000 annually for the American Antislavery Society.

After the twenty-fourth Boston Bazaar closed its doors in December 1857, Maria Weston Chapman and her sisters issued a unilateral 'decree' to terminate the annual sale. In its place, Chapman proposed to organize an annual subscription campaign, which she argued would raise more money and expend considerably less effort than the Bazaar had. '[F]airs' she wrote to a friend, 'are like an Excise; good only if no other mode is practicable.'[85] News of the Bazaar's demise was received with a mixture of shock, disapproval, anger and eventual resignation by abolitionists on both sides of the Atlantic. Chapman justified her decision to end the Fair by claiming that it had become *passé*; she argued that the Anniversary – an

---

[83] In this context I am referring to the classic 19th-century liberalism that espoused free trade, capitalist commerce and free labour. The idea of hard work and profit making, the achievement of position or policy based on merit, as opposed to inheritance, or corrupt influence.

[84] Chapman's invocation of a professionalized commercial discourse in her newspaper article, as well as the more generalized use of accounting precepts in female charity reports, reflects what Beverly Lemire describes in her study of domestic accounting as 'an intensification of numerate capitalist culture and an emphasis on quantitative measurement' that reached its apogee in the nineteenth-century (p. 209). Chapman's reporting on the Boston Bazaar would have been read by a mid-nineteenth-century audience in the context of a wide range of charitable and financial information that appeared in newspapers and in periodical literature of the first half of the nineteenth century. Mary Poovey argues in her analysis of Victorian financial writing, which she identifies as starting in the mid-1840s, that numerical accounts (of the kind that dominated merchant's lists and government reports) and narrative forms (borrowed from contemporary fiction) began to overlap, creating what she terms 'financial journalism'. See: Mary Poovey, 'Writing about Finance in Victorian England: Disclosure and Secrecy in the Culture of Investment', *Victorian Studies*, 45/1 (2002): p. 25.

[85] Maria Weston Chapman to E.P. Nichols, 25 January 1860, as cited in Quarles, 'Sources of Abolitionist Income', p. 75.

exclusive, invitation-only soiree featuring music, food and speeches – was more *à la mode* and would bring in more money than the Bazaar.

In the end, the Boston Bazaar succumbed to the same forces that had made it such a popular and successful form of antislavery activism. By the late 1850s, fashion, entertainment and the market had moved on. Charity fairs, while still a popular mode of fundraising, were no longer new, the goods they sold and the forms of entertainment they featured were readily available elsewhere by mid-century. Moreover, by the 1850s, antislavery itself had become, if not a fashionable, at least acceptable to the majority of American Northerners. Antislavery bazaars and the women who managed them played a central role in the movement of abolitionism from the margins to the centre of American consciousness. They, along with innumerable other charity fair organizers, also played an important role in creating an alternative language of commerce, one which embraced the tropes of femininity, claiming a space in the antebellum economy where domesticity and the market were not a contradiction in terms.

Chapter Seven
Silk and Sartorial Politics in the Sokoto Caliphate (Nigeria), 1804–1903[1]

Colleen E. Kriger

> He said men should take up their bows and quivers
> As well as swords, you hear his command.
> He said, 'Make ready the horses, and firm up your intention
> To prepare for the jihad'.
> He sent messages to all the major towns,
> Calling everybody who would listen to him.
> He said, 'Show by your dress who you are and what you intend.
> Make up your minds what to do, and be prepared'.[2]

Proper clothing for Muslim believers was a serious political matter in the years leading up to the 1804 jihad that created the Sokoto Caliphate (now northern Nigeria – see Map 7.1). The Fulbe scholar Shaikh Uthman dan Fodio (b. 1754, d. 1817), intent on teaching and administering a more uniform and more orthodox version of Muslim law, had attracted a devoted circle of followers in the predominantly Hausa-speaking kingdom of Gobir throughout the 1780s and 1790s. In his preaching, he was openly critical of the nominally-Muslim leaders of Gobir and the other Hausa kingdoms, accusing them of corruption and 'unbelief'. Charges such as these were not new in West Africa, where Islam's long history of coexistence with different local religions had led to the creation of many forms of 'mixed practice', or syncretism.[3] Along with other religious reformers of his time, the Shaikh took it upon himself to eradicate the mixing of Islam with what he considered to be unlawful rituals and unseemly behaviour, and his preaching had the result of exacerbating divisions within the broader Muslim community. Tensions between the Shaikh's followers and the Gobir court intensified during the reign of Nafata

---

[1] This article is based on a paper given at the XIV World Economic History Congress held in Helsinki, Finland, 21–25 August 2006. I would like to thank Beverly Lemire for inviting me to take part in her panel, 'Fashion, Material Culture, and Economic Life: Perspectives across Time, Place, and Politics, 1600–2000', and for her apt and very useful editorial questions and comments.

[2] From the poem 'The Journey', written originally in Fulfulde and Hausa by Nana Asma'u, daughter of Shaikh Uthman dan Fodio. Jean Boyd and Beverly Mack (eds and trans.), *One Woman's Jihad* (Bloomington, IN, 2000), pp. 157–8.

[3] Mervyn Hiskett, *The Course of Islam in Africa* (Edinburgh, 1994), Chapter 4.

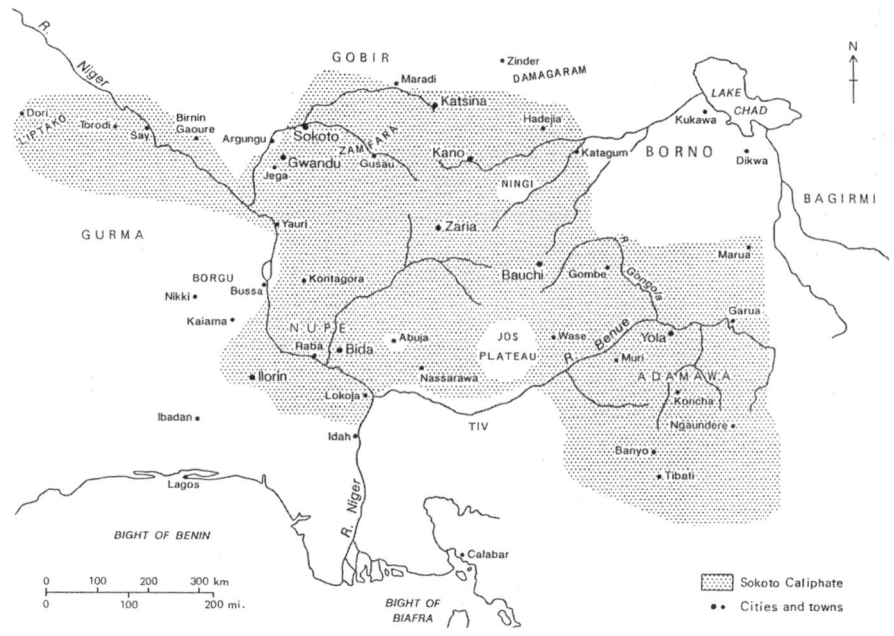

Map 7.1   The Sokoto Caliphate, now northern Nigeria

(1794–1801) who placed restrictions on the believers in an attempt to diminish their growing influence among the general population. Nafata ordered that only the Shaikh himself would be allowed to preach publicly, that boys were not to be converted to a faith different from the one their fathers practised, and introduced stringent sumptuary regulation stipulating that the wearing of turbans (by men) and veils (by women) was to be no longer allowed. These edicts, and the climate of persecution they created, served as a prelude to the series of kidnappings and raids that eventually sparked the jihad.[4] They also explain why, in the section of Nana Asma'u's poem that describes the preparation for war (in the epigraph above), she portrays the Shaikh calling for his followers to identify themselves 'by dress'. At that time, on the eve of the jihad, wearing turbans and veils was a political act of defiance against the Gobir court and a pledge of solidarity with the Shaikh and his community.

This paper presents another example of sartorial politics in the Sokoto Caliphate, one that concerned legal questions and controversies over the wearing of silk. The 'problem of silk' – who could legally wear it and when – is believed to go all the way back to the seventh century and the time of Muhammad, and recurring discussions of it reveal the variability of opinions on the social and ethical

---

[4]   Mervyn Hiskett, *The Sword of Truth* (New York, 1973), pp. 42–104; Murray Last, *The Sokoto Caliphate* (New York, 1967), Chapters 1 and 2.

significance of Muslim dress. This specific study of silk in the Sokoto Caliphate is based on two independent sets of primary sources: translations of texts written by leaders of the jihad; and special garments made by and for the Caliphate's male literati. Silk and sumptuous clothing were criticized in the writings of Shaikh Uthman dan Fodio and his brother, Abdullah, who were the intellectual architects of the jihad.[5] Their harshest pronouncements against silk suggest that they may well have prohibited their male followers from wearing fabrics made with this fibre. To test this proposition, I turn my attention to the production and distribution of men's robes in the Caliphate. Caliphate robes were well known and were far from ordinary items of clothing. Among them there was a signature type of elaborately embroidered garment that was worn by members of the Muslim male elite, with some select examples serving as 'robes of honour'.[6] My analyses of such robes – what they looked like, how they were made, and what the role of silk was in their manufacture – offer a unique perspective on Caliphate society that is quite different from the impression conveyed by the writings of the Shaikh and his brother. Attitudes toward dress were varied, complex, and sometimes contradictory, for the wearing of silk by Muslim men was tolerated and, in some ways, actively promoted.

By examining the politics of silk I aim also to historicize dress and textile manufacture in this particular part of West Africa. In doing so, I challenge an entrenched convention among Africanist scholars who attach ethnic or linguistic characterizations to these very same robes – calling them 'Hausa', 'Fulani', 'Nupe', or 'Yoruba' garments. Such apparently timeless descriptors misrepresent the robes and their historical significance by disregarding why they existed and why their

---

[5] Works cited in this paper are English translations of three writings attributed to Shaikh Uthman dan Fodio and one attributed to Abdullah. Each text is a critical edition collated from authenticated copies, all in Arabic. The originals were authored during the period *circa* 1793–1808.

[6] The idea and principle of the 'robe of honour' was very likely well known to Muslim scholars in West Africa. An early reference noted that the Sultan of Cairo awarded robes of honour to Mansa Musa, the king of Mali, as he passed through Cairo on his pilgrimage to Mecca in 1324. Other devout West African Muslims making the pilgrimage would also have been familiar with the 'robe of honour' institution. Shaikh Uthman never actually made the pilgrimage himself, but he was well connected in international scholarly networks and was visited by scholars on their way to and from Mecca. N. Levtzion and J.F.P. Hopkins (eds and trans.), *Corpus of Early Arabic Sources for West African History* (Cambridge, 1981), p. 270; Hiskett, *Sword*, Chapters 2 and 4. The age and origin of the specific garment type I analyse here is not known. Early tailored tunics found in burial caves farther west (in the upper Niger region) dating to the eleventh century were tailored in a different way. Seventeenth-century robes in the Ulmer Museum in Germany (collected on the coast, west of the lower Niger) were also tailored in a different way. Linguistic, visual, and technical evidence suggest the particular robe type assessed in this chapter originated in desert-side Muslim communities. See Colleen Kriger, 'Robes of the Sokoto Caliphate', *African Arts*, 21/3 (1988): pp. 52–7, 78–9, 85–6.

popularity lingered on into the period of British colonial rule in the twentieth century. Men who wore such robes cannot be neatly categorized in ethnic terms – they spoke a number of different languages, as did the many artisans who engaged in all stages of textile manufacture. Most importantly, the robes were serving a Muslim, and therefore a unifying and pan-ethnic, ideal. Over time they came to be so well known, prestigious, and widely imitated that non-Muslim men wore them as well. Consideration of these garments as specifically Muslim and Caliphate robes illuminates their important institutional roles and, by extension, their social complexity and cultural significance. It then becomes much more understandable why they were in such high demand across language groups and how this broad consumer market stimulated an expansion in the production of robes at varying prices. This new trend in male 'fashion' was historically rooted *not* in ethnic identity but in the realms of religious politics and governmental administration distinct to that region and time period.

Silk and the Sunna

For Muslim scholars, it was not at all an easy task to distinguish what was proper Muslim clothing from what was not. Silk had long been a subject of special concern, given its history as a textile fibre used for making costly and luxurious fabrics, but it is portrayed very differently in each of the three main textual sources forming the basis of Islamic law. In the Quran, for example, Paradise is a place where true believers will be rewarded with, among other things, rich jewellery and beautiful garments of silk and brocade.[7] But silk was expressly forbidden to male believers during their earthly existence, according to accounts of the Prophet Muhammad in the *hadith* literature. Then there are the detailed and sometimes conflicting legal opinions on the permissibility of silk that were written over the centuries by Muslim legal scholars. Attitudes about silk could thus be particularly contentious in scholarly circles, which certainly was the case in the early years of the Sokoto Caliphate.

Mervyn Hiskett confirms the conflicted attitudes towards silk in his biography of the Shaikh Uthman dan Fodio, who himself lived the austere and disciplined life of a deeply learned Sufi scholar, one that he modelled after the Prophet Muhammad. Even as a young man the Shaikh had been recognized for his piety. Among the outward signs that conveyed his disinterest in material goods was his exceptionally simple wardrobe, which apparently consisted of one gown, one pair of trousers, and one turban. Beginning in 1794, the Shaikh dedicated himself to educating and uplifting his society by identifying and criticizing sinful customs and urging that people adopt the Sunna, or customs of the Prophet. In his preaching he warned audiences about the dangers of envy, ostentation, and the seeking of wealth for display, referring to these and other behaviours as destructive to the

---

[7] Suras 18:31, 22:23, 35:33, 76:12, 76:21.

human soul. He advised that, for those who wished to enter Paradise, the true path to salvation was to be found by avoiding the corrupting effects of possessions and comfort.[8] Dress, considered as an expression of inner character and faith, was therefore not at all trivial.

It would be a mistake, however, to overestimate the degree to which the Shaikh and his community of followers were willing to enforce strict orthodoxy in matters of apparel. In one of his early writings from about 1793, he displayed a moderate tone as he explained the reasoning and sense of duty underlying his decision to travel and preach among the common folk and to teach them the Sunna, by word and by example. He emphasized the importance of proper intent – that this educational process should be for the benefit of the people and should not become an opportunity for excessive fault-finding and the casting of blame. He was also careful to define orthodoxy, which he was attempting to revive, as opposed to 'innovation', which he was hoping to eradicate. He defined as innovation anything that was extraneous to the Quran, Sunna, and the consensus of Muslim legal scholars. By embracing the latter, that is, the body of established legal opinion, as an authoritative guide in making judgements about legal issues and proper conduct, the Shaikh set himself apart from narrower, more fundamentalist approaches to shari'a law.[9] Moreover, even those innovations that he disapproved of were not all singled out for outright prohibition. Two examples of permissible innovations were the wearing of beautiful clothes and living in impressive houses. He recommended that reformers should object only to certain specific innovations that had to do with religious practice and political administration. An example he gave of a forbidden innovation was the appointment of an unqualified person to a position of authority, that is, assuming a position solely on the basis of inheritance.[10] In short, the Shaikh adopted a relatively pragmatic approach to the problem of legal and social reform.

But as conflicts between the Shaikh's community and the rulers of Gobir continued, the possibility of reform faded and his authorial tone changed. Predatory raids by the Gobir army and counter-attacks in defense of the believers and their allies hardened positions on both sides, leading the Shaikh to formally declare war in 1804. Over the next four years, military commanders were appointed and sent on campaigns to depose the leaders of the other major Hausa kingdoms. This period generated more writings by the Shaikh and his circle. Silk was now seen as a prime example of luxurious worldly trappings, and was such a cause of concern that dan Fodio included a legal opinion about it in a work written two years after the jihad had begun. Citing a variety of references in the *hadith* literature, his

---

[8] Hiskett, *Sword*, pp. 31, 50–51.
[9] Hiskett, *Sword*, pp. 137–8.
[10] Ismail A.B. Balogun (trans.), 'A critical edition of the *Ihya Al-Sunna Wa-Ikhmad Al-Bida* of Uthman b. Fudi, popularly known as Usumanu Dan Fodio' (Unpublished Ph.D. dissertation, University of London, 1967), pp. 81–5; Hiskett, *Sword*, pp. 51–3.

judgement presents us with a complex picture of what scholars might consider permissible and proper dress to be, on what occasions and for whom.

Gender was a central issue. As the Shaikh saw it, there was a clear consensus that women were not restricted from wearing silk clothing, but there were serious questions as to whether it was illegal and/or sinful for men to do so. He quoted Al-Bukhari and others, whose collections repeated the putative sayings of Muhammad where the Prophet either discouraged or outlawed the wearing of silk by men: 'Do not wear silk, for whosoever wears it in this world shall not wear it in the hereafter'; 'Only a worthless fellow wears silk'; and 'There will certainly be among my community people who consider [the wearing of] silk to be lawful; they will be transformed into monkeys and pigs until the Day of Resurrection'. Other accounts stated that the Prophet had held a piece of silk in one hand and a piece of gold in the other, saying 'Verily, these two are forbidden to the males of my community'. The Shaikh also quoted others who stated that men could wear silk in a jihad, or when travelling, or when it was used as an ornamental border on a cloth. But in the end, he pronounced that the most reliable and accepted view was that it should be 'forbidden for men to wear pure silk even in a jihad', and that the Maliki school of law and the majority of scholars considered silk to be permissible for women and not for men.[11] In other words, the 'problem of silk' was a problem having to do primarily with the proper attire of adult males.

Another of the Shaikh's writings, composed around 1808, set out in some detail the criticisms he and his community had levelled against the Hausa kings and then by way of contrast provided an account of what he considered to be the correct form of government under shari'a law. It was meant to be both a justification of the jihad as well as a guide for officials and teachers in the new administration they were establishing. Referring to the Hausa kings as 'unbelievers', the Shaikh itemized the many practices that were deemed objectionable, from the way public policies such as government appointments and taxation were handled to matters having to do with marriage and slavery.[12] Taken together, they portray a much more critical view of Hausa society at that time, especially its Muslim rulers, with ostentation being only one of the many sins that were being committed:

> One of the ways of their governments is their intentionally eating whatever food they wish, whether it is religiously permitted or forbidden, and wearing whatever clothes they wish, whether religiously permitted or forbidden, and drinking what beverages they wish, whether religiously permitted or forbidden, and riding

---

[11] Uthman dan Fodio, 'On the Law Concerning the Wearing of Silk in a Jihad' in Fathi Hasan Masri (trans.), *Bayan wujub al-hijra ala l-ibad* (New York, 1978), pp. 91–2.

[12] For a discussion of the issues related to defining 'unbelievers' see M.G. Smith, 'The jihad of Shehu dan Fodio' in I.M. Lewis (ed.), *Islam in Tropical Africa* (London, 1966), especially pp. 412–15; and D.M. Last and M.A. Al-Hajj, 'Attempts at Defining a Muslim in 19th century Hausaland and Bornu', *Journal of the Historical Society of Nigeria*, 3 (1965): pp. 231–40.

whatever riding beasts they wish, whether religiously permitted or forbidden, and taking what women they wish without marriage contract, and living in decorated palaces, whether religiously permitted or forbidden, and spreading soft carpets as they wish, whether religiously permitted or forbidden.[13]

His brother Abdullah catalogued similar complaints, but the sinners he targeted were amongst his own commanders and soldiers:

> [Their] purpose is the ruling of the countries and their people
> In order to obtain delights and acquire rank
> According to the custom of the unbelievers, and the titles of their sovereignty.
> And the appointing of ignorant persons to the highest offices,
> And the collecting of concubines, and fine clothes
> And horses that gallop in the towns, not on the battlefields,
> And the devouring of the gifts of sanctity, and booty and bribery,
> And lutes, and flutes, and the beating of drums.
> Their activities weaken those charged with managing affairs.[14]

Many of these allegations of corruption and disregard for shari'a law in the Hausa kingdoms are corroborated by testimony from other contemporary sources, as Hiskett has shown.[15] But even so, the early Caliphate leaders were more successful in pointing out these problems than they were in eradicating them. What was certainly the most important issue for the Shaikh and his immediate circle was not so much the prevalence of sinful behaviour but other kinds of acts that constituted 'unbelief', examples of which were polytheistic ritual practices or deliberate armed attacks on Muslims. These, too, proved to be a matter of scholarly dispute as can be seen in the surviving correspondence with Al-Kanemi.[16]

After the initial battles between 1804 and 1808 were over, the Shaikh set about organizing the institutional structure of a new government. Those Hausa kingdoms that had been defeated now became emirates, all joined together for the first time under a central administration headed by the office of Caliph.[17] In 1812, the Shaikh withdrew from political affairs in order to spend his time writing scholarly works and engaging in diplomatic correspondence, whereupon he divided the Caliphate into two parts that were to be administered by his brother, Abdullah, and his son,

---

[13] Mervyn Hiskett (trans.), '*Kitab al-farq*: A Work on the Habe [Hausa] Kingdoms attributed to Uthman dan Fodio', *Bulletin of the School of Oriental and African Studies* 23/3 (1960): p. 567.

[14] Mervyn Hiskett (trans.), *Tazyin al-waraqat* (Ibadan, Nigeria, 1963), pp. 121–2.

[15] Hiskett, '*Kitab al-farq*', pp. 572–9.

[16] Last and Al-Hajj, 'Attempts'.

[17] For the historical model he followed, see Hiskett, *Sword*, pp. 136–46.

Muhammad Bello. He himself died in 1817.[18] It was then left to his successors to carry on the work of renewing the faith and governing in accordance with shari'a law.

What they achieved, while falling short of the Shaikh's ambitious goals and ideals, was nevertheless of great consequence for the history of the region. They expanded the Caliphate beyond Hausaland and held it together for almost a century, which helped create and foster an economic expansion the likes of which had not been seen for several centuries. Agricultural output grew and contributed to the high volume of craft production and inter-regional trade that made the Caliphate so famous in the second half of the nineteenth century. Slaveholding also expanded, setting the stage for sharp criticisms by Christian missionaries after mid-century. At the same time there were advances in Quranic education within that new political territory, along with much scholarly writing and copying of manuscripts, not only in Arabic but also in the vernacular languages of Hausa and Fulfulde.[19]

It is within this ideological and economic context – the significance of dress to the ethos of the Shaikh and his community, and the period of prosperity ushered in by their government – that we may most profitably examine men's embroidered robes, which were among the most prominent textile products made in the Sokoto Caliphate. It has been stated very generally, based upon the Shaikh's written pronouncements, that vividly coloured clothing and elaborately embroidered garments would have been discouraged after the jihad, and that government officials, especially, would have preferred wearing plain white cotton cloth.[20] Whether or not this was so can only be ascertained by looking at what Muslim men actually wore, that is, by systematically documenting and analysing the material and visual features of nineteenth- and early twentieth-century robes.

Robes for Kings and Commoners

Tailored garments, especially embroidered robes, mattered a great deal to the founders and administrators of the Caliphate government. Following on the historical precedents set by the early Muslim caliphates,[21] they promoted textile

---

[18] Hiskett, *Sword*, pp. 110–15, 138–50; Last, *Sokoto Caliphate*, Chapter 3.

[19] Murray Last, 'The Sokoto Caliphate and Borno' in J.F. Ade Ajayi, *Africa in the Nineteenth Century until the 1880s* UNESCO General History of Africa series, Vol. VI. (Berkeley, 1989), pp. 555–99.

[20] Last, 'Sokoto', p. 579; David Heathcote, *The Arts of the Hausa* (Chicago, 1977), p. 17.

[21] R.B. Serjeant, *Islamic Textiles* (Beirut, 1972); Maurice Lombard, *Les Textiles dans le Monde Musulman* (Paris, 1978); Yedida Kalfon Stillman, *Arab Dress: A Short History, from the Dawn of Islam to Modern Times* (Leiden, 2000); Stewart Gordon (ed.), *Robes and Honor: The Medieval World of Investiture* (New York, 2001), especially Chapters 6, 8, 9, 12 and 17.

manufacture in general and also encouraged the production of a particular type of robe that came to signify the new regime. European explorers regularly commented on these characteristic 'tobes' or gowns which were commonly worn by the Caliphate's male elite.[22] What made these robes so recognizable were three consistent features that they shared: the specific patterns or colours of locally-woven cloth from which they were made (Appendix A); the particular cut and style of tailoring;[23] and the special design composition and stitching of the embroidery (Illustrations 7.1 and 7.2 below). Women's clothing, in contrast, was un-tailored, and their wardrobes consisted of rectangular textiles of various sizes that were wrapped around and draped over the body.

Men's robes and women's wrappers were both sometimes made with silk. Many types of fabrics were woven on Caliphate looms, with certain ones having been especially popular and well known by name. Appendix A lists the major textile products of the Caliphate. As well, this Appendix includes information about the type of garment for which each textile was customarily used, the gender of the wearer, and whether silk fibre was included in the fabric. Of the six fabrics used to create men's robes, three contained silk. In most cases the silk was in the form of discrete fibres rather than a single filament and therefore it had to be spun. *Tsamiya* [*sanyan* in Yoruba] was a beige and white cloth made with silk fibre that was gathered in the wild, processed, and spun locally from the cocoons of several moth species. *Sak'i*, or 'guinea fowl' cloth, was the fabric most closely identified with the garb of Caliphate officials and notables. A variant of it had a stripe of imported magenta or green silk in the warp. *Barage* was a red and white cloth, the 'red' referring to magenta silk fibre that was imported from North Africa.[24] Which came first, the local wild silk or the imports, is not known, but unspun silk fibre

---

[22] European accounts sometimes refer to them as 'tobes', an Anglicization of the Arabic word *thawb*, meaning a gown. Dixon Denham, Hugh Clapperton, and Walter Oudney, *Travels and Discoveries in Northern and Central Africa in 1822, 1823, and 1824* (4 vols, London, 1831), vol. 4, p. 146; William Allen and T.R.H. Thomson, *A Narrative of the Expedition to the River Niger* (2 vols, New York, 1967), vol. 1, p. 395; Heinrich Barth, *Travels and Discoveries in North and Central Africa* (3 vols, London, 1965), vol. 1, pp. 345, 512–13; Gustav Nachtigal, *Sahara and Sudan* (4 vols, London, 1980), vol. 2, pp. 181–3.

[23] The robe was characterized by a rectangular neckline, long body with large sleeves, and a single patch pocket over the chest. There were two main types: called *gare* in Hausa (*gari* in Nupe), with a single layer of cloth strips sewn edge to edge; and *girke* or *shaya* in Hausa (*giwa* or *tasi* in Nupe), which had a double thickness of fabric in the body of the garment. G.P. Bargery and D. Westermann, *A Hausa-English Dictionary and English-Hausa Vocabulary* (London, 1934), pp. 365, 390, 934; Brigitte Menzel, *Textilien aus Westafrika* (3 vols, Berlin, 1972–74), vol. 2, nos. 599, 600/601; A.W. Banfield, *Dictionary of the Nupe Language* (2 vols, Farnborough, UK, 1969), vol. 1, pp. 150–51.

[24] Called *alharini* in Hausa (from Arabic, *al-harir*), *alali* in Nupe, and *alari* in Yoruba. Silk imported from the coast was called *seda* in Yoruba (from Portuguese, *seda*). Bargery and Westermann, *Hausa-English*; Samuel Crowther, *A Grammar and Vocabulary of the Nupe Language* (London, 1864); S. Crowther, *A Vocabulary of the Yoruba Language* (London,

was being transported by caravan across the Sahara to Katsina and Borno from at least the late eighteenth century.[25]

A sample of 23 standard 'Caliphate robes' is listed in Appendix B. They are all now housed in museum collections, and were almost all acquired during the formal period of Caliphate rule between 1804 and 1903. Analyses of their features show no evidence of a strictly enforced code of dress or severe restrictions on silk. Cotton was certainly the most common textile fibre for men's robes overall, but silk was used in the weaving of certain fabrics, in the embroidery of robes and trousers, and in the weaving of border linings for robes. Even the plain white cotton robes [*fari* in Hausa, *dekun* in Nupe], which were the preferred form of dress for Quranic scholars and other pious believers, were embroidered in silk and lined with fabric containing stripes of brightly coloured imported silk. In total, 14 out of the 23 robes contained silk either in the fabric, embroidery, or border lining. Thus, material evidence challenges a simplistic understanding of clothing practices in this region and time period.

What is most striking about the robes is that there was such general visual uniformity and, at the same time, such variability in detail within this one single garment type. Individual robe specimens would appear to be very similar from a distance, yet they could differ markedly when the materials and quality of workmanship were viewed up close – and close attention to detail reveals critical features about the context and significance of these garments. Robes ranged from the simpler ones that were available for purchase in markets in and around the Caliphate to the most elaborate ones that circulated selectively as gifts or as 'robes of honour'.[26] Such a range in quality and in contexts of distribution and use makes it difficult therefore to fit this robe into one single overriding category of analysis: some examples served either as ceremonial or official dress while others were purchased to be worn as an item of male fashion; the robes likely signalled a common purpose through emulation or identification with the rulers and notables of the new regime. A comparison of two individual robes, which come from each end of the quality spectrum, will help to explain and illustrate this important point.

Of all the Caliphate robes I have seen, the finest example is housed in the ethnology collections of the British Museum (Illustration 7.1).[27] It was brought back to England in April of 1863 by Arthur P. Eardley Wilmot, Commander of the British naval ship *Rattlesnake*, who had just returned from a voyage to the

---

1852); T. J. Bowen, *Grammar and Dictionary of the Yoruba Language* (Washington, DC, 1858).

[25] *Proceedings of the Association for Promoting the Discovery of the Interior Parts of Africa* (London, 1967), vol. 1, pp. 172–3, 182–6; Marion Johnson, 'Calico Caravans: The Tripoli-Kano Trade after 1880', *Journal of African History*, 17/1 (1976): pp. 100–102.

[26] Kriger, 'Robes'. For definitions of the 'robe of honour' (*khil'a*), and the Sufi cloak or mantle (*khirka*), see *The Encyclopaedia of Islam* (12 vols, Leiden, 1986), vol. 5, pp. 6–7 and 17–19.

[27] Accession number 1920.2–11.1.

Illustration 7.1 Sokoto Caliphate robe with white silk embroidery on magenta silk narrow strip cloth (barage). White 'lining' on the inside of the robe can be seen through the neck opening. Collected by Wilmot in Dahomey Kingdom, 1862. Ethnology Department, British Museum, accession # 1920.2-11.1. Photograph by the author. Courtesy of the Trustees of the British Museum, UK

west coast of Africa. On an official visit to the King of Dahomey the previous December, Wilmot had been presented with this garment, clearly a Caliphate robe and not a product of the Dahomey kingdom.[28] Precisely how and when it had reached the king and his court is not clear, but neither is it surprising. Exceptional robes such as this one were not usually available for purchase but instead were awarded ceremonially as 'robes of honour' to designate special political or social relationships. They also accompanied messages and written correspondence; some might be taken as spoils of war.[29] Dahomey, as a slave-trading kingdom with a powerful army, was no stranger to war or to complex regional and international

---

[28] Log book, *HMS Rattlesnake*, 20 Aug. 1862–11 April 1863, ADM 53/8428, The National Archives, Kew, UK; and accession information, Ethnology, British Museum.

[29] Kriger, 'Robes'.

diplomatic relationships. And as was the case with other so-called 'pagan' states in West Africa that were incorporated into Muslim trading networks, the kingdom hosted resident Muslim communities as well as routine visits by travelling Muslim merchants and scholars. Hence this splendid robe could readily have made its way into the Dahomey capital during the early- to mid-nineteenth century, by any one of several possible avenues.[30]

This robe is visually and technically impressive in every respect. First, it is made of two versions of a type of narrowly woven strip cloth called *barage* [*baraze* in Nupe, *alari* in Yoruba], each one designed according to specifications in the tailoring. One version was specially made for the body of the garment: half of the strip was woven of vivid imported magenta silk with narrow stripes, the other half plain white silk. The other version was specially made for the sleeves and gussets: the strip was woven with two repeats of a striped pattern on a magenta silk ground. Both versions were skilfully woven using imported silk in the warp and a weft of indigo blue cotton that serves to deepen the luminous colour. Second, the cut of the robe follows the standard form, but the tailoring method is unusually elaborate. In constructing the robe's main body, the tailor overlapped the special half-magenta, half-white strips and sewed each strip's edge to the centre of the strip below it. This technique creates a brightly coloured striped magenta outer fabric and a solid white inner lining. In other words, the garment has a cleverly constructed and sturdy double thickness, matched by contrasting inner and outer colours. For the broad sleeves, the all-magenta strips were simply sewn together edge to edge to form a single thickness of fabric. Third, the embroiderer was a master. He composed the standard embroidery design in a particularly elegant manner and sewed the couching and eyelet stitches very densely and consistently. Finally, the robe has a band of bias silk lining at the hem, which was also woven with imported silk in the warp and indigo cotton in the weft. In all, the construction of this garment was planned out very thoughtfully, and then was skilfully worked at all stages, using costly materials and the most demanding, labour-intensive techniques.

The Wilmot robe represents the important multiple roles of these garments in government as official and honorific dress, as diplomatic symbol and as revenue. Robes were awarded, along with turbans, to office-holders and were given as special gifts to political allies, potential converts and foreign guests. Caliphate administrators made sure they had a steady supply of robes at their disposal by establishing textile workshops in Sokoto and encouraging the manufacture of textiles in the capitals of the major emirates. Administrative centres received thousands of robes as tribute payments and as the government's share of spoils of

---

[30] Mahdi Adamu, *The Hausa Factor in West African History* (Zaria, Nigeria, 1978), Chapter 5; Richard Burton, *A Mission to Gelele, King of Dahome* (New York, 1966), pp. 157, 159–60, 183. For an example of the complexity of Muslim communities in non-Muslim polities in West Africa, see Robert S. Kramer, 'Islam and Identity in the Kumase Zongo' in John Hunwick and Nancy Lawler (eds), *The Cloth of Many Colored Silks* (Evanston, IL, 1996), pp. 287–96.

war, while individual specimens came in as gifts from visitors or accompanying scholarly or diplomatic correspondence.[31] Moreover, the encouragement of robe production and distribution upheld the faith by supporting Quranic scholars and their students, many of whom engaged part-time in the work of tailoring and embroidering men's garments.[32]

Another robe, along with a batch of 102 embroidery fragments, was collected by the German ethnographer Frobenius in Bida in 1911, over 50 years after the Wilmot robe arrived in England and just eight years after Sokoto fell to the British. These textiles were all undoubtedly purchased in Bida's thriving and lamp-lit evening market, and together they present a dramatically different method of robe manufacture, one that is clearly commercial in orientation.[33] Frobenius's written account of his visit to Bida conveys, among other things, a sense of how industrious the townsfolk were and the complexity of labour divisions by occupation and by gender. He noted, for example, that in one section of the market an open square contained nothing but small embroideries – mostly rectangular pockets embellished with the standard robe designs. These were apparently the work of young boys who belonged to the upper strata of Nupe society. In another section of the market he saw stalls where master tailors sold embroidered robes, which continued to remain in steady demand during the colonial era. Frobenius also remarked on the acuity of consumer taste in textiles. Passersby engaged in intense and shrewd commentary on the quality of individual robes as potential customers inspected all aspects of the workmanship, even counting the number of cloth strips in the garments' construction.[34]

More complete and precise details about techniques, specialization and the production process can be gleaned from the visual features of the robe and embroidery fragments Frobenius brought back to Europe. The robe depicted in Illustration 7.2 is made of *sak'i* cloth [*zabo* in Nupe, *etu* in Yoruba, *tailelt* in Tamashek], otherwise known as 'guinea fowl' or 'pepper and salt', a patterned

---

[31] Last, *Sokoto Caliphate*, pp. 70, 105 n. 59; Denham et al., *Travels*, p. 146; Paul Staudinger, *In the Heart of the Hausa States* (2 vols, Athens, OH, 1990), vol. 1, p. 181; T.J. Hutchinson, *Narrative of the Niger, Tshadda, and Binue Expedition* (London, 1966), pp. 111, 164; Charles H. Robinson, *Hausaland: or, Fifteen Hundred Miles through the Central Soudan* (London, 1900), p. 105; Adamu Fika, *The Kano Civil War and British Over-rule, 1882–1940* (Ibadan, Nigeria, 1978), p. 63, Plate 1; Michael Mason, *Foundations of the Bida Kingdom* (Zaria, Nigeria, 1981), pp. 29, 44 n. 59; Siegfried Nadel, *A Black Byzantium* (London, 1942), p. 91 n. 1; Christraud Geary, *Images from Bamum* (Washington, DC, 1988), pp. 18–23.

[32] Kriger, 'Robes'; Nadel, *Black Byzantium*, p. 379; David Heathcote, 'A Hausa Embroiderer of Katsina', *Nigerian Field*, 37/3 (1972): pp. 123–31; D. Heathcote, 'Insight into a Creative Process: A Rare Collection of Embroidery Drawings from Kano', *Savanna*, 1/2 (December 1972): pp. 165–74.

[33] Accession numbers 15-26-56 through 15-26-157, Staatliches Museum für Völkerkunde, Munich, Germany.

[34] Leo Frobenius, *The Voice of Africa* (2 vols, London, 1913), vol. 2, pp. 411–20.

Illustration 7.2   Unfinished robe made of indigo and white cotton narrow strip cloth (sak'i or zabo). Embroidered in white cotton, with raw edges remaining at the hem. Collected by Frobenius in Bida, 1911. Staatliches Museum für Völkerkunde, Munich, accession # 15-26-56. Photograph by S. Autrum-Mulzer. Courtesy of the Staatliches Museum für Völkerkunde, Munich, Germany

fabric for which the Caliphate was especially renowned. The checkered pattern, of narrow indigo and white stripes in both the warp and the weft, creates a very delicate speckled effect which is likened to the feathers of the local guinea fowl, hence the name for the cloth in the Caliphate's major vernacular languages.[35] In this case, the robe is light in weight, having only a single thickness of narrow all-cotton strip cloth sewn edge to edge to make up the garment. The cut of the robe is standard, but the tailor left it unfinished, with raw edges remaining at the bottom of the arm openings and along the hem for later finishing, perhaps with silk lining fabric. The embroidery design, too, is standard, with some of the white cotton stitches done by hurried or less practised hands. As for the embroidery fragments, they appear to be intended for at least two different purposes. Some

---

[35]   Colleen Kriger, *Cloth in West African History* (Lanham, MD, 2006), pp. 85–92.

are embroidered pockets, finished and unfinished, that could potentially be sewn onto the body of a robe. Others, however, are irregular fragments. It is likely that these latter pieces were workshop models – remnants of old robes that could serve as guides for learning the correct layout and proportions of the composition. In any event, as a group the fragments indicate that *sak'i* and plain white *dekun* cloth were the fabrics most commonly used for making men's robes in Bida. They also suggest a division of labour in embroidery, with beginning students learning their trade on the motifs that were sewn with chain and eyelet stitches, and more highly skilled embroiderers specializing in the motifs that were sewn on later, with delicately patterned couching stitches.[36]

The Frobenius robe represents another important function of robes in the Caliphate economy: as an item of male fashion that was vital to domestic production and the export trade. Textile manufacture in general became a crucially important economic sector, linking the countryside to towns and cities. Wealthy officials, many of them having been granted tracts of land along with their positions, amassed large numbers of slaves to produce and harvest, among other things, cotton and indigo. Skilled workers – men and women, slave and free – spent much of the dry seasons cleaning cotton, spinning it into thread and weaving it into narrow strips of cloth. Dyeing, tailoring and embroidery were more often than not carried out in urban and village workshops. Expanding robe production spawned a regional trade in wild silk and a new skill for Quranic scholars – spinning silk embroidery thread.[37] Centres of large-scale textile production for export were concentrated in the emirates of Katsina, Kano and Zaria, and in the southern emirates of Bida and Ilorin. Finished and semi-finished cotton textiles and tailored garments were traded south to the coast, north across the Sahara and along the savanna belt eastward to Lake Chad and beyond and westward all the way to the Atlantic. In other words, the region's economic growth during the nineteenth century was fuelled in large part by the multiplier effects of agricultural and craft production, much of it directed at the manufacture and trade of textiles, including robes.[38]

When and where the first examples of this special type of Caliphate robe were made is not known, nor is it known whether these were generally available for

---

[36] Accession numbers 15-26-126, 15-26-129, and 15-26-130.

[37] Philip Shea, 'Kano and the Silk Trade', *Kano Studies*, n.s. 2/1 (1980): pp. 96–112; Douglas Ferguson (trans.), 'Nineteenth Century Hausaland being a description by Imam Imoru of the Land, Economy, and Society of his People' (Unpublished Ph.D. dissertation, University of California, Los Angeles, 1973), p. 304; in the Nupe language, *ku* = to spin or twist *alali*, '*bagi nana eku alali*' = 'this man is spinning red silk'. Banfield, *Nupe*, vol. 1.

[38] Colleen Kriger, 'Textile Production and Gender in the Sokoto Caliphate', *Journal of African History*, 34 (1993); Ann O'Hear, 'The Economic History of Ilorin in the 19th and 20th Centuries: The Rise and Decline of a Middleman Society' (Ph.D. dissertation, University of Birmingham, 1983), pp. 122–36; Philip Shea, 'Big is Sometimes Best: The Sokoto Caliphate and Economic Advantages of Size in the Textile Industry', *African Economic History* 34 (2006): pp. 5–21.

purchase from the beginning of the Caliphate. A British visitor to Sokoto in 1824 noted that robes made of *sak'i* cloth were being manufactured there and exported, but did not specify whether they were being sold or distributed officially or both. Later observers described robes of this type that were available in markets, and their prices ranged widely. In 1841, for example, modestly priced versions could be purchased for 7,000 cowries while others made of silk *barage* cloth could cost 200,000 cowries or more, that is, about 30 times as much.[39] Staudinger wrote that in 1886 the main clothing for men, rich or poor, was the long gown made of cloth strips. A white one made with cheap cloth went for 8,000 cowries, the dark indigo-blue *kore* robes sold at 15,000 to 60,000, while the 'guinea fowl' robe sold for 30,000 to 60,000 and more for very expensive ones. He considered fine white robes with red silk lining to be the most expensive ones, priced at 100,000 cowries, but he apparently did not observe any examples made with silk *barage* cloth.[40]

Not surprisingly, this range in price corresponded to the wide range in quality of the robes. My analyses of price factors for woven cloth indicated that the fineness of thread, density of the weave, depth of dye colour and the presence or absence of silk were important features affecting price, and that these qualities were clearly visible to discerning consumers.[41] In the simplest robes, ones that were sold in the market or exported in the caravan trade, the narrow strips of cloth were sewn edge to edge and the hem was left unfinished. More costly ones were finished with a silk border lining.[42] The embroidery, too, could vary from the simple to the elaborate. On simpler robes it was stitched in cotton, while the embroidery of the finest robes was stitched very densely and consistently, and entirely with silk. Master embroiderers sometimes monopolized the use of silk for sewing only certain motifs, leaving their students to sew the rest of them in cotton. In short, there were some versions of this robe that were affordable to a large cross-section of the male population while high prices kept other versions well out of their reach.

There were as well differing ways of seeing and understanding the robe's embroidered imagery. Nevertheless, its standard motifs, which were related to Quranic illumination and also to pan-Islamic talismans, would have been meaningful to a wide audience of literate, semi-literate, and non-literate viewers. Well-traveled literati would have seen similar imagery abroad in the greater Muslim world, where it was drawn, engraved and sewn on surfaces as a device

---

[39] Kriger, 'Robes', pp. 54–5, 85 n. 6. For cowries as money and for a discussion of inflation during the nineteenth century, see Jan Hogendorn and Marion Johnson, *The Shell Money of the Slave Trade* (Cambridge, 1986), Chapter 9.

[40] Staudinger, *Heart*, vol. 1, p. 181, vol. 2, pp. 201–2.

[41] Colleen Kriger, 'Textile Production in the Lower Niger Basin: New Evidence from the 1841 Niger Expedition Collection', *Textile History*, 21/1 (1990): pp. 31–56.

[42] In the Hausa language: *shafi* = lining to sleeve or shirt of a gown; *wa'ddare* = coloured lining of the bottom of a gown (Sokoto and Katsina). In the Nupe language: *egba* = border on a garment. Bargery and Westermann, *Hausa-English*; Banfield, *Nupe*, vol. 1.

for protection from malevolent spirits and misfortune.[43] Closer to home, some of these very same motifs – magic squares, knot forms, and interlaces – were drawn on the popular calligraphic amulets and charm gowns made by Quranic scholars in the Caliphate and in neighbouring kingdoms.[44] Even the uninitiated could not have failed to notice this special robe embroidery. Soldiers, renegade slave-raiders and tax collectors were among the men who wore these designs. Such embroidery was also worn by 'palace mallams' – the Muslim scholars who served as advisors to emirs and to 'pagan' kings and who performed prayers and divination rituals that influenced critical decisions of public policy, including the timing of military campaigns.[45] The embroidery conveyed to all a very powerful message, thus lending another very special and potent dimension to this particular robe's desirability (Illustration 7.3).

Caliphate robes developed a unique authority. Indeed, they became a widespread male fashion that lasted longer than the Caliphate itself. By the end of the nineteenth century, versions of these robes were being worn by men – Muslim and non-Muslim – beyond the Caliphate's borders in the forest kingdoms of Yorubaland and the Niger delta, in communities along the caravan routes to Asante, in Borno, and in many towns across the west African savanna and Sahel regions. European explorers, merchants, and missionaries wore them as well, commenting sometimes on how popular they were. The German geographer Heinrich Barth, for example, writing in 1851, described the famous 'guinea fowl' robe, adding that it had been his own preferred form of dress in his travels across West Africa. Gustav Nachtigal, too, adopted the local mode of male dress, choosing to wear the 'guinea fowl' robe during his diplomatic mission to Borno between 1870 and 1874. He considered it to be better adapted to the climate and added that it offered valuable social benefits as well – whenever he wore this robe he garnered more respect and trust from the general population.[46] A similar experience was recorded some years later in the early 1890s. A group of British missionaries living in Lokoja, at the southern edge of the Caliphate, adopted a policy of wearing these robes,

---

[43] Kriger, 'Robes'; Kriger, *Cloth*, Chapter 3.

[44] David Heathcote, 'A Hausa Charm Gown', *Man*, n.s. 9 (1974): pp. 620–24; Arnold Rubin, 'Layoyi: Some Hausa Calligraphic Charms', *African Arts*, 17/2 (1984): pp. 67–70, 91–2; Labelle Prussin, *Hatumere: Islamic Design in West Africa* (Berkeley, 1986), pp. 90–91; René Bravmann and Raymond Silverman, 'Painted Incantations: The Closeness of Allah and Kings in 19th-century Asante' in Enid Schildkrout (ed.), *The Golden Stool: Studies of the Asante Center and Periphery* (New York, 1987), pp. 93–108; René Bravmann, *African Islam* (Washington, DC, 1983), pp. 22–5.

[45] Adamu, *Hausa*, pp. 114–22, 130–34; Geary, *Images*, p. 23; Allen and Thomson, *Narrative*, vol. 1, p. 294; Ivor Wilks, 'The Position of Muslims in Metropolitan Ashanti in the early Nineteenth Century' in I.M. Lewis (ed.), *Islam in Tropical Africa* (Oxford, 1966), pp. 318–39.

[46] Barth, *Travels*, vol. 1, pp. 345, 512–13 and Berlin Museum für Völkerkunde accession number IIIC 15288; Nachtigal, *Sahara*, vol. 2, pp. 179–80, vol. 4, frontispiece.

Illustration 7.3   British missionaries G. Wilmot Brooke (left) and J.A. Robinson (right) wearing Sokoto Caliphate robes, which they called 'native dress' or 'Hausa dress', c. 1891. They were stationed at Lokoja, on the southern border of the Sokoto Caliphate. Source: C.H. Robinson 1900.

which they referred to more generically as 'native dress' (see above, Illustration 7.3). They concurred with Nachtigal's assessment of the robe's comfort and social advantages, claiming that by wearing the 'flowing garments of the Hausas [sic]' they were able to mix freely with all classes of the local people.[47] 'Guinea fowl' robes were also worn by European colonial officers in the early twentieth century, and were still being purchased by European travellers and ethnographers into the 1960s.[48]

Conclusion: Wearing Silk in the Sokoto Caliphate

Evidence from actual specimens of Caliphate robes complicates the question of silk and its legality, thus shedding new light on Shaikh Uthman dan Fodio's condemnation of silk as sinful for men. His strongly argued pronouncement is

---

[47]   J.A. Robinson, 'Sudan and Upper Niger Mission', *The Church Missionary Intelligencer*, (February 1891): p. 111; C.H. Robinson, *Hausaland*, p. 90 and frontispiece.

[48]   Adam Mischlich, *Über die Kulturen im Mittel-Sudan* (Berlin, 1942), frontispiece and pp. 115–16; Menzel, *Textilien*, Vol. II, nos. 629/30.

directly contradicted by the discovery that Muslim scholars in the Caliphate worked with silk and often wore it. Perhaps the paradox can be reconciled by appreciating that the text written in the early years of the jihad and the Shaikh's uncharacteristically harsh tone of that era were the products of a particular and passing historical moment. It might be more appropriate to interpret the Shaikh's pronouncement as a reflection of the specific time of urgency in which it was written, that is, during the jihad and all the horrors, human losses and upheavals that it unleashed. His intended audiences – the literate elites – were among those commanders and soldiers who were seizing as spoils of war the rich wardrobes and opulent trappings of the Hausa kings. He was moved to write at this time in order to instruct his followers in the recommended ways of government and the correct handling of property.[49]

However, Shaikh Uthman dan Fodio's judgement on the 'problem of silk' was most assuredly not an attempt to enforce strict orthodoxy regarding men's dress in the Sokoto Caliphate. On the contrary, for the combined evidence suggests that a relatively tolerant attitude toward such matters prevailed during the Caliphate's century of existence. Clothing, along with horses and riding equipment, served as indicators of status and wealth for the male elite, with some office-holders amassing very large wardrobes. One official in Kano, for example, left behind an estate that included 53 robes and gowns of various colours made with either silk or cotton fabrics, locally-made and imported.[50] Trusted slaves and poor men could acquire fine garments as gifts, or they could purchase a less expensive robe or pair of trousers in the market. In short, men across the social spectrum were not prohibited from wearing silk and were not confined to wearing plain white garments, but could display their taste and status through their chosen apparel.

My sample of robes represents official attitudes toward dress in the Caliphate much more fully than do the didactic writings of the jihad's leaders. Moreover, the standard features of the robes show clearly that silk was not forbidden to Muslim men. Stunning 'robes of honour' such as the Wilmot robe were made of fabric containing colourful imported silk and were elaborately embroidered with lustrous silk thread. They and similar but less costly robes were integrated into the workings of government, formally bestowed as rewards for service and as diplomatic gifts. Of the many robes that administrators welcomed into their treasuries, it was this garment type in particular that had been singled out for favour. It was a robe worn regularly by Caliphate elites, and it was replicated in tailoring and embroidery workshops across the land. But it was not reserved for official circles alone. This special robe came to signify the Caliphate administration, its notables, and its economic successes throughout much of West Africa. More and more men chose to

---

[49] Masri, *Bayan*, pp. 13–28.

[50] The estate also included skeins of silk thread, presumably for embroidery. Mervyn Hiskett (trans.), 'Materials relating to the cowrie currency of the western Sudan – I: A late nineteenth-century schedule of inheritance from Kano', *Bulletin of the School of Oriental and African Studies*, 29/1 (1966): pp. 122–42.

wear it as merchants and messengers carried versions of it across political, language and religious boundaries. This robe became emblematic of the Caliphate.

If there were any scholarly disputes over proper Muslim dress that persisted, they were not a deterrent to the manufacture of embroidered robes made with silk. Quranic scholars were certainly not averse to wearing them – silk was oftentimes noticeably present in the elegant and vividly coloured linings of their white cotton robes. And they, the most highly respected members of the Caliphate's male elite, were themselves largely responsible for the silk content of men's garments. Expansion of Quranic teaching in the Caliphate meant, ironically, an expansion in silk production, since scholars worked with silk in a number of ways. As tailors, they might commission or choose a fabric with silk for piecing together the robes and their linings. And Muslim traders supplied them with local and imported silk which they spun into thread for embroidery. This thread, in turn, was transformed by scholars into hand sewn talismanic imagery. Then, by organizing tailoring and embroidery workshops in their Quranic schools, they trained their students to be the next generation of skilled tailors and embroiderers. Scholars thus ensured that there would be silk in the finest and most prominent Caliphate robes, even beyond their own lifetimes.

Appendix A: Major Textile Products, Sokoto Caliphate

Name	Robe	Wrapper	Veil	Male	Female	Silk*
Barage	X	X		X	X	X
Tsamiya	X	X		X	X	X
Sak'i/zabo	X	X		X	X	X
Kore	X	X		X	X	
Fari/dekun	X	X		X	X	
Gwanda	X			X		
Turkudi			X	X		
Jimada		X			X	X
Keke		X			X	
Ridi		X			X	X
Zalwami		X			X	X
Bununuwa		X			X	
Godo		X			X	
Shata		X			X	

* Silk fiber included in the woven textile.
Names in bold are cloth types used for making the standard 'Caliphate robe'

Appendix B: The Standard 'Caliphate Robe'

Date Collected	Cloth Type	Cloth Fibre	Embroidery Fibre	Border Lining	Source/Accession
1841	kore	C	?	none	BM 43.3-11.53
1841	tsamiya	C/S	C/S	none	BM 43.3-11.22
1841	fari/dekun	C	C/S	yes, C/S	WF 1.xii.1856
1850?	sak'i	C	n.a.	yes, n.a.	L/H: p.70, fig.94
1851?	sak'i	C	C/S	none	B IIIC 15288
1862	barage	C/S	S	yes, C/S	BM 1920.2-11.1
1863	sak'i	C	C	none	NMS 1878.1.2
1880?	sak'i	C	C/S	yes, S	MT R85.1291
1880?	barage	C/S	C	yes, C/S	MT R85.1290
1890	sak'i	C	C	none	B IIIC 5058
1890?	sak'i	C	C/S	none	BM 1934.3-7.215
1897	fari/dekun?	C?	C/S	yes, C/S?	B XI/1897
1900	import(white)	C	W	yes, importC	B XI/1900
1900	fari/dekun	C	C	none	B IIIC 41026
1900	fari/dekun	C	C/S?	yes, C/S?	B IIIC 41027
1900	tsamiya?	C/S?	C/S	yes, C/S?	B no # (II, 627)
1900	sak'i	C	C/S	none	B IIIC 41025
1903	barage	C/S	C	yes, C	NMS 1903.354
1903	fari/dekun	C	C/S	yes, C?	L 5.10.1906.2
1903	sak'i	C	C	none	L 5.10.1906.1a
1903	import(white)	C	C?	yes, C?	L 5.10.1906.3a
1911	sak'i	C	C?	none	M 15-26-56
1929	zaboyeko	C	C/S	yes, C?S	ROM 950.126.2

Key: (B) Museum für Völkerkunde, Berlin; (BM) British Museum, London; (L) Liverpool Museum; (L/H) Lamb and Holmes, image of robe in Pitt-Rivers Museum, Oxford, reproduced without accession number in V. Lamb and J. Holmes, *Nigerian Weaving*; (M) Staatliches Museum für Völkerkunde, Munich; (MT) Textile Museum of Canada, Toronto; (NMS) National Museum of Scotland, Edinburgh; (ROM) Royal Ontario Museum, Toronto; (WF) Wisbech and Fenland Museum, Wisbech, UK. Berlin robe with no number is published in Brigette Menzel, *Textilien aus Westafrika*, vol. 2 (3 vols, Berlin, 1972-4), #627.

PART THREE
Fashion Strategies, Global Practice

Chapter Eight
Designing, Producing and Enacting Nationalisms: Contemporary Amerindian Fashions in Canada[1]

Cory Willmott

Today, generations after the adoption of European styles, Amerindian people's everyday clothing is almost indistinguishable from that of other residents of North America. Until recently their culturally distinct clothing has been mainly reserved for ceremonial occasions such as powwows and religious rituals. This bifurcation of clothing styles and contexts parallels the dichotomy between 'traditional' and 'assimilated' Native identity that has been imposed by the dominant society. The dichotomy is a double bind: adopting 'traditional' identities, Native peoples are cast into a static ahistorical frame, while appearing 'assimilated' erases cultural distinctiveness.[2] In both cases, Native peoples cannot effectively stake claims to a place in contemporary society. Whereas Jennifer Kramer and Rosemary Coombe advocate 'double-voiced rhetoric', that is, 'oscillation between opposing cultures and systems',[3] I suggest that First Nations contemporary fashion designers have integrated the opposing identity poles in new clothing styles for everyday

---

[1] I am grateful for the support of the Social Science and Humanities Research Council of Canada for funding for three main periods of fieldwork for this research: 1998–2000, William Taylor Doctoral Fellowship; 2001–2002, Postdoctoral Fellowship; and 2003–2004, with Dr Raymond Wiest for Project 4 of the MRA project, Community Economic Development in the New Economy, headed by John Loxley. I am thankful to Zeek Cywink and Jessie Silverstein who contributed original artwork for this chapter, as well as Temperance McDonald who conducted interviews during the MRA phase of the research. Thanks also to the fashion designers and others who kindly participated in interviews, as well as the Victoria & Albert Museum, the Minnesota Historical Society and the National Archives and Records Administration who gave permission to reproduce visual images.

[2] Cory Silverstein-Willmott, 'Men or Monkeys?: The Politics of Clothing and Land within Ontario First Nations, 1830–1900', in Jill Oakes (ed.), *Native Voices in Research* (Winnipeg, MB, 2003), pp. 127–40.

[3] Jennifer Kramer, *Switchbacks: Art, Ownership, and Nuxalk National Identity* (Vancouver and Toronto, 2006), pp. 119–20; Rosemary Coombe, 'The Properties of Culture and the Possession of Identity: Postcolonial Struggle and the Legal Imagination', in Bruce Ziff and Pratima V. Rao (eds), *Borrowed Power: Essays on Cultural Appropriation* (New Brunswick, NJ, 1997), p. 91.

wear that simultaneously combine 'traditional' and 'contemporary' elements. The strategies they use to create this new integrated Aboriginal identity subvert colonial oppression through nation-building initiatives that contribute significantly to fluid and multi-levelled constructions of intertribal Native nationhood. To demonstrate this thesis, I will survey nation-building projects among established nation-states, and show how these historical processes are strikingly similar to the social movement among urban North American Native peoples from the 1960s to the 1970s. I will then demonstrate how contemporary Native Canadian fashion designers use strategies that both materialize and enact intertribal nationhood in the realms of design, production and cultural performance.

Nations and Nation-building Processes

As Benedict Anderson points out, Western concepts and manifestations of nationhood are historically contingent: 'nationality, ... nation-ness, as well as nationalism, are cultural artefacts of a particular kind'[4] that came into being towards the end of the eighteenth century. Anderson further notes that 'the nation' is 'an imagined political community' that is imagined as 'both limited and sovereign'.[5] Whereas Anderson identified the crucial role of mass media in the formation of nations, Orvar Löfgren conceives the role of cultural phenomena on a much broader basis. In contrast to the 'traditional patriotism linking the sovereign to his people', the new 'idea of the nation ... proceeded from the belief that the boundaries of the political state should coincide with a national culture'. Löfgren observes that the idea of the nation is 'an international ideology that is imported for national ends', which provides 'fixed ideas about what a national cultural heritage should include'. Hence, nations 'amass a symbolic capital of myths, heroes, occasions of national destiny and pomp, and develop patterns for national iconography and aesthetics'. Clothing was an important component of these international 'building instructions'. For example, all over Europe, Löfgren observes, the 'dress of the peasantry was synthesized into national costume and displayed at folk dance performances, which became an important way to stage national distinctiveness and cohesion'.[6] Patricia Williams observed a similar phenomenon with regard to peasant dress in Norway, as did Ruta Saliklis for Lithuania.[7]

---

[4] Benedict Anderson, *Imagined Communities: Reflections on the Origin and Spread of Nationalism* (London, 1991), p. 4.

[5] Anderson, *Imagined Communities*, pp. 6–7.

[6] Orvar Löfgren, 'Materializing the Nation in Sweden and America', *Ethnos*, 58/3–4 (1993): pp. 162–3.

[7] Patricia Williams, 'From Folk to Fashion: Dress Adaptations of Norwegian Immigrant Women in the Midwest', in Patricia Cunningham and Susan Voso Lab (eds), *Dress in American Culture* (Bowling Green OH, 1993), pp. 95–108; Ruta Saliklis, 'The Dynamic Relationship Between Lithuanian National Costumes and Folk Dress', in Linda

At the same time, certain cultural forms of nation-ness are so entirely integrated into daily life that they appear self-evident until a national border crossing confronts one with different everyday forms and practices. Löfgren observes that a 'prominent feature of the international paradigm' is that the existence of nations depends on their mutual recognition. Not only are there losers in this 'identity game', specifically the ethnic groups that are not recognized as nations, but there is also a hierarchy among the recognized nations. Nations are in a competitive relationship that was formally enacted through international expositions, but has now turned mainly to international sports events.[8]

Löfgren's analysis of the historical construction of modern nation-states makes clear the difficulties confronting communities that 'imagine' alternative constructions of nationhood, particularly among would-be nations that lack recognition of political sovereignty. According to Partha Chatterjee, 'anticolonial nationalists rose to this challenge in Asia and Africa by 'dividing the world of social institutions and practices into two domains – the material and the spiritual', in which the former represents outer/colonial and the latter inner/native. In this way, 'anticolonial nationalism creates its own domain of sovereignty within colonial society well before it begins its political battle with the imperial power'. The nationalist project within the inner domain, however, is not to create a 'traditional' native 'self' in contrast to the modern colonial 'other', but rather to 'fashion a modern national culture that is nevertheless not Western'.[9] Historically, Chatterjee argues, this project took place in India in the realms of language, drama performances, art, education and the family, all of which are facets of what cultural anthropologists would call 'culture'.[10] Chatterjee's analysis of anti-colonial national projects demonstrates the crucial role of culture in the creation of national identities prior to political sovereignty. His discussion is confined, however, to the histories of postcolonial states that have, in fact, now achieved international recognition as sovereign nation-states.

The term 'cultural nationalism' is often applied in situations where national identities are imagined by communities that have all the features of the international standards for nationhood except political sovereignty. Ireland is a classic case of this scenario where national dress was also a prominent feature of the nineteenth-century Irish nationalist cultural revival movement.[11] 'Cultural nationalism' is

---

Welters (ed.), *Folk Dress in Europe and Anatolia: Beliefs about Protection and Fertility* (Oxford, 1999), pp. 106–7.

[8] Löfgren, 'Materializing the Nation in Sweden and America', pp. 166, 168–70, 189–90.

[9] Partha Chatterjee, *The Nation and its Fragments: Colonial and Postcolonial Histories* (Princeton, 1993), p. 6.

[10] Chatterjee, *Nation and its Fragments*, pp. 7–9.

[11] Hilary O'Kelly, 'Reconstructing Irishness: Dress in the Celtic Revival, 1880–1920', in Juliet Ash and Elizabeth Wilson (eds), *Chic Thrills: A Fashion Reader* (London, 1992), pp. 75–83.

a misleading term if we accept Anderson's argument that nationhood itself is a 'cultural artefact' and, following Löfgren and Chatterjee, that the mobilization of cultural forms and practices is indispensable to successful nation building. From this point of view, the term 'cultural nationalism' reinforces the illusion that internationally recognized nations are 'natural', as if they did not also depend on cultural forms for their creation and maintenance. Whereas deep, subconscious cultural processes thereby undermine the legitimacy of politically dominated, but geographically bounded, nations, more severe challenges confront groups that lack both political sovereignty and geographical territories. The question then becomes: is it possible to imagine nationhood without either of these key factors in the international paradigm?

In response to this challenge, Renato Rosaldo argues for a redefinition of nationhood premised on the concept of 'cultural citizenship', which emphasizes 'local, informal notions of membership, entitlements and influence', as well as 'vernacular definitions of community, identity, and human dignity, particularly those of subordinate groups'. Rosaldo's strategy circumvents the international conventions for 'nationhood' and shifts attention instead to indigenous constructions of 'Native nationhood'.[12] Building upon my work on Anishnaabe narrative and social structure, I can illustrate this concept for Algonquian-speaking Native nations in the Great Lakes region throughout the period of contact with colonial powers. At time of first contact, these Native nations were neither dynasties nor nation-states. Their borders and boundaries were not determined, demarcated or enforced by central governments and armies. Rather their membership was determined by kinship, while their boundaries were enforced by customary practices such as the Calumet Ceremony and small-scale warfare.[13] Most groups had both hereditary and acquired leadership roles, but in either case leadership depended upon personal powers of persuasion rather than authority deriving from the position.[14] These nations were made up of a number of kin groups that shared cultural traits such as language, dress, religion and oral traditions. The kin groups

---

[12] Renato Rosaldo, 'Social Justice and the Crisis of National Communities', in Francis Parker, Peter Hulme and Margaret Iverson (eds), *Colonial Discourse/Postcolonial Theory* (Manchester, 1994), pp. 243–4, 251.

[13] Cory Silverstein, '"That's just the kind of thing this lake does": Anishnaabe reflections on knowledge, experience and the power of words', in David Pentland (ed.), *Papers of the 28th Algonquian Conference* (Winnipeg, MB, 1998); 'Clothed Encounters: The Power of Dress in Relations between Anishnaabe and British Peoples in the Great Lakes Region, 1760–2000' (Unpublished PhD Dissertation, McMaster University, 2000); Cory Silverstein and Zeek Cywink, 'From Fireside to TV Screen: Self-Determination and Anishnaabe Storytelling Traditions', *Canadian Journal of Native Studies*, 20/1 (2000): pp. 35–66.

[14] Cory Willmott and Kevin Brownlee, 'Dressing for the Homeward Journey: Western Anishnaabe Leadership Roles Viewed Through Two Nineteenth-Century Burials', in Laura Peers and Carolyn Podruchny (eds), *Gathering Places: Essays on Aboriginal Histories* (Vancouver, BC, 2010), pp. 58–61.

were allied through marriage and trade. Their socio-economic bonds were renewed annually at shared religious and political ceremonies. Kinship and alliance were the two most significant determinants of group boundaries and identities. They were the root principles that bonded larger groups together, and hence, informed concepts of 'nationhood'.[15]

Similar in its fluidity to pre-nineteenth century constructions of Native nationhood, those promoted by contemporary Native fashion designers may be seen in the light of an intertribal nation composed of several levels of allied groups. The members of this 'imagined community' share a vision of the structure of borders that are conceptually firm and clear even though they may be blurred and dynamic in social practice. During my seven years of embedded participation in the Native community of Toronto and Southern Ontario (1993–2000), I developed the understanding that the borders of the intertribal nation do not correspond to precise geographic territories. This is in contrast to the unequivocally geographical orientation of individual First Nations or American Indian tribal land claims, and in spite of the profound consequences the geographic boundary imposed by the colonial nation-states has had upon Aboriginal nations that were divided arbitrarily down the centre. Rather, one might imagine the intertribal nation's 'territory' as a cosmological map that is oriented to the four cardinal directions. But it also employs shifting variables of race, ethnicity, cultural competency and social action as determinants of boundaries. This intertribal nation tends towards inclusiveness more so than the legal definitions of the Canadian Indian Act or the constitutions of American tribes.

Direct expressions of intertribal nationhood based on principles of cultural/ spiritual solidarity are found in the histories of twentieth century urban Native communities. For example, Adam (Nordwall) Fortunate Eagle describes the 'new Indian clubs' in the San Francisco Bay Area during the 1950s: 'Some of them, such as the Sioux Club and the Navajo Club, were formed around tribal identities, others, such as the Four Winds Club, focused on social objectives.' In 1961, an umbrella organization was founded, called the United Bay Area Council of American Indian Affairs, Inc. The United Council, as it was called for short, was 'an Indian mini-version of the United Nations'.[16] The events surrounding the United Council's 1969 occupation of Alcatraz Island were directly related to the founding of the American Indian Movement, or AIM, which brought the new urban political consciousness 'back home' to the American reservations. In Canada, the cultural and intertribal aspects of American Indian activism helped fuse the ideas of 'Native Art', 'high art' and Canadian national identity in the Indians of Canada

---

[15] Heidi Bohaker, 'Nindoodemag: The Significance of Algonquian Kinship Networks in the Eastern Great Lakes Region, 1600–1701', *William and Mary Quarterly*, 3rd Series, 63/1 (2006): pp. 25–52.

[16] Adam (Nordwall) Fortunate Eagle, 'Urban Indians and the Occupation of Alcatraz Island', in Troy Johnson, Joane Nagel and Duane Champaigne (eds), *American Indian Activism: Alcatraz to the Longest Walk* (Chicago, 1997), pp. 54–5.

Pavilion at Expo 67.[17] For both sides of the border, this political movement rested on the principle, identified by Chatterjee, in which would-be nations established sovereignty in an inner/spiritual realm that was sharply contrasted to the outer/material realm of the colonizers. As in Chatterjee's examples, 'the spiritual' consisted of things that were culturally distinctive, yet were adapted, revised or reinvented to suit modern urban life. This cultural movement consisted of a 'supratribal popular culture in areas such as music, films, dress and jewelry, and crafts' whose message urged 'intertribal unity' and 'adherence to spiritual values and cultural traditions'.[18]

Scholars usually apply the term 'Pan-Indianism' to the distinctive values, social conventions and cultural expressions of urban Native communities. As 'Pan-Indianism' developed, common history, culture and concerns began to determine membership more than tribal affiliation as increasing numbers of second and third generation urban Natives made up its membership.[19] Reminiscent of Rosaldo's interpretation of 'cultural citizenship', Susan Lobo suggests that urban Indian community boundaries are determined by 'strongly situational and to some degree negotiable criteria', in particular: ancestry, appearance, cultural knowledge and Indian community participation. These criteria, she elaborates, are 'perhaps reflecting a reality closer to that of Native homelands prior to the imposition of reservation borders'.[20] In the history of the urban Indian political mobilization we see the adoption of certain aspects of the 'international blueprint', including an organizational structure that demands nation-to-nation negotiation and the development of a distinctive intertribal national culture. The fact that historically colonial nation states once recognized and dealt with Native nations as 'nations' forms the basis of a unique conception of intertribal nationhood today. In the remaining sections I will illustrate how contemporary Native fashion designers manipulate the cultural symbols of intertribal nationhood through the realms of design, production and cultural performance.

Designing Nationalisms

The individuals included in the term 'contemporary Native Canadian fashion designers' are entrepreneurial small business owners whose main product lines

---

[17] Karen Duffek, 'Northwest Coast Indian Art from 1950 to the Present', in *Shadows of the Sun: Perspectives on Contemporary Native Art* (Ottawa, 1993), p. 221.

[18] Joane Nagel, *American Indian Ethnic Renewal: Red Power and the Resurgence of Identity and Culture* (New York, 1996), p. 203.

[19] Terry Straus and Debra Valentino, 'Retribalization in Urban Indian Communities', in Susan Lobo and Kurt Peters (eds), *American Indians and the Urban Experience* (Walnut Creek, CA, 2001), p. 89.

[20] Susan Lobo, 'Is Urban a Person or a Place?: Characteristics of Urban Indian Country', in Susan Loba and Kurt Peters (eds), *American Indians and the Urban Experience* (Walnut Creek, CA, 2001), p. 81.

are non-ceremonial clothing and accessories. Although they may design some ceremonial regalia, their main focus is on 'everyday wear', by which I mean all categories of dress that are not intended specifically for ethnic events such as powwows and/or religious ceremonies – from T-shirts to evening gowns. I include small-scale designers who have local businesses based on made to order one-of-a-kind pieces through large-scale ones who have both high and low end lines that ship nationally and internationally. I also consider fashion show producers and production managers who have contributed to the contemporary First Nations fashion movement.

One of Native fashion designers' main objectives is to use mainstream fashion styles to create culturally distinct clothing. As Navajo journalist Linda Martin explains, they attempt to 'balance innovative adaptations and clothing heritage preservation'.[21] Similarly, Haida designer Dorothy Grant's vision is to: 'Merge art with fashion and forge a link between ancient heritage and modern society.'[22] Native designers use two main design strategies to achieve this goal. Most commonly, they apply easily recognized 'Indian' motifs on garments made in mainstream silhouettes and styles. Alternatively, they create garments in mainstream silhouettes and styles using materials associated with 'Indianness', such as blankets, fur, deerhide, hair pipe beads, animal teeth, silver conches, ribbons or shells.

With regard to the first strategy, First Nations designers whose design strategies draw heavily upon aesthetic traditions tend to frame their work within the category of 'wearable art'. Under the mentorship of a long lineage of esteemed Northwest Coast artists, as well as her former husband, Haida artist Robert Davidson, Dorothy Grant was one of the first Native Canadian designers to incorporate 'formline' motifs into contemporary fashion. Beginning in the 1980s, prestigious museums such as the Canadian Museum of Civilization, the National Museum of Natural History, the de Young Art Museum and others have collected her pieces.[23] There are now over a dozen Northwest Coast fashion designers who apply 'formline' motifs to evening wear, outerwear and sportswear. Ron Everett Green, for example, explains that he wants to teach people about his Tsimshiam heritage by 'pushing the boundaries' and 'making new and innovative ways to show heritage, not just the Melton wool coats'. Rather, he wants to 'show it in a contemporary way' for an international audience and clientele. He has incorporated 'formline' designs into satin and velvet evening ensembles (Illustration 8.1). He has also used an airbrush technique to apply Native themed motifs to his 'day wear, casual fun wear, and funky little tops'. Most recently he applied both 'formline' and feather motifs to

---

[21] Linda Martin, 'Navajo Style: Fashions for all Seasons', *Native Peoples Magazine*, 13/4 (2000): p. 31.

[22] Dorothy Grant Website, 'The Company' page: http://www.dorothygrant.com/content.cfm?cmd=Company, accessed 17 April 2001.

[23] Dorothy Grant Website, 'Fashion Designer – Dorothy Grant', article by Vesta Giles in *Indian Artist*, Fall 1997, reproduced with permission at: http://www.dorothygrant.com/content.dfm?cmd=HaidaArt&ID=12, accessed 17 April 2001.

Illustration 8.1   Ron Everett Green's formline motifs on evening ensemble worn by Amerindian professional model at Aboriginal Voices Festival in Toronto, 1999 (Photo by Cory Willmott)

micro-suede evening gowns and tailored winter coats.[24] Concerning the second strategy, those First Nations designers and/or companies whose work focuses more on indigenous materials tend to orient their marketing towards ecological lifestyles. D'Arcy Moses and Dene Fur Clouds are good examples of this strategy. Moses designs coats of wild fur and the latter specializes in contemporary uses of fur, most particularly, beaver fur strips knit into mittens, scarves, vests and hats (Illustration 8.2). The Dene Fur Clouds 'design team has drawn inspiration and materials from habitat and history in the design and making of their line of sustainable urban accessories for people and homes'.[25]

Both of these design strategies blend global modernity with timeless indigenous tradition. Remarkably, this is exactly the same formula that characterizes the nation-

---

[24]   Ronald Everett interviews with Temperance McDonald, 30 May (informal) and 22 June 2004 (taped). Ronald Everett Design website, 'Gowns in Micro Suede' page: http://ronaldeverettdesign.com/PhotoAlbums/-album_1216076720/, accessed 26 November 2008.

[25]   Dene Fur Clouds website, http://www.ek-o.net/ accessed 25 May 2009.

Illustration 8.2   Tammy Beauvais, Dene Fur Clouds and D'Arcy Moses designs at Fashion-Nation, international annual trade show at Toronto, 2004 (Photo by and courtesy of Jessie Silverstein)

building projects of recognized nation-states.[26] Under the influence of evolutionism, however, different rules applied to 'folk art' and 'primitive art'. Where the latter was concerned, scholars and the public alike previously regarded such 'mixing of genres' as indicative of aesthetic degeneracy or cultural contamination.[27] Postmodernists, however, have embraced cultural mixture, a phenomenon that is intimately connected to the burgeoning interest in globalization and diasporas. Hence, a series of descriptive explanatory concepts have arisen, which include 'syncretism', 'bricolage', 'creolization', 'conflation',[28] 'transculturation'[29] and

---

[26]   Chatterjee *The Nation and its Fragments*, p. 6; Löfgren, 'Materializing the Nation in Sweden and America', p. 169.

[27]   Deborah Kapchan and Pauline Turner Strong, 'Theorizing the Hybrid', *Journal of American Folklore*, 112/ 445 (1999): pp. 140–41, 149; Ruth Phillips, *Trading Identities: The Souvenir in Native North American Art from the Northwest, 1700–1900* (Seattle and London, 1998), pp. 18, 163–7.

[28]   Kapchan and Strong, 'Theorizing the Hybrid', pp. 240–41, 249.

[29]   Phillips, *Trading Identities*, p. 16; Wolfgang Welsch, 'Transculturality: The Puzzlin Form of Cultures Today', in Mike Featherstone and Scott Lash (eds), *Spaces of Culture: City, Nation, World* (London, 1999), pp. 194–213.

'hybridity'. This last concept has become so ubiquitous that it appears to offer a self-evident and 'natural' explanation.

All of these concepts celebrate the emergence of 'the new' and the 'transcendence of boundaries'.[30] They also share, however, a spurious 'background of authenticity' that assumes original discrete units that join together to create new forms.[31] Another problem with an analytic approach that ends with the blurring of genres and a homogeneous 'new' form is that it focuses on the genealogy of the object or cultural form, as if objects had reproductive powers of their own. In fact, scholars formerly referred to such objects as 'promiscuous'. The main problem with these explanatory models, however, is that they actually serve to 'reinforce the notion of static and unequal set of power relations' that such objects embody.[32] Instead of reproducing these biologically-based metaphors of object evolution, scholars should examine the history of the social movement of which a cultural form is a part, and/or the biographies of its producers.

Clothing, in particular, is always about identity. I agree with Jonathan Friedman that hybridity is 'only significant where it is practiced as a self-identification'. When we reframe the question to focus on peoples' identities, it appears that hybridity is especially the identity project of diasporic 'cosmopolitan elites'.[33] Native peoples have suffered successive waves of diasporic experiences, the most recent of which was the mass migrations to cities that began in the late 1950s, a process that has continued ever since. I previously mentioned that the project of intertribal nationhood developed in the crucible of urban Native communities. One might therefore suppose that the projects of intertribal nationhood and diasporic nationhood are similar. As James Clifford astutely points out, however, in contrast with diasporic discourse, the claims of indigenous peoples

> challenge the hegemony of the modern nation-state in a different way. Tribal or Fourth World assertions of sovereignty and 'first-nationhood' do not feature histories of travel and settlement, though these may be part of the indigenous historical experience. They stress continuity of habitation, aboriginality, and often a 'natural' connection to the land.[34]

---

[30] Kapchan and Strong 'Theorizing the Hybrid', p. 242; Jonathan Friedman, 'The Hybridization of Roots and the Abhorrence of the Bush', in Mike Featherstone and Scott Lash (eds), *Spaces of Culture: City, Nation, World* (London, Sage, 1999), p. 247.

[31] Friedman, 'Hybridization of Roots', p. 237.

[32] Avtar Brah and Annie E. Coombes, 'Introduction: the Conundrum of "Mixing"', in Avtar Brah and Annie Coombes (eds), *Hybridity and its Discontents: Politics, Science and Culture* (London and New York, Routledge, 2000), p. 12.

[33] Friedman, 'Hybridization of Roots', p. 252.

[34] James Clifford, *Routes: Travel and Translation in the Late Twentieth Century* (Cambridge, MA, 1997), p. 252.

The reclamation of 'traditional' clothing was a feature of the urban Native political movement from its inception. Anny Hubbard told me that AIM members organized the first powwow that she attended in Sault St. Marie, Michigan. Although they did not have regalia at that first event, subsequently they were 'really working hard on [their] outfits'. Taking elements from pageant regalia and 'historical stuff', a 'contemporary traditional' style emerged. As Anny put it: 'Oh man, it was seventies!'[35] This style was politically significant because it holistically integrated the old and the new, as well as the 'ethnic' and the 'mainstream', and thereby transcended the dichotomy between the modernity of 'world fashion' everyday wear and 'past-oriented' 'ethnic' ceremonial dress that characterizes the historical experience of most ethnic groups.[36]

I suggest that the 'ethnification' of the national dress styles of minority peoples is one way that their subordinate status is maintained. As I mentioned earlier, often nation-states appropriate these styles for the purpose of creating and maintaining *their* national identities. The particular design strategy of using Native national symbols with mainstream fashion styles for everyday wear is no exception to this historical trend. It was first developed and promoted by American and Canadian fashion designers, textile manufacturers, anthropologists and government officials. Despite diverging interests between these disparate groups, their common purpose was to create distinctly North American fashions. These fashions were symbols of Canadian and American nationalism, made to be worn by North Americans and tourists. In the United States, for example, during the first few decades of the twentieth century the Pendleton Blanket Company bought Navajo blanket designs from Southwestern trading companies and developed a product line that included fashionable women's coats.[37] During World War I, severance of trade with Paris stimulated efforts to promote culturally distinct American fashions. This trend produced many Pendleton imitators, such as those produced by Powers Fashions in 1925 (Illustration 8.3).

In the late 1930s under President Roosevelt's administration, Rene D'Harnoncourt was hired to develop markets for Native arts and crafts. His idea was to create high-end markets by changing the image of crafts to fine arts, and retaining their 'exotic' character while simultaneously re-contextualizing them in modern consumer settings. For the influential exhibition he produced at the Museum of Modern Art in 1940, D'Harnoncourt provided fashion designer Fred Picard with 'articles of Indian manufacture' that he used in his line of women's

---

[35] Anny Hubbard taped interview with Cory Willmott, 14 December 1999.

[36] Joanne Eicher and Barbara Sumberg, 'World Fashion, Ethnic, and National Dress', in Joanne Eicher (ed.), *Dress and Ethnicity: Change Across Space and Time* (Oxford, 1995), pp. 300–302.

[37] Kathy M'Closkey, 'Marketing Multiple Myths: The Hidden History of Navajo Weaving', *Journal of the Southwest*, 36/3 (1994): pp. 202–3.

Illustration 8.3　　Flapper Southwestern Blanket Coats by Powers Fashions of Minneapolis, 1925 (Courtesy of Minnesota Historical Society, Loc# GT1.4i r8 Neg# 8463-A)

wear[38] (Illustration 8.4). Anthropologist Fred Douglas used Native women's ensembles from the Denver Art Museum in a *haute couture* fashion show that was produced from 1942 to 1972, and even appeared on TV. Imitations were soon available in major department stores across America.[39] While American nationalist initiatives such as Pendleton, D'Harnoncourt and Douglas succeeded in creating mainstream markets for Native-inspired fashions, they did not link these markets to Native producers. That was not their intent.

Native fashion designers view this 'borrowing' of cultural symbols by and for the colonizers as a form of appropriation. This legacy has in large part provided the

---

[38]　W. Jackson Rushing, 'Marketing the Affinity of the Primitive and the Modern: René D'Harnoncourt and "Indian Art of the United States"', in Janet Berlo (ed.), *The Early Years of Native North American Art History* (Vancouver, 1992), p. 215.

[39]　Nancy J. Parezo, 'The Indian Fashion Show', in Ruth Phillips and Christopher Steiner (eds), *Unpacking Culture: Art and Commodity in Colonial and Postcolonial Worlds* (Berkeley, 1999), pp. 258–9.

Illustration 8.4   Fred Picard dress at Museum of Modern Art show in New York City, 1940: Creating a high end fashion market (Courtesy of National Archives and Records Administration, Photo # 75-CL-1R-3)

nation-building context in which Native fashion designers from different Native nations bond together to form an intertribal unity. Very often, they express this unity by using style genres whose markets were previously created and monopolized by non-Natives. Literally dozens of Native designers from all parts of North America design outerwear using Southwestern themes, including Pendleton blankets. For example, Northwest Coast designer Shannon Kilroy and Mohawk designer Sandra Jean Lazore showed vests and coats made from Pendleton blankets at the Canadian Aboriginal Festival fashion shows in 1998 and 2000, respectively. The widespread use of the Southwestern blanket theme gives form to intertribal nationhood. In order to redefine Native identity, and to encompass both Native and non-Native markets, contemporary Native fashion must convey messages that are in some respects different for the two groups, yet at the same time reasonably coherent to both. Perhaps ironically, easily recognized symbols of 'Indianness', even stereotypical symbols, seem to be the most effective for these purposes.

   Outside the intertribal nation, the merging of cultural symbols and markets tends to blur the boundary between Native and non-Native cultures and nations, in part because clothing messages are seldom if ever perfectly coherent across cultures. To achieve economic and representational control, however, it is necessary for Native designers to maintain the distinction between themselves and the non-Native producers who presently enjoy the bulk of the market for contemporary Native fashions. For example, two different applications of Plains-style hair pipe bead decorations illustrate differences between appropriation, on the one hand, and intertribal nationalism on the other. In 1992, the London-based Turkish designer, Rifat Ozbek, produced an ensemble inspired by the movie 'Dances With Wolves', displayed in the Victoria and Albert Museum, London, in 2001 (Illustration 8.5).

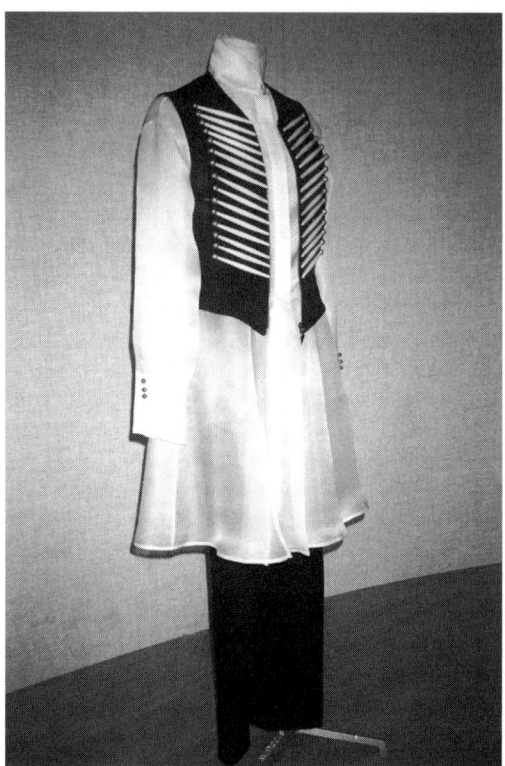

Illustration 8.5   Design by Rifat Ozbek, Spring/Summer 1992, on display at Victoria and Albert Museum in London, UK, 2001 (Photo by Cory Willmott; courtesy of Victoria and Albert Museum, Catalogue # T.99 to 101–2001).

Dave Jones of Garden River, Ontario, the founder of Turtle Concepts Inc., designed a set of tuxedo vests for the fashion finale at the Native Music Awards held at Toronto's Canadian Aboriginal Festival in 1999 (Illustration 8.6). Jones uses fashion as a means through which to build self-esteem and self-presentation skills among Native youth. These models are among the many graduates of his six-week

Illustration 8.6   Turtle Concepts tuxedo vests modelled by Amerindian youths at Canadian Aboriginal Festival (CANAB) at Toronto, 1999 (Photo by Cory Willmott)

'Self-Improvement Course (S.I.C.)'. They wear the tuxedo vests to convey Turtle Concepts' message, 'Its O.K. to feel good about yourself'.

Like the Southwestern blankets, Plains-style hair pipe beads embody a unified intertribal identity. Angela Gonzales, a Hopi sociologist, similarly remarks that as 'both an identity and a culture', the pan-Indianism that characterizes most urban Native communities 'draws heavily from popular images and traditions of Plains Indians, namely the Lakota (Sioux). Such ethnic markers are normative, ahistorical and often based on stereotypes.'[40] It would be virtually impossible to determine the racial affiliations of these garments if the Ozbek and Jones vests were placed side by side in a department store. Although they may look alike, there are major differences in their meanings and values that arise from the contexts of the museum mannequin versus the Native models. The issue of appropriation hinges on the criteria of proximity to, and control by, Native peoples in the processes of design, production and distribution, as well as the enactment of identity through ownership and display. Appropriation is not simply a good versus bad racial dichotomy, however. Like Ozbek's forerunners in mainstream fashion discussed above, the 'Dances

---

[40] Angela Gonzales, 'Urban (Trans)Formations: Changes in Meaning and Use of American Indian Identity', in Susan Lobo and Kurt Peters (eds), *American Indians and the Urban Experience* (Walnut Creek, CA, 2001), p. 177.

with Wolves' couture outfit may function to create and/or maintain a niche market demand for ethnic styles. In turn, this consumer demand enables Amerindian designers to counter appropriate the salient symbols of the genre to profitable and political effect.

Whereas American and Canadian nation-building projects strove to modernize Native fashion for the modern North American consumer, the intertribal nation-building project of contemporary Native fashion designers strives to 'indigenize' the modern for both Native *and* non-Native consumers. For Native consumers, their objective is to claim a specifically Native modernity. For non-Native consumers, their aim is to reclaim the market and the power of representation from non-Native producers. In order to claim a new Native modernity, contemporary Native designers must counteract the stereotypes that 'Indianness' entails static traditionalism and chronic poverty. Rather, many Native designers insist that 'Indianness' is contemporary, professional and high class, and therefore partakes of all the privileges of twenty-first-century civilization. This fashion statement empowers Native people to be current, successful and glamorous without sacrificing cultural identity. Significantly, it also enables and encourages them to wear culturally distinct styles for everyday wear which, as Aaron Glass points out, become 'indexical vehicle(s) for relations of belonging and affiliation ... the objective basis for claims about personhood and kinship'.[41]

Despite the apparent 'mixing of genres', contemporary Native fashion designers express an unequivocally First Nations identity, one that is self-consciously contemporary and forward-looking. Simultaneously, however, this vision enables 'Indian fashion' to be stylish and appealing for non-Native consumers because it allows them to be 'exotic' without sacrificing privileges. Moreover, this design strategy stimulates both Native and non-Native markets. The foregoing examples demonstrate that design alone is not sufficient to mark the distinction between appropriation and intertribal nationalism. Rather, the critical factor is that of proximity to Native people, in terms of both economic production and cultural enactments.

Economic Nationalism

One of the international standards for nationhood is that nations produce commodities that are marketable to other nations. Contemporary Native fashion designers employ a number of strategies that approximate the economic nationalisms of established nation-states, even though, or perhaps because, the intertribal nation does not have the sort of borders over which imports and exports can be monitored. As I mentioned, the issue of who makes the blanket coat, or the hair pipe beaded vest, is a critical component of Native fashion designers' desire

---

[41] Aaron Glass, 'Crests on Cotton: "Souvenir" T-Shirts and the Materiality of Remembrance among the Kwakwaka'wakw of British Columbia', *Museum Anthropology*, 31/1 (2008): p. 3.

to reclaim economic control and monetary gain from colonial and Third World usurpers. Many designers choose to produce one-of-a-kind originals, or made-to-order custom work, in order to keep all aspects of production within their own hands (often literally). Sue Smoke, for example, told me that she only does one-of-a-kind garments. Although she said she would like eventually to mass produce 'smaller end items like vests', she is apprehensive: 'I think that's where you get into problems with mass production and things being shipped everywhere ... and then having them take those apart, make the patterns, and then mass produce them ... And that's why I didn't go into that, even off the internet.'[42]

In contrast to 'indie' Native designers like Smoke, Dinawo was a Native owned-and-operated business that mass-produced a product line of active wear aimed at a Native youth market. Dinawo combined cultural representation and economic nationalism in strategies designed to improve self-esteem among Native youth while at the same time creating employment for Native people, and reclaiming the Native market from labels such as Nike, Hilfiger and Adidas. In 1999, the company's former General Manager, Shelley Burnham, explained: '[Dinawo's founders] wanted to create a label that would not only be cool, but give First Nations kids a meaning ... that would motivate them in a positive way to believe and achieve in their goals.' Additionally, Dinawo aimed to employ all Native people at their plant at Six Nations of Grand River in Ohsweken Ontario (just south of Toronto): 'That would fulfil the whole Dinawo dream, not only to be giving back to the community by sending out a really strong message but also building the base up as far as jobs and employment.'[43]

Dinawo's dream, as well as their fashions, fit well with Dave Jones' Turtle Concepts Inc. which takes a holistic approach to economic nationalism by working with Native youth to develop the human resource potential of the intertribal nation.[44] Turtle Concepts youth at the 1999 Canadian Aboriginal Festival in Toronto performed a 'Health and Fitness' skit wearing active wear separates designed and distributed by Dinawo. The company also launched a widespread publicity campaign involving high profile Native performers and athletes. The Dinawo dream was not realized, however. Despite professional finance management advice, the high costs of production and transportation proved prohibitive and Burnham moved on to other entrepreneurial initiatives.[45]

On the West Coast, Pam Baker has been more successful integrating design, production, and training First Nations youth, while using fashion shows to promote self-esteem. Her renovated loft includes not only a design studio and production factory, but also a fashion school. She initiated the 'Self-Esteem One' programme for youth, and has organized tours to Los Angeles and China for up-and-coming Native entrepreneurs to gain first-hand experience in the fashion world and to

---

[42] Sue Smoke taped interview with Cory Willmott, 15 July 2001.
[43] Shelley Burnham taped interview with Cory Willmott, 15 December 1999.
[44] Dave Jones taped interview with Cory Willmott, 6 December 1999.
[45] Anonymous interviews with Cory Willmott, 26 November 2008.

make connections for sourcing fashion materials.⁴⁶ Her business and training programmes have operated successfully for over a decade. Although she aspires to employ mainly Native people in her production process, in 2004 she hired a highly qualified Korean production manager and resorted to outsourcing much of her production due to time constraints in making up orders.⁴⁷

As the retail industry is reorganizing towards consolidation of retail and production in large multinational companies, and small niche market entrepreneurial boutiques, it will become more and more difficult for mid-sized companies such as Baker's TOC/Touch of Culture Legends to find markets. This will put increasing pressure upon First Nations entrepreneurs to turn towards fast and inexpensive production, principles that work against their ability to create sustainable and equitable jobs within their communities. Like clothing manufacturers in all segments of Canadian society, First Nations designers must often rely upon government subsidies to start and/or continue operating their businesses.⁴⁸ Yet, First Nations fashion is a category that often slips through the cracks of government granting agencies. As Pam Baker explained: 'For Native designers one of the main obstacles is getting money from Arts Canada or the Canada Arts Council. They don't look at our work as art.'⁴⁹ Conversely, fashion projects are rarely considered for economic development funding, which tends to support local service industries, and/or modern industrial initiatives. For example, case studies considered for the comprehensive 1993 Royal Commission on Aboriginal Peoples Report included forestry, a mechanical testing company, a hunters and trappers income security programme, a chocolate product line, a local daycare, pizza parlour and pub, hair salon, banking, and an industrial park that housed production of heating and cooling aids.⁵⁰ Fashion initiatives escaped their attention.

The Arctic Co-operatives are in some respects an exception to these trends, probably due to the importance of fur harvesting to their local economy. In 1995, Dene designer D'Arcy Moses enjoyed a stellar career with Natural Furs International based in New York and Montreal.⁵¹ Representatives of the territorial government invited him to Northwest Territories to lead workshops with local artisans that year. Connecting with his heritage for the first time, he decided to stay

---

⁴⁶ Jamie Monastyrski, 'Pam Baker: High End Fashion', *Aboriginal Voices*, 6/1 (1999): p. 18; TOC Legends: Touch of Culture, http://www.toclegends.com/enter/ accessed 25 May 2009.

⁴⁷ Pam Baker taped interview with Temperance McDonald, 27 May 2004.

⁴⁸ Raymond Wiest and Cory Willmott, 'Aboriginal Labour and the Garment Industry in Winnipeg', in John Loxley, Jim Silver and Kathleen Sexsmith (eds), *Doing Community Economic Development* (Winnipeg MB and Black Point NS, 2007), pp. 142–55.

⁴⁹ Pam Baker taped interview with Temperance McDonald, 27 May 2004.

⁵⁰ Royal Commission on Aboriginal Peoples (RCAP). *Sharing the Harvest: The Road to Self-Reliance. Report of the Round Table on Aboriginal Economic Development and Resources* (Ottawa, 1993), p. 268.

⁵¹ Millie Knapp, 'D'Arcy Moses: Ready-to-Wear', *Aboriginal Voices*, 3/1 (1995): p. 15.

and has been there ever since.⁵² Setting up shop in Fort Simpson, Moses designed for Genuine MacKenzie Valley Furs (GMVF), sponsored by the Northwest Territories Development Corporation (NTDC), to promote international sales for locally harvested wild furs.⁵³ Simultaneously, he trained and hired local Dene in production and marketing so that by 1998 he employed seven full time and three part time in-house workers, as well as 25–30 piecework sewers. He is also contracting with the Winnipeg-based union shop, Midwest Garment Apparel (MWG), for production and marketing of his Natsenelu sportswear line, which has sold to retailers such as Orvis Limited, Marks Work Warehouse and others. Moses also mentors another NTDC sponsored fashion company, Dene Fur Clouds, which employs five full-time and five part-time local Dene employees.⁵⁴

Like all companies in the garment industry in Canada, First Nations designers are experiencing varying degrees of financial distress, which makes it difficult to meet their ideals of creating jobs in the garment industry. However, a significant number of these entrepreneurs have endured throughout the decade of my study (1998–2008). Designers such as Dorothy Grant and D'Arcy Moses had already achieved significant success in the 1990s and they continue to expand and gain in prominence in the 2000s. Likewise Pamela Baker, Ronald Everett and Dene Fur Clouds, not previously well known, are now achieving national and international recognition. Economic viability is crucial to the success of these designers' intertribal nation-building process. Sustained public exposure will help ensure the transformation of social categories and cultural values that the identity project entails.

Enacting Nationalisms

Enactment and exposure imply performance and audience. Because proximity to Native actors is crucial to the distinction between intertribal nationhood and appropriation, I consider only those performance events in which there is significant Native participation in production, fashion design or modelling. A Native audience is an important but insufficient component of the nation-building process. On the one hand, it is obvious that Native audiences to non-Native productions, designs and models will not fulfil the objectives of intertribal nationhood. On the other

---

⁵² CBC Radio North Website, 'Home Again in Fashion', by Alison Dempster: http://north.cbc.ca/north/archive/-fur/simpfur.htm, accessed 17 April 2004.

⁵³ Fred Koe interview with Cory Willmott, 7 May 2001.

⁵⁴ NWT Assembly Proceedings Website: Friday, 4 December 1998: http://www.assembly.gov.nt.ca/_live/-documents/documentManagerUpload/Hn981204.pdf, accessed 27 November 2008; Turtle Island News Archives: 'D'Arcy Moses': http://www.assembly.gov.nt.ca/_live/documents/documentManagerUpload/Hn981204.pdf, accessed 8 October 2005; Northern News Services Ltd. Website, 'Fur Clouds Makes a Comeback': http://www.nnsl.com/-frames/newspapers/2001-11/nov19_01fur.html, accessed 3 July 2005.

hand, returning to Löfgren's observation that the existence of nations depends on their mutual recognition, it also becomes obvious that the performance of the new culturally distinct modern identity must be recognized by other nation-states in the international structure.[55] Therefore contemporary Native Canadian fashion designers must penetrate the world of mainstream fashion in order to achieve this recognition, not simply as token representatives of Canadian nationalism, but as representatives of a self-defined collective identity. Overcoming tokenism requires unification on the intertribal level in order to reach the critical mass necessary to make an effective statement.

Fashion shows are one of the most dramatic contexts for the enactment of intertribal nationhood envisioned by contemporary Native fashion designers. Fashion shows play powerful political roles. Yet, as with production costs, getting a foothold in this domain has depended on government sponsorships. Although government-produced initiatives often took the competitive form of the international paradigm for nationhood, conformity to these conventions was not necessarily a bad thing for the intertribal nation-building project. For example, in 1993 the Canadian government sponsored the gala 'Winds of Change' fashion show in which Aboriginal designers competed against one another for prizes. Dorothy Grant won the prize for the best fashion designer in Canada, which included a trip to Paris where her work was showcased at the Canadian embassy.[56] In this international venue, the symbols of 'Indianness' on Grant's designs served to embody nationhood at the levels of the nation-state, the intertribal nation and the Haida nation. This example illustrates how the multivalency of contemporary Native fashion design contributes to its power to manifest cultural sovereignty, if not political recognition. As long as 'Indian' symbols on Western-styled garments remain associated with their Native creators, they are capable of simultaneously personifying Native and non-Native national identities. As well, non-Native consumers contribute to the economic independence of the intertribal nation.

Within the intertribal nation, however, contemporary Native fashion designers stress co-operation rather than competition. When asked why she works hard to build alliances among designers, designer and fashion show producer, Sue Smoke explained: 'It's just like our sweetgrass. They say that one blade is easily broken but when braided together there is a lot of strength and it cannot be broken. And that's what I feel when I work with all these other designers.'[57] Lacking substantial resources, often without any financial backing, Aboriginal producers of fashion shows must rely on the collaborative effort of all participants: designers, models, stylists, technicians, dressers and others who help produce a show. Likewise,

---

[55] Löfgren, 'Materializing the Nation in Sweden and America', p. 166.

[56] Dorothy Grant Website, 'Fashion Designer – Dorothy Grant', article by Vesta Giles in *Indian Artist*, Fall (1997), reproduced with permission at: http://www.dorothygrant.com/content.dfm?cmd=HaidaArt&ID=12, accessed 17 April 2001.

[57] Video recording of fashion show at Toronto International Powwow (CANAB) by Zeek Cywink, 21 November 1998.

because most individual designers lack widespread brand recognition, they multiply their audience by billing under a group identity. Famous First Nations designers lend their brand name to such events to promote the aims of the contemporary Native fashion movement as a whole. They thereby broaden recognition among non-Native audiences and validate modern identities within Native communities, breaking down dichotomies of colonial oppression such as: urban/rural, lower/upper class, traditional/contemporary and material/spiritual.

The function of fashion shows – to validate these new roles, promote social cohesion and raise community esteem – is particularly apparent where local youth model the fashions or where the proceeds are donated to local Native charities. In 1999, one such small-scale fashion show at the First Nations School of Toronto featured grade school and high school models wearing designs by Dinawo, M.J. Helmer, Barbara Owl, and other First Nations designers, as well as those by Linda Lundstrom.[58] The latter is a Canadian designer who has lived and worked in the Canadian north, loans clothes for local fashion shows, hires First Nations artists to design motifs and donates her high end duffel coats to Native community fundraising events. The Home and School Liaison Coordinator who organized this show explained the inspiration behind the show was to 'give the kids an opportunity to raise self-esteem and build confidence about themselves through getting up in front of a crowd, and through the role model mentorship of the older kids involved in the show'.[59] The event opened with an elder offering a traditional prayer. It also included a traditional feast featuring corn soup, bannock, deer meat, wild rice casserole and berry desserts. The audience consisted almost exclusively of parents and relatives of the youth in the show: members of the Toronto Native community. The occasion served to validate the ties between old and new traditions, as well as between elders and youth in the community.

On a much broader scale, the Canadian Aboriginal Festival (CANAB) held annually at the Rogers Center in Toronto since 1993 is one of the most influential promoters of contemporary First Nations fashion. This festival and powwow, which draws both Native and non-Native crowds from Canada and the United States, has featured a fashion design component since 1995. Dave Jones of Turtle Concepts Inc. has produced these events for the last decade, using graduates of his 'Self Improvement Course' (SIC) as models. These 'Turtles' are ordinary First Nations youths whom Jones and his team of SIC graduates have trained to employ fashion as a means to raise self-esteem, improve social skills and make positive lifestyle choices. They also create personal identities that bridge traditional and contemporary paradigms.[60] Since 2001, Jones and his 'Turtles' have also produced a show for the annual Canadian Aboriginal Music Awards (CAMA), a similarly

---

[58] First Nations School of Toronto, 31 March 1999: 'Fashion/Talent Show', video recording by Zeek Cywink and Cory Willmott.

[59] Anonymous interview with Cory Willmott, 27 March 1999.

[60] Dave Jones taped interviews with Cory Willmott, 6 December 1999 and 30 August 2001.

large-scale event at the same venue. The history of CANAB tells a story about the effectiveness of fashion as a medium of identity transformation. The earliest fashion shows were tucked into make-shift plastic tents in the back corners of the stadium, while the 2008 CANAB Festival includes not only a significant role in the CAMA award extravaganza, but also a 'fashion alley' for designers' booths, graphic marketing of their products, and six high profile fashion shows over the three day festival period.[61] The growing role of the fashion shows in the largest national Aboriginal gathering in Canada suggests that the fashion designers' message of 'contemporary' intertribal national identity in everyday life is finding a place side-by-side with the celebration of 'traditional' ethnic identity embodied in the ceremonial powwow regalia.

The nation-building potential of fashion shows is most effectively realized when the venue is manipulated to strengthen group identity. For example, at the CANAB fashion show in 2000, the stage was adorned with banners in the four sacred colours (yellow, red, black, white), which in essence created an intertribal nationalist space. For the finale of the show, the models, who were all members of the 'Turtle team', were each introduced individually. With the exception of those wearing Turtle Concepts gowns, they all wore jackets with the Turtle Concepts logo on the back. This performance thereby enacted the principle of nationhood based on unity in diversity. Moreover, the 'Turtle team' is suggestive of a kin group. Dave Jones's own *doodem* [clan] is the Loon, but his Anishnaabe name is *Mishiikenh*, a kind of snapping turtle.[62] Although it was not his conscious intention to create a sort of extended kinship network among his students, he is pleased that his 'Turtles' share a strong sense of belonging. Just as historically clan members helped each other even if they were strangers, Turtles do the same when they are travelling in each other's territories, or when they meet each other at schools away from home. Jones complains that it is hard to maintain this community across the wide distances that separate the Turtles, but, he jokes, 'Thank god for the internet!'[63]

If there are challenges to be overcome gaining recognition within the intertribal Native community, the same may be said of national and international audiences, but for different reasons. Although designers such as D'Arcy Moses and Dorothy Grant have individually participated in mainstream fashion shows among internationally prominent designers, occasions for making a collective statement on the mainstream international fashion stage have been rare. One such opportunity occurred during Toronto's 2004 Fashion Week, which included a highly visible and well promoted show devoted entirely to contemporary Native

---

[61] Canadian Aboriginal Festival Website, 'Designer Package': http://www.canab.com/pdfs/fashion/2008/-designer_package2008.pdf, and Turtle Concepts: http://www.turtleconcepts.com/UploadedFiles/File/-2008_designer_package_for_website.pdf, accessed 26 November 2008.

[62] Dave Jones taped interview with Cory Willmott, 30 August 2001.

[63] Dave Jones taped interview with Cory Willmott, 30 August 2001. See Turtle Concepts' website: http://www.turtleconcepts.com.

Canadian designers. 'Fashion-Nation', as the show was called, included Pam Baker, Ronald Everett, D'Arcy Moses, Tammy Beauvais, Dene Fur Clouds and Angela DeMontigne (Illustration 8.2). The nationalism function of these 'fashion weeks', staged annually in different cities around the world, can be seen in Vittorio Missoni's statement about his role as sponsor for the event: 'I'll be a good ambassador for' Canadian designers in the international fashion world. Of Fashion-Nation he said, 'I think the idea of these young Canadian designers was great, to use their origins and translate it into the fashion world'.[64] Missoni, the leader of a world-renowned Italian fashion house, appears to understand and play his role in recognizing the distinctive identity of the First Nations' designers among the Canadian designers. Yet, within Canada the deeply embedded stereotypes of 'Indianness' make it difficult to walk the fine line between racial stereotyping and recognizable symbols of cultural identity. For example, one probably well-intended reporter evoked racial stereotyping in her 'praise' of the show: 'Given the rich history of handicraft in this country's aboriginal culture, its no wonder that some of the details in the Fashion-Nation show were also standouts.'[65] The problem with this statement is that the observer 'sees' only the surface detail that conveys the ethnic identity, without 'seeing' the whole composition of its integration with contemporary fashion. It is only the complete picture, or total clothed appearance, that embodies the identity of intertribal nationhood.

Conclusion

As with all would-be nations, the 'bottom line' will ultimately be economic viability. This may depend upon the designers' success at translating the complex world of fashion into a contemporary First Nations identity that resonates with the imagined nation's citizens' everyday lives, with lifestyles ranging from backwoods bush life to cocktail parties with international celebrities. Whereas individual designers and companies come and go, First Nations designers' contribution to the intertribal nationalist movement continues to grow and gather strength, ensuring that their messages win a foothold in society at large.

Contemporary Native fashion designers are continually navigating paths and negotiating borders between multiple constructs of nationhood. Their cultural productions engage significantly with both Native and non-Native nations and cultures. They use design strategies that embody intertribal nationhood to accomplish their fundamental goals of gaining control over representation and economies. The enactment of nationhood through fashion shows and Native

---

[64] Fashion-Nation, http://www.canada.com/topics/lifestyle/fashionweek/story html?id=b42e0e6b-5513-47e5-8786-46af39cddc40&k=47127, accessed 25 May 2009.

[65] Deborah Fulsang, 'Star Power on the Catwalk', *Globe and Mail*, 3 April 2004: http://www.globeandmail.com/-servlet/ArticleNews/TPPrint/LAC/20040403/CATWALK03/TPEntertainment, accessed 5 April 2004.

peoples' everyday wear achieves a political unity and economic strength that bolsters their collective position in relation to non-Native competitors. It does so by creating and validating a contemporary Native identity that transcends the oppressive binary opposition between 'traditional' and 'assimilated'. In a broader context, the counter appropriation of high fashion and active wear from the non-Native producers, for Native everyday wear, reflects and influences the growing political power of Native peoples more generally. In this way, contemporary Native fashion designers' enactment of intertribal nationhood ultimately serves the critical political interests of tribal nations and local Native communities.

Chapter Nine

Reclaiming Materials and Fashion-Work in the Urban Philippines[1]

B. Lynne Milgram

In 1996, Patricia Manolo,[2] a 32-year-old agricultural worker and seamstress, moved with her husband and three children from Benguet province, northern Philippines to an inner-city Manila community in order to find more secure employment. Drawing on her sewing skills and on her network of relatives who had migrated to Manila a few years earlier, Patricia obtained employment in a small workshop manufacturing children's clothing. Paid on a piecework basis, Patricia earned an average daily income of 150 pesos ($US 3.00).[3] In 2003, to increase her earnings and gain access to social support services, Patricia joined the Artisan Multipurpose Cooperative (AMC), a producer collective in her community that manufactures a range of carrying bags made from recycled plastic juice drink containers – materials that organization members collect locally. Patricia's first job was to sort the used containers by colour and quality as they arrived at the cooperative. After attending training sessions on AMC manufacturing processes generally, Patricia started a new job distributing to sewers the specific materials they require, such as recycled juice containers, thread, fabric or zippers, to manufacture AMC products. To earn additional income, Patricia has the option to work overtime sewing bags that clients have ordered.

---

[1] Field research for this paper has been conducted in the Philippines over several periods from 1998 to 2008. Financial support was provided by the Social Sciences and Humanities Research Council of Canada (SSHRC) through a Post-doctoral fellowship (1997–99) and Standard Research Grants (2000–2003; 2004–2007; 2008–11) and by the Ontario College of Art & Design, Faculty Research Grants. In the Philippines I am affiliated with the Cordillera Studies Center, University of the Philippines Baguio, Baguio City. I thank my colleagues at CSC for their generous support of my research. The members of this cooperative organization generously and repeatedly gave their time to answer my questions and I thank them for their efforts to facilitate my research. I also thank the volume editor, Beverly Lemire, and the anonymous reviewers for their thoughtful comments on earlier versions of this chapter.

[2] All personal names of individuals are pseudonyms including the name of the cooperative, the Artisan Multipurpose Cooperative (AMC).

[3] I use the average rate of exchange of $US 1.00 = 50 Philippine pesos.

As a work-option to the farm and factory, artisan trades, such as Patricia Manolo's work in the Artisan Multipurpose Cooperative, have increased worldwide, and most prominently, in those countries that have embraced pro-market reforms such as the Philippines. In the late 1990s, to explore the parameters of such informal sector artisanal work, I conducted research on microfinance development programmes and women's weaving cooperatives in the northern Philippines.[4] In this earlier research, as in my current engagement with the AMC, my conversations with artisans highlight the extent to which women can access new work opportunities and negotiate constraints across production spheres within a cooperative framework. While most women, such as Patricia Manolo, report that they benefit from working in such collectives as a result of fair wages, regular employment or skills training, others outline the challenges they continue to confront balancing work with domestic responsibilities or gaining access to, and training in, leadership roles. Female artisans, in particular, have increasingly looked to collective production as the Philippine government's structural adjustment policies have brought few work options to rural and urban household-based producers, generally.[5] Excluded from development decisions that affect their lives and looking to participate in global markets more on their own terms, artisans have thus carved innovative arenas of work while simultaneously negotiating the challenges to their small-scale engagements.

To understand the dynamics of female artisans' collective work in fashion-based production, I focus here on the Artisan Multipurpose Cooperative (AMC) – an inner-city Manila enterprise whose operations, like those of artisan collectives worldwide, seek to design distinctive goods that can resonate with shifting global tastes while achieving sustainable livelihoods for members.[6] Specifically, I explore the channels through which AMC producers navigate the cooperative alternative to affect the very globalized circuits that have reconfigured the networks on which they once relied.

---

[4] B. Lynne Milgram, 'Reorganizing Production for Global Markets: Women and Craft Cooperatives in Ifugao, Upland Philippines', in Kimberly M. Grimes and B. Lynne Milgram (eds), *Artisans and Cooperatives: Developing Alternative Trade for the Global Economy* (Tuscon, AZ, 2000), pp. 107–28; B. Lynne Milgram, 'Banking on Bananas, Crediting Crafts: Financing Women's Work in the Philippine Cordillera', *Atlantis: A Women's Studies Journal*, 26/2 (2002): pp. 109–19.

[5] See for example, Arsenio Balisacan, 'Anatomy of Poverty during Adjustment: The Case of the Philippines', *Economic Development and Cultural Change*, 44/1 (1995): pp. 33–62; Sylvia Chant, 'Women's Roles in Recession and Economic Restructuring in Mexico and the Philippines', *Geoforum*, 27/3 (1996): pp. 297–327.

[6] This paper significantly expands the empirical data documented in an earlier published article, B. Lynne Milgram, 'Juicing Up for Fair Trade', *Cultural Survival Quarterly*, 29 (2005): pp. 47–9, and it differentially contextualizes and uses new empirical findings and insights documented in, B. Lynne Milgram, 'From Trash to Totes: Recycled Production and Cooperative Economy Practice in the Philippines', *Human Organization*, 69/1 (2010): 75–85.

The AMC's distinctive manufacture of a wide range of carrying bags, footwear and furnishing accessories made from recycled plastic juice drink containers responds to contemporary consumers' growing demand for environmentally friendly and ethically produced goods. In addition, the AMC operates as a multipurpose cooperative that provides poor urban women with local employment, social support services as well as the financial benefits of a profit-sharing organizational structure. The cooperative, however, faces growing competition from artisans who manufacture similarly conceived products constructed from their particular regional solid waste or recyclables in countries such as South Africa, Mexico, Brazil, Chile, India, Nepal and Vietnam (with organizations like Ecoist; Escama Studio; Nahui Ollin; Olly Molly; Spiral Foundation).[7] In order to maintain their competitive edge, AMC artisans must continually negotiate complex and culturally mediated design processes – diversifying production and developing new techniques – in order to successfully transform recyclable materials into middle- and high-end fashion goods. That the cooperative's local and export sales have steadily increased since its inception in 1998, means that cooperative members have been able to maintain some degree of autonomy as producers and traders despite the broader market forces that challenge such small independent enterprises.[8]

Drawing on analyses of women's craft cooperatives and of emergent personalized 'ethnic business landscapes' in fashion,[9] I argue that Philippine women working within associations such as the Artisan Multipurpose Cooperative similarly reconfigure 'lines of flow'[10] that mediate among local producers, national buyers and global trade organizations. The linkages they develop shift attention from the logical hand of the market and the dichotomies it creates to the 'interweavings' and *situatedness* of people, social institutions, fashion trends and knowledge and frame these as always contextual and in process.[11] I suggest,

---

[7] Ecoist 2008, URL: www.ecoist.com, accessed 18 December 2008; Escama Studio 2009, URL: www.escamastudio.com, accessed 20 September 2009; Nahui Ollin 2008, URL: www.nahuiollin.com, accessed 18 December 2008; Olly Molly 2008, URL: www.ollymolly.co.za, accessed 18 December 2008; Spiral Foundation 2009, URL: www.spiralfoundation.org, accessed 20 April 2009. I thank Karen Tranberg Hansen for drawing my attention to some of these organizations and for the insights she offered on this issue through her comments on an earlier version of this paper.

[8] For example, Andrea M. Singh and Anita Kelles-Viitanen (eds), *Invisible Hands: Women in Home-Based Production* (London, 1987); Virginia A. Miralao, *Labor Conditions in Philippine Craft Industries*, Ramon Magsaysay Research and Working Papers (Manila, 1986).

[9] Parminder Bhachu, *Dangerous Designs: Asian Women Fashion the Diaspora Economies* (New York and London, 2004), p. 129.

[10] Sarah Whatmore and Lorraine Thorne, 'Nourishing Networks: Alternative Geographies of Food', in David Goodman and Michael Watts (eds), *Globalising Food: Agrarian Questions and Global Restructuring* (London and New York, 1997), p. 287.

[11] The italics in *situatedness* is in the original, Whatmore and Thorne, 'Nourishing Networks', pp. 288–9; Mike Featherstone, *Global Culture: Nationalism, Globalisation and Modernity* (London, 1990).

however, that at the same time that women's work in this sphere refashions spaces of consumption and livelihood, it may also produce cleavages in material well-being.[12] The extent to which different artisans working within such production collectives can access opportunities and mitigate constraints on their actions thus depends on how effectively they can work together to shape, not just respond to, the forms global capital takes in any location.[13]

Women's Artisanal Work in the Philippines

Philippine women's work within artisanal cooperatives offers a particularly useful lens for the analysis of gender and economic outcomes with globalizing markets, as women's workforce participation throughout the Philippines is among the highest and most varied in countries of the Global South.[14] Recent studies examining women's micro-activities clearly demonstrate that women work across different spheres including household and market, rural and urban spaces, formal and informal economic sectors and local-to-national-to-global economic arenas.[15] Their multifaceted activities dissolve determinist ideas about discrete and bounded socioeconomic categories. As Wazir Karim argues for Southeast Asia, women secure a 'continuous chain of productive enterprises' for family and personal well-being by establishing 'a repertoire of social units' linked to household, market and environmental resources; and they 'unlink' themselves when situations change. Women thus create an 'open-ended' and 'multi-focal' system of socioeconomic relations with 'undifferentiated boundaries' and 'varying connotations of space'.[16] In this light, AMC female artisans, for example, can combine their objective of profit

---

[12] Rudi Colloredo-Mansfeld, 'An Ethnography of Neoliberalism: Understanding Competition in Artisan Economies', *Current Anthropology*, 43/1 (2002): p. 114.

[13] Carla Freeman, 'Is Local: Global as Feminine: Masculine? Rethinking the Gender of Globalization', *Signs: Journal of Women in Culture and Society*, 26/4 (2001): pp. 1008–9.

[14] Balisacan, 'Anatomy of Poverty during Adjustment', pp. 33–62; Robin Broad, *Unequal Alliance: The World Bank, the International Monetary Fund and the Philippines* (Berkeley, CA, 1988); Rene E. Ofreneo and Esther P. Habana, *The Employment Crisis and The World Bank's Adjustment Program – Philippines* (Quezon City, Philippines, 1987); Vergara R. Pineda, 'Domestic Outwork for Export-Oriented Industries', in Amaryllis T. Torres (ed.), *The Filipino Woman in Focus* (Manila, Philippines, 1995), pp. 153–67.

[15] For example, Sylvia Chant and Cathy McIlwaine, *Women of a Lesser Cost: Female Labour, Foreign Exchange and Philippine Development* (London and East Haven, CT, 1995); B. Lynne Milgram, 'Crafts, Cultivation and Household Economies: Women's Work and Positions in Ifugao Northern Philippines', *Research in Economic Anthropology*, 20 (1999): pp. 221–61; Rhacel S. Parreñas, *Servants of Globalization: Women, Migration & Domestic Work* (Stanford, CA, 2001).

[16] Wazir Jahan Karim, 'Introduction: Genderising Anthropology in Southeast Asia', in Wazir J. Karim (ed.), *'Male' and 'Female' in Developing Southeast Asia* (Oxford and Washington, 1995), p. 28.

maximization to secure the needs of their families with their goals to build information and social networks, maintain autonomy and achieve personal recognition.[17]

Studies of development in regions of the South, clearly demonstrate that the imposition of national macro-economic policies also contributes to the varying control women have over their labour in both formal and informal work sectors.[18] In many cases, women are disadvantaged by neoliberal policies which have fuelled the gap separating rich and poor, segmented labour conditions and often undermined women's consumption base as men and women with less income-generating work, logically, have less money to spend. Indeed, since the 1986 restoration of democratic government in the Philippines, successive national leaders have failed to institute economic and political reforms that effectively act 'on behalf of the public interest'; instead, state politics continue to put forward anti-poverty programmes that rarely come to fruition. In artisan trades, development programmes have targeted larger mainstream urban-based enterprises – such as, rattan and bamboo furniture and furnishing accessories – leaving home-based, and often poor, individual rural and urban artisans to fend for themselves.[19]

Some informal sector and home-based workers such as those in the AMC thus sought to identify new market-desirable, niche commodities that could fulfil their need for work. Since the early 1990s, for example, the growing global concern for eroding environmental resources has prompted increasing ethical and environmentally friendly consumption practices, as noted.[20] By recycling used plastic juice drink containers into functional carrying bags and home décor items, with no initial guarantee that their goods would indeed prove fashionable, AMC artisans developed products that resonated with this emergent wave in informed consumption.[21] The AMC, however, as noted, must continue to distinguish its line of goods from those of artisanal collectives worldwide that also innovatively

---

[17] Milgram, 'Reorganizing Production for Global Markets', pp. 107–28; see also Beverly Lemire, 'Introduction. Women, Credit and the Creation of Opportunity: A Historical Overview', in Beverly Lemire, Ruth Pearson and Gail Campbell (eds), *Women and Credit: Researching the Past, Refiguring the Future* (Oxford and New York, 2002), pp. 3–14.

[18] Chant, 'Women's Roles in Recession', pp. 297–327; Linda J. Seligmann, 'Introduction: Mediating Identities, Marketing Wares', in Linda J. Seligmann (ed.), *Women Traders in Cross-Cultural Perspective: Mediating Identities, Marketing Wares* (Stanford, CA, 2001), pp. 1–24; Deborah Winslow, 'Pottery, Progress, and Structural Adjustments in a Sri Lankan Village', *Economic Development and Cultural Change*, 44/4 (1996): pp. 701–26.

[19] Paul D. Hutchcroft and Joel Rocamora, 'Strong Demands and Weak Institutions: The Origins and Evolution of the Democratic Deficit in the Philippines', *Journal of East Asian Studies*, 3/2 (2003): pp. 260 and 281; Filomeno V. Aguilar and Virginia A. Miralao, *Rattan Furniture Manufacturing in Metro Cebu: A Case Study of an Export Industry*, Ramon Magsaysay Handcraft Project Paper Series No. 6 (Manila, Philippines 1985).

[20] Stephanie Barrientos and Catherine Dolan (eds), *Ethical Sourcing in the Global Food System* (London, UK, 2006).

[21] Erin Kobayashi, 'Buy Into It: BYO Bag', *Toronto Star* (21 April 2007): pp. 1 and 3; Beverly Natividad, 'Packaging firm strengthens push to recycle used Tetra Pak Cartons',

use local recyclable materials (paper, plastic, metal) in their ethically-rooted production. To foster their personalized and cooperative fashion economy and 'capture [such] contested spaces' of consumption,[22] AMC artisans then, look beyond culling livelihood tactics from economic relations of production alone. Rather, they simultaneously build on their knowledge of how to sustain and enable culturally-grounded social networks while keeping informed of transnational fashion trends and demands.

A Cooperative Production Alternative

The growing scholarship on women's cooperatives explores the extent to which artisans' work within such collectives can facilitate their transition from producing goods for local sale and trade to producing for national and international markets. The experience of artisans engaged in the AMC reflects many of the benefits and challenges women have experienced elsewhere. Research on women's craft cooperatives in Latin America, in particular, identifies a number of the positive outcomes for participants. These include, in particular: skills training in product development and business accounting, increased control over, and more direct access to, distribution channels and markets, expansion of social support networks beyond those of one's family and augmented participation in local and regional politics.[23] In addition, in the Philippines, women's enhanced positions due to their cooperative membership earnings do not meet resistance from men as has been documented in similar circumstances in Latin America, for example,[24] because women in the Philippines customarily manage and allot household finances and, through history, have actively engaged in local and national trade.

While most accounts of women's participation in cooperatives demonstrate members' ability to garner some benefits, the potential of collectives to equally support all women's group and individual objectives is often not realized. The role

---

*BW Weekender (*Philippines*)* (10 June 2006): p. 8; *Toronto Star* staff, 'Recycled Juice Containers Make Fun Totes', *Toronto Star* (19 February 2004): p. L2.

   [22]   Whatmore and Thorne, 'Nourishing Networks', p. 290.

   [23]   Lynn Stephen, 'Women's Weaving Cooperatives in Oaxaca', *Critique of Anthropology*, 25/3 (2005): pp. 253–78; Karen E. Tice, *Kuna Crafts, Gender, and the Global Economy* (Austin, TX, 1995); Gabriela Vargas-Cetina, 'Anthropology and Cooperatives: From the Community Paradigm to the Ephemeral Association in Chiapas, Mexico', *Critique of Anthropology*, 25/3 (2005): pp. 229–51. See also, Kimberly M. Grimes and B. Lynne Milgram, 'Introduction: Facing the Challenges of Artisan Production in the Global Market', in Kimberly M. Grimes and B. Lynne Milgram (eds), *Artisans and Cooperatives: Developing Alternative Trade for the Global Economy* (Tucson, AZ, 2000), pp. 3–10.

   [24]   Christine Eber, '"That They be in the Middle, Lord": Women, Weaving, and Cultural Survival in Highland Chiapas, Mexico', in Kimberly M. Grimes and B. Lynne Milgram (eds), *Artisans and Cooperatives: Developing Alternative Trade for the Global Economy* (Tucson, AZ, 2000), pp. 45–64.

of women as primary caregivers in raising children, for example, may hinder their engagement in leadership roles as these women cannot assume administrative responsibilities beyond a certain level of commitment. The AMC's recent initiative then, to provide childcare within the cooperative can enable more members to operationalize potential administration and production options as they arise. Instances may also occur in which participation in collectives can advantage those who are already in stronger economic positions, that is, those with established complementary businesses such as grocery stores, rather than those in the poorest sectors.[25] Thus, the AMC's outreach programme that offers piecework employment to women in the community's squatter quarter starts to readdresses the potential of such imbalances across class groups.

Most women, such as AMC artisans then, view positively the social and economic options that cooperative membership can offer. The broader potential of such collective enterprises, moreover, lies in opening up international markets to small community producers and educating consumers (particularly those in the 'North') to more often select ethically manufactured goods such as those of the AMC.

Personalized Fashion Economies

The establishment of the Artisan Multipurpose Cooperative in the late 1990s, coincided with both a growing global demand for indigenous crafts,[26] and quite unrelated, the 1990s Asian fashion diasporas in which Asian fashion became a noticeable worldwide trend, changing the way that people inside and outside Asia think about dress.[27] Within this context, the AMC's initiative to develop niche fashion items provides a critical forum within which to discuss how such goods visually mark broader social, economic and cultural shifts in consumption and in identity construction. Clothing and textiles are not just any type of commodity, but ones that 'mediate between self and society' in ways that highlight how people choose to reposition themselves in times of dramatic change.[28] By using recycled materials to manufacture fashion goods for a varied clientele, AMC designers have forged a cultural space that speaks of ethical production, in particular, and of Asian identity more generally. That the AMC's production is 'recoding and

---

[25] Milgram, 'Reorganizing Production for Global Markets', pp. 110–2.

[26] June Nash (ed.), *Crafts in the World Market: The Impact of Global Exchange on Middle American Artisans* (Albany, NY, 1993).

[27] Bhachu, *Dangerous Designs*; Carla Jones and Ann Marie Leshkowich, 'Introduction: The Globalization of Asian Dress: Re-Orienting Fashion or Re-Orientalizing Asia?' in Sandra Niessen, Ann Marie Leshkowich and Carla Jones (eds), *The Globalization of Asian Dress: Re-Orienting Fashion* (Oxford and New York, 2003), pp. 1–48.

[28] Karen Tranberg Hansen, *Salaula: The World of Secondhand Clothing and Zambia* (Chicago, 2000), p. 4 and Karen Tranberg Hansen, 'Fashioning', *Journal of Material Culture*, 8/3 (2003): pp. 301–9.

reimagining' previously denigrated domains of cultural production resonates with material culture studies as in food and music that similarly document a trickle-up of goods from margin to mainstream as such edgy production is widely adopted across race and class.[29]

Carla Jones's and Ann Marie Leshkowich's study of Asian fashion traces such a flow of goods from periphery to centre and back again. On the one hand, they demonstrate how fashion elites and celebrities selectively don elements of Asian style in their dress as items such as sarongs and kimono jackets have become 'regularly featured aspects of American fashion designers' product lines.[30] On the other hand, they note how Asian consumers, across class, ethnicity and gender, decide on what occasions they should wear Western or Asian clothing – the former affording anonymity, the latter proclaiming personal ethnic identity.[31] Indeed, the women most likely to don the AMC carrying bags and footwear are those who are economically well-off – tourists, resident foreigners or middle- to upper-income Filipinas – women whose socioeconomic security affords them some distance from the origins of the solid waste products they sport. Increasingly, however, these products are gaining popularity among Filipino consumers generally, and AMC artisans, buoyed by the positive reception of their goods, confidently use the recycled bags that they make to identify themselves with their nationally-rooted production.

The line of handbags that AMC artisans produce are functional goods whose history is rooted in textile and garment construction generally, but not in the production of these specific items. AMC producers then, have the production freedom to invent their own set of meanings for this material culture form. Their goods enter the contemporary global world of fashion, but the graphics and patterns illustrated on each juice pack speak generally of locally identifiable consumer waste materials. AMC artisans thoughtfully compose the product label text that they attach to each item to identify the recycled character of their goods and to specify that these products have been manufactured within an owner-operated cooperative. AMC artisans thus construct a 'discourse of cultural pride' and act 'as agents of cultural pedagogy' by using their particularized manufacture to educate

---

[29] For a further discussion with regard to Asian fashion, see Ann Marie Leshkowich and Carla Jones, 'What Happens when Asian Chic Becomes Chic in Asia?' *Fashion Theory*, 7/3-4 (2003): pp. 281–300. With regard to food, see for example, Penny Van Esterik, 'From Hunger Foods to Heritage Foods: Challenges to Food Localization in Lao PDR' in Richard Wilk (ed.), *Fast Food/Slow Food: The Cultural Economy of the Global Food System* (Lanham, MD, 2006).

[30] Jones and Leshkowich, 'Globalization of Asian Dress', p. 2.

[31] Jones and Leshkowich, 'Globalization of Asian Dress', p. 5. Jones and Leshkowich argue further here that while the global interest in Asian dress might seem to open new democratic forms of cross-cultural exchange, studies also highlight that some aspects of Asian dress – due to their repeated north-south travels – have been continually reworked to the extent that these features might be characterized as 'homogenized heterogeneity'.

the Asian and Euro-American public about aspects of Philippine material culture and livelihood, as the following case study demonstrates.[32]

The Artisan Multipurpose Cooperative

In late 1997, in order to provide viable and locally-based work for poor and unemployed urban women, municipal officials in an inner-city Manila community organized local residents to collect recyclable waste such as paper, plastic and metal. These items were then sold to registered local 'junk' dealers and the income from these sales was used to support community programmes. In 1998, the women in these organized groups established a project to manufacture a range of carrying bags made from the used plastic juice drink containers they had been collecting. These bags include shoulder bags, handbags, clutch purses, backpacks, small utility bags and large tote bags (Illustration 9.1). Subsequently, some artisans took the lead to establish links with a Manila-based, fair trade organization, Associated Partners for Fairer Trade, Inc. (APFTI), to avail of this organization's low interest loans, product development and skills training workshops and international market connections.[33] APFTI's financial support, for example, enabled AMC artisans to upgrade their manual treadle sewing machines to more heavy-duty industrial models. In 1999, collective members registered with the Securities Employment Commission (SEC) as the Artisan Multipurpose Cooperative (AMC) to formalize their production initiatives.

The Artisan Multipurpose Cooperative's projects provide work for approximately 400 women who live within this inner city community. Some women work in the cooperative's building while others choose to work on a piecework basis from their homes. Working at the AMC enables women to remain living with their families and balance domestic and childcare responsibilities with earning an income. In all aspects of production, the AMC provides artisans with the required raw materials and women are paid for their labour. Those women working full time (eight hours a day, five days a week) earn from 200 to 250 Philippine pesos

---

[32] Bhachu, *Dangerous Designs*, p. 40.

[33] Associated Partners for Fairer Trade, Inc. (APFTI), 2002 and 2003 *Annual Reports* (Quezon City, Philippines, 2002 and 2003). For a full discussion of fair trade organizations see Kimberly M. Grimes, 'Democratizing International Production and Trade', in Kimberly M. Grimes and B. Lynne Milgram (eds), *Artisans and Cooperatives: Developing Alternative Trade for the Global Economy* (Tuscon, AZ, 2000), pp. 11–24; Kimberly M. Grimes, 'Changing the Rules of Trade in Global Partnerships: The Fair Trade Movement', in June Nash (ed.), *Social Movements: A Reader* (Oxford, 2005), pp. 235–48; Mary Ann Littrell and Marsha Ann Dickson, *Social Responsibility in the Global Market: Fair Trade of Cultural Products* (London, 1999). The growing fair trade movement has also seen the emergence of a number of recent studies analysing both the 'pros' and 'cons' of this initiative. See for example, Sarah Lyon and Mark Moberg (eds), *Fair Trade and Social Justice: Global Ethnographies* (Albany, NY, 2010).

Illustration 9.1 Two carrying bags made from recycled plastic juice drink containers. These bags, made by women working in the Artisan Multipurpose Cooperative, feature the Philippine juice drink manufacturer's brand name along with the fruit motif. Photograph by B.L. Milgram, Manila, Philippines, 2007

($US 4.00–$US 5.00) a day – salaries that, while minimally sustainable, are still less than that recommended by Philippine government guidelines, which is PHP 350 or $US 7.00/day. Working on a piecework basis, most applicable to artisans engaged in washing and sewing the recycled juice packs, facilitates a more flexible schedule and higher earnings than the regular full-time rate depending upon the number and type of units artisans sew or wash. The AMC obtains information about the specific tastes of their consumers and consults with their distributors to develop particular types, sizes and designs for bags suitable for different geographically-located orders. In addition, a standard line of ready-to-purchase goods is illustrated in the association's product catalogue. In 2008, the AMC manufactured 35,000 carrying bags per month, the majority of which were exported to Japan, Korea, Canada, Australia, the United States and Europe. The growing popularity of these bags means that the cooperative has formalized its global distribution networks by allocating exclusive distribution rights to specific dealers in designated country locations. In turn, distributors commit to generate an agreed-upon volume of sales per month for the AMC to enable the cooperative to more accurately plan their production schedule and ensure salaries to cooperative members.

In order to keep pace with the growing demand for their recycled goods, the AMC has streamlined its operation such that separate sections handle specialized stages of manufacturing in what Ursula Franklin terms 'prescriptive' technology.[34] The challenge that emerges for the collective then, is to balance success in the transnational fashion business with support of employees in line with the AMC's community-based philosophy.

Reclaiming Materials, Refashioning Work

Throughout Southeast Asia, within the context of a growing world concern for environmental sustainability, collecting waste products for recycling in both state-sponsored and independent enterprises has emerged as a viable income-generating activity for men and women.[35] To expand its earlier waste collection activities, the AMC established its own Ecology Centre in which women sort the solid waste products (metal, paper, cardboard, assorted plastic) that they have collected from their own and, currently, from a growing number of neighbouring communities. The income from sales of the waste material not used in AMC manufacturing supports the cooperative's social welfare programmes, while the plastic juice drink containers that members collect contribute to the AMC's daily need for thousands of juice packs to sustain its production quota. The AMC Ecology Centre supervisor outlines that members' collections earn the cooperative approximately 2,000 pesos ($US 40.00) a week from sales of assorted plastic and scrap metal and approximately 2,500 pesos ($US 50.00) a week from sales of used cardboard boxes.

The AMC purchases used juice containers in all brand names and pays collectors according to the quality of the juice packs they have assembled – ten cents for each juice container classified as 'slightly used' (a juice container with minor damage) and 20 cents for each juice container classified as being in 'good' condition. Collectors usually accumulate used juice packs until they can fill two to three rice sacks; each sack, which formerly held 50 kilos of rice, can hold 6,500 to 7,000 used plastic juice containers. Vendors deliver their goods to the AMC and return the following week to receive their payment after cooperative members have counted and assessed the quality of the delivery. Those collecting these goods

---

[34] Ursula Franklin, *The Real World of Technology* (Toronto, 1999), pp. 10–13.

[35] Michael DiGregorio, *Urban Harvest: Recycling as a Peasant Industry in Northern Vietnam* (Honolulu, Hawaii, 1994); Virginia Maclaren and Nguyen Thi Anh Thu (eds), *Gender and the Waste Economy: Vietnamese and International Experiences* (Hanoi, Vietnam, 2003).

obtain them from locations where they are consumed and subsequently discarded in large quantities such as in schools, parks and at public events.[36]

When the used juice packs arrive at the cooperative, designated workers thoroughly wash the containers. In 2003, to fulfil its mandate to provide employment across the community, the AMC started an outreach programme for women and their families living in the area's squatter settlement. Currently, 40 to 50 women from this community, who are not necessarily cooperative members, work in their homes cleaning the used juice packs on a piecework basis. These women receive 200 pesos ($US 4.00), the regular AMC daily wage, to wash 2,000 juice packs (equivalent to the contents of one-third rice sack) and some families report that when a number of family members work together, they can wash as many as 6,000 packs (the contents of one rice sack) in one day.

Artisans then sort the washed juice containers dividing the packs into groups based on colour, brand name, and the type of fruit juice drink they once contained. Allie Mendes, who oversees the AMC's stock of used juice packs, explains that these containers fall into a hierarchy of goods that ranges from highly to less desirable. Expressing the knowledge and passion of an art connoisseur, Allie outlines that the AMC consistently has an oversupply of Zesto orange juice drink containers, in particular, as this brand is one of the least expensive to buy and thus the most often consumed. 'Some of our regular clients are currently more discriminating', she explains, 'about the type of juice containers they want featured in the products they order. These distributors thus request that we do not include, in their orders, the more commonly occurring packs such as Zesto orange.' Allie points out that such specialized design directives from distributors means that, at times, AMC artisans may have the orders they seek, but lack the specific type of juice drink packs they require to complete these requests. 'In late 2006', Allie explains, 'the AMC decided to stop purchasing Zesto orange brand juice packs, but we had to abandon this restrictive purchasing strategy within a few months because this tactic led to steep decreases in the overall volume of packs that waste pickers delivered to us'. The AMC is thus developing different products, such as home furnishing accessories, which can utilize the types of juice drink packs that are not in demand for their bags. Allie reports that the juice drink containers currently most in fashion are those that picture Asian 'exotic' fruits such as mango, passion fruit, kiwi, coconut, calamunsi (orange/lime) and durian. A rainbow-like display board mounted in the cooperative's showroom features each type of used juice drink pack highlighting the wide variety that is available.

After sorting, the used juice containers travel to the sewing department (Illustration 9.2). The two or three women who work here as material controllers distribute the different component parts – juice packs, thread, zippers and fabric – used in product construction; the amount of each item given to artisans depends

---

[36] Collectors estimate that they can earn, on average, about 150 pesos a day – a minimally subsistence income that is consistent with the earnings of many Philippine street vendors.

Illustration 9.2 Artisans working in the sewing section of the Artisan Multipurpose Cooperative. Photograph by B.L. Milgram, Manila, Philippines, 2007

upon the types of bags that the sewer will be making. As Patricia Manolo, whom we met earlier, outlines:

> I have been a member in this cooperative since 2003, but I first worked as a washer and sorter. When I wanted to use my former sewing skills and learn something new, I attended training sessions and then transferred to this job. Here I estimate the amount of materials such as thread, fabric, zippers, buttons, and juice containers or 'doy packs' that each sewer needs for the products she will manufacture. I am also distributing the raw materials to those working in the footwear section and in the recycled paper beads section. I am responsible for all of these materials so I really have a demanding job.

Sample makers plan the patterns for the differently designed bags based on colour, brand name and on the sequence in which the component parts – the individual juice packs – are to be arranged. The designs in the AMC's lines of bags are also classified as to whether they are simple or complex as these criteria determine the piecework rate paid to sewers. Sewers are also encouraged to create new bag designs which, if accepted by the cooperative's review committee, earn the artisan a bonus payment and are named based on the artisan's initials and a number; the latter indicates the accumulated number of styles designed by a particular maker. This system of labelling clearly identifies the producer's skill and instills pride in her production (Illustration 9.3). Among the compositions of sewer-designer Alice Talango, for example, one of the AMC's prominent pattern makers, are bags that combine juice pack patterns of native Philippine fruits with panels of hard-wearing fabrics in a 'this plus that sort of construction' – the 'this' of a locally identifiable material plus the 'that' of a fashionable modernity.[37] By increasing the proportion of commercial fabric used in selected bags, moreover, AMC artisans are able to fulfil their production quotas at those times when supplies of juice drink packs may be low. In addition, the increased availability of such suitably coloured and textured hard-wearing fabrics means that designers can more easily respond to clients' recent requests for AMC bags to be equipped with secure closing systems. Alice Talango has devised such a locking feature by sewing one panel of fabric to each of the upper sections of a plastic juice bag and then attaching a zipper to enable the bag to remain closed while it is being used.

Home decorating magazines with up-to-date information on colour, design and fashion trends sit displayed on tables throughout the workshop for artisans' reference. Sewer-designers explain:

> One year the colour yellow is popular, so we accumulate mango juice drink packs, for example, in order to design bags that showcase this colour trend; the

---

[37] Cory Silverstein, 'Clothed encounters: The power of dress in relations between Anishnaabe and British peoples in the Great Lakes region 1760–2000' (Unpublished PhD Dissertation, McMaster University, Canada, 2000), p. 23.

Illustration 9.3 A sewer-designer from the Artisan Multipurpose Cooperative proudly displays some of the hats and bags that she has designed and sewn from recycled plastic juice drink packs. Photograph by B.L. Milgram, Manila, Philippines, 2008

next year graphics may be in demand and thus we use juice drink brands such as *Big* or *Plus* as these companies prominently feature their names along with the fruit motifs of the juice drink, and so on'. (See Illustration 9.1)

These mosaic juice drink bags visibly showcase the pioneering skills of AMC artisans. Some bag designs feature the same type of fruit pattern in a strong regular repeat arrangement; other products include only two or three types of fruit motifs arranged in various configurations; still other bags offer a catalogue of the available flavours as each sewn section displays the pattern of a different fruit. To improve product quality, designer-sewers currently reinforce the seams along the outer bag edges with hardwearing synthetic fabric bias tape whose colours match those in the fruit drink packs. As one sewer, explains, 'We regularly consult with each other to stay informed about global fashion tastes such that our bags can remain up-to-date and competitive in changing markets'.

Sewers attend training workshops, as each sewer must have the knowledge of different design configurations, both simple and complex. Because not all women have a background in sewing, the training sessions become essential tools for enabling women to learn new skills or improve already existing skills. As sewer Cecille Tabriz explains:

> Before joining the AMC, I worked altering women's clothing. When I had my third child, it became more difficult for me to leave the house for my job. I decided to join the cooperative as our mandate gives us the option to complete our assignments in our homes especially if we have young children. Now the AMC has established a children's play area to assist those women who need to bring their children with them to work. But before, this was not an option.
>
> If I want to work at home, I obtain the items and the pattern codes I need to sew from the material distributors such as Patricia Manolo. When I have completed the products, I deliver them to the AMC's receiving section. In this arrangement, I can determine my personal work schedule.

In order to assist women who wish to purchase their own sewing machines for home-based work, the AMC enables the sewer to pay for the machine on an instalment basis with lower-than-market interest rates. The AMC deducts the monthly payment instalments for the sewing machine, usually 500 pesos ($US 10.00) per month, from the value of the products sewers complete.

The rate of pay that sewers can earn varies according to the size and to the type of bags completed, with larger bags earning a higher rate. The rate also varies according to the type of design that producers sew – simple or complex. Artisans explain that they can make approximately 40 to 50 bags a day if the design is simple and the bag is small and 20 to 30 medium-size bags a day if the pattern is familiar to them; if the designs are intricate, women explain that they can make only 10 to 15 pieces a day. The rate of pay for the larger more complex designs ranges from 40 to 60 pesos ($US 0.80 – $1.20) per piece, 25 pesos ($US 0.50) per piece for medium-size bags with familiar designs, while the rate for simple patterns in small bags is 7 to 10 pesos ($US 0.10 – $US 0.20) per piece. A rough calculation of these rates of pay illustrates that sewers can earn from 300 to 500 pesos ($US 6.00 – $US 10.00) a day and both rates are higher than the 200- to 250-peso ($US 4.00 – $US 5.00) daily wage earned by women in the other areas of processing. Sewers also confirm that they consider those times during which their salary may decrease while they learn new patterns, as an investment for future production. 'Learning new designs', Cecille explains, 'increases our repertoire of skills and knowledge and provides us with the flexibility to produce a wider range of products.'

As required in manufacturing generally, all AMC products must meet quality control standards. Anne Reyes has been supervising the quality control process for over five years (Illustration 9.4). She explains that she and the other women in her section try to be as instructive as possible to sewers when they find bags with construction flaws as they realize that such mistakes cost the sewers labour time as well as a part of their earnings if the flaws cannot be mended. At the same time, however, the women in this section have their own daily quota of bags that they must check – 300 small bags and 100 large bags per day. This means that when women inspecting bags find a defective piece, their rate of inspection tends to slow down. Thus, while those assessing quality want to be as supportive of sewers as they can, the workload expectations of their department and the high quality standards demanded by the international fashion circles in which these goods circulate, can constrain their efforts.

While a formal market mode of production and distribution is present in the AMC's operation, it is often mediated through channels of connectivity. Product labels developed, for example, by one of the AMC's distributors in California – '*Re-bagz*: Eco-Chic Handbags', make such linkages explicit:

> *Re-bagz* – The next evolution in style – as stylish as they are sustainable. Once upon a time the vivid weaves and fabric in our *Re-bagz* handbags had another job. Some...were fruit juice packs – the kind you stick a straw in and slurp from. But after those jobs were done, these packs...were just too colorful to throw away. So instead they're rescued and transformed into our whimsical bags, handmade especially for you, by a wonderful women's cooperative in the Philippines. Wear, enjoy – and recycle.[38]

Such labelling establishes the cooperative's philosophy as well as a physical connection between those who produce and those who buy such goods.

---

[38] 'Re-bagz'. Product label text that was attached to a rectangular clutch purse I purchased in Los Angeles, CA on 3 April 2009. See also URL: www.rebagz.com, accessed 7 April 2009.

Illustration 9.4 Women working in the Artisan Multipurpose Cooperative inspect some recycled plastic juice drink bags for quality and pack other bags for their export shipments. Photograph by B.L. Milgram, Manila, Philippines, 2008

Strategizing Cooperative Practice

Working within a collective context does not insulate organizations like the Artisan Multipurpose Cooperative from the discipline of global markets – delivery deadlines, trading regulations, changing consumer tastes and quality standards, as noted – all have to be met. David Lewis suggests that a key challenge in alternative trade practice involves converting producers and their organizations into enterprises with the ability to sell high quality goods in competitive, complex and rapidly changing international markets.[39] Given that the AMC produces goods in the field of fashion where designs and colours change with the seasons, members' initiatives need to be that much more innovative. The AMC is thus expanding its manufacturing base by producing new product lines in footwear, selected garments, household furnishing accessories made from recycled juice drink packs and jewellery fashioned from the discarded, used coloured waste paper that members collect.

The cooperative members who manufacture footwear (primarily different types of open-toe shoes), for example, receive training in how to cut and proportion the juice containers and the corkboard used in basic shoe construction, as well as how to glue and sew the components together. In the spring of 2005, when a Japanese client ordered 1,000 pairs of shoes with a two-month delivery deadline, the AMC expanded its outreach programme by training 15 community artisans to manufacture these goods outside the collective's building – an initiative that was largely successful and on which the AMC continues to build.

In their efforts to consolidate their association with contemporary fashion spheres, artisans have also developed different garment types – hats, aprons and vests – whose physical construction benefits from the rigidity of the juice packs. Neda Ballan, another AMC pattern maker, combines fabric elements with juice packs to construct a variety of playfully designed and functional hats; such hats are popular in the Philippines as well as abroad as they offer protection from both the sun and the rain (see Illustration 9.3). AMC artisans also construct women's vests made from juice drink packs that have been cut into different shapes and then either sewn together to form a solid piece or applied to a flexible fabric backing. This new garment style enables the cooperative to use juice drink containers that have been more than minimally damaged as artisans can adapt the intact pieces of containers to where they most appropriately fit into the vest's design. AMC artisans have also started to produce a line of kitchen aprons constructed from recycled plastic tomato sauce containers. These plastic packs are produced by international brand names such as Del Monte as well as by well-known national companies such as Jufran, Magnolia, and Mama Sita who manufacture the Philippines' distinctive banana ketchup and sauce – a product combining tomatoes and bananas.

---

[39] David Lewis, 'Non-governmental Organizations, Business and the Management of Ambiguity: Case Studies from Nepal and Bangladesh', *Nonprofit Management and Leadership*, 9/2 (1998): pp. 135–52.

The larger size of these containers and the subject of their designs are aptly suited for use in these kitchen aprons each of which features two front pockets fashioned from plastic tomato sauce or banana ketchup containers.

The cooperative has further expanded its product line by including household furnishing accessories whose outer surfaces sport the wide array of recycled plastic juice drink containers that are locally available. Some of these goods include: vertical Venetian blinds, differently sized cardboard storage and file boxes, screens, cushion covers, garment and shoe storage bags, file folios and brief cases, and a variety of table coverings (Illustration 9.5). In addition, the AMC's new range of jewellery – necklaces, bracelets and earrings – made from rolled up and lacquered coloured waste paper beads that artisans assemble has proven particularly popular in the growing market for inexpensive 'quirky' costume jewellery.

Illustration 9.5   The showroom at the Artisan Multipurpose Cooperative displays the variety of home furnishing accessories that cooperative artisans construct from recycled plastic juice drink packs and cardboard. Photograph by B.L. Milgram, Manila, Philippines, 2008

The AMC is actively developing its on-line catalogue in order to provide its international clients with more complete and faster access to its new product lines, but this technology remains very much a work in progress. Wholesale clients usually visit the AMC showroom twice a year and it is at these face-to-face meetings that most product development for specific export orders takes place. At the same time, the AMC is devoting substantial resources to enhance its local profile and access to its goods through repeated renovations to its showroom. The AMC's global sales success has resulted in a number of local newspaper articles heralding the collective's success and vividly describing its products.[40] Such publicity has made the AMC one of the most popular shopping destinations for the resident expatriate community and for foreign embassy officials looking for typically appropriate Filipino gifts for friends and family abroad. The paradox that emerges here is that these goods, in effect, represent an invented tradition whose manufacture is more closely connected to the broader context of recycling and sustainable production practiced by artisans worldwide, than it is to any long-standing and distinctly Philippine craft custom.

The AMC also fosters ongoing, cross-sector partnerships with organizations such as the Philippine Design Centre (operated by the federal Department of Trade and Industry) enabling cooperative members to access services such as product development and skills training seminars. To showcase their goods to global audiences, the AMC participates in two yearly Philippine craft trade fairs (Manila FAME and CITEM) that attract international buyers looking for unique and fashionable Philippine products. In this way, AMC artisans emerge as 'cultural and commodity brokers' who foster personalized 'rhythms of fashion' and design.[41] They use the market in different ways, not just as a mechanism of economic exchange, but also as an avenue through which they can activate for the social, economic and political conditions of where they work and live.

Conclusion

Through their cooperative work in artisanal fashion, AMC producers innovatively contribute to a niche market – local, national and transnational – for commodities that simultaneously speak of commercial, cultural and ethical production. They are 'savvy design agents' who work within capitalist markets while asserting their 'politically and culturally inflected fashion agendas'.[42] To address the risks in such

---

[40] Vince Cabreza, 'Fashion from Recycled Materials is the New Rage, *Philippine Daily Inquirer* (7 July, 2006): p. B 2; Natividad, 'Packaging firm strengthens push to recycle used Tetra Pak Cartons', p. 8.

[41] Bhachu, *Dangerous Designs*, p. 5.

[42] Parminder Bhachu, 'Designing Diasporic Markets: Asian Fashion Entrepreneurs in London', in Sandra Niessen, Ann Marie Leshkowich and Carla Jones (eds), *Re-Orienting Fashion: The Globalization of Asian Dress* (Oxford and New York, 2003), p. 140.

production, AMC artisans diversify the goods they manufacture, actively consult clients, mobilize a variety of resources and consolidate networks across social and economic spheres.

The current marketing success of the Artisan Multipurpose Cooperative does not mean that issues of contention do not arise with regard to production and design practices. A number of artisans explain, for example, that the general daily wage of 200 pesos is often insufficient to meet their families' subsistence needs. The AMC's mandate, however, identifies members' early goals to support social welfare services, profit sharing schemes and provide work for as many community producers as possible, rather than paying higher wages to fewer cooperative members. As commendable as this outreach policy may be, in on-the-ground practice, many artisans currently outline the different 'sidelines' in which they need to engage on Saturdays and Sundays (like factory production or washing and ironing clothes) to earn the income they require to sustain their families.

Instances of dissention may also arise given the differential between the class-based positions of cooperative managers (e.g., executive director, treasurer, secretary and marketing manager), on the one hand, and those of most members, on the other. Women currently working as management officers, for the most part, have some college education and have spouses who are employed enabling them to attain middle-class (albeit lower middle-class) standing. Many cooperative members, however, are single mothers or have husbands who work only periodically in contract wage labour or are unemployed. Although the cooperative encourages women's movement horizontally across jobs and vertically up to the level of department head, there have been few women who have risen from the rank of production worker to that of manager. But this situation has recently started to shift. In mid-2007, following substantial training, two young women have assumed the responsibilities of the former Manager of Export Orders – a move that potentially opens avenues for similar internal vertical promotion for other artisans. Given the youth of the AMC and the continuing challenge to provide sustainable work for more community members, artisans explain, moreover, that they remain committed to developing AMC practice alternatives in response to the ways in which global capital has transformed their livelihoods at so many levels.

Examining the dynamics of the AMC's cooperative and fashion-niche production thus push analyses of such enterprises beyond simple trickle-down flows from North to South. By operationalizing social and economic resources and their design expertise, artisans activate multiple spaces that resist and indeed compromise the singular neoliberal model of global capitalist enterprise. Artisans' initiatives in the AMC demonstrate how a ubiquitous commodity – fashion accessories made from recycled materials – can reconfigure livelihoods and commodity flows by connecting institutions and sectors of societies not previously linked or by connecting them in different ways.[43] The increasing distribution of the AMC's local and ethically

---

[43] Theodore Bestor, 'Supply-Side Sushi: Commodity, Market, and the Global City', *American Anthropologist*, 103/1 (2001): p. 77.

manufactured, yet globally-linked products, highlight how these women, while still facing challenges, have crafted current 'market moments'[44] to transform the conditions within which they work through their expressive practice.

---

[44] Bhachu, *Dangerous Designs*, p. 6.

Chapter Ten

The City, Clothing Consumption, and the Search for 'the Latest' in Colonial and Postcolonial Zambia

Karen Tranberg Hansen

'Watch Lusaka', argued Samuel Ngoma, a feature writer for one of the daily newspapers in Zambia. 'All who are gorgeously attired mostly get their clothes abroad.' The capital's so-called boutiques, he went on, 'have become rather like museums ... Neither Lusaka's Cairo Road nor Kamwala shopping area is the place to look. You have a better chance at the second-hand clothes dealer, the flea market or even the city centre market dealer who jaunts between Lusaka and Johannesburg.'[1] Of course, people in Zambia have shaped their material culture, including their dress, with commodities and ideas from far away as Samuel Ngoma acknowledged in this excerpt from 1995. Yet a lively interest in clothing is not a new thing in Zambia. The anthropologists who conducted urban research there during the colonial period were struck by the active interest Africans took in dress.[2] Their preoccupations were with Western-style dress, a matter that many scholars examining dress in Africa have understood only through its Western origin rather than with reference to local use.

Dressed bodies are the points of contact between local knowledge and broader global influences, historically as well as at the present time. To explain consumer demand and the desire for fashion that have driven preoccupations with bodies and dress, we must bring the local geography of consumption with its spaces, agents, and performances into the global story. It is from this angle that I approach my discussion of dress practice, including that of secondhand clothing, in Zambia.

Across Africa, engagements with Western-styled clothing varied by place and time, reflecting diverse prior dress traditions as well as changing cultural and economic politics. I argue in this chapter that labour migration and urban living were key processes in turning Africans into active consumers of clothing

---
[1] *Times of Zambia.* Samuel Ngoma, 'Wanted: Quality Clothing in Zambia', 26 August 1995, p. 4.
[2] Godfrey Wilson, 'An Essay on the Economics of Detribalization', *Rhodes-Livingstone Papers*, 5–6 (2 vols, 1941–42); Clyde J. Mitchell, 'The Kalela Dance', *Rhodes-Livingstone Papers*, no. 27, 1956; Arnold L. Epstein, *Urbanization and Kinship: The Domestic Domain on the Copperbelt of Zambia, 1950–1956* (New York, 1981).

for the case of Northern Rhodesia, as Zambia was known from the late 1800s until independence from British colonial rule in 1964. And cities remain key sites for fashionable clothing consumption in the present because they serve as stages for the translation of global influences into local terms. Dressing and dressing well is at the heart of modern sensibilities about living better lives. In making this argument, I touch on both the supply and demand side of the growing consumerism that involved clothing: the expansion of clothing access through new sales techniques and shopping venues, and the development of aesthetic sensibilities regarding dress.[3]

This paper's first half offers a brief discussion of the appropriation of Western-styled garments in African exposures to trade cloth and imported clothing and turns then to labour migration and town life as key processes in exposing Africans both to new dress styles and conventions about how to dress. By the mid-twentieth century, African urban residents in Northern Rhodesia obtained clothes from several sources: imported factory made, imported secondhand, locally produced by small-scale tailors, and to a very limited extent, garments manufactured in local factories. The second half of the paper concerns the period after independence where active preoccupations with clothing and intense interests in 'the latest', encompassing fashion influences from across Africa and beyond continue to flourish in spite of the economic situation. I showcase the results: youth dress styles, secondhand clothing ensembles, and new versions of pan-African influenced outfits worn with pride by consumers who differ by class, generation, and gender.

Clothing Encounters

Cloth and clothing were central commodities in the long-term transformations that brought the market to this part of Africa and gradually made people dependent on it as consumers. These processes entailed the kind of personal identity space we usually associate with modernity. The new outlook made claims at village, urban, and state levels for sensibilities of space, time, and the self that detached individuals, to varying degrees, from larger kin groupings and polities in an ongoing engagement with the developmental aspects of the modern: education, occupation and wealth. In local experiences a commodity like clothing went to the heart of widespread notions of well being, playing active roles in constructing visions of the future.

Calico and cotton cloth had already penetrated the interior by the mid-nineteenth century. Functioning as media of exchange and measures of wealth, these new commodities were initially the monopoly of kings and chiefs who extended their use through tribute channels and distributed them through the kinship system. As trade slipped away from local power and kinship connections, becoming increasingly oriented toward market exchange, the role of kings and chiefs as

---

[3] Peter N. Stearns, *Consumerism in World History: The Global Transformation of Desire* (New York, 2001).

clearing agents weakened. Clothing became a commodity that was exchanged for labour, service, or other goods, and it was increasingly purchased with money. A rare thing had become a necessity that people craved.

People in Zambia have been clothing conscious for a long time. Throughout most of the nineteenth century, ordinary people's dress in this part of Africa exposed the body. It consisted of bark cloth, skin, and hides, and a variety of body adornment. Unlike in many countries in West Africa, cotton weaving had been practised only on a very limited scale. First traders and prospectors, then missionaries, white settlers, and government officials were among the many actors introducing both cloth and clothing, and along with them new notions of the body and propriety, including dress conventions. Because African engagements with dress in this region are enmeshed with issues of Western influence, it is a challenge to insist, as I do, on the power of local appropriation. Missionaries who have received prominent attention in scholarship on early clothing encounters in southern Africa[4] were not the first or only actors to introduce new dress conventions. Many African men from Northern Rhodesia had already begun labour migration to the Belgian Congo, Southern Rhodesia and South Africa, where they had direct access to a wide range of desirable commodities. The clothing practices that arose in these many encounters drew on influences from the missions, migration, and school as well as on African normative notions about the body and sexuality. What is at issue in these encounters was not so much antecedents and origins as Africans making these practices their own.

The imposition of taxes in the early 1900s provided additional incentive for men to leave their home villages in search of jobs to earn cash. By the mid-1930s, more than 50 per cent of the able-bodied male population from Northern Rhodesia was working for wages away from home, as many outside the territory as within it.[5] In this changing regional socioeconomic context, new ideas of wealth, civilization, and maturity came together in clothing, the acquisition of which for a long time hinged on labour migration.[6]

---

[4] John L. Comaroff and Jean Comaroff, 'Fashioning the Colonial Subject: The Empire's Old Clothes' in John L. Comaroff and Jean Comaroff (eds), *Of Revelation and Revolution, The Dialectics of Modernity on a South African Frontier* (2 vols, Chicago, 1997), vol. 2, pp. 218–73; Kristen Reuter, 'Heated Debates over Crinolines: European Clothing on Nineteenth-Century Lutheran Mission Stations in the Transvaal', *Journal of Southern African Studies*, 28/2 (2002): pp. 359–78.

[5] Andrew D. Roberts, *A History of Zambia* (London, 1976), p. 171.

[6] Leroy Vail and Landeg White, *Power and the Praise Poem: Southern African Voices in History* (London, 1991) pp. 256–61.

Labour Migration, Urban Life and Clothing Consumption

Cities and towns were crucial settings where migrants acquired not only knowledge about consumption practices but also insights into how to pursue them. New consumption spaces and shopping venues gave Africans direct access to traders in towns, enabling them to pursue their clothing desires unsupervised by, for instance, missionaries and employers. Many migrants worked in domestic service, which was the chief labour relationship in which African men were socialized into working for whites from early on; for most of the colonial period it remained the second-largest African employment sector, after mining.[7] Because of their knowledge of the European way of life, including dress etiquette, style and care, domestic servants were often consulted by workers in other jobs. But their privileged access to their employers' hand-me-downs must not be interpreted merely as emulation. Servants had little choice in this matter. Their substandard wages, partly paid in kind, limited their ability to purchase clothes.

Clothing competence was far from a servants' monopoly, especially after some job mobility and more disposable income came within reach of African men during the late colonial period. Inspired by his observations while working for the London Missionary Society on the Copperbelt from 1933 until his death in 1943, R.J.B. Moore had a good eye for detail when characterizing this period's African dress practice.

> The African urban dweller to-day, whatever his work, can no more exist without a smart rig-out of clothes than he could have managed yesterday without bow and arrow...Crowds at beer halls and football matches where everyone is dressed in European fashion show how universal is the new standard of clothing.[8]

Clothing remained a high priority in African consumption decisions throughout this period as the migratory process moved people, goods, and ideas across the wider region. The mine workers Godfrey Wilson studied in Broken Hill in the late 1930s spent more than half of their cash wages on clothes.[9] Clothing was the primary consumer good that migrants transferred to rural areas. 'The new ambitions of the country dwellers', Wilson noted in 1941–42, 'have reduced the proportional significance of food to them; they still want food, but wanting clothes, saucepans

---

[7] Karen Tranberg Hansen, *Distant Companions: Servants and Employers in Zambia, 1900–1985* (Ithaca, NY, 1989).

[8] R.J.B. Moore, *These African Copper Miners*. Revised, with appendices by A. Sandilans (London, 1948), pp. 72–3.

[9] Wilson, 'Economics of Detribalisation', vol. 2, p. 80. At the time of Wilson's study, African workers received food rations as part of their compensation. If the proportion of wages they spent on food was compared to that on clothing, food expenses are likely to have been larger, judging from later consumption surveys. Karen Tranberg Hansen, *Salaula: The World of Secondhand Clothing and Zambia* (Chicago, 2000), pp. 260–61.

and bicycles too, they would rather go hungry than do without them ... the wealth which young men send or give them is hardly ever turned into food.'[10]

The volume and variety of clothing in travel kits of returning migrants illustrate the high value migrants and people in their home villages attached to clothes. David Mwanza, who went with his father from the Eastern Province to Southern Rhodesia when he was 12 years old in 1936, worked on a European farm for one year. Before beginning their return journey, he related that 'we went to the store. I bought shorts, a shirt, a belt, a sweater, a hat and tennis shoes'.[11] When he was nearly 16-years-old in 1949, Sindikani Phiri left home in the same region to seek work in Southern Rhodesia. He first worked on a dairy farm, then in a shoe factory. 'When I was in Southern Rhodesia', he explained, 'I was earning good money and on returning [in 1951] I had thirteen pounds, a bicycle and other things, such as shorts, [long] trousers, six shirts and a jacket.'[12]

Observations like these are available from many regions, for example, in a detailed recording of travel kits of migrants returning home from the Copperbelt in the early 1930s, which lists a profusion of clothes.[13] Transfers of clothes from towns to rural areas continued well into the 1950s in Luapula Province (bordering the Belgian Congo) as Aron Chinanda remembered: 'those who had relatives working on the Copperbelt used to send money, and a person would take the money to one of the shops in Mansa and buy clothes ... he would buy clothes for himself and his wife'.[14] While statements such as these do not distinguish between new and used clothing, a good proportion of what migrants brought home when returning from the Belgian Congo consisted of *kombo*, as secondhand clothing was called in Luapula at that time.

By late World War II, 'the once familiar blue print dress ha[d] almost entirely been replaced by these Congo dresses'.[15] At this time, clothing no longer served as a store of wealth in the manner described for the 1930s. Wilson had noted that the 'possession of unused clothes enables the Africans to visit their rural homes ..., and provides security against the sudden loss of a job ... These clothes are kept, sometimes in boxes in their own houses, sometimes in the stores where they

---

[10] Wilson, 'Economics of Detribalisation', vol. 2, p. 52.

[11] Max Marwick, *Some Labour Histories. Appendix B in Helmuth Heisler, Urbanisation and the Government of Migration: The Interrelation of Urban and Rural Life in Zambia* (New York, 1974) p. 145.

[12] Marwick, *Labour Histories*, p. 145.

[13] J. Merle Davis, *Modern Industry and the African: An Enquiry into the Effect of the Copper Mines of Central Africa upon Native Society and the Work of the Christian Missions*, 2nd edn (1933, reprinted New York 1968), pp. 401–2.

[14] Mwelwa Musambachime, *The Oral History of Mansa, Zambia*. Edited and annotated version of oral-history research conducted by second-year students Raban Chanda and Daniel Yambayamba. N.D. Department of History, University of Zambia. Number 26.

[15] NAZ/SEC2/875. Kawambwa Tour Reports. No.3 of 1948. Appendix 8: Trade. National Archives of Zambia, Lusaka.

are purchased.'[16] A legal ordinance from 1915 had regulated the box system that enabled migrant workers to accumulate clothing in stores, either for safekeeping or as a security against payment. Developments in society at large during the war made this arrangement obsolete, and in 1948 the ordinance was repealed.[17]

The first call on wages by migrants in town was a visit to the stores to buy clothing, according to an official publication on trade, noting that 'the Native coming in or back from the reserves usually arrives and returns in rags'. The priority items were 'khaki shorts and shirts and the wardrobe will then gradually be built up with fancy shirts, hat, shoes, socks, belt and possibly a suit'.[18] Secondhand clothing represented the first type of ready-made clothing Africans could afford to buy, especially when considering their limited income and the poor quality of imported Indian and Japanese garments available in the local shops. Older people with whom I discussed clothing consumption spoke of *kombo* as garments with a better fit, superior quality, lasting longer, and as generally being more fashionable. 'These clothes were not seen in the shops', recalled Geoffrey Mee from his youth in Luapula during the war.[19] Still, the tailor played an insufficiently recognized role in responding to clothing demands and desires, not only by fabricating very basic garments such as shorts and school uniforms but also by fashioning clothes requiring more skills such as suits and elaborately styled dresses. Aside from mining and domestic labour, which employed a great number of migrants, the tailor's craft was an important activity that enabled men to find employment almost everywhere. Translating clothing needs and desires into garments, tailors contributed importantly to the process of making Africans knowledgeable and discriminating consumers of clothing.

Consumption Space, Trading Place, and African Opportunity

Questions about African clothing needs and desires cannot be explained without reference to the social, economic, and political conditions that structured their livelihoods during the last decades of colonial rule. Between 1939 and 1947 the cost of living for Africans increased by almost 100 per cent; most retail prices of textiles and clothing more than doubled between 1939 and 1943.[20] Because of wartime restrictions, clothing demand far outstripped supply, and Africans, as I briefly mentioned above, eagerly purchased *kombo* supplied by traders from the Belgian Congo.

---

[16] Wilson, 'Economics of Detribalisation', vol. 2, p. 35.

[17] NAZ/SEC2/294, 1939-47. Box System, National Archives of Zambia, Lusaka.

[18] Board of Trade, *The African Native Market in the Federation of Rhodesia and Nyasaland* (London, 1954), p. 11.

[19] Interview, 16 May 1995, Lusaka.

[20] Hansen, *Salaula*, p. 45.

When African pay scales finally increased and real wages improved in the post-war period, more Africans had the ability to buy, but their possibilities were still limited. Colonial urban town planning continued to segregate social and economic opportunity by race, restricting African trade to a limited array of goods in designated places and providing practically no credit arrangements to stimulate the development of entrepreneurship. Africans were expected to purchase goods for their households in the townships and in so-called second-class trading areas where largely Indian-owned stores sold a larger and more varied stock than traders in the African townships. Because the colonial government was reluctant to develop a manufacturing sector in Northern Rhodesia other than in industries supporting the mines, most textiles and garments were imported. Imports from South Africa and Southern Rhodesia enjoyed 'empire preference' on customs and tariffs. Textiles, clothing, and other commodities were also imported from Great Britain, India, Hong Kong and, in the early 1950s, from Japan while the early 1950s saw the imported, *kombo*, arrive from the Congo.[21]

Because of the limited scope of the colony's domestic garment manufacture, Africans turned to many other sources for their clothing needs. Tailors experienced brisk business, judging from the steep rise in the importation of sewing machines. Used clothing from many sources found a popular market. In the early 1940s, according to R.J.B. Moore, 'a European only has to tell the houseboy that there are some old clothes for sale, for a large and interested crowd to throng at the back door. At police sales of deceased's estates [Africans] run each other up to absurd prices for socks, shirts and old suits. A European church wanting to raise money only has to organize a jumble sale of clothes in a compound to be sure of successful results.'[22] Also, of course, there was the *kombo*. It is important here to recall Geoffrey Mee's comments about secondhand clothing from his youth on the Copperbelt in the 1940s, namely that 'these clothes were not seen in the shops'.

Mail-order firms in the United Kingdom and South Africa were already a dynamic presence by 1932. J. Merle Davis commented on the growth of a flourishing mail-order business by the English J.D. Williams and Oxendale companies among African miners on the Copperbelt, where numbers of workers would pool their orders to avoid processing charges.[23] During World War II, when import quotas and currency restrictions reduced the volume and variety of clothing available for purchase, more Africans eagerly turned to mail-order firms abroad. R.J.B. Moore reported from around 1943 that 'a man in town becomes a catalogue fiend. Overseas mails are loaded with catalogues from Oxendales and other mail order forms. Almost any evening a group of men may be seen in the compound or location sitting on dirty boxes poring over a catalogue for clothes, while one who can write makes out the order.'[24] Some elderly men in Luapula with whom

---

[21] Hansen, *Salaula*, p. 47.
[22] Moore, *African Copper Mines*, p. 58.
[23] Davis, *Modern Industry and the African*, pp. 73–4.
[24] Moore, *African Copper Mines*, pp. 57–8.

I discussed clothing access prior to independence recalled that quality shoes and good-looking jackets were purchased from mail-order firms, among them Edwards and Oxendale in England. Drawing on his detailed memory about clothing style, Mr Kamuti described a particularly well-liked blazer from the early 1960s in brightly coloured narrow stripes of yellow, green, red and with gold metal buttons.[25]

Hortense Powdermaker's paraphrase of a conversation between two African miners provides an example of the types of garments Africans purchased from mail-order catalogues as well as of local reactions to their acquisition. The prime attraction was an overcoat from Oxendales. One of the men described three other overcoats featured in the catalogue but added, '[T]hey are not good. The one which this man ordered is wonderful. In June [the coldest month in this part of Africa] he will be wearing it to the beer hall, since he is a strong drinker, and people will all be looking at him. The coat is brown in colour and has very long hair. If he wears it in town, a policeman can ask him from where he got it.'[26] The two friends both wanted such a coat, one of them wanting to order it before visiting in his village: 'People at home will just fall off the chair when they see that coat.'

Judging from the contemporary descriptions and recollections, on which I have drawn so far, it no longer makes sense to speak of Africans wearing European clothes in this period. In their active engagement with a changing world, Africans had clearly made European-styled dress conventions their own. They eagerly dressed in clothing they appropriated from a wide variety of domestic and foreign sources: shops, stores and hawkers; tailors; mail-order firms; locally obtained second-hands and imported *kombo*. The dress practices that arose from this medley of sources were not much influenced by local print advertising that rarely features textiles and clothing. Their knowledge about clothing consumption was above all practical knowledge acquired from participation in group activities and individual networks in urban life both at work and at home, in recreation and entertainment and at markets and in the streets. In such interactions, the visual impact of being noticed was paramount, requiring a sharp eye for detail, active recall of bodies in dress, and constant and detailed talk about clothing matters. In short, the dressed body mediated new aspirations with a lot of verve through display and eye-catching styling that made the European origin of garment/styles merely one of many inspirations.

The Gender Story: 'We want dresses'

The colonial period's clothing discussion pushed African women into the background for three reasons. One is the deeply gendered history of clothing consumption that through labour migration drew in African men much earlier

---

[25] 29 May 1925, *Oral History of Mansa*.

[26] Hortense Powdermaker, *Copper Town: Changing Africa. The Human Condition on the Rhodesian Copperbelt* (New York, 1962), p. 94.

than African women. For a long time, for example, men dominated in gender-typed occupations such as domestic service and tailoring. Another reason concerns normative assumptions about gender and authority that had men as heads of households, as the authority in charge of clothing transfers to wives and dependents. A third reason has to do with the available sources which, although they were not all written by men, overwhelmingly report the opinions of men, both African and European, about African women's clothing needs and desires.

Women had more limited access to and choice of clothing than men who had been migrant workers. When trading *kombo* in Luapula villages in the 1940s, hawkers were often pressed with specific orders from women. 'What I want is a dress' was a common demand with specification of size and style.[27] When women came to the towns in larger numbers during and after World War II, they were eager for new fashions.[28] A report on the commercial prospect of the colony in the early 1950s when purchasing power had improved somewhat noted that a man's:

> first expenditure is on clothing for himself and his womenfolk and the latter usually see to it that they are not overlooked… [T]he native woman…attaches considerable importance to matters of design, style and fashion in her dress goods and she generally knows just what she wants in the way of cloth[ing] when she goes shopping. Just as fashions change in our western world, so, often for unaccountable reasons, certain designs or colours in cotton piece-goods, for instance, suddenly lose popularity and become quite unsaleable.[29]

It was a cultural expectation that husbands provide wives with clothes. Some women 'judged husbands and lovers according to the amount of money they are given to spend on clothes'.[30] The normative expectation that men dress women gave rise to suspicion when women's clothes looked expensive. The flashily dressed woman and her paramours is a well-worked theme in popular songs of this era. Yet in the urban settings some women did earn money in their own right, largely through small-scale trade and services as very few had yet found wage-labour jobs. Tensions in gender relations on the domestic front and beyond were fuelled by rapid socioeconomic change, including women's growing consumption abilities and new dress options.[31]

---

[27] Ellie Mukonko, 25 May 1995, *Oral History of Mansa*.

[28] Jane L. Parpart, '"Where is Your Mother?" Gender, Urban Marriage, and Colonial Discourse on the Zambian Copperbelt, 1924–1945', *International Journal of African Historical Studies*, 27/2 (1994): pp. 250–54.

[29] Overseas Economic Surveys, *Southern and Northern Rhodesia and Nyasaland* (London: Her Majesty's Stationery Office, 1950) p. 28.

[30] Wilson, 'Economics of Detribalisation', vol. 2, p. 18.

[31] Epstein, *Urbanization and Kinship*; Powdermaker, *Coppertown*.

Lusaka: Postcolonial Experiments with Fashion, Looks and Style

Across southern Africa today, people from Zambia are known as good dressers. Zambian women are noted for dressing more smartly and fashionably than women elsewhere in the region and Zambian elite men love suits from areas such as Savile Row (Illustration 10.1). Small-scale tailors in Lusaka produce highly styled outfits from *chitenge* fabric (distinguished by its colourful prints) for resale by suitcase traders in South Africa where such outfits are called 'Zambia'. Women's *chitenge* outfits and men's suits are part of a dress universe that has diversified dramatically since the opening up of the economy when compared to the restricted clothing access of both the colonial period and the one-party state (1972–91). When import restrictions were relaxed in the late 1980s, secondhand clothing from the United States and Europe rapidly became a popular trade and consumption item, as I describe below. After a period of rapid growth during the first half of the 1990s, the import and local trade in secondhand clothes appears to have become an established part of the clothing scene in the 2000s, rarely causing any public debate. In fact, with the growth of imported new garments from China in recent years, secondhand clothing's share of total clothing imports has actually declined.

As stated previously, since the mid-1980s, imported secondhand clothing has been referred to as *salaula* which in the Bemba language means approximately 'selecting from a pile by rummaging' or for short, 'to pick'. The term describes vividly the process that takes place once a bale of imported secondhand clothing

Illustration 10.1   Fashion sign. Photograph by Karen Tranberg Hansen, 2004

has been opened in the market and consumers select garments to satisfy both their clothing needs and wants. The shop window of Zambia's secondhand clothing trade, the big public markets, create an atmosphere much like the West's shopping malls where consumers can find what they want in a way not possible in the formal stores, where Zambian consumers are often dealt with offhandedly or are pressured to purchase.

Consumers in Zambia go to secondhand clothing markets for many reasons. White-collar workers of both sexes in Lusaka's city centre often spend their lunch hour going through the secondhand clothing stalls, sometimes making purchases at whim. Others go to find just that right item to match a particular garment. Some women who tailor in their homes search the markets for interesting buttons, belts, and trim to decorate garments. And some go to purchase garments with the intention to resell. But the vast majority shop from *salaula* for clothing for themselves and their families. Secondhand clothing does not serve only poorer consumers. People come into the city centre from residential areas like those in which I examined clothing consumption and where roughly two-thirds of all households supplied most of their members' clothing from secondhand clothing markets.

Only the very tiny high-income group in Zambia has an effective choice in the clothing market. This group, called *apamwamba*, a term in the Nyanja language that means approximately 'those on the top', purchases clothing everywhere, including from upscale stores and boutiques in Lusaka's new shopping malls as well as from secondhand clothing markets. People from these better-off households spend more money on tailor-made clothing than do poor households. Recent years have witnessed the emergence of some entrepreneurs launching themselves as local clothing designers who are beginning to make a mark with 'African designs' in *chitenge* fabrics that may add new value to the local fashion scene.[32]

Space and Place in the *Salaula* Market

Salaula is the centrepiece of activity in public markets in Zambia's cities and towns, taking up more vending space than foodstuffs. The value consumers in Zambia attribute to *salaula* is created through a process of re-commodification involving several phases. The chief source of the international secondhand clothing trade is the charitable organizations that dispose of their enormous surplus of donated clothing to textile recyclers.[33] In the United States and Europe, the sorting

---

[32] *Weekend Post*, 2 December 2005, Augustine Mukota and Photos by Collin Phiri, 'Lookout for "Fresh" Designs … as two Young Designers Churn out Their First Dresses', p. 4.

[33] As I have discussed in my larger work (Hansen 2000), the consequences of this trade are manifold and controversial. For a discussion of popular reactions, see Hansen, 'Helping or Hindering? Controversies around the International Second-hand Clothing Trade', *Anthropology Today*, 20/4 (2004): pp. 3–9.

and compressing of secondhand clothing into bales in the clothing recycler's warehouse strip used garments which had any connection with their past. The decommissioned value of the West's unwanted but still wearable clothing is then re-activated on local terms in transactions between overseas suppliers and local importers. Through subsequent transformations the meanings shift in ways that help redefine used clothing into 'new' garments. These transformations begin in communications between exporters and importers and in on-site visits, continue at wholesale outlets and in public markets, and they show how consumers feel about *salaula*. In addition to these processes through which the register of meaning of clothing shifts, there are also physical and material changes involving alteration, mending and recycling.

On first sight, the *salaula* markets meet the non-local observer's eye as a chaotic mass of secondhand clothing hung up on flimsy wood contraptions, displayed on tables or dumped in piles on the ground. That view is deceptive. A variety of informal rules organize vending space and structure sales practices. Both vendors and customers know these practices. A prospective customer looking for a specific garment will go to a particular part of the market. The vendors of men's suits, for example, one of the most expensive items, tend to be located in a part of the outdoor market that is near to major thoroughfares such as a main road passable by automobiles. So are vendors of other high demand garments, such as women's skirts and blouses, and the best selling item of all, at least in Zambia, baby clothes. There are spatial clusters of vendors selling shoes and, during the winter in the southern hemisphere, cold weather clothing.

The display on most secondhand clothing stands is carefully designed. High quality items are hung on clothes hangers on makeshift walls. A clothing-line or a wood stand may display a row of cotton dresses (Illustration 10.2). Everything that meets the eye has been carefully selected with a view both to presentation and sales strategy. Lively discussions and price negotiations accompany sales. The piles on the ground include damaged items and garments that have been around for a while. Such items are sold at a discount, and they are often purchased by rural customers who take them to the villages to resell.

Near the high-end of the secondhand clothing display, and near the major roads of the market section are the 'boutiques'. Boutiques in these markets sell specially pre-selected items, coordinated to form stylish matched outfits. They tend to be operated by young vendors who 'pick', in the language of the market. Once other traders open secondhand clothing bales, the pickers descend on them, selecting garments they buy on the spot. Then they make up, for instance, women's two-piece ensembles, men's suits, and leisure wear (Illustration 10.3). Most of the boutique operators I met were young men who were very skilled at choosing quality stock with a fine eye for what might sell, a great sense of style, and a flair for making stunning combinations. I also met boutique operators who were women. Some of them had tailoring skills and they sewed clothing to order from their own homes.

The Search for 'the Latest' in Colonial and Postcolonial Zambia 227

Illustration 10.2 Salaula market. Photograph by Karen Tranberg Hansen, 1992

Clothing Competence

A vital dimension of the demand for modern clothing involves cultural taste and style issues that come together in the creation of a 'total look'. Concerns with fabric quality, texture, and construction precede that creation which in turn revolves around the anticipated dress needs of the specific situation. The chief attraction of garments from 'outside' is style and variety, not price, which is why everyone regardless of class, shops from *salaula*. *Salaula* fashions bring consumers into a bigger world: the world of awareness. It is the search for the look, rather than brand-names, that guide how people shop although of course neither style issues nor clothing markets are ever static but develop in complex ways, one of which might be the preoccupation with brand names in the secondhand clothing markets in the future.

When shopping from secondhand clothing markets, consumers' preoccupation with creating particular appearances is inspired by trends from across the world. Consumers draw on these influences in ways that are informed by local norms about bodies and dress. The desired clothing silhouette for both adult women and men is neat and tidy. It is a product of immaculate garment care and of wearing

Illustration 10.3   Chitenge outfits. Photograph by Karen Tranberg Hansen, 2006

clothes in ways that are not considered to be too revealing. Even then, women's and men's garments are understood differently. The cultural norms about how to dress weigh down on women more heavily than on men. In effect, women feel restrained in their freedom to dress so as not to provoke men.[34] Women should not

---

[34] Karen Tranberg Hansen, 'Dressing Dangerously: Miniskirts, Gender Relations, and Sexuality in Zambia' in Jean Allman (ed.), *Fashioning Africa: Power and the Politics of Dress* (Bloomington, 2004), pp. 166–85.

expose their shoulders. Above all, they must cover their 'private parts', which in this region of Africa includes their thighs. This means that dress length, tightness and fabric transparency become issues when women interact with men and elders both at home and in public.

The desire for uniqueness, to stand out, while dressing the body on Zambian terms entails considerable skill in garment selection from the abundance of *salaula*, making discriminating decisions concerning quality, style, and value for money, in garment co-ordination to fit specific occasions and contexts, and in the overall presentation and comportment of the dressed body to produce a 'total look'. Many consumers are extraordinarily aware when it comes to clothing purchases aimed at producing particular effects. In order to highlight that shopping from *salaula* does not mean that anything goes, I describe as 'clothing competence' the skill that is critical to the successful business of clothes shopping . The underlying sensibility is a visual aesthetic that on first sight cultivates endless variation of dress, yet on closer analysis is also in the service of continuity. In this creative process, consumers are active in putting together an attractive and unique look for themselves reflecting an approach I saw expressed in a caption to a recent news story about fashion: 'where others imitate, we originate'.[35]

Suit Aesthetics and Provocative Wear: Young Men's Dress Dilemmas

Unlike young women who carefully monitor the way they dress in public, young men like to draw attention to themselves in various ways, depending on their socioeconomic circumstances and regional location in Zambia's declining economy. They actively seek to present a smart appearance that is both fashionable and neat. Young men's self-conscious preoccupations with suits and jeans illustrate different constructions of these types of dress.

Suits are worn widely in the civil service and other white-collar jobs in Zambia. Formal suits show young urban men's desire to become adult, hold jobs, and head households. Cutting a fine figure in a smart suit conveys something important about personal background, respectability, and responsibility – suits are identified with patriarchal social power that is widespread throughout Zambia. Most of the young men in their late teens or early twenties in a secondary school in Lusaka who in 1995 described for me where they bought their clothes and how they liked to dress aspired to this dress practice and the ideal it conveys. 'Suits are the clothes I like most', explained Simon, 'because they make me look decent and soon I will be joining the society of workers.' Morgan, his class mate, described a pair of trousers and a jacket he recently had received: 'I was full of joy ... I like these clothes because a lot of people say that I look like a general manager and not only that, they also say that I look like a rich man.' And Moses' delight in a double-

---

[35] *Weekend Post*, 2 December 2005.

breasted jacket his father had given him is evident: 'I like jackets because they suit me like a second skin.'

Other classmates liked jeans, particularly because of their durability but also because 'they are in style now'. But wearing jeans had a downside that too often made some people think of scruffy youths and street vendors, who are popularly associated with illegal activities. According to Moses, 'I hate wearing jeans because people may fail to distinguish between cigarette sellers and myself.'

If suits and jeans frame young urban men's desires for a better life, young men in rural areas have similar desires but are more circumscribed by the conditions in which they live. Secondary school students in Mansa, a provincial town in Luapula Province, explained this clearly. Joshua explained: 'Of all the clothes, I like strong ones which can serve me longer such as jeans. I like them because it is not easy for me to buy soap, and most of the time I do manual work in order to earn my living.' The suit figures in the desires of these young rural men mostly by its absence. Describing why the suit combination did not fit his situation, Nicholas explained: 'Such clothes can easily be torn and I think they are for office working people, so they don't suit me.' Yet he added as an afterthought, 'If I had a choice, I would really like to wear suits.'

Jeans are a must in the evolving street vendor style. Lusaka's downtown streets are full of young male traders in all kinds of goods, many of whom put much effort into being seen, and many of whom dress in a striking manner. In addition to the style explanations I describe below, the preference of street vendors for denim has an obvious practical reason. Jeans, one of them explained, 'are durable; they are nice and easy to keep especially for bachelors like me who have no one to look after our clothes'. What the young vendors my assistant interviewed in 1997 did for their own pleasure was to dress up in public in variations on the baggy jeans look. The layered look was in vogue that year as were knitted caps referred to as head-socks and shoes with thick rubber soles, often worn without socks.

The secondary school students and the young street vendors purchased their clothes from a variety of sources. Some bought imported clothing from 'suitcase' traders who bring in garments from abroad, some went to the tailor for specific wear, and all of them scoured the *salaula* market for just the right items. As one of the street vendors explained, 'In *salaula* you will find things you can't believe how good they are'. When shopping for clothes, the young vendors look for garments that will contribute to the overall creation of a particular style, which in the late 1990s was 'the big look', rather than for brand-name items. 'I wear the big look because it is fashion', one said while another explained how he liked to 'move with time'. I don't like 'common clothes and imitations', said yet another.

Making associations between specific articles of clothing and behaviour, young people construct an understanding of their world and how they inhabit it. Young male secondary students with high economic aspirations for themselves do not want to be mistaken for the school drop-outs turned street vendors. They want suits. The vendors, for their part, wear clothes they equate with the power and success achieved by popular performers both in Africa and beyond. Putting themselves together with clothing the major part of which is from *salaula*, both groups of young people are dressing to explore who they are and who they would like to become.³⁶

Dress Codes and Choices: *Apamwamba* Women's Dress Practice

If suits are the garments to wear for young men who wish to be upwardly mobile, decent dress that does not reveal too much is the clothing style for young women, including young women of better means who have real options in the clothing market because of their economic background. The dress presentation by male and female announcers of the daily evening news on national television in Zambia, the government controlled Zambia National Broadcasting Corporation (ZNBC), illustrates the almost iconic status of the suit and decent dress in Zambia.

I tracked these dress presentations over the course of my two-month stay in Lusaka during the southern hemisphere's cold months of July and August both in 2003 and 2004. Back in 1995, I had interviewed then popular TV announcer Mary Phiri about dress protocol for the news announcers. There were none, she said, other than 'decent'. Unlike on South African TV where clothing firms sometimes dress announcers for advertising value, clothing firms do not (to my knowledge) dress the news announcers on Zambian TV.³⁷ The announcers purchase their own clothes, including garments from *salaula*. Without exception, men announcers always wore a suit and tie. While the severity of their suits varied from striped, check, to single colours of very dark, grey and beige, ties and pocket handkerchiefs offered variation. By contrast, the women announcers' clothes were more diverse. Some women announcers were more likely than others to wear *chitenge* suits or dresses, that is, the very ornamented outfits, elaborately tailored from colourful printed fabric. This dress presentation sometimes included complicated head-ties inspired by West African head dressing practices. A global fashion fusion is evident here, as some Zambian women refer to such headdresses as *dukas*, a term that derives from the Afrikaans word *doek* for scarf. More women news announcers wore *chitenge* dresses in 2003 than in 2004 for reasons that may have to do with the temporary absence of some very popular announcers. The rest of the women news announcers most frequently wore jackets with contrasting shirt or blouse with a variety of decorative trim. Zambian women refer to the skirt and jacket combination as office- or corporate wear.

---

³⁶ Eileen Moyer offers very comparable insights in her research on young men working and living on the streets of Dar es Salaam, Tanzania. While influenced by American hip-hop culture and Jamaican Rastafari ideals, they work to achieve a look that is suitable to their living environment and reflective of their own desires. Eileen Moyer, 'Keeping up Appearances: Fashion and Function among Dar es Salaam Street Youth', *Etnofoor*, 16/2 (2003): pp. 88–105.

³⁷ I have seen hairdressers' names acknowledged on Zambian TV.

Interacting with young people of both sexes of mid- to upper-income background in 2002 and 2003, an assistant and I sought to learn where they go in their free time, with whom, and how they dress on such occasions. I focus on the women we interviewed here. Such women constitute a very small segment of Lusaka's huge youth population. Pursuing further education at a variety of colleges, training institutions, and universities, including some abroad in Australia and the United States, most of these young women have the means, usually because of wealthy parents, to hang out with friends at Lusaka's new shopping malls, other shopping venues, popular pool halls, bars and parks. There is a nightclub scene which some of them visit. In their day-time interaction, aside from gossiping about friends, talking about relationships, sex, the entertainment scene, and their futures, these young women spend considerable time discussing 'looks', exchanging information about the availability of particularly desired garments, and who has been seen wearing what and where. Most of them love clothes. Their interest in dress is valued in positive terms by the friends they associate with and they all spend considerable time and effort discussing the latest fashions. 'It is the combination of clothing', said a 22-year-old psychology student, 'that demonstrates your sense of style'.

'Clothes', said a 24-year-old marketing student, 'place me in my class.' Like many others, she did not like baggy jeans, 'no boring loose slacks' as one expressed it,' because they are tomboyish, and gangsta', a comparison that we also heard some young men make. During the daytime interactions when we interviewed the young women, they dressed decently but casually, meaning – controlling for body size – in tight jeans, or knee length jeans skirts resting on the hips with waistlines accentuated by cropped short tops. Young women who were heavy-set wore long, fitted skirts with slits. A 22- year-old university student explained that her outfit, combining jeans, matching tops, and smart shoes 'make me look mature and outline my model body'. Altogether by Zambian norms, there was nothing too revealing in the way these young women dressed when out in public. Their hair was either richly braided or cut short, the most popular women's hairstyles at the time. Their overall look was accessorized by cell phones, handbags, shoes and jewellery.

These young women sourced most of their clothing from stores and boutiques, including from abroad. They also, as I indicated earlier, shop from *salaula*, but as a pastime, not a need. Some had never been to a tailor. They were not keen to wear *chitenge* dresses, and they did not all own one. Young women's attitude to wearing *chitenge* outfits revolves around body size and age. Looking best on 'traditionally built women', these elaborately styled dresses evoke a level of maturity which some young women consider to be old, something that they associate with what their mothers and grandmothers wear.[38] With an outlook such as this, it is no surprise that 'casual' is the thing to wear.

---

[38] Karen Tranberg Hansen, 'Gender and Differnece: Youth, Bodies, and Clothing in Zambia' in Victoria Goddard, ed., *Gender, Agency, and Change: An Anthropological Perspective* (London, 2000), p. 265.

'Everything I wear', said a 21-year-old woman, 'should make people look and say "wow, she is nice".' In their concern to create their own fashion statements and demonstrate an individual sense of style, these young women emphasize their *apamwamba* status. While their self-styling has something in common with the hip, cutting-edge, middle-class life-styles that Sarah Nuttall has described for the Y generation of Rosebank in Johannesburg (2004), it does not come close to the sartorial, visual, and sonic dimensions of youth culture of Rosebank.[39] The reasons may have to do with Zambia's status as one of the world's least developed countries. In their self-styling through dress, *apamwamba* women in Lusaka seek to avoid 'sliding down' in local socio-economic terms. While they wear world/global fashions, the strategic presentation of their dressed bodies becomes meaningful on Zambian terms, that is, in the local context of economic decline, urban poverty, and other processes set into motion by Zambia's unequal place in the global economy.

Conclusion: The City and Fashion on Zambian Terms

'Watch Lusaka', argued Samuel Ngoma, when drawing attention to the many sources that enlivened the capital's fashion scene. In the past, cities like Lusaka were the prime stages for the cultivation of dress styles and dress conventions from which developed a local dress aesthetics. Migration and town life helped translate dress inspirations from across the world into local understandings and experiences. The link between city life and fashion continues strongly in the present with the proliferation and broadening of dress exposures that we associate with globalization. Across class in Zambia, dress invokes aspirations, desires, and imaginaries that vary by gender and generation and have changed over time. But one thing remains in place and that is a widely shared dress aesthetics that, as I have demonstrated in this paper, surprises, delights and gives positive reactions.

In Zambia, dressing, and dressing up, are both an end and a means. Dress is a resource as well as a technique. There is genuine pleasure to be gained from being dressed well which in the view of local observers is a sign of wellbeing. But while preoccupations with the dressed body are of long standing, specifically styled garments have come and gone. This preoccupation constitutes an aesthetic sensibility, implicating discerning skills from a variety of sources in creating an overall look that results in pride, pleasure, and experiences of feeling good. In this way, clothing is part of the aesthetic of everyday urban life. Mediating between self and society, the dressed body also construes desires, including global imaginaries. As a cultural and material resource, secondhand clothing does all of these things.

In their engagements with the West's used clothing, consumers in Zambia reconstruct these garments as 'new' or 'fresh' and transform them by notions of

---

[39] Sarah Nuttall, 'Stylizing the Self: The Y Generation in Rosebank, Johannesburg', *Public Culture*, 16/3 (2004): pp. 430–52.

taste and selection to fit the embodied dress norms of their local clothing universe. It is by crafting themselves through dress that Zambian wearers of secondhand clothing achieve the look they call 'the latest', that fluid appearance of change and novelty that we tend to associate with fashion.[40] But if the effect of such appearances rarely is precise or explicit but fluid and volatile, appearance itself is not arbitrary. Rather it is the product of a set of clearly identifiable, interacting practices, the effects of which converge in the moment of display. In Lusaka, this performance expresses itself in a vibrant aesthetic sensibility of cultivating appearances that makes people take notice, with admiration or opprobrium as the case may be.

---

[40] Joanne Finkelstein, *Fashion: An Introduction* (New York, 1998).

Bibliography

Primary Sources

Archive of Americana Database. www.infowebnewsbank.com.
Arxiu Històric Comarcal de Vilafranca del Penedés, APN, Joan Rovira, P-XVIII-63-1, f. 62.; J. Mullol, P-XVIII-131-1, s/n; 'Documents pendent de classificar', Llibreta de las sabatas y roba se ha feta per compte de la Sra. Francisca Nin, viuda, comensant en lo any 1727'.
Boston Public Library Collections, Rare Books Department, Chapman-Weston Papers.
British Museum, London, UK, Department of Ethnology, Africa Collections, accession information and accession number BM 43.3-11.53; BM 43.3-11.22; BM 1920.2-11.1; BM 1934.3-7.215.
Canadian Aboriginal Festival Website, 'Designer Package': http://www.canab.com/pdfs/fashion/2008/designer_package2008.pdf, accessed 26 November 2008.
Dene Fur Clouds, http://www.ek-o.net/ accessed 25 May 2009.
Everett, Ronald, interviews with Temperance McDonald, 30 May (informal) and 22 June 2004 (taped). Ronald Everett Design Website, 'Gowns in Micro Suede' page:http://ronaldeverettdesign.com/PhotoAlbums/album_1216076720/, accessed 26 November 2008.
Grant, Dorothy, Website, 'The Company' page: http://www.dorothygrant.com/content.cfm?cmd=Company, accessed 17 April 2001. 'Fashion Designer – Dorothy Grant,' article by Vesta Giles in *Indian Artist*, Fall 1997, reproduced with permissionat:http://www.dorothygrant.com/content.dfm?cmd=HaidaArt&ID=12, accessed 17 April 2001.
Guerlain Archives, Paris. Guerlain, *Prix-courant de Guerlain, Parfumeur breveté (S.G.D.G.), 15 rue de la Paix* (Paris, Imprimerie de T. Jeunet, 1878); *Prix-courant de Guerlain, Parfumeur breveté (S.G.D.G.), 15 rue de la Paix* (Paris, 1882).
Kawambwa Tour Reports. No.3 of 1948. Appendix 8: Trade.
Liverpool Museum, UK, L 5.10.1906.2; L 5.10.1906.1a; L 5.10.1906.3a.
Municipal Archives Antwerp, Guilds & Corporations, nr. 4006; Chamber of Insolvent Inventories, nr. 2363; Pamphlets, nr. 531/2; Chamber of Privileges, nr. 788; Lawsuit Supplements, nr. 6732.
Museum für Völkerkunde, Berlin, B IIIC 15288; B IIIC 5058; B XI/1897; B XI/1900; B IIIC 41026; B IIIC 41027; B no # (II, 627); B IIIC 41025.
National Archives, Kew, UK, ADM 53/8428, Log book, *HMS Rattlesnake*.
National Archives of Zambia, Lusaka, NAZ/SEC2/294, 1939-47. Box System; NAZ/SEC2/875.
National Museum of Scotland, Edinburgh, NMS 1878.1.2; NMS 1903.354.

Pitt-Rivers Museum, Oxford, V. Lamb and J. Holmes, *Nigerian Weaving*, p.70, fig.94.
Royal Ontario Museum, Toronto, ROM 950.126.2.
Staatliches Museum für Völkerkunde, Munich, Germany, Department of Ethnology, Africa Collections, accession information and accession numbers 15-26-56 through 15-26-157.
Textile Museum of Canada, Toronto, MT R85.1290; MT R85.1291.
TOC Legends: Touch of Culture, http://www.toclegends.com/enter/ accessed 25 May 2009.
Turtle Concepts: http://www.turtleconcepts.com/UploadedFiles/File/2008 designer_package_for_website.pdf, accessed 26 November 2008.
University of Zambia, Ellie Mukondo, Mwelwa Musambachime, *The Oral History of Mansa, Zambia*. Edited and annotated version of oral-history research conducted by second-year students Raban Chanda and Daniel Yambayamba. N.D. Department of History, Number 26.
Victoria and Albert Museum Digital Database. http://images.vam.ac.uk/
Wisbech and Fenland Museum, Wisbech, UK, WF 1.xii.1856.

Consultants

Anonymous, 27 March 1999. Home and School Liaison Coordinator, First Nations School of Toronto, informal telephone interview by Cory Willmott.
Anonymous, 26 November 2008. Two different residents of Six Nations of Grand River Reserve concerning fate of Dinawo after 2002, informal telephone interviews by Cory Willmott.
Baker, Pam, 27 May 2004. Kwakiutl/Squamish, Capilano Reservation, North Vancouver,
BC Designer/Proprietor of TOC (Touch of Culture) Legends; Owner/Instructor of TOC Native Training Institute. Taped telephone interview by Temperance McDonald. Video-taped recording 1 June 1999, by Zeek Cywink.
Burnham, Shelley, 15 December 1999. Onieda, Six Nations, Ont. – General Manager of Dinawo, Ohsweken, Ontario. Taped telephone interview by Cory Willmott.
Everett, Ron, 30 May 2004; 22 June 2004. Tsimshian, Lax Kwalaams/Toronto, ON – fashion designer; proprietor of Ronald Everett Design. Untaped telephone interview and taped telephone interview by Temperance McDonald. Video-taped recording 1 June 1999, by Zeek Cywink.
Heese George, Tracey, 5 December 1999; 1 June 2000. Cree, Ochaponace First Nation/Regina, Saskatchewan - fashion designer and fashion show co-ordinator. Taped interview: Sky Dome Powwow, Toronto by Cory Willmott; untaped telephone interview by Cory Willmott.

Hubbard, Anny, 14 December 1999. Anishnaabe/Metis; Sault St. Marie, MI - multi-media artist, birch bark cut-out artist, regalia artist, poet, teacher and workshop instructor. Taped telephone interview by Cory Willmott.

Jones, Dave, 6 December 1999; 30 August 2001. Anishnaabe, Garden River First Nation – founder and director of Turtle Concepts Inc., fashion photographer, fashion show producer and MC. Taped interviews at SkyDome Powwow and Dave Jones' house at Garden River by Cory Willmott. Video-taped recordings, Nov. 25th and 26th, 2000, by Zeek Cywink.

Koe, Fred E., 7 May 2001. Executive Director, Northwest Territories Development Corporation, informal face to face interview at North American Fur and Fashion Emporium at Montreal (NAFFEM) by Cory Willmott.

Smoke, Suzanne 1998-2001, Anishnaabe, Alderville First Nation, Ontario - Peterborough, ON - fashion designer and fashion show producer and MC. Taped interview: 11 July 2001 (and informal conversations on a number of occasions).

Video-Taped Recordings

CANAB, 21 November 1998: Toronto International Powwow Fashion Shows, Skydome, by Zeek Cywink.

CANAB, 25 November 2000: Toronto International Powwow Fashion Shows, Skydome, by Zeek Cywink.

FNST, 31 March 1999: 'Fashion/Talent Show', First Nations School of Toronto, by Zeek Cywink and Cory Willmott.

Printed Primary Sources

'Académie des sciences – séance du 25 octobre 1893', *La Nature*, 2 (1893).

Allen, William and T.R.H. Thomson, *A Narrative of the Expedition to the River Niger* (2 vols, 1848 reprinted New York: Johnson Reprint, 1967).

APFTI (Associated Partners for Fairer Trade, Inc.). *2002 and 2003 Annual Reports* (Quezon City, Philippines: APFTI, 2002 and 2003).

Balzac, Honoré de, 'Une double famille', *La Comédie humaine. Œuvres complètes de M.de Balzac* (12 vols, Paris: Furne, Dubochet et Cie, 1842), vol. 1.

—, 'Histoire de la grandeur et de la décadence de César Birotteau', *La Comédie humaine. Œuvres complètes de M. de Balzac* (12 vols, Paris: Furne, Dubochet et Cie, 1844), vol. 10.

Barreswil, Charles-Louis, 'La parfumerie en 1862', in Charles Laboulaye (ed.), *Annales du Conservatoire Impérial des Arts et Métiers* (8 vols, Paris: Librairie scientifique industrielle et agricole de Eugène Lacroix, 1863), 1st series, vol. 4.

Barth, Heinrich, *Travels and Discoveries in North and Central Africa* (3 vols, 1857; reprinted London: Cass, 1965).

Board of Trade, *The African Native Market in the Federation of Rhodesia and Nyasaland.* (London: Her Majesty's Stationery Office, 1954).
Bon Ton, Le, 26/2 (1 July 1860).
Bowen, T.J., *Grammar and Dictionary of the Yoruba Language* (Washington, DC: Smithsonian Institution, 1858).
Boyd, Jean and Mack, Beverly (eds and trans.), *One Woman's Jihad: Nana Asma'u, Scholar and Scribe* (Bloomington, IN: Indiana University Press, 2000).
Burton, Richard, *A Mission to Gelele, King of Dahome* (New York: Praeger, 1966).
Campbell, R., *The complete London tradesman* (London, 1757).
[Cardon, Pieter], *Den oorspronck van de ruïne en armoede der Spaensche Nederlanden alsmede de aenwijsingen der hulpmiddelen om de selve landen wederom te herstellen ende in de selve te doen herleven den afgestorven koophandel, schipvaert, landtbouw, 't maecken van manufacturen ende alderhande soorten van handtwercken, tot een algemeyne welvaeren van de ingesetenen van de selve landen* (Liège, 1699).
Casanovas i Canut, Sebastià, *El manuscrit de Palau-Saverdera: Memòries d'un pages empordanès del segle XVIII (Figueres: El corral del vent, 1986).*
Catalogue général de la fabrication des savons et parfums de Violet (Paris: 1865).
Cavendish, Margaret, *The life of William Cavendish, Duke of Newcastle,* ed. C.H. Firth, (London: John C. Nimmo, 1886).
CBC Radio North Website, 'Home Again in Fashion,' by Alison Dempster: http://north.cbc.ca/north/archive/fur/simpfur.htm, accessed 17 April 2004.
Crowther, Samuel, *A Vocabulary of the Yoruba Language* (London: Seelys, 1852).
—, *A Grammar and Vocabulary of the Nupe Language* (London: Church Missionary House, 1864).
Dan Fodio, Uthman, 'On the Law Concerning the Wearing of Silk in a Jihad', in Fathi Hasan Masri (trans.), *Bayan wujub al-hijra ala l-ibad* (New York: Oxford University Press, 1978).
De Gencé, Comtesse, *Code Mondain de la Jeune Fille* (Paris: 1909).
—, *Le cabinet de toilette d'une honnête femme* (Paris: Pancier, 1909).
Denham, Dixon, Clapperton, Hugh and Oudney, Walter, *Travels and Discoveries in Northern and Central Africa in 1822, 1823, and 1824* (4 vols, London: John Murray, 1831).
Douglass, Frederick, *Narrative by of the Life of Frederick Douglass An American Slave. Written Himself* (Dublin: Webb and Chapman, 1845).
Dufaux de la Jonchère, Ermance, *Le savoir-vivre dans la vie ordinaire et dans les cérémonies civiles et religieuses* (Paris: Garnier Freres, 1883).
Frobenius, Leo, *The Voice of Africa* (2 vols, London: Hutchinson and Co., 1913).
Gazette van Antwerpen (1700–1705, 1723–7, 1743–7).
Harrison, William, *The Description of England,* ed. Georges Edelen (Ithaca: Cornell University Press, 1968).

Hennequin, G., 'Boutique de parfumerie, à Paris, boulevard des Italiens', *La Construction Moderne*, 9 (1893): pp. 126–7.
Hermant, A., 'Grandes industries françaises: la parfumerie, La Maison L.T. Piver', *Le Monde illustré*, (1862).
Hibernian Anti-slavery Society, (ed.), *Some Particulars of the late Boston Antislavery Bazaar: With a Sketch of the Antislavery Movement in the United States* (Dublin: Webb and Chapman, 1842).
Hiskett, Mervyn (trans.), '*Kitab al-farq*: A Work on the Habe [Hausa] Kingdoms attributed to Uthman dan Fodio', *Bulletin of the School of Oriental and African Studies*, 23/3 (1960): pp. 558–79.
— (trans.), *Tazyin al-waraqat* (Ibadan, Nigeria: Ibadan University Press, 1963).
— (trans.), 'Materials relating to the cowrie currency of the western sudan – I: A late nineteenth-century schedule of inheritance from Kano', *Bulletin of the School of Oriental and African Studies*, 29/1 (1966): pp. 122–42.
Hutchinson, T.J., *Narrative of the Niger, Tshadda, and Binue Expedition* (1855, reprinted London: Cass, 1966).
Levtzion, N. and Hopkins, J.F.P. (eds and trans.), *Corpus of Early Arabic Sources for West African History* (Cambridge: Cambridge University Press, 1981).
Maryan, M. and Béal, G., *Le Fond et la forme: le savoir-vivre pour les jeunes filles*, (Paris: Blond & Barrai, 1896).
Masri, Fathi Hasan (trans.), *Bayan wujub al-hijra ala l-ibad* (New York: Oxford University Press, 1978).
Menzel, Brigitte, *Textilien aus Westafrika* (3 vols, Berlin: Museum für Völkerkunde, 1972–74).
Mischlich, Adam, *Über die Kulturen im Mittel-Sudan* (Berlin: Dietrich Reimer, 1942).
Mode Illustrée, La, 37/24 (14 June 1896).
Morrall, Abel, *Needles in their Principal Stages ...Prepared for the Boston Anti-Slavery Bazaar, 1855* (Manchester: n.p., 1855).
Nachtigal, Gustav (trans.), *Sahara and Sudan* (4 vols, 1879, reprinted London: Hurst and Company, 1980).
Overseas Economic Surveys, Southern and Northern Rhodesia and Nyasaland (London: Her Majesty's Stationery Office, 1950).
Owen, Mrs Henry, *The Illuminated Book of Needlework: Comprising Knitting, Netting, Crochet, and Embroidery, Proceeded by a History of Needlework, Including an Account of the Ancient Historical Tapestries*. Countess of Wilton (ed.), (London: H.G. Bohn, 1847).
Parfumerie, La, 'Le musc en parfumerie', 2/25 (12 August 1888).
Picard, Alfred, *Exposition universelle internationale de 1900 à Paris. Le bilan d'un siècle (1801–1900)*, (6 vols, Paris: Imprimerie Nationale, 1906) vol. 5.
Piesse, Septimus, *Chimie des parfums et fabrication des essences ... Édition française mise au courant des progrès de la chimie, etc.* (Paris: Bibliothèque des connaissances utiles, 1903).

Poirters, Adrianus, *Het masker van de wereldt afgetrocken* (Antwerp: By de weduwe, ende erfgenaemen Ian Cnobbaerts, 1646).

Proceedings of the Association for Promoting the Discovery of the Interior Parts of Africa (2 vols, London: Dawsons of Pall Mall, 1967. Facsimile of 1810 edition).

Pyrard, François, *The Voyage of Francois Pyrard of Laval to the East Indies, the Maldives, the Moluccas and Brazil* (London: Printed for the Hakluyt Society, 1887–88).

Rancé, François, *Prix courant des parfumeries de la fabrique de François Rancé* (Grasse: n.p., n.d.). *Rapports du jury mixte international publiés sous la dir. de S.A.I. le Prince Napoléon, président de la commission impériale* (Paris : Imprimerie Impériale, 1856).

Report of the Twentieth National Antislavery Bazaar (Boston: J.B. Yerrinton & Son, Printers, 1854).

Report of the Twenty-First National Antislavery Bazaar (Boston: J.B. Yerrinton & Son, Printers, 1855).

Robert-André, Jacqueline, 'A la Reine des fleurs', *La Tribune Piver*, 1/5 (1960): p. 9.

Robinson, Charles H., *Hausaland: or, Fifteen Hundred Miles through the Central Soudan* 3rd edn, (London: S. Low Marston, 1900).

Robinson, J.A., 'Sudan and Upper Niger Mission', *The Church Missionary Intelligencer*, February (1891): p. 111.

Roger & Gallet: parfumeurs et créateurs, 1806-1989, Exposition du Musée municipal de Bernay, 3 juin–3 septembre 1898 (Bernay: Association pour la promotion de la culture à Bernay, 1987).

Royal Commission on Aboriginal Peoples (RCAP), *Sharing the Harvest: The Road to Self-Reliance. Report of the Round Table on Aboriginal Economic Development and Resources* (Ottawa: Minister of Supply and Services, 1993).

Russell, John, 'Boke of Nurture', in F.J. Furnivall (ed.), *Early English Meals and Manners: John Russell's Boke of Nurture* (London: Early English Text Society, 1868).

Sempere y Guarinos, Juan, *Historia del lujo y de las leyes suntuarias en España* (2 vols, Madrid: Imprenta Real, 1788).

Sentiments de monseigneur Jean Joseph Languet eve'que de Soissons, et de quelques autres Savants & Pieux écrivains de la compagnie de Jésus, sur le faux bonheur & la vanité des plaisirs mondains, spécialement des bals, des comédies et autres amusements dangereux nouvellement recueillis par Jean Baptiste Vermeersch, curé de S. Michel à Gant, (Ghent: Michel De Goesin, 1738).

Shaw, John, *Sketches of the history of the Austrian Netherlands* (London: Robinson, 1786).

Smith, Adam, *An Inquiry into the nature and causes of the wealth of nations...* (1776, London: T. Nelson and Sons, 1852),

Staffe, Baronne, *Règles du savoir-vivre dans la société moderne* (Paris: Victor-Havard, 1892).

Staudinger, Paul, *In the Heart of the Hausa States* (2 vols, 1889 edn, trans. and reprinted Athens, OH: Ohio University Center for International Studies, 1990).
Zola, Emile, *Thérèse* (Paris: Raquin, Lacroix, Verbockhoven et Cie, 1868).
—, *Nana* (1880, Paris, 1994).
—, *Au Bonheur des dames* (1883, reprinted Paris: 1984).

Printed Secondary Sources

Abelson, Elaine S., *When Ladies Go A-Thieving: Middle-Class Shoplifters in the Victorian Department Store* (London: Oxford University Press, 1989).
Adamu, Mahdi, *The Hausa Factor in West African History* (Zaria, Nigeria: Ahmadu Bello University Press, 1978).
Adshead, S. A. M., *Material Culture in Europe and China, 1400-1800: the rise of consumerism* (New York: St Martin's Press, 1997).
Aguilar, Filomeno V. and Miralao, Virginia A., *Rattan Furniture Manufacturing in Metro Cebu: A Case Study of an Export Industry*, Handcraft Project Paper Series No. 6 (Manila, Philippines: Ramon Magsaysay Award Foundation, 1985).
Ajmar-Wollheim, Marta, and Dennis, Flora (eds), *At Home in Renaissance Italy* (London: Victoria & Albert Museum, 2006).
Albert de la Bruhèze, Adri and de Wit, Onno, 'De productie van consumptie. De bemiddeling van productie en consumptie en de ontwikkeling van de consumptiesamenleving in Nederland in de twintigste eeuw', *Tijdschrift voor Sociale Geschiedenis*, 28 (2002): pp. 257–72.
Allen, D.E., 'Fashion as a Social Process', *Textile History*, 22/2 (1991): pp. 347–58.
Allman, Jean (ed.), *Fashioning Africa: Power and the Politics of Dress* (Bloomington: University of Indiana Press, 2004).
Anderson, Benedict, *Imagined Communities: Reflections on the Origin and Spread of Nationalism* (London, Verso, reprinted 1991).
Andersson, Gudrun, 'A Mirror of Oneself: Possessions and the Manifestation of Status among a Local Swedish Elite, 1650–1770', *Cultural and Social History*, 3/1 (2006): pp. 21–44.
Appadurai, Arjun (ed.), *The Social life of Things: Commodities in Cultural Perspective* (Cambridge: Cambridge University Press, 1986).
Atkin, Andrea M., '"When Pincushions are Periodicals" Women's Work, Race and Material Objects in Female Abolitionism', *American Transcendental Quarterly*, 11/2 (1997): pp. 93–113.
Auslander, Leora, 'Beyond Words', *American Historical Review*, 110/4 (2006): pp. 1015–44.
Baldwin, Frances Elizabeth, *Sumptuary Legislation and Personal Regulation in England* (Baltimore: Johns Hopkins Press, 1926).
Balisacan, Arsenio, 'Anatomy of Poverty during Adjustment: The Case of the Philippines', *Economic Development and Cultural Change*, 44/1 (1995): pp. 33–62.

Banfield, A.W., *Dictionary of the Nupe Language* (2 vols, 1914 reprinted, Farnborough, UK: Gregg International, 1969).

Barba i Roca, Manuel, *El corregiment i partit de Vilafranca del Penedès a l'últim terç del segle XVIII* (Vilafranca del Penedès: Museu de Vilafranca, 1991).

Bargery, G.P. and D. Westermann, *A Hausa-English Dictionary and English-Hausa Vocabulary* (London: Oxford University Press, 1934).

Barker-Benfield, G. J., *The culture of sensibility. Sex and society in Eighteenth-century Britain* (Chicago: The University of Chicago Press, 1992).

Barrera, Albert, *Casa, herencia y familia en la Cataluña rural* (Madrid: Alianza, 1990).

Barrientos, Stephanie and Dolan, Catherine (eds), *Ethical Sourcing in the Global Food System* (London: Earthscan, 2006).

Barthes, Roland, *The Fashion System*, translated by Matthew Ward and William Howard (New York: Hill & Wang, 1983).

Bauland, Micheline, Schuurman, Anton J. and Servais, Paul (eds), *Inventaires Apres-Deces et Vented de Meubles: Apports à une histoire de la vie économique et quotidienne (XIVe – XIXe siècle* (Louvain-la-Neuve: Académia, 1988).

Baulant, Micheline, 'Typologie des inventaires après décès', in Ad Van der Woude and A. Schuurman (eds), *Probate inventories. A new source for the historical study of wealth, material culture and agricultural development*, (Utrecht: HES Publishers, 1980) pp. 33–42.

—, 'Nécessité de vivre et besoin de paraître. Les inventaires et la vie quotidienne', in M. Baulant, A.J. Schuurman, P. Servais (eds), *Inventaires après-décès et ventes de meubles* (Louvain-la-Neuve: Académia, 1988), pp. 9–14.

Baumgarten, Linda, *What Clothes Reveal: The Language of Clothing in Colonial and Federal America* (New Haven, CT: Yale University Press and The Colonial Williamsburg Foundation, 2002).

Beachy, Robert, Craig, Béatrice and Owens, Alastair (eds), *Business, and Finance in Nineteenth-Century Europe: Rethinking Separate Spheres* (Oxford and New York: Berg Publishers, 2006).

Beaudry, Mary C., *Findings: The Material Culture of Needlework and Sewing* (New Haven, CT: Yale University Press, 2007).

Bennassar, Bartolomé, 'Los inventarios post-mortem y la historia de las mentalidades', in *Actas II Coloquio de Metodología Histórica Aplicada* (2 vols, Santiago de Compostela: Universidad de Santiago, 1984), vol 2, pp. 139–52.

Benson, Susan, *Counter Cultures: Saleswomen, Managers, and Customers in American Department Stores, 1890–1940* (Urbana: University of Illinois Press, 1988).

Berg, Maxine, *A Woman in History: Eileen Power 1889–1940* (Cambridge: Cambridge University Press, 1996).

—, 'Women's Consumption and the Industrial Classes in Eighteenth-Century England', *Journal of Social History*, 30/2 (1996): pp. 414–34.

—, 'Product innovation in core consumer industries in eighteenth-century Britain', in Maxine Berg and Kristine Bruland (eds), *Technological revolutions in Europe. Historical perspectives* (Cheltenham: Elgar, 1998), pp. 138–57.

—, 'New Commodities, Luxuries and Their Consumers in Eighteenth-Century England', in Maxine Berg and Helen Clifford (eds), *Consumers and Luxury: Consumer Culture in Europe, 1650–1850* (Manchester, 1999), pp. 63–85.

—, 'French fancy and cool Britannia: the fashion markets of Early Modern Europe', in Simonetta Cavaciocchi (ed.), *Fiere e mercati nella integrazione delle economie Europee secc. XIII–XVIII* (Firenze: Monnier, 2001), pp. 519–56.

—, 'From imitation to invention: creating commodities in eighteenth-century Britain', *Economic History Review*, 55 (2002): pp. 1–30.

—, *Luxury and Pleasure in Eighteenth-Century Britain* (Oxford: Oxford University Press, 2005).

Berry, Christopher J., *The Idea of Luxury: a conceptual and historical investigation* (Cambridge: Cambridge University Press, 1994).

Bestor, Theodore C., 'Supply-Side Sushi: Commodity, Market, and the Global City', *American Anthropologist*, 103/1 (2001): pp. 76–95.

Bhachu, Parminder, 'Designing Diasporic Markets: Asian Fashion Entrepreneurs in London', in Sandra Niessen, Ann Marie Leshkowich and Carla Jones (eds), *Re-Orienting Fashion: The Globalization of Asian Dress* (Oxford and New York, 2003), pp. 139–58.

—, *Dangerous Designs: Asian Women Fashion the Diaspora Economies* (New York and London: Routledge, 2004).

Bianchi, Marina (ed.), *The active consumer. Novelty and surprise in consumer choice* (London: Routledge, 1998).

Biow, Douglas, *The Culture of Cleanliness in Renaissance Italy* (Ithaca, NY and London: Cornell University Press, 2006).

Blewett, Mary H., *Men, Women, and Work: Class, Gender, and Protest in the New England Shoe Industry, 1780–1910* (Urbana: University of Illinois Press, 1988).

Blondé, Bruno, 'Indicatoren van het luxeverbruik? Paardenbezit en conspicuous consumption te Antwerpen (zeventiende-achttiende eeuw)', *Bijdragen tot de Geschiedenis*, 84 (2001): pp. 497–512.

—, 'Art and economy in seventeenth- and eighteenth-century Antwerp: a view from the demand side', in Simonetta Cavaciocchi, (ed.), *Economia e arte secc. XIII–XVIII* (Firenze: Monnier, 2002), pp. 379–91.

—, 'Tableware and changing consumer patterns. Dynamics of material culture in Antwerp, 17th–18th centuries', in Johan Veeckman (ed.), *Majolica and glass. From Italy to Antwerp and beyond. The transfer of technology in the 16th–early 17th century* (Antwerp: Antwerpen, Stad. Afdeling Archeologie, 2002), pp. 295–311.

—, 'Cities in decline and the dawn of a consumer society: Antwerp in the 17th–18th centuries', in Bruno Blondé, Eugénie Briot, Natacha Coquery and Laura Van Aert (eds), *Retailers and consumer changes in Early Modern Europe.*

England, France, Italy and the Low Countries (Tours: Presses Universitaires François-Rabelais, 2005), pp. 37–52.

—, Eugénie Briot, Natacha Coquery and Laura Van Aert (eds), *Retailers and consumer changes in Early Modern Europe. England, France, Italy and the Low Countries* (Tours: Presses Universitaires François-Rabelais, 2005).

— and De Laet, Veerle, 'Owning paintings and changes in consumer preferences in the Low Countries, seventeenth-eighteenth centuries', in Neil De Marchi and Hans J. Van Miegroet (eds), *Mapping markets for paintings in Europe, 1450–1750* (Turnhout: Brepols, 2006), pp. 69–84.

— and Greefs, Hilde, '"Werk aan de winkel", De Antwerpse meerseniers: aspecten van de kleinhandel en het verbruik in de 17de en 18de eeuw', *Bijdragen tot de Geschiedenis: De lokroep van het bedrijf. Handelaars, ondernemers en hun samenleving van de zestiende tot de twintigste eeuw. Liber amicorum Roland Baetens*, 84 (2001): pp. 216–20.

—, Stabel, Peter, Stobart, Jon and Van Damme, Ilja, 'Retail circuits and practices in medieval and early modern Europe: an introduction', in Bruno Blondé, Peter Stabel, Jon Stobart and Ilja Van Damme (eds), *Buyers and sellers. Retail circuits and practices in medieval and early modern Europe* (Turnhout: Brepols, 2006), pp. 7–29.

— and Van Damme, Ilja, 'Low Countries: Southern Netherlands between 1585 and 1830', in Joel Mokyr (ed.), *The Oxford encyclopedia of economic history* (5 vols, Oxford: Oxford University Press, 2003), vol 3, pp. 392–4.

— and —, '11 augustus 1723. Indische Compagnie trekt naar de beurs', in Gustaaf Asaert (ed.), *De 25 dagen van Antwerpen* (Amsterdam: Waanders, 2006), pp. 274–95.

— and —, 'Retail growth and consumer changes in a declining urban economy: Antwerp (1650–1750)', *Economic History Review*, 62 (2009): forthcoming.

Blumer, Herbert, 'Fashion: From Class Differentiation to Collective Selection', *Sociological Quarterly*, 10/3 (1969): pp. 275–91.

Bohaker, Heidi, 'Nindoodemag: The Significance of Algonquian Kinship Networks in the Eastern Great Lakes Region, 1600–1701', *William and Mary Quarterly*, 3rd Series 63/1 (2006): pp. 25–52.

Boucher, François, *20,000 Years of Fashion: the history of costume and adornment* (New York, 1967, new edition 1987).

Bourdieu, Pierre, *Distinction: a social critique of the judgement of taste* translated by Richard Nice (French edition 1979, Cambridge MA: Harvard University Press, 1984).

Boydston, Jeanne, *Home and Work: Housework, Wages, and the Ideology of Labor in the Early Republic* (New York: Oxford University Press, 1994).

—, 'The Woman Who Wasn't There: Women's Market Labor and the Transition to Capitalism in the United States', *Journal of the Early Republic*, 16/2 (1996): pp. 183–206.

Brah, Avtar and Coombes, Annie E., 'Introduction: the Conundrum of "Mixing"', in Avtar Brah and Annie Coombes (eds), *Hybridity and its Discontents: Politics, Science and Culture* (London and New York, Routledge, 2000), pp. 1–16.

Branson, Susan, 'Women and the Family Economy in the Early Republic: The Case of Elizabeth Meredith', *Journal of the Early Republic*, 16/1 (1996): pp. 47–71.

Braudel, Fernand, *Capitalism and Material Life, 1400–1800* translated by Miriam Kochan (New York: Harper & Row, 1973).

—, *Civilization & Capitalism 15th–18th Century: The Structure of Everyday Life*, translated by Siân Reynolds (New York: Harper & Row, 1985).

Bravmann, René, *African Islam* (Washington, DC: Smithsonian Institution Press, 1983).

Brewer, John and Porter, Roy (eds), *Consumption and the World of Goods* (London: Routledge, 1993).

— and Silverman, Raymond, 'Painted Incantations: The Closeness of Allah and Kings in 19th–century Asante' in Enid Schildkrout (ed.), *The Golden Stool: Studies of the Asante Center and Periphery* (New York: American Museum of Natural History, 1987), pp. 93–108.

Briot, Eugénie, 'César Birotteau et ses pairs: poétiques et mercatique des parfumeurs dans le Paris du XIXe siècle', in Bruno Blondé, Eugénie Briot, Natacha Coquery and Laura Van Aert (eds), *Retailers and consumer changes in Early Modern Europe. England, France, Italy and the Low Countries* (Tours: Presses Universitaires François-Rabelais, 2005), pp. 71–102.

Broad, Robin, *Unequal Alliance: The World Bank, the International Monetary Fund and the Philippines* (Berkeley: University of California Press, 1988).

Brook, Timothy, *The confusions of pleasure: commerce and culture in Ming China* (Berkeley: University of California Press, 1998).

Brown, Frank E., 'Continuity and Change in the Urban House: Developments in Domestic Space Organisation in Seventeenth-Century London', *Comparative Studies in Society and History*, 28/3 (1986): pp. 558–90.

Buck, Anne, 'Clothing and textiles in Bedfordshire inventories, 1617–1620', *Costume*, 34 (2000): pp. 25–38.

Burke, Peter, '*Res et verba*: conspicuous consumption in the early modern world', in John Brewer and Roy Porter (eds), *Consumption and the World of Goods* (London: Routledge, 1993), pp. 148–61.

Burman, Barbara (ed.), *The Culture of Sewing: Gender, Consumption and Home Dressmaking* (Oxford and New York: Berg Publishers, 1999).

Cabreza, Vince, 'Fashion from Recycled Materials is the New Rage', *Philippine Daily Inquirer*, 7 July 2006: B 2.

Campbell, Colin, *The romantic ethic and the spirit of modern consumerism* (Oxford: Oxford University Press, 1987).

—, 'The desire for the new. Its nature and social location as presented in theories of fashion and modern consumerism', in Miller, Daniel (ed.), *Consumption. Critical concepts in the social sciences* (4 vols, London and New York: Routledge, 2001), vol 1, pp. 247–50.

Carbonell, Montserrat, *Sobreviure a Barcelona. Dones, pobresa i assistència al segle XVIII* (Vic: Eumo Editorial, 1997).

Carr, Lois Green and Walsh, Lorena S., 'Changing Lifestyles and Consumer Behavior in the Colonial Chesapeake', in Cary Carson, Ronald Hoffman and Peter J. Albert, (eds), *Of consuming interests: the style of life in the eighteenth century* (Charlottesville, NC: Published for the United States Capitol Historical Society by the University Press of Virginia, 1994), pp. 59–166.

Carson, Cary, Hoffman, Ronald and Albert, Peter J. (eds), *Of consuming interests: the style of life in the eighteenth century* (Charlottesville, NC: Published for the United States Capitol Historical Society by the University Press of Virginia, 1994).

Castañeda, Luis, 'Ensayo metodológico sobre los inventarios post–mortem en el análisis de los niveles de vida material: el ejemplo de Barcelona entre 1790–1794' in *Actes Primer Congrés d'Història Moderna de Catalunya* (Barcelona: Universitat de Barcelona, 1984), pp. 757–69.

Chambers-Schiller, Lee, "'A Good Work Among the People': The Political Culture of the Boston Antislavery Fair,' in Jean Fagan Yellin and John C. Van Horne (eds), *The Abolitionist Sisterhood: Women's Political Culture in Antebellum America* (Ithaca, 1994), pp. 249–74.

Chandler, Daniel, *Semiotics: The Basics* (London: Routledge, 2004).

Chant, Sylvia, 'Women's Roles in Recession and Economic Restructuring in Mexico and the Philippines', *Geoforum*, 27/3 (1996): pp. 297–327.

— and McIlwaine, Cathy, *Women of a Lesser Cost: Female Labour, Foreign Exchange & Philippine Development* (London and East Haven, CT: Pluto Press, 1995).

Chatterjee, Partha, *The Nation and its Fragments: Colonial and Postcolonial Histories* (Princeton: Princeton University Press, 1993).

Cherry, Deborah and Helland, Janice (eds), *Local/Global: Women Artists in the Nineteenth Century* (Aldershot, UK: Ashgate Publishers, 2006).

Clark, Alice, *Working Life of Women in the Seventeenth Century* (London: George Routledge & Sons, 1919).

Clark, Anna, 'The Rhetoric of Chartist Domesticity: Gender, Language, and Class in the 1830s and 1840s', *The Journal of British Studies*, 31/1 (1991): pp. 62–88.

Clifford, Helen, 'A commerce with things: the value of precious metalwork in Early Modern England', in Maxine Berg and Helen Clifford (eds), *Consumers and luxury. Consumer culture in Europe 1650–1850* (Manchester: Manchester University Press, 1999), pp. 147–68.

Clifford, James, *Routes: Travel and Translation in the Late Twentieth Century* (Cambridge, MA: Harvard University Press, 1997).

Clunas, Craig, 'Modernity Global and Local: Consumption and the Rise of the West', *American Historical Review*, 104/5 (1999): pp. 1497–511.

Cochrane, Laura, 'From the Archives: Women's History in Baker Library's Business Manuscripts Collection', *Business History Review*, 74/3 (2000): pp. 465–76.

Codina, Jaume, *Delta del Llobregat. la gent del fang (El Prat; 965–1965)* (Barcelona: Montblanc, 1966).

Coleman, D.C., 'Ken Ponting: An Appreciation', *Textile History*, 14/2 (1983): pp. 108–13.

Collins, Brenda, 'Matters Material and Luxurious – Eighteenth and Early Nineteenth-Century Irish Linen Consumption', in Jacqueline Hill and Colm Lennon (eds), *Luxury and Austerity: Papers Read before the 23rd Irish Conference of Historians* (Dublin: University College Dublin Press, 1999), pp. 106–20.

Colloredo-Mansfeld, Rudi, 'An Ethnography of Neoliberalism: Understanding Competition in Artisan Economies', *Current Anthropology*, 43/1 (2002): pp. 113–37.

Comaroff, John L. and Comaroff, Jean, 'Fashioning the Colonial Subject: The Empire's Old Clothes', in John L. Comaroff and Jean Comaroff (eds), *Of Revelation and Revolution, The Dialectics of Modernity on a South African Frontier* (Chicago: University of Chicago Press, 1997), pp. 218–73.

Coombe, Rosemary, 'The Properties of Culture and the Possession of Identity: Postcolonial Struggle and the Legal Imagination', in Bruce Ziff and Pratima V. Rao (eds), *Borrowed Power: Essays on Cultural Appropriation* (New Brunswick, NJ: Rutgers University Press, 1997), pp. 74–96.

Coppens, Marie, '"Au magasin de Paris". Une boutique de mode à Anvers dans la première moitié du XVIIIe siècle', *Belgisch Tijdschrift voor Oudheidkunde en Kunstgeschiedenis*, 52 (1983): pp. 81–107.

Coquery, Natacha (ed.), *La boutique et la ville : commerces, commerçants, espaces et clientèles, XVIe–XXe siècle: actes du colloque des 2, 3 et 4 décembre 1999* (Tours: Centre d'histoire de la ville moderne et contemporaine, Université François Rabelais, 2000).

—, *L'hôtel aristocratique: le marché du luxe à Paris au XVIIIe siècle*, (Paris: Publications de la Sorbonne, 1998).

Corbin, Alain, *Le Miasme et la jonquille: l'odorat et l'imaginaire social XVIIIe–XIXe siècles* (Paris: Aubier-Montaigne, 1982).

—, *The Foul and the Fragrant: Odor and the French Social Imagination* (Cambridge, MA: Harvard University Press, 1986).

Corner, David, 'The tyranny of fashion: the case of the felt-hatting trade in the late seventeenth and eighteenth centuries', *Textile History*, 22 (1991): pp. 153–78.

Cornette, Joël, 'La révolution des objets: le Paris des inventaires apres décès (XVIIe–XVIIIe siècles)', *Revue d'Histoire Moderne et Contemporaine*, 36 (1989): pp. 476–86.

Corrigan, Peter, *The sociology of consumption* (London: Sage, 1997).

Craske, Matthew, 'Plan and control: design and the competitive spirit in early and mid-eighteenth-century England', *Journal of Design History*, 12 (1999): pp. 187–216.

— and Berg, Maxine, 'Art and industry. The making of modern luxury in eighteenth-century Britain', in Simonetta Cavaciocchi (ed.), *Economia e arte secc. XIII–XVIII* (Firenze: Monnier, 2002), pp. 823–35.

Crowley, John E., 'The Sensibility of Comfort', *American Historical Review*, 104/3 (1999): pp. 749–82.
—, *The Invention of Comfort: Sensibilities and Design in Early Modern Britain and Early America* (Baltimore: Johns Hopkins University Press, 2001).
Crowston, C.H., '"The queen and her minister of fashion": gender, credit and politics in pre-revolutionary France', *Gender & History*, 14 (2002): pp. 96–116.
Csergo, Julia, *Liberté, égalité, propreté: la morale de l'hygiène au XIXe siècle* (Paris: Albin Michel, 1988).
'Cultures of Clothing in Later Medieval and Early Modern Europe', Special Issue, *Journal of Medieval and Early Modern Studies*, 39/3 (2009).
Cunnington, C. Willett and Cunnington, Phillis, *Handbook of English Mediaeval Costume* (London: Faber and Faber, 1952).
— and —, *Handbook of English Costume in the Sixteenth Century* (London: Faber & Faber, 1954).
— and —, *Handbook of English Costume in the Seventeenth Century* (London: Faber & Faber, 1955).
— and —, *Handbook of English Costume in the Eighteenth Century* (London: Faber & Faber, 1957).
D'Amat, Rafael and Baró de Maldà, Margarida Aritzeta, *Viles i ciutats de Catalunya* (Barcelona: Barcino, 1994).
Daumard, Adeline, 'Structures sociales et classement socioprofessionel. L'apport des archives notariales au XVIIIe et XIXe siècle', *Revue Historique*, 227/1 (1962): pp. 139–54.
Davidoff, Leonore & Hall, Catherine, *Family Fortunes: Men and women of the English middle class 1780–1850* (Chicago: Hutchinson Education, 1987).
Davis, J. Merle, *Modern Industry and the African: An Enquiry into the Effect of the Copper Mines of Central Africa upon Native Society and the Work of the Christian Missions*, 2nd edn (1933, reprinted New York: St Martin's Press, 1968).
Deceulaer, Harald, *Pluriforme patronen en een verschillende snit. Sociaaleconomische, institutionele en culturele transformaties in de kledingsector in Antwerpen, Brussel en Gent, 1585–1800* (Amsterdam: Aksant, 2001).
De Grazia, Victoria and Furlough, Ellen (eds), *The Sex of Things. Gender and Consumption in Historical Perspective* (Berkeley: University of California Press, 1996).
De Marchi, Neil and Van Miegroet, Hans J., 'Transforming the Paris art market, 1718–1750', in Neil De Marchi and Hans J. Van Miegroet (eds), *Mapping markets for paintings in Europe, 1450–1750* (Turnhout: Brepols, 2006), pp. 383–404.
De Meuter, Ingrid, 'De wandtapijtindustrie te Brussel ten tijde van het Oostenrijks bewind. De bestellingen geplaatst door keizerin Maria-Theresia', in *De Oostenrijkse Nederlanden, het Prinsbisdom Luik en het Graafschap Loon in de 18de eeuw. Bijdragen over cultuur, politiek en economie* (Hasselt: Provinciebestuur van Limburg, 1989), pp. 79–90.

Deneckere, M., 'Histoire de la langue française dans les Flandres (1770–1823)', *Handelingen der Maatschappij voor Geschiedenis en Oudheidkunde te Gent*, 6 (1952): pp. 131–255.

De Schrijver, Reginald, 'Oorlog en vrede voor de Zuidelijke Nederlanden 1678–1700', in *Algemene Geschiedenis der Nederlanden* (12 vols, Haarlem: Fibula-Van Dishoeck, 1979), vol 8, pp. 308–19.

Despretz-Van de Casteele, S., 'Het protectionisme in de Zuidelijke Nederlanden gedurende de tweede helft der 17de eeuw', *Tijdschrift voor Geschiedenis*, 78 (1965): pp. 294–317.

De Vlieger-De Wilde, Koen, *Adellijke levensstijl. Dienstpersoneel, consumptie en materiële leefwereld van Jan van Brouchoven en Livina de Beer, graaf en gravin van Bergeyck (ca. 1685–1740)* (Brussels: Verhandelingen van de Koninklijke Vlaamse Academie voor Wetenschappen en Kunsten, 2005).

De Vries, Jan, *European Urbanization, 1500–1800* (London: Methuen 1984).

—, 'Between purchasing power and the world of goods: understanding the household economy in early modern Europe' in John Brewer and Roy Porter (eds), *Consumption and the world of goods* (London: Routledge, 1993), pp. 85–132.

—, 'The industrious revolution and economic growth, 1650–1830', in Paul A. Davids and Mark Thomas (eds), *The economic future in historical perspective* (Oxford: Oxford University Press, 2003), pp. 43–71.

De Zamora, Francisco, *Diario de los viajes hechos en Cataluña* (Barcelona: Curial, 1973).

Dibbits, Hester C., 'Between Society and Family Values: The Linen Cupboard in Early-Modern Households', in Anton Schuurman and Pieter Spierenburg (eds), *Private Domain, Public Inquiry: Families and Life-Styles in the Netherlands and Europe, 1550 to the Present* (Hilversum, NL: Verloren, 1996), pp. 125–45.

Diefendorf, Barbara, 'Women and property in *ancien régime* France. Theory and practice in Dauphiné and Paris' in John Brewer and Susan Staves (eds), *Early Modern Conceptions of Property* (London: Routledge, 1996), pp. 170–93.

Díez, Fernando, 'La apología ilustrada del lujo en España. Sobre la configuración del *hombre* consumidor', *Historia Social*, 37 (2000): pp. 3–26.

—, *Utilidad, deseo y virtud. La formación de la idea moderna del trabajo* (Barcelona: Ediciones Península, 2001).

DiGregorio, Michael, *Urban Harvest: Recycling as a Peasant Industry in Northern Vietnam* (Honolulu, Hawaii: East-West Center Occasional Papers, Environment Series. No. 17, 1994).

Douglas, Mary, *Thought Styles: Critical Essays on Good Taste* (London: Sage, 1996).

— and Isherwood, Baron *The World of Goods: Towards an Anthropology of Consumption* (New York: Basic Books, 1979).

Dublin, Thomas, *Transforming Women's Work: New England Lives in the Industrial Revolution* (Ithaca: Cornell University Press, 1994).

Duby, Georges (ed.), *A History of Private Life. Revelations of the Medieval World*, vol. 2, (5 vols, Cambridge, MA and London: Harvard University Press, 1988).

Duffek, Karen, 'Northwest Coast Indian Art from 1950 to the Present', in *Shadows of the Sun: Perspectives on Contemporary Native Art* (Ottawa: Canadian Museum of Civilization, 1993).

Earle, Alice Morse, *Costume in Colonial Times* (New York: Empire State Book Company, 1924).

Eber, Christine, '"That They be in the Middle, Lord": Women, Weaving, and Cultural Survival in Highland Chiapas, Mexico', in Kimberly M. Grimes and B. Lynne Milgram (eds), *Artisans and Cooperatives: Developing Alternative Trade for the Global Economy* (Tuscon, AZ: University of Arizona Press, 2000), pp. 45–64.

Ecoist, URL: www.ecoist.com (December 18, 2008).

Edelstein, T.J., 'They Sang the 'Song of the Shirt': The Visual Iconography of the Seamstress', *Victorian Studies*, 23 (1980): pp. 183–210.

Edwards, Clive D., 'Floorcloth and Linoleum: Aspects of the History of Oil-coated Materials for Floors', *Textile History*, 27/2 (1996): pp. 148–71.

—, *Turning houses into Homes: A History of the Retailing and Consumption of Domestic Furnishings* (Aldershot, UK: Ashgate, 2005).

—, 'The upholsterer and the retailing of domestic furnishings 1600–1800', in Bruno Blondé, Eugénie Briot, Natacha Coquery and Laura Van Aert (eds), *Retailers and consumer changes in Early Modern Europe. England, France, Italy and the Low Countries* (Tours: Presses Universitaires François-Rabelais, 2005), pp. 53–69.

Edwards, Ralph, *A History of the English Chair* (London, 1951).

Edwards, Tim, *Contradictions of consumption: concepts, practices and politics in consumer society* (Buckingham: Open University Press, 2000).

Eicher, Joanne and Sumberg, Barbara, 'World Fashion, Ethnic, and National Dress', in Joanne Eicher (ed.), *Dress and Ethnicity: Change Across Space and Time* (Oxford: Berg Publishers, 1995), pp. 295–306.

Eiras Roel, Antonio, 'La documentación de protocolos notariales en la reciente historiografía modernista', *Estudis Històrics i Documents dels Arxius de Protocols*, 8 (1980): pp. 7–28.

Elias, Norbert, *El proceso de la civilización* (México: Fondo de Cultura Económica, 1989).

The Encyclopaedia of Islam (12 vols, Leiden: Brill, 1960–2004).

Epstein, Arnold L., *Urbanization and Kinship: The Domestic Domain on the Copperbelt of Zambia, 1950–1956* (New York: Academic Press, 1981).

Escama Studio, URL: www.escamastudio.com, accessed 20 September 2009.

Estabrook, Carl B., *Urbane and Rustic England: Cultural Ties and Social Spheres in the Provinces 1660–1780* (Manchester: Manchester University Press, 1998).

Everaert, John, 'Een "nobele besogne" in verval. De kwijnende trafiek in kunst en edelstenen tussen Vlaanderen en Spanje (1650–1685)', in Hugo Soly and René

Vermeir (eds), *Beleid en bestuur in de Nederlanden. Liber amicorum Prof. Dr. M. Baelde* (Ghent: Rijksuniversiteit Gent, 1993), pp. 183–88.
Fair, Laura. 'Dressing Up: Clothing, Class and Gender in Post-Abolition Zanzibar', *Journal of African History*, 39/1 (1998): pp. 63–94.
Fairchilds, Cissie, 'The Production and Marketing of Populuxe Goods in Eighteenth-Century Paris', in John Brewer and Roy Porter (eds), *Consumption and the World of Goods* (London: Routledge, 1993), pp. 228–48.
—, 'Consumption in Early Modern Europe. A review article', *Comparative Studies in Society and History*, 35 (1993): pp. 850–58.
—, 'Determinants of Consumption Patterns in Eighteenth-Century France', A.J. Schuurman and L.S. Walsh (eds), *Material culture, life-style, standard of living, 1500–1900, Proceedings of the XI International Economic History Congress* (Milan: Bocconi University Press, 1994), pp. 50–70.
Fashion-Nation, http://www.canada.com/topics/lifestyle/fashionweek/story html?id=b42e0e6b-5513-47e5-8786-46af39cddc40&k=47127, accessed 25 May 2009.
Fauve-Chamoux, Antoinette, 'Vedove di città e vedove di campagna nella Francia preindustriale: Aggregato domestico, trasmissione e strategie familiari di sopravvivenza', *Quaderni Storici*, 98 (1998): pp. 301–32.
Featherstone, Mike, *Global Culture: Nationalism, Globalisation and Modernity* (London: Sage, 1990).
Ferrero, Pat, Hedges, Elaine and Silber, Julie, *Hearts and Hands: The Influence of Women & Quilts on American Society* (Chicago: Quilt Digest Press, 1987).
Fika, Adamu, *The Kano Civil War and British Over-rule, 1882–1940* (Ibadan, Nigeria: Oxford University Press, 1978).
Finkelstein, Joanne, *Fashion: An Introduction* (New York: New York University Press, 1998).
Finn, Margot, 'Men's Things: Masculine Possession in the Consumer Revolution', *Social History*, 25/2 (2000): pp. 133–55.
Finnane, Antonia, *Changing Clothes in China: Fashion, History, Nation* (New York: Columbia University Press, 2008).
Foley, Caroline, 'Fashion' *The Economic Journal*, 3/11 (1893): pp. 458–74.
Fontaine, Laurence, *Histoire du colportage en Europe. XVe–XIXe siècle* (Paris: Albin Michel, 1993).
—, 'The circulation of luxury goods in eighteenth-century Paris: social redistribution and an alternative currency', in Maxine Berg and Elizabeth Eger (eds), *Luxury in the eighteenth century. Debates, desires and delectable goods* (Basingstoke, UK: Palgrave Macmillan, 2003), pp. 89–102.
— and Schlumbohm, Jürgen (eds), *Household strategies for survival 1600–2000: fission, faction and cooperation* (Cambridge: Cambridge University Press, 2000).
Fortunate Eagle, Adam (Nordwall), 'Urban Indians and the Occupation of Alcatraz Island', in Troy Johnson, Joane Nagel and Duane Champaigne (eds), *American*

Indian Activism: Alcatraz to the Longest Walk (Chicago: University of Illinois Press, 1997), pp. 52–73.

Fox, Robert and Turner, Anthony (eds), *Luxury, trades and consumerism in ancient regime Paris* (Aldershot, UK: Ashgate, 1998).

Franklin, Ursula, *The Real World of Technology*, Revised Edition (Toronto, ON: Anasi, 1999).

Freeman, Carla, 'Is Local: Global as Feminine: Masculine? Rethinking the Gender of Globalization', *Signs: Journal of Women in Culture and Society*, 26/4 (2001): pp. 1007–37.

Freudenberger, Herman, 'Fashion, Sumptuary Laws, and Business', *Business History Review*, 37/1/2 (1963): pp. 37–48.

Friedman, Jonathan, 'The Hybridization of Roots and the Abhorrence of the Bush', in Mike Featherstone and Scott Lash (eds), *Spaces of Culture: City, Nation, World* (London, Sage, 1999), pp. 230–56.

Fulsang, Deborah, 'Star Power on the Catwalk,' *Globe and Mail* 3 April 2004: http://www.globeandmail.com/servlet/ArticleNews/TPPrint/LAC/20040403/CATWALK03/TPEntertainment, accessed 5 April 2004.

Gamber, Wendy, *The Female Economy: The Millinery and Dressmaking Trades, 1860–1930* (Urbana: University of Illinois Press, 1997).

—, 'A Gendered Enterprise: Placing Nineteenth-Century Businesswomen in History', *Business History Review*, 72/2 (1998): pp. 188–217.

—, *The Boardinghouse in Nineteenth-Century America* (Baltimore: Johns Hopkins University Press, 2007).

García, Máximo and Yun, Bartolomé, 'Pautas de consumo, estilos de vida y cambio político en las ciudades castellanas a fines del Antiguo Régimen', in J.I. Fortea Pérez, (ed.), *Imágenes de la diversidad. El mundo urbano en la Corona de Castilla (s.XVI–XVIII)* (Santander, 1997), pp. 245–82.

Geary, Christraud, *Images from Bamum* (Washington, DC: Smithsonian Institution Press, 1988).

'Gender and Business History: Special Section', *Business History Review,* 72/2 (Summer 1998): pp. 185–249.

Geuter, Ruth, 'Reconstructing the Context of Seventeenth-Century English Figurative Embroideries', in Moira Donald and Linda Hurcombe (eds), *Gender and Material Culture in Historical Perspective* (London: Longmans, 2001), pp. 97–111.

Glass, Aaron, 'Crests on Cotton: "Souvenir" T-Shirts and the Materiality of Remembrance among the Kwakwaka'wakw of British Columbia', *Museum Anthropology*, 31/1 (2008): pp. 1–18.

Goldin, Claudia, *Understanding the Gender Gap: An Economic History of American Women* (New York: Oxford University Press, 1990).

Gondola, Didier, 'Dream and Drama: The Search for Elegance among Congolese Youth', *African Studies Review*, 42/1 (1999): pp. 23–48.

Gonzales, Angela, 'Urban (Trans)Formations: Changes in Meaning and Use of American Indian Identity', in Susan Lobo and Kurt Peters (eds), *American*

Indians and the Urban Experience (Walnut Creek, CA: Alta Mira Press, 2001), pp. 169–85.

Goody, Jack, *The Theft of History* (Cambridge: Cambridge University Press, 2007).

Gordon, Beverly, *Bazaars and Fair Ladies: The History of the American Fundraising Fair* (Knoxville: University of Tennessee Press, 1998).

Gordon, Sarah A., '"Boundless Possibilities": Home Sewing and the Meanings of Women's Domestic Work in the United States, 1890–1930', *Journal of Women's History*, 16/2 (2004): pp. 68–91.

Gordon, Stewart (ed.), *Robes and Honor: The Medieval World of Investiture* (New York: Palgrave, 2001).

Goubert, Pierre, 'Intérêt et utilisation historique des papiers de succesions: inventaires aprés décès, partages, comptes de tutelle', *Revue d'Histoire Moderne et Contemporaine*, 1/1 (1954): pp. 22–38.

Grassby, Richard, 'Material Culture and Cultural History', *Journal of Interdisciplinary History*, 35/4 (2005): pp. 591–603.

Greenfield, Kent Roberts, *Sumptuary Law in Nürmberg: a Study in Paternal Government* (Baltimore: Johns Hopkins Press, 1918).

Greig, Hannah and Riello, Giorgio, 'Eighteenth-Century Interiors – Redesigning the Georgian: Introduction', *Journal of Design History*, 20/4 (2007): pp. 273–89.

Griffin, Patrick, 'The Pursuit of Comfort: the Modern and the Material in the Early Modern British Atlantic World', *Reviews in American History*, 30 (2002): pp. 365–72.

Grimes, Kimberly M., 'Democratizing International Production and Trade: North American Alternative Trading Organizations', in Kimberly M. Grimes and B. Lynne Milgram (eds), *Artisans and Cooperatives: Developing Alternative Trade for the Global Economy* (Tuscon, AZ: University of Arizona Press, 2000), pp. 9–25.

—, 'Changing the Rules of Trade in Global Partnerships: The Fair Trade Movement', in June Nash (ed.), *Social Movements: A Reader* (Oxford: Basil Blackwood, 2005), pp. 237–48.

— and Milgram, B. Lynne, 'Introduction: Facing the Challenges of Artisan Production in the Global Market', in Kimberly M. Grimes and B. Lynne Milgram (eds), *Artisans and Cooperatives: Developing Alternative Trade for the Global Economy* (Tuscon, AZ: University of Arizona Press, 2000), pp. 3–10.

Guenther, Irene V., 'Nazi "Chic"? German Politics and Women's Fashions, 1915–1945', *Fashion Theory*, 1/1 (1997): pp. 29–58.

Habib, Vanessa, 'Scotch Carpets in the Eighteenth and Early Nineteenth Centuries', *Textile History*, 28/2 (1997): pp. 161–75.

Hall, Stuart, (ed.), *Representation: Cultural Representations and Signifying Practices* (London: Sage, 1997).

Handler, Sarah, *Austere Luminosity of Chinese Classic Furniture* (Berkeley: University of California Press, 2001).

Hansen, Debra Gold, *Strained Sisterhood: Gender and Class in the Boston Female Anti-Slavery Society* (Amherst: University of Massachusetts Press, 1993).
Hansen, Karen Tranberg, *Distant Companions: Servants and Employers in Zambia, 1900–1985* (Ithaca, NY: Cornell University Press, 1989).
—, 'Gender and Difference: Youth, Bodies, and Clothing in Zambia', in Victoria Goddard (ed.), *Gender, Agency, and Change: An Anthropological Perspective* (London: Routledge, 2000), pp. 32–55.
—, *Salaula: The World of Secondhand Clothing and Zambia* (Chicago: University of Chicago Press, 2000).
—, 'Fashioning', *Journal of Material Culture*, 8/3 (2003): pp. 301–9.
—, 'The World in Dress: Anthropological Perspectives on Clothing, Fashion, and Culture', *Annual Review of Anthropology*, 33 (2004): pp. 369–92.
—, 'Helping or Hindering? Controversies around the International Second-hand Clothing Trade', *Anthropology Today*, 20/4 (2004): pp. 3–9.
—, 'Dressing Dangerously: Miniskirts, Gender Relations, and Sexuality in Zambia', in Jean Allman (ed.), *Fashioning Africa: Power and the Politics of Dress* (Bloomington: Indiana University Press, 2004), pp. 166–85.
Harris, Beth, *Famine and Fashion: Needlewomen in The Nineteenth Century* (Aldershot, UK: Ashgate Publishing, 2005).
Harte, Negley, 'Foreward' in 'Fabrics and Fashions: Studies in the economic and Social History of Dress', *Textile History*, 22/2 (1991): p. 150.
—, 'The Economics of Clothing in the Late Seventeenth Century', *Textile History*, 12/2 (1991): pp. 277–96.
Heathcote, David, 'A Hausa Embroiderer of Katsina', *Nigerian Field*, 37/3 (1972): pp. 123–31.
—, 'Insight into a Creative Process; A Rare Collection of Embroidery Drawings from Kano', *Savanna*, 1/2 (December 1972): pp. 165–74.
—, 'A Hausa Charm Gown', *Man*, n.s. 9 (1974): pp. 620–24.
—, *The Arts of the Hausa* (Chicago: University of Chicago Press, 1977).
Hellman, Mimi, 'Furniture, Sociability, and the Work of Leisure in Eighteenth-Century France', *Eighteenth-Century Studies*, 32/4 (1999): pp. 415–44.
Hiler, David and Wiedmer, Laurence, 'Le rat de ville et le rat des champs. Une approche comparative des intérieurs ruraux et urbains à Genève dans la seconde partie du XVIIIe siècle', in M. Baulant (ed.), *Inventaires apres-décès et ventes de meubles. Actes du séminaire tenu dans le cadre du 9ème Congrès International d'Histoire Economique de Berne (1986)* (Louvain-la Neuve: Acadèmia, 1988), pp. 146–7.
Hill, A.O. and Hill, B.H., 'Marc Bloch and Comparative History', *American Historical Review*, 85/4 (1980): pp. 828–57.
Hiskett, Mervyn, *The Sword of Truth* (New York: Oxford University Press, 1973).
—, *The Course of Islam in Africa* (Edinburgh: Edinburgh University Press, 1994).
Hoffmann, Paul, *La femme dans la pensée des lumières* (Strasbourg, 1977).
Hoffman, Ronald, and Albert, Peter J. (eds), *Women in the Age of the American Revolution* (Charlottesville: University of Virginia Press, 1989).

Hogendorn, Jan and Johnson, Marion, *The Shell Money of the Slave Trade* (Cambridge: Cambridge University Press, 1986).
Hollander, Anne, *Sex and Suits: The Evolution of Modern Dress* (New York: Knopf, 1994).
Hood, Adrienne D., 'The Material World of Cloth: Production and Use in Eighteenth-Century Rural Pennsylvania', *William and Mary Quarterly*, 53/1 (1996): pp. 48–50.
—, *The Weaver's Craft. Cloth, Commerce, and Industry in Early Pennsylvania* (Philadelphia: University of Pennsylvania Press, 2003).
Hooper, Wilfrid, 'The Tudor Sumptuary Laws', *English Historical Review*, 30 (1915): pp. 433–49.
Hudson Turner, T., *Some Account of Domestic Architecture in England from Richard II to Henry VIII* (2 vols, Oxford: John Henry and James Parker, 1859).
Hufton, Olwen, *The Prospect Before Her. A History of Women in Western Europe. 1500–1800*, vol. 1 (2 vols, London: Harper Collins, 1995).
Hunt, Alan, *Governance of the Consuming Passions: A History of Sumptuary Law* (Basingstoke, UK: Macmillan, 1996).
Hutchcroft, Paul D. and Rocamora, Joel, 'Strong Demands and Weak Institutions: The Origins and Evolution of the Democratic Deficit in the Philippines', *Journal of East Asian Studies*, 3/2 (2003): pp. 259–92.
Israel, Jonathan I., *Conflicts of empires. Spain, the Low Countries and the struggle for world supremacy. 1585–1713* (London and Rio Grande: Hambledon, 1997).
Jeffrey, Julie Roy, *The Great Silent Army of Abolitionism: Ordinary Women in the Antislavery Movement* (Chapel Hill: University of North Carolina Press, 1998).
—, '"Stranger, Buy ... Lest Our Mission Fail": The Complex Culture of Women's Abolitionist Fairs', *American Nineteenth Century History*, 4/1 (2003): pp. 1–24.
Jenkins, David, 'Textile History: 40 Years On', *Textile History*, 39/1 (2008): pp. 4–15.
Johnson, Marion, 'Calico Caravans: The Tripoli–Kano Trade after 1880', *Journal of African History*, 17/1 (1976): pp. 95–117.
Jones, Ann Rosalind and Stallybrass, Peter, *Renaissance Clothing and the Materials of Memory* (Cambridge: Cambridge University Press, 2000).
Jones, Carla and Leshkowich, Ann Marie, 'Introduction: The Globalization of Asian Dress: Re-Orienting Fashion or Re-Orientalizing Asia?', in Sandra Niessen, Ann Marie Leshkowich and Carla Jones (eds), *The Globalization of Asian Dress: Re-Orienting Fashion* (Oxford and New York: Berg, 2003), pp. 1–48.
Jones, E.L., 'The Fashion Manipulators: Consumer Tastes and British Industries, 1660–1800', in L.P. Cain and P.J. Uselding (eds), *Business Enterprise and Economic Change* (Kent, OH: Kent State University Press, 1973), pp. 198–226.
Jones, Jennifer, '*Coquettes* and *Grisettes*. Women Buying and Selling in Ancien Régime Paris' in Victoria de Grazia and Ellen Furlough (eds), *The Sex of Things. Gender and Consumption in Historical Perspective.* (Berkeley: University of California Press, 1996), pp. 25–53.

—, *Sexing La Mode: Gender, Fashion and Commercial Culture in Old Regime France* (Oxford and New York: Berg Publishers, 2004).

Kapchan, Deborah and Turner Strong, Pauline, 'Theorizing the Hybrid', *Journal of American Folklore*, 112/ 445 (1999): pp. 239–53.

Karim, Wazir Jahan, 'Introduction: Genderising Anthropology in Southeast Asia', in Wazir J. Karim (ed.), *'Male' and 'Female' in Developing Southeast Asia* (Oxford and Washington: Berg 1995), pp. 11–34.

Kay, Alison C., 'Revealing her assets: Liberating the Victorian businesswoman from the sources', *Business Archives: Sources and History*, 96 (2006): pp. 1–16.

—, 'Retailing, Respectability and the Independent Woman in Nineteenth-century London', in Robert Beachy, B. Craig and A. Owens (eds), *Women, Business and Finance in Nineteenth-Century Europe: Rethinking Separate Spheres* (Berg, 2006), pp. 152–66.

Kessler-Harris, Alice, *Out to work: a history of wage-earning women in the United States* (New York: Oxford University Press, 1982).

Kowaleski-Wallace, Elizabeth, *Consuming Subjects: Women, Shopping, and Business in the Eighteenth Century* (New York: Columbia University Press, 1997).

Kramer, Jennifer, *Switchbacks: Art, Ownership, and Nuxalk National Identity* (Vancouver and Toronto: University of British Columbia Press, 2006).

Kramer, Robert S., 'Islam and Identity in the Kumase Zongo', in John Hunwick and Nancy Lawler (eds), *The Cloth of Many Colored Silks* (Evanston, IL: Northwestern University Press, 1996), pp. 287–96.

Kriger, Colleen, 'Robes of the Sokoto Caliphate', *African Arts*, 21/3 (1988): pp. 52–7, 78–9, 85–6.

—, 'Textile Production in the Lower Niger Basin: New Evidence from the 1841 Niger Expedition Collection', *Textile History*, 21/1 (1990): pp. 31–56.

—, 'Textile Production and Gender in the Sokoto Caliphate', *Journal of African History*, 34 (1993): pp. 361–401.

—, *Cloth in West African History* (Lanham, MD: Alta Mira Press, 2006).

Kusamitsu, T., 'Novelty, give us novelty: London agents and northern manufacturers', in Maxine Berg (ed.), *Markets and manufacture in early industrial Europe* (London: Routledge, 1991), pp. 114–38.

Kelly, F.M., 'The Iconography of Costume', *The Burlington Magazine*, 64/375 (June 1934): pp. 278–84.

Knapp, Millie, 'D'Arcy Moses: Ready-to-Wear', *Aboriginal Voices*, 3/1 (1995): p. 15.

Kobayashi, Erin, 'Buy Into It: BYO Bag', *Toronto Star*, (21 April 2007): pp. 1, 3.

Kwolek-Folland, Angel, *Incorporating Women: A History of Women and Business in the United States* (New York: Twayne Publishers, 1998).

Lamb, V. and Holmes, J., *Nigerian Weaving* (Hertingfordbury, UK: Roxford Books, 1980).

Lanoë, Catherine, *La poudre et le fard: une histoire des cosmétiques de la Renaissance aux Lumières* (Paris: Éditions Champ Vallon, 2009).

Last, Murray, 'The Sokoto Caliphate and Borno', in J.F. Ade Ajayi, *Africa in the Nineteenth Century until the 1880s*, UNESCO General History of Africa series, vol. 6 (8 vols, Berkeley: University of California Press, 1989).
Last, D.M. and Al-Hajj, M.A., 'Attempts at Defining a Muslim in 19th century Hausaland and Bornu', *Journal of the Historical Society of Nigeria*, 3 (1965): pp. 231–40.
Leach, William R., 'Transformations in a Culture of Consumption: Women and Department Stores, 1890–1925', *Journal of American History*, 71/2 (1984): pp. 319–42.
Leibenstein, Harvey, 'Bandwagon, snob, and Veblen effects in the theory of consumers' demand', *Quarterly Journal of Economics*, 64 (1950): pp. 183–207.
Lemire, Beverly, *Fashion's Favourite: the Cotton Trade and the Consumer in Britain 1669–1800* (Oxford: Oxford University Press, 1991).
—, 'Introduction. Women, Credit and the Creation of Opportunity: A Historical Overview', in Beverly Lemire, Ruth Pearson and Gail Campbell (eds), *Women and Credit: Researching the Past, Refiguring the Future* (Oxford and New York: Berg, 2001), pp. 3–14.
—, 'Domesticating the Exotic: Floral Culture and the East India Calico Trade with England, c. 1600–1800', *Textile: The Journal of Cloth and Culture*, 1/1 (2003): pp. 65–85.
—, *The Business of Everyday Life: Gender, Practice and Social Politics in England, c. 1600–1900* (Manchester and New York: Manchester University Press, 2005).
—, and Riello, Giorgio, 'East and West: Textiles and Fashion in Eurasia in the Early Modern Period', *Journal of Social History*, 41/4 (2008): pp. 887–916.
Lencina Pérez, Xavier, 'Los inventarios post-mortem en el estudio de la cultura material y el consumo. Propuesta metodologica. Barcelona, siglo XVII', in Jaume Torras and Bartolomé Yun (eds), *Consumo, condiciones de vida y comercialización. Cataluña y Castilla, siglos XVII–XIX* (Junta de Castilla y León: Caja Duero, 1999), pp. 41–59.
Leshkowich, Ann Marie and Jones, Carla, 'What Happens when Asian Chic Becomes Chic in Asia?', *Fashion Theory*, 7/3–4 (2003): pp. 281–300.
Levy Peck, Linda, *Consuming Splendor: Society and Culture in Seventeenth-Century England* (Cambridge: Cambridge University Press, 2005).
Lewis, David, 'Non-governmental Organizations, Business and the Management of Ambiguity: Case Studies from Nepal and Bangladesh', *Nonprofit Management and Leadership*, 9/2 (1998): pp. 135–52.
Lewis, Susan Ingalls, 'Female Entrepreneurs in Albany, 1840–1885', *Business and Economic History*, 21(1992): pp. 65–73.
Lipovetsky, Gilles, *The Empire of Fashion: Dressing Modern Democracy*, translated by Catherine Porter, (Princeton: Princeton University Press, 1994).
Littrell, Mary Ann and Dickson, Marsha Ann, *Social Responsibility in the Global Market: Fair Trade of Cultural Products* (London: Sage, 1999).

Lobo, Susan, 'Is Urban a Person or a Place?: Characteristics of Urban Indian Country', in Susan Loba and Kurt Peters (eds), *American Indians and the Urban Experience* (Walnut Creek, CA: Alta Mira Press, 2001), pp. 73–84.

Löfgren, Orvar, 'Materializing the Nation in Sweden and America', *Ethnos*, 58/3–4 (1993) pp. 161–96.

Lombard, Maurice, *Les Textiles dans le Monde Musulman* (Paris: Mouton, 1978).

Long, Helen C., *The Edwardian House. The Middle-Class Home in Britain 1880–1914* (Manchester: Manchester University Press, 1993).

Lynn, Hyung Gu, 'Fashioning Modernity: Changing Meanings of Clothing in Colonial Korea', *Journal of International and Area Studies*, 11/3 (2005): pp. 75–93.

Lyons, Sarah and Moberg, Mark (eds), *Fair Trade and Social Justice: Global Ethnographies* (Albany, NY: SUNY Press, 2010).

McCracken, Grant, *Culture and Consumption: New Approaches to the Symbolic Character of Consumer Goods and Activities* (Bloomington, IN: Indiana University Press, 1987).

Mack, Rosamund E., *Bazaar to Piazza: Islamic Trade and Italian Art 1300–1600* (Berkeley: University of California Press, 2002).

McKendrick, Neil, Brewer, John and Plumb, J.H., *The Birth of a Consumer Society: the Commercialization of Eighteenth-Century England* (London: Hutchinson, 1982).

Maclaren, Virginia and Nguyen, Thi Anh Thu (eds), *Gender and the Waste Economy: Vietnamese and International Experiences* (Hanoi, VN: National Political Publisher, 2003).

M'Closkey, Kathy, 'Marketing Multiple Myths: The Hidden History of Navajo Weaving', *Journal of the Southwest*, 36/3 (1994): pp. 185–220.

McNeill, J.R. and McNeill, William H., *The Human Web: A Bird's Eye View of World History* (New York: W.W. Norton, 2003).

McNeil, Peter, 'Everlasting: The Flowers in Fashion and Textiles', in *Everlasting: The Flowers in Fashion and Textiles* (Victoria, Australia: National Gallery of Victoria, 2005), pp. 17–22.

— and Riello, Giorgio, 'The Art and Science of Walking: Gender, Space and the Fashionable Body in the Long Eighteenth Century', *Fashion Theory*, 9/2 (2005): pp. 175–204.

Main, Gloria L., 'Gender, Work, and Wages in Colonial New England', *The William and Mary Quarterly*, 51/1 (1994): pp. 39–66.

Malanima, Paolo, *Il lusso dei contadini. Consumi e industrie nelle campagne toscane del sei e settecento* (Bologna: Il Mulino, 1990).

—, *Economia preindustriale. Mille anni: dal IX al XVIII secolo* (Milano: Mondadori: 1995).

Mander, Nicholas, 'Painted Cloths: History, Craftsmen and Techniques', *Textile History*, 28/2 (1997): pp. 119–48.

Martin, Ann Smart, *Buying into the World of Goods: Early Consumers in Backcountry Virginia* (Baltimore: Johns Hopkins University Press, 2008).

Martin, Linda, 'Navajo Style: Fashions for all Seasons', *Native Peoples Magazine*, 13/4 (2000).

Marwick, Max, 'Some Labour Histories', Appendix B in Helmuth Heisler, *Urbanisation and the Government of Migration: The Interrelation of Urban and Rural Life in Zambia* (New York: St Martin's Press, 1974).

Mason, Michael, *Foundations of the Bida Kingdom* (Zaira, Nigeria: Ahmadu Bello University Press, 1981).

Mauss, Marcel, *The Gift, Forms and Functions of Exchange in Archaic Societies*, translated by Ian Cunnison (London: Cohen & West, 1954).

Meganck, Linda, 'Architectuur als décor voor het sociale leven in de 18de eeuw', in Jaak Van Schoor, Christel Stalpaert and Bram Van Oostveldt (eds), *Performing arts in the Austrian 18th century: new directions in historical and methodological research* (Ghent: Academia Press, 1999), pp. 9–10.

Melis, François, *Poortersboeken* (Antwerp: Stadsarchief Antwerpen, 1977).

Midgley, Clare, *Women Against Slavery: The British Campaigns 1780–1870* (London and New York: Routledge, 1992).

—, *Feminism and Empire: Women Activists in Imperial Britain, 1790–1865* (London and New York: Routledge, 2007).

Miles, Steven, *Consumerism as a way of life* (London: Sage, 1998).

Milgram, B. Lynne, 'Crafts, Cultivation and Household Economies: Women's Work and Positions in Ifugao Northern Philippines', *Research in Economic Anthropology*, 20 (1999): pp. 221–61.

—, 'Reorganizing Production for Global Markets: Women and Craft Cooperatives in Ifugao, Upland Philippines', in Kimberly M. Grimes and B. Lynne Milgram (eds), *Artisans and Cooperatives: Developing Alternative Trade for the Global Economy* (Tuscon, AZ: University of Arizona Press, 2000): pp. 107–28.

—, 'Banking on Bananas, Crediting Crafts: Financing Women's Work in the Philippine Cordillera', *Atlantis: A Women's Studies Journal*, 26/2 (2002): pp. 109–19.

—, 'Juicing Up for Fair Trade', *Cultural Survival Quarterly*, 29/3 (2005): pp. 47–9.

—, 'From Trash to Totes: Recycled Production and Cooperative Economy Practice in the Philippines', *Human Organization*, 69/1 (2010).

Miller, Daniel, *Material Culture and Mass Consumption* (Oxford: Blackwell Publishers, 1987).

Minchinton, W.E., 'Convention, fashion and consumption: aspects of British experience since 1750', in H. Baudet and M. Bogucka (eds), *Types of consumption, traditional and modern* (Budapest: Akademiai Kiado, 1982), pp. 31–40.

Miralao, Virginia A., *Labour Conditions in Philippine Craft Industries*, Research and Working Papers (Manila, Philippines: Ramon Magsaysay Award Foundation, 1986).

Mitchell, Clyde J., 'The Kalela Dance', *Rhodes-Livingstone Papers*, 27 (1956).

Monastyrski, Jamie, 'Pam Baker: High End Fashion', *Aboriginal Voices*, 6/1 (1999): p. 18.

Moore, R.J.B., *These African Copper Miners: a study of the industrial revolution in Northern Rhodesia, with principal reference to the copper industry.* Revised, with appendices by A. Sandilands (London: Livingston Press, 1948).

Moreno Claverías, Belén, 'Pautas de consumo en el Penedés del siglo XVII. Una propuesta metodológica a partir de inventarios sin valoraciones monetarias', *Revista de Historia Económica*, 20 (2003): pp. 207–45.

—, 'Mito y realidad de la 'feminización del consumo' en la Europa Moderna: Las pautas de consumo de las mujeres en el Penedés preindustrial', *Arenal*, 11/1 (2004): pp. 119–52.

—, '*Révolution de la Consommation Paysanne*? Modes de Consommation et Differentiation Sociale de la paysannerie catalane, 1670–1790', *Histoire et Mesure*, 21/1–2 (2006): pp. 141–83.

—, *Consum i condicions de vida a la Catalunya Moderna. El Penedès, 1670–1790* (Vilafranca del Penedès: Andana, 2007).

Morris, Frances, 'An Elizabethan Embroidery', *The Metropolitan Museum of Art Bulletin*, 18/10 (1923): pp. 228–30.

Moyer, Eileen, 'Keeping up Appearances: Fashion and Function among Dar es Salaam Street Youth', *Etnofoor*, 16/2 (2003): pp. 88–105.

Mui, Hoh-Cheung and Mui, Lorna H., *Shops and shopkeeping in eighteenth-century England* (Kingston: McGill-Queen's University Press, 1989).

Mukerji, Chandra, *From graven images: patterns of modern materialism* (New York: Columbia University Press, 1983).

Muldrew, Craig, 'Hard food for Midas: cash and its social value in Early Modern England', *Social History*, 18 (1993): pp. 163–83.

—, *The economy of obligation: the culture of credit and social relations in Early Modern England* (New York: Palgrave, 2001).

Mukota, Augustine and photos by Phiri, Collin, 'Lookout for "Fresh" Designs… as two Young Designers Churn out Their First Dresses', *Weekend Post* (2 December 2005): p. 4.

Musgrave, Pieter, *The Early Modern European economy* (Basingstoke, UK: MacMillan, 1999).

Nadel, Siegfried, *A Black Byzantium* (London: Oxford University Press, 1942).

Nagel, Joane, *American Indian Ethnic Renewal: Red Power and the Resurgence of Identity and Culture* (New York: Oxford University Press, 1996).

Nahui Ollin, URL: www.nahuiollin.com, accessed 18 December 2008.

Nash, June (ed.), *Crafts in the World Market: The Impact of global Exchange on Middle American Artisans* (Albany, NY: SUNY Press, 1993).

Nash, Mary (ed.), *Més enllà del silenci: les dones a la història de Catalunya* (Barcelona: Generalitat de Catalunya, 1988).

Natividad, Beverly, 'Packaging firm strengthens push to recycle used Tetra Pak Cartons', *BW Weekender* (10 June 2006): p. 8.

Nenadic, Stana, 'Middle-Rank Consumers and Domestic Culture in Edinburgh and Glasgow, 1720–1840', *Past and Present*, 145 (1994): pp. 122–56.

Neuschel, Kristen B., 'Noble Households in the Sixteenth Century: Material Settings and Human Communities', *French Historical Studies*, 15/4 (1988): pp. 595–622.

Ngoma, Samuel, 'Wanted: Quality Clothing in Zambia', *Times of Zambia*, (26 August 1995).

Niessen, Sandra, 'Re-Orienting Fashion Theory', in Linda Welters and Abby Lillethun (eds), *The Fashion Reader* (London and New York: Berg Publishers, 2007), pp. 105–10.

Nijboer, Harm, 'Fashion and the Early Modern consumer evolution. A theoretical exploration and some evidence from seventeenth century Leeuwarden', in Bruno Blondé, Eugénie Briot, Natacha Coquery and Laura Van Aert (eds), *Retailers and consumer changes in Early Modern Europe. England, France, Italy and the Low Countries* (Tours: Presses Universitaires François-Rabelais, 2005), pp. 21–36.

Northern News Services Ltd. Website, 'Fur Clouds Makes a Comeback': http://www.nnsl.com/frames/newspapers/2001-11/nov19_01fur.html, accessed 3 July 2005.

Northwest Territories Assembly Proceedings Website: Friday, 4 December 1998: http://www.assembly.gov.nt.ca/_live/documents/documentManagerUpload/Hn981204.pdf, accessed 27 November 2008.

Nuttall, Sarah, 'Stylizing the Self: The Y Generation in Rosebank, Johannesburg', *Public Culture*, 16:3 (2004): pp. 430–52.

Ofreneo, Rene E. and Esther P. Habana, *The Employment Crisis and The World Bank's Adjustment Program – Philippines* (Quezon City, Philippines: University of the Philippines Press, 1987).

Ogborn, Miles, 'Georgian Geographies?', *Journal of Historical Geography*, 24/2 (1998): 218–23.

—, *Spaces of Modernity: London's Geographies, 1680–1780* (New York and London: Guilford Press, 1998).

— and Withers, Charles W.J. (eds), *Georgian Geographies: Essays on Space, Place and Landscape in the Eighteenth Century* (Manchester: Manchester University Press, 2004).

O'Kelly, Hilary, 'Reconstructing Irishness: Dress in the Celtic Revival, 1880–1920', in Juliet Ash and Elizabeth Wilson (eds), *Chic Thrills: A Fashion Reader* (London: Harper Collins, 1992) pp. 75–83.

Olly Molly, URL: www.ollymolly.co.za, accessed 18 December 2008.

Overton, Mark, 'Prices from probate inventories', in Tom Arkell, Nesta Evans and Nigel Goose (eds), *When death do us part: understanding and interpreting the probate records of Early Modern England* (Oxford: Leopard, 2000), pp. 120–42.

—, Whittle, Jane, Dean, Darron and Hann, Andrew, *Production and Consumption in English Households, 1600–1750* (London and New York: Routledge, 2004).

Oxford English Dictionary. 2nd edn 1989. *OED Online*. Oxford University Press, accessed 20 October 2009.

Panhuysen, Bibi, *Maatwerk. Kleermakers, naaisters, oudkleerkopers en de gilden (1500–1800)* (Amsterdam: Aksant, 2000).

Pardailhé-Galabrun, Annik, *The Birth of Intimacy: Privacy and Domestic Life in Early Modern Paris* (Philadelphia: University of Pennsylvania Press, 1991).

Parés i Puntals, Antoni, *Tots els refranys catalans* (Barcelona: Edicions 62, 1999).

Parezo, Nancy J., 'The Indian Fashion Show', in Ruth Phillips and Christopher Steiner (eds), *Unpacking Culture: Art and Commodity in Colonial and Postcolonial Worlds* (Berkeley: University of California Press, 1999), pp. 243–63.

Parker, Rozsika, *The Subversive Stitch: Embroidery and the Making of the Feminine* (London: Women's Press Ltd, 1996).

Parpart, Jane L., '"Where is Your Mother?" Gender, Urban Marriage, and Colonial Discourse on the Zambian Copperbelt, 1924–1945', *International Journal of African Historical Studies*, 27/2 (1994): pp. 241–71.

Parreñas, Rhacel S., *Servants of Globalization: Women, Migration & Domestic Work* (Stanford, CA: Stanford University Press, 2001).

Pascual, Jean-Paul, 'Meubles et objets domestiques quotidiens des intérieurs damascains du XVIIIe siècle', *Revue du Monde Musulman et de la Méditerranée*, 55–56 (1990): pp. 197–207.

Peck, Linda Levy, *Consuming Splendor: Society and Culture in Seventeenth-Century England* (Cambridge: Cambridge University Press, 2005).

Peiss, Kathy, 'Vital Industry and Women's Ventures: Conceptualizing Gender in Twentieth-Century Business History', *Business History Review*, 72/2 (1998): pp. 219–41.

Pellegrin, N. and Péret, J., 'Meubles et vêtements dans les inventaires après décès poitevins au XVIIIe siècle: une source et ses problèmes', in Joseph Goy and Jean Pierre Wallot (eds), *Évolution et Éclatement du Monde Rural* (Paris-Montréal: Editions EHESS, 1986), pp. 469–73.

Petrov, Julia, '"The habit of their age". English genre painters, dress collecting, and museums, 1910–1914', *Journal of the History of Collections*, 20/2 (2008): pp. 237–51.

Perrot, Philippe, *Le corps féminin: le travail des apparences XVIIIe–XIXe s* (Paris: Seuil, 1984).

—, *Le luxe. Une richesse entre faste et confort. XVIIIe–XIXe siècle*, (Paris: Edition Du Seuil, 1995).

Pineda, R. Vergara, 'Domestic Outwork for Export-Oriented Industries', Amaryllis T. Torres (ed.), *The Filipino Woman In Focus* (Manila, Philippines: University of the Philippines Press, 1995), pp. 153–67.

Phillips, Ruth B., *Trading Identities: The Souvenir in Native North American Art from the Northeast, 1700–1900* (Washington: University of Washington Press, 1998).

Pinchbeck, Ivy, *Women Workers and the Industrial Revolution* (London: George Routledge & Sons, 1930).

Pomeranz, Kenneth *The great divergence. China, Europe, and the making of the modern world economy* (Princeton: Princeton University Press, 2000).

Ponsonby, Margaret, 'Towards an Interpretation of Textiles in the Provincial Domestic Interior: Three Homes in the West Midlands, 1780–1848', *Textile History*, 38/2 (2007): pp. 165–78.

—, *Stories from Home: English Domestic Interiors, 1750–1850* (Aldershot, UK: Ashgate, 2007).

Poovey, Mary, 'Writing about Finance in Victorian England: Disclosure and Secrecy in the Culture of Investment ', *Victorian Studies*, 45/1 (2002): pp. 17–41.

Poulot, Dominique, 'Une nouvelle histoire de la culture matérielle?', *Revue d'Histoire Moderne et Contemporaine*, 44/2 (1997): pp. 344–57.

Powdermaker, Hortense, *Copper Town: Changing Africa. The Human Condition on the Rhodesian Copperbelt* (New York: Harper & Row, 1962).

Prestholdt, Jeremy, 'On the Global Repercussions of East African Consumerism', *American Historical Review*, 109/3 (2004): pp. 755–81.

Priestley, Ursula, 'The marketing of Norwich stuffs, c. 1660–1730', *Textile History*, 22 (1991): pp. 193–209.

—, and Corfield, Penelope J., 'Rooms and Room Use in Norwich Housing, 1580–1730', *Post–Medieval Archaeology*, 16 (1982): pp. 93–123.

Prochaska, F.K., 'Charity Bazaars in Nineteenth-Century England', *The Journal of British Studies*, 16/2 (1977): pp. 62–84.

—, *Women and Philanthropy in Nineteenth-Century England* (New York: Oxford University Press, 1980).

Prown, Jules, 'Mind into Matter: An Introduction to Material Culture Theory and Method', *Winterthur Portfolio*, 17/1 (1982): pp. 1–19.

Prussin, Labelle, *Hatumere: Islamic Design in West Africa* (Berkeley: University of California Press, 1986).

Quarles, Benjamin, 'Sources of Abolitionist Income', *The Mississippi Valley Historical Review*, 32/1 (1945): pp. 63–76.

Quemin, Alain, 'Luxe, ostentation et distinction : Une lecture contemporaine de *La théorie de la classe de loisir* de Thorstein Veblen', in Olivier Assouly (ed.), *Le luxe : Essais sur la fabrique de l'ostentation* (Paris : Editions de l'Institut Français de la Mode, 2005), pp. 137–52.

Queniart, Jean, 'L'utilisation des inventaires en histoire socio-culturelle', in Bernard Vogler (ed.), *Les Actes Notariés. Sources de l'Histoire Sociale XVIe–XIXe Siècles. Actes du Colloque de Strasbourg (mars 1978)* (Strasbourg, France: Librairie Istra, 1979).

Ramos Palencia, Fernando, 'Una primera aproximación al consumo en el mundo rural castellano a través de los inventarios post-mortem: Palencia, 1750–1840' in Jaume Torras and Bartolomé Yun (eds), *Consumo, Condiciones de vida y Comercialización. Cataluña y Castilla, siglos XVII–XIX* (Junta de Castilla y León: Caja Duero, 1999), pp. 107–31.

Re-bagz, URL: www.rebagz.com, accessed 7 April 2009.

Reuter, Kristen, 'Heated Debates over Crinolines: European Clothing on Nineteenth-century Lutheran Mission Stations in the Transvaal', *Journal of Southern African Studies*, 28/2 (2002): pp. 359–78.

Riello, Giorgio, 'Asian Knowledge and the Development of Calico Printing in Europe in the Seventeenth and Eighteenth Centuries', *Journal of Global History*, 5 (2010).

—, 'Geography and Environment', in James Marten and Elizabeth Foyster (eds), *A Cultural History of Childhood and Family. The Age of Enlightenment (1650– 1800) vol 4* (6 vols, Oxford: Blackwell, 2010).

Rosaldo, Renato, 'Social Justice and the Crisis of National Communities', in Francis Parker, Peter Hulme and Margaret Iverson (eds), *Colonial Discourse/Postcolonial Theory* (Manchester: Manchester University Press, 1994), pp. 239–52.

Rendell, Jane, *The Pursuit of Pleasure: Gender, Space and Architecture in Regency London* (London, 2002).

Roberts, Andrew D., *A History of Zambia* (London: Heinemann, 1976).

Robinson, Dwight E., 'The Importance of Fashions in Taste to Business History: An Introductory Essay', *Business History Review*, 37/1/2 (1963): pp. 5–36.

Roche, Daniel, *La culture des apparences. Une histoire du vêtement (XIIIe–XVIIIe siècle)* (Paris: Fayard, 1989).

—, *The culture of clothing: dress and fashion in the 'ancien régime'*, translated by Jean Birrell (Cambridge: Cambridge University Press, 1994).

—, *Histoire des choses banales. Naissance de la consommation XVIIe–XIXe siècle* (Paris : Fayard, 1997).

—, *A History of Everyday Things. The Birth of Consumption in France, 1600– 1800* (Cambridge: Cambridge University Press, 2000).

Rose, Clare, 'The Manufacture and Sale of "Marseilles" Quilting in Eighteenth-Century London', *CIETA Bulletin*, 76 (1999): pp. 104–11.

Ross, Robert, *Clothing: A Global History. Or, the Imperialists New Clothes* (Cambridge: Polity Press, 2008).

Rothstein, Natalie and Levey, Santina M., 'Furnishings, c. 1500–1780', in David Jenkins (ed.), *The Cambridge History of Western Textiles*, vol. 1 (2 vols, Cambridge: Cambridge University Press, 2003), pp. 631–58.

Rotsaert, Katelijne, *Tussen Eva en Maria. De vrouw volgens de predikanten van de 17de en 18de eeuw* (Aartrijke: Decock, 1992).

Rubin, Arnold, 'Layoyi: Some Hausa Calligraphic Charms', *African Arts*, 17/2 (1984): pp. 67–70, 91–2.

Rushing, W. Jackson, 'Marketing the Affinity of the Primitive and the Modern: René D'Harnoncourt and "Indian Art of the United States"', in Janet Berlo (ed.), *The Early Years of Native North American Art History* (Vancouver, BC, University of British Columbia Press, 1992), pp. 191–236.

Saez, Barbara, 'The Discourse of Philanthropy in Nineteenth-Century America', *American Transcendental Quarterly*, 11/3 (1997): pp. 163–70.

Saliklis, Ruta, 'The Dynamic Relationship Between Lithuanian National Costumes and Folk Dress', in Linda Welters (ed.), *Folk Dress in Europe and Anatolia:*

Beliefs about Protection and Fertility (Oxford: Berg Publishers, 1999), pp. 211–34.

Sargentson, Carolyn, *Merchants and luxury markets. The marchands merciers of eighteenth-century Paris* (London: Victoria and Albert Museum, 1996).

—, 'The manufacture and marketing of luxury goods: the marchands merciers of late 17th- and 18th-century Paris', in Robert Fox and Athony Turner (eds), *Luxury trades and consumerism in Ancien Régime Paris. Studies in the history of the skilled workforce* (Aldershot, UK: Ashgate, 1998), pp. 104–37.

Sarin, Sophie, 'The Floorcloth and Other Floor Coverings in the London Domestic Interior 1700–1800', *Journal of Design History*, 18/2 (2005): pp. 133–45.

Sarti, Raffaella, *Vita di casa. Abitare, mangiare, vestire nell'Europa moderna* (Rome and Bari: Laterza, 1999).

—, *Europe at Home: Family and Material Culture, 1500–1800*, translated by Allan Cameron (New Haven CT and London, 2002).

Scanlon, Jennifer, *Inarticulate Longings: The Ladies' Home Journal, Gender and the Promise of Consumer Culture* (New York: Routledge, 1995).

—, *The Gender and Consumer Culture Reader* (London: New York University Press, 2000).

Schama, Simon, *The Embarrassment of Riches: An Interpretation of Dutch Culture in the Golden Age* (London, 1987).

Schuurman, A.J., 'Probate inventory Research: Opportunities and Drawbacks', in M. Baulant, A.J. Schuurman, P. Servais (eds), *Inventaires après-décès et ventes de meubles* (Louvain-la-Neuve: Académia, 1988), pp. 19–28.

Scott, Joan W., 'Comment: Conceptualizing Gender in American Business History', *Business History Review*, 72/2 (1998): pp. 242–9.

Scranton, Philip, 'Introduction: Gender and Business History', *Business History Review*, 72/2 (1998): pp. 185–7.

Sekules, Veronika, 'Spinning Yarns: Clean Linen and Domestic Values in Late Medieval French Culture', in Anne L. McClanan and Karen Rosoff Encarnación (eds), *The Material Culture of Sex, Procreation, and Marriage in Premodern Europe* (Basingstoke, UK: Palgrave, 2001), pp. 79–91.

Seligmann, Linda J., 'Introduction: Mediating Identities, Marketing Wares', in Linda J. Seligmann (ed.), *Women Traders in Cross-Cultural Perspective: Mediating Identities, Marketing Wares* (Stanford, CA: Stanford University Press, 2001), pp. 1–24.

Serjeant, R.B., *Islamic Textiles* (Beirut: Librairie du Liban, 1972).

Servais, Pierre, 'Inventaires et ventes de meubles: apports a l'histoire économique', in M. Baulant, A.J. Schuurman, P. Servais (eds), *Inventaires après-décès et ventes de meubles* (Lauvain-la-Neuve: Académia, 1988), pp. 29–35

Shammas, Carole, 'The Domestic Environment in Early Modern England and America', *Journal of Social History*, 14/1 (1980): pp. 3–24.

—, *The Pre-Industrial Consumer in England and America* (New York: Oxford University Press, 1990).

—, 'The decline of textile prices in England and British America prior to industrialisation', *Economic History Review*, 47/3 (1994): pp. 483–507.

Shea, Philip, 'Kano and the Silk Trade', *Kano Studies*, 2/1 (1980): pp. 96–112.

—, 'Big is Sometimes Best: The Sokoto Caliphate and Economic Advantages of Size in the Textile Industry', *African Economic History*, 34 (2006): pp. 5–21.

Silverstein, Cory, '"That's just the kind of thing this lake does": Anishnaabe reflections on knowledge, experience and the power of words', in David Pentland (ed.), *Papers of the 28th Algonquian Conference* (Winnipeg, MB: University of Manitoba Press, 1998), pp. 354–64.

— and Cywink, Zeek, 'From Fireside to TV Screen: Self-Determination and Anishnaabe Storytelling Traditions', *Canadian Journal of Native Studies*, 20/1 (2000): pp. 35–66.

Silverstein-Willmott, Cory, 'Men or Monkeys?: The Politics of Clothing and Land within Ontario First Nations, 1830–1900', in Jill Oakes (ed.), *Native Voices in Research* (Winnipeg, MB: Aboriginal Issues Press, 2003), pp. 127–40.

Simmel, Georg, 'Fashion', *International Quarterly*, 10 (1904): pp. 130–55.

Singh, Andrea M. and Kelles-Viitanen, Anita (eds), *Invisible Hands: Women in Home-Based Production* (London: Sage, 1987).

Smekens, Fernand, 'Ambachtswezen en "nieuwe nijverheid"', in *Antwerpen in de 18de eeuw* (Antwerp: Genootschap voor Antwerpse Geschiedenis, 1952), pp. 65–79.

Smith, M.G., 'The jihad of Shehu dan Fodio', in I.M. Lewis (ed.), *Islam in Tropical Africa* (London: Oxford University Press, 1966).

Sombart, Werner, *Lujo y capitalismo* (Madrid: Alianza, 1979).

Spiral Foundation, URL: www.spiralfoundation.org, accessed 20 April 2009.

Spufford, Margaret, *The Great Reclothing of Rural England: Petty Chapmen and their Wares in the Seventeenth Century* (London: Hambledon Press, 1984).

—, 'The limitations of the probate inventory', in John Chartres and David Hey (eds), *English rural society, 1500–1800* (Cambridge: Cambridge University Press, 1990), pp. 139–75.

Stansell, Christine, *City of Women: Sex and Class in New York, 1789–1860* (Urbana: University of Illinois Press, 1987).

Stearns, Peter N., 'Stages of consumerism: recent work on the issues of periodization', *Journal of Modern History*, 69 (1997): pp. 102–17.

—, *Consumerism in World History: The Global Transformation of Desire* (New York: Routledge, 2001).

Steer, Francis W., *Farm and Cottage Inventories of Mid-Essex, 1635–1749* (Colchester: Essex Record Office, 1950).

Stephen, Lynn, 'Women's Weaving Cooperatives in Oaxaca', *Critique of Anthropology*, 25/3 (2005): pp. 253–78.

Stewart, Mary Lynn, *Dressing Modern Frenchwomen: Marketing Haute Couture, 1919–1939* (Baltimore: Johns Hopkins University Press, 2008).

Stillman, Yedida Kalfon, *Arab Dress: A Short History, from the Dawn of Islam to Modern Times* (Leiden: Brill, 2000).

Straus, Terry and Valentino, Valentino, 'Retribalization in Urban Indian Communities', in Susan Lobo and Kurt Peters (eds), *American Indians and the Urban Experience* (Walnut Creek, CA: Alta Mira Press, 2001), pp. 85–94.

Styles, John, 'Product innovation in Early Modern London', *Past & Present*, 168 (2000): pp. 124–69.

—, 'Lodging at the Old Bailey: Lodgings and their Furnishings in Eighteenth-Century London', in John Styles and Amanda Vickery (eds), *Gender, Taste and Material Culture in Britain and North America, 1700–1830* (New Haven and London, 2006), pp. 61–80.

—, *The Dress of the People: Everyday Fashion in Eighteenth-Century England* (New Haven and London: Yale University Press, 2007).

— and Vickery, Amanda (eds), *Gender, Taste, and Material Culture in Britain and North America, 1700–1830* (New Haven and London: Yale University Press, 2006).

Sullerot, Evelyne, *La Presse féminine* (Paris, 1963).

Sussman, Charlotte, *Consuming Anxieties: Consumer Protest, Gender & British Slavery, 1713–1833* (Stanford: Stanford University Press, 2000).

Taylor, Clare, *British and American Abolitionists: An Episode in Transatlantic Understanding* (Edinburgh: Edinburgh University Press, 1974).

Taylor, Lou, *The Study of Dress History* (Manchester: Manchester University Press, 2002).

Thijs, Alfons K.L., *De zijdenijverheid te Antwerpen in de zeventiende eeuw* (Antwerp: Pro Civitate, 1969).

—, 'Structural changes in the Antwerp industry from the fifteenth to eighteenth century', in Herman Van der Wee (ed.), *The rise and decline of urban industries in Italy and in the Low Countries (late Middle Ages-Early Modern Times)* (Leuven: Leuven University Press, 1988), pp. 207–12.

—, 'De nijverheid', in *Antwerpen in de XVIIde eeuw* (Antwerp: Genootschap voor Antwerpse Geschiedenis, 1989), pp. 131–51.

—, *Van geuzenstad tot katholiek bolwerk. Antwerpen en de contrareformatie* (Turnhout: Brepols, 1990).

—, 'Antwerp's luxury industries: the pursuit of profit and artistic sensitivity', in Jan Van der Stock (ed.), *Antwerp, story of a metropolis, 16th and 17th century* (Ghent: Snoeck-Ducaju, 1993), pp. 105–13.

Thirsk, Joan, 'The Fantastical Folly of Fashion: the English Stocking Knitting Industry, 1500–1700', in N.B. Harte and K.G. Ponting, (eds.), *Textile History and Economic History: Essays in Honour of Miss Julia de Lacy Mann* (Manchester: Manchester University Press, 1973), pp. 50–73.

—, *Economic Policy and Projects: The Development of a Consumer Society in Early Modern England* (Oxford: Clarendon Press, 1978).

Tice, Karin E., *Kuna Crafts, Gender, and the Global Economy* (Austin, TX: University of Texas Press, 1995).

Tilly, Louis and Scott, Joan W., *Women, Work and Family* (New York, 1978).

Toronto Star, 'Recycled Juice Containers Make Fun Totes', *Toronto Star*, 19 February, 2004, L2.

Turtle Island News Archives: 'D'Arcy Moses': http://www.assembly.gov.nt.ca/_live/documents/documentManagerUpload/Hn981204.pdf, accessed 8 October 2005.

Vail, Leroy and White, Landeg, *Power and the Praise Poem: Southern African Voices in History* (London: Currey, 1991).

Van Aert, Laura and Van Damme, Ilja, 'Retail dynamics of a city in crisis: the mercer guild in pre-industrial Antwerp (c. 1648–c. 1748)', in Bruno Blondé, Eugénie Briot, Natacha Coquery and Laura Van Aert (eds), *Retailers and consumer changes in Early Modern Europe. England, France, Italy and the Low Countries* (Tours: Presses Universitaires François-Rabelais, 2005), pp. 139–67.

Van Broekhoven, Deborah Bingham, '"Better than a clay club": The organization of anti-slavery fairs, 1835–60', *Slavery and Abolition*, 19/1 (1998): pp. 24–45.

—, *Devotion of These Women: Rhode Island in the Antislavery Network* (Amherst: University of Massachusetts Press, 2002).

Van Damme, Ilja, 'Het vertrek van Mercurius. Historiografische en hypothetische verkenningen van het economisch wedervaren van Antwerpen in de tweede helft van de zeventiende eeuw', *NEHA-Jaarboek*, 66 (2003): pp. 18–36.

—, 'Zotte verwaandheid. Over Franse verleiding en Zuid-Nederlands onbehagen, 1650–1750', in de Raf Bont and Tom Verschaffel (eds), *Het verderf van Parijs* (Leuven: Leuven University Press, 2004), pp. 187–203.

—, 'Changing consumer preferences and evolutions in retailing. Buying and selling consumer durables in Antwerp (c. 1648–c. 1748)', in Bruno Blondé, Peter Stabel, Jon Stobart and Ilja Van Damme (eds), *Buyers and sellers. Retail circuits and practices in medieval and early modern Europe* (Turnhout: Brepols, 2006), pp. 199–223.

—, 'A city in transition. Antwerp after 1648', in Ben Van Beneden and Nora De Poorter (eds), *Royalist refugees. William and Margaret Cavendish in the Rubens house 1648–1660* (Antwerp: Rubenshuis en Rubenianum, 2006), pp. 55–62.

—, *Verleiden en verkopen. Antwerpse kleinhandelaars en hun klanten in tijden van crisis (ca. 1648–ca. 1748)* (Amsterdam: Aksant, 2007).

Van der Wee, Herman, 'Industrial dynamics and the process of urbanization and de-urbanization in the Low Countries from the Late Middle Ages to the eighteenth century. A synthesis', in Van der Wee, Herman (ed.), *The rise and decline of urban industries in Italy and in the Low Countries (late Middle Ages-Early Modern Times)* (Leuven: Leuven University Press, 1988), pp. 307–81.

Van der Woude, Ad and Schuurman, Anton, *Probate inventories. A new source for the historical study of wealth, material culture and agricultural development* (Utrecht: HES Publishers, 1980).

Van Esterik, Penny, 'From Hunger Foods to Heritage Foods: Challenges to Food Localization in Lao PDR', in Richard Wilk (ed.), *Fast Food/Slow Food: The Cultural Economy of the Global Food System* (Lanham, MD: Altamira Press, 2006).

Van Horne, John C. and Yellin, Jean Fagan (eds), *The Abolitionist Sisterhood: Women's Political Culture in Antebellum America* (Ithica: Cornell University Press, 1994).

Vargas-Cetina, Gabriela, 'Anthropology and Cooperatives: From the Community Paradigm to the Ephemeral Association in Chiapas, Mexico', *Critique of Anthropology*, 25/3 (2005): pp. 229–51.

Veblen, Thorstein, *The Theory of the Leisure Class: an economic study of institutions* (1899, reprinted New York: Huebsch, 1919).

—, *The Theory of the Leisure Classes: an Economic study of Institutions* (1899) translated, *Teoría de la clase ociosa* (Madrid: Alianza, 1988).

Velut, Christine, 'Between Invention and Production: The Role of Design in the Manufacture of Wallpaper in France and England at the Turn of the Nineteenth Century', *Journal of Design History*, 17/1 (2004): pp. 55–69.

Verlet, Paul, 'Le commerce des objets d'art et les marchands merciers à Paris au XVIIIe siècle', *Annales. Economies. Sociétés. Civilisations*, 13 (1958): pp. 10–29.

Vickery, Amanda, 'Women and the world of goods: a Lancashire consumer and her possessions, 1751–81', in John Brewer and Roy Porter (eds), *Consumption and the World of Goods* (London: Routledge, 1993), pp. 274–304.

—, *Behind Closed Doors: At Home in Georgian England* (London and New Haven: Yale University Press, 2010).

Vigarello, Georges, *Le Propre et le sale: l'hygiène du corps depuis le Moyen âge* (Paris: Seuil, 1985).

—, *Concepts of Cleanliness: Changing Attitudes in France since the Middle Ages* (Cambridge: Cambridge University Press, 1988).

Vincent, John Martin, *Costume and Conduct in the Laws of Basel, Bern and Zurich 1370–1800* (Baltimore: Johns Hopkins University Press, 1935).

Wallace, Anne D., '"Nor in Fading Silks Compose": Sewing, Walking and Poetic Labor in Aurora Lee', *English Literary History*, 64/1 (1997): pp. 223–56.

Walton, Whitney, '"Life is Nothing Without Furniture": Consumer Practices of the Parisian Bourgeoisie 1814–1870', *Proceeding of the Annual Meeting of the Western Society for French History*, 17 (1990): pp. 278–85.

Weatherill, Lorna, 'Consumer Behaviour and Social Status in England, 1660–1750', *Continuity and Change*, 1/1 (1986): pp. 191–216.

—, 'A Possession of One's Own: Women and Consumer Behaviour in England, 1660–1740', *Journal of British Studies*, 25/2 (1986): pp. 131–56.

—, *Consumer Behaviour and Material Culture in Britain 1660–1760* (London: Routledge, 1988).

Welsch, Wolfgang, 'Transculturality: The Puzzlin Form of Cultures Today', in Mike Featherstone and Scott Lash (eds), *Spaces of Culture: City, Nation, World* (London: Sage, 1999), pp. 194–213.

Welters, Linda and Lillethun, Abby (eds), *The Fashion Reader* (Oxford and New York: Berg Publishers, 2007).

Whatmore, Sarah and Thorne, Lorraine, 'Nourishing Networks: Alternative Geographies of Food', in David Goodman and Michael Watts (eds), *Globalising*

Food: Agrarian Questions and Global Restructuring (London and New York: Routledge, 1997), pp. 287–304.

White, Sophie, '"Wearing three or four handkerchiefs around his collar, and elsewhere about him": Constructions of Masculinity and Ethnicity in French Colonial New Orleans', *Gender & History*, 15/3 (2003): pp. 528–49.

Wiest, Raymond and Willmott, Cory, 'Aboriginal Labour and the Garment Industry in Winnipeg', in John Loxley, Jim Silver and Kathleen Sexsmith (eds), *Doing Community Economic Development*. (Winnipeg MB and Black Point NS: Fernwood Publishing, 2007), pp. 142–55.

Wilks, Ivor, 'The Position of Muslims in Metropolitan Ashanti in the early Nineteenth Century', in I.M. Lewis (ed.), *Islam in Tropical Africa* (Oxford: Oxford University Press, 1966).

Williams, Patricia, 'From Folk to Fashion: Dress Adaptations of Norwegian Immigrant Women in the Midwest', in Patricia Cunningham and Susan Voso Lab (eds), *Dress in American Culture* (Bowling Green OH: Bowling Green State University Press, 1993), pp. 95–108.

Willmott, Cory and Brownlee, Kevin, 'Dressing for the Homeward Journey: Western Anishnaabe Leadership Roles Viewed Through Two Nineteenth-Century Burials', in Laura Peers and Carolyn Podruchny (eds), *Gathering Places: Essays on Aboriginal Histories* (Vancouver, BC: University of British Columbia Press, 2010).

Wilson, Godfrey, 'An Essay on the Economics of Detribalization', *Rhodes-Livingstone Papers*, nos. 5 and 6, (2 vols. 1941–42).

Winslow, Deborah, 'Pottery, Progress, and Structural Adjustments in a Sri Lankan Village', *Economic Development and Cultural Change*, 44/4 (1996): pp. 701–26.

Wischerman, Clemens 'Placing advertising in the modern cultural history of the city', in Clemens Wischerman and Elliott Shore (eds), *Advertising and the European city: historical perspectives* (Aldershot: Ashgate, 2000), pp. 1–31.

Yellin, Jean Fagan, *Women and Sisters: Antislavery Feminists in American Culture* (New Haven: Yale University Press, 1992).

Zboray, Ronald J. and Zboray, Mary Saracino, 'Books, Reading and the World of Goods in Antebellum New England', *American Quarterly*, 48/4 (1996): pp. 587–622.

Unpublished Sources

Balogun, Ismail A.B. (trans.), 'A Critical Edition of the *Ihya Al-Sunna Wa-Ikhmad Al-Bida* of Uthman b. Fudi, popularly known as Usumanu Dan Fodio' (Unpublished PhD dissertation, University of London, 1967).

Bruno Blondé, Van Aert, Laura and Van Damme, Ilja, unpublished database based on François Melis, *Poortersboeken* (Antwerp, 1977).

Cowen Orlin, Lena, 'Walls and their Chinks in Early Modern England' (Unpublished Paper presented at the Workshop 'Putting Objects in Their Places', Shakespeare Institute, Stratford, 18 June 2005).

Evans, Adrian B., 'Consumption and the Exotic in Early Modern England: A Socio-Material Investigation of the Retail, Domestic Ownership and Use of Exotic Goods in Suffolk and Bristol' (Unpublished PhD thesis, University of Bristol, 2001).

Ferguson, Douglas (trans.), 'Nineteenth Century Hausaland being a description by Imam Imoru of the Land, Economy, and Society of his People' (Unpublished PhD Dissertation, University of California, Los Angeles, 1973).

Fuller, Rachel, 'Out of Sight, Out of Mind? The Meaning of the Linnenkast in the Material and Conceptual Landscape of the Seventeenth-Century Dutch Republic' (Unpublished MA Thesis, V&A/RCA History of Design Programme, 2004).

L'heureux-Icard, Rosine, 'Les parfumeurs entre 1860 et 1910 d'après les marques, dessins et modèles déposés à Paris' (2 vols, Unpublished Thesis, Ecole Nationale des Chartes, 1994).

Luypaers, Carolien, *'Le goût pour les spectacles est tellement devenu à la mode'. Spektakelcultuur in het achttiende-eeuwse Antwerpen* (unpublished Master-dissertation, Catholic University of Leuven, 2001).

Moreno Claverías, Belén, *Pautas de consumo y diferenciación social en la Cataluña preindustrial* (Unpublished PhD Dissertation, European University Institute, Florence, 2002).

O'Hear, Ann, 'The Economic History of Ilorin in the 19th and 20th Centuries: The Rise and Decline of a Middleman Society' (Unpublished PhD dissertation, University of Birmingham, 1983).

Riello, Giorgio, '"Things Seen and Unseen": Inventories and the Representation of the Domestic Interior in Early Modern Europe' (Unpublished paper, V&A/RCA conference on Inventories in Renaissance and Early Modern Europe, May 2004).

—, 'The Ecology of Textiles in Early Modern Europe: Possibilities and Potentials' (Unpublished paper presented at the GEHN Conference on 'A Global History of Cotton Textiles', University of Padua, 17–19 November 2005).

Silverstein, Cory, 'Clothed encounters: The power of dress in relations between Anishnaabe and British peoples in the Great Lakes region 1760–2000' (Unpublished Ph.D. Dissertation, McMaster University, Canada, 2000).

Willems, Bart, *Krediet, vertrouwen en sociale relaties: kleine producenten en winkeliers te Antwerpen in de 18de eeuw* (Unpublished PhD dissertation, Free University of Brussels, 2006).

Index

References to illustrations are in **bold**.

Adshead, S.A.M. 44
aesthetics, textiles 60
Africans
    dress practice
        and labour migration 219–20
        Moore on 218
        second hand clothing 219, 220, 221, 222
        women 222–3
    and Western-styled clothes 215
    see also Zambia
agency concept, textiles 59
Alcatraz Island, Native American occupation of 171
American Antislavery Society 118, 131
American and Foreign Antislavery Society 132
Anderson, Benedict 168
anti-fashion 14–15
antislavery
    potholder 123–4, **123**
    reticule, silk **122**, 124
antislavery sewing circles 119–20
    antislavery slogans 121, 122, 123
    needlework, importance of 124–5
    products 121
Antwerp 17
    Au magasin de Paris 34, 37
    consumer demand 33–5, 37–8
    economic riots 29
    exports, decline 28, 29
    French
        clothing 25, 27
        culture 23
        fashion 22, 25, 29
        theatre 25, **26**
    Huguenot artisans 27
    periwig-makers 27
    retailers, increase 31–2
    textile sector, decline 29
Appadurai, Arjun 61
Artisan Multipurpose Cooperative (Philippines) 191, 192–3
    childcare 197
    craft fairs, participation in 211
    cultural space 197
    Ecology Centre 201
    establishment 199
    fabrics, use of 204, 209
    global sales 200–201, 211
    juice packs, used 201–2, 206, **208**
    labelling 198, 207
    online catalogue 211
    outreach programme 202, 212
    partnerships 211
    products
        bags 195, 198, 199, 200, **200**, **205**
        footwear 209
        hats **205**, 209
        home furnishing accessories 195, 209, 210, **210**
        jewellery 209, 210
        kitchen aprons 210
    publicity 211
    quality control 207, **208**
    recyclable waste, use of 199, 201–2, 209–10
    sewing
        department 202–3, **203**, **205**
        training 206
    show room **210**, 211
    social class issues 212
    wages 199–200, 206–7, 212
    workers 199
Associated Partners for Fairer Trade (Philippines) 199

Baker, Pam 185, 189

'Self-Esteem One' programme 183–4
Balzac, Honoré de 97
Barth, Heinrich 159
Barthe, Roland 8
Baumgarten, Linda 4
Beauvais, Tammy 189
Beaux, Ernest, creator, Chanel No.5 107
beds
    feather 53
    four-poster **50**
    function 50
    investment in 49–50, 79
    textiles for 49
    types 50–51
Berg, Maxine 35, 57, 75
Bigg, William Redmore, Old Woman Preparing Tea **46**
books, possession of 78
Boston Antislavery Bazaar 115–16, 117, 119
    British contributions 130–31, 132, 133
    demise 141–2
    'Fair Report' 119
    food donations 129
    goods
        fancy, prevalence of 129
        foreign 131, 133–4, 141
        pricing of 134–5
        professionally-made 128
        sources 119
    inventory sell-off 135
    local merchants, competition from 128
    male criticism of 139–40
    needlebook 125, **126**
    organization of 119
    profit issues 135, 140
    rural women's contribution 129–30
    unsold goods 131
    venues 140
Bourdieu, Pierre 8
Braudel, Fernand 10–11, 44, 46
    Civilization and Capitalism 11
    on fashion 11
Brewer, John 10
Briot, Eugénie 17
Broekhoven, Deborah van 118
buildings, use of wood 46
Burke, Peter 12
Burnham, Shelley 183

Calumet Ceremony 170
Campbell, Colin 34
Canadian Aboriginal Festival 187
Canadian Aboriginal Music Awards 187–8
Cardon, Pieter 21, 22, 29, 38
Carpenter, Mary 133
Catalonia, rural consumption patterns 68–71, 77–82, 85–93
    see also under consumption
Cavendish, Margaret, Duchess of Newcastle 23–4
chairs 77, 78, 81
    easy 86, 87, 90
    rush-bottomed 27
    upholstered 43
Chapman, Anne 120
Chapman, Maria Weston 115, 127, 129, 130, 131, 133, 134, 135, 136, 140, 141
charity bazaars 117–19, 142
    and consumption 138
    elitist criticism 139
    male criticism of 139
    and women in business 138–9
    see also Boston Antislavery Bazaar
'chase-and-flight' trendsetters 33
Chatterjee, Partha 169, 172
chocolate consumption 75, 78, 82
Claverías, Belén Moreno 17
Clifford, James 176
clothes
    African interest in 215
    consciousness, Zambia 217
    as cultural communication 100
    and identity 176, 177, 198
    peasant, and national distinctiveness 168
    Roche on 97, 100
    silk *see under* Sokoto Caliphate
    as wealth indicator 219
    Western-styled, and Africans 215
    see also sumptuary laws
Clunas, Craig 15
comfort
    idea of 43
    and textiles 43–4, 60
consumer society, development 9–10
consumers, and middlemen 36, 37, 38
consumption
    and charity bazaars 138

conspicuous 68
    perfume as 102, 104
heiresses 88
patterns, post-mortem inventories 68–9
of perfume, as fashion act 100
revolution 68
rural Catalonia 68–71, 77–82, 85–93
    auction evidence 86–8
    chocolate 82
    and dowry system 85–6
    inventory evidence 77–81
    religious prints 80
    widows 89–90
and social class 67
studies 76
urban, and luxury 75–6
widows 88–9
Coombe, Rosemary 167
cooperatives, women's
    Latin America 196
    scholarship on 196
    Southeast Asia 194
    see also Artisan Multipurpose
        Cooperative
Corbin, Alain 100
    Le Miasme et la jonquille 98
cottage, interior **46**
couture houses, and perfume 114
Crowley, John 51
Csergo, Julia 98, 100
cultural
    citizenship 170, 172
    space, Artisan Multipurpose
        Cooperative (Philippines) 197
culture, role in nation-building 169
Cunnington, Phillis 5
curtains 78
    window, rural/urban use 57, 77
cutlery, use 77

Dahomey Kingdom 153
Damme, Ilja van 17
dan Fodio, Shaikh Uthman 143, 145
    dress, attitude to 146–7
    on the Hausa kings 148–9
    innovation, attitude to 147
    on silk wearing 147–8, 160–61
    see also Sokoto Caliphate

Davis, J. Merle 221
DeMontigne, Angela 189
Dene Fur Clouds company 174, **175**, 185, 189
D'Harnoncourt, Rene 177
Dinawo, Native fashion company 183
domesticity, commodification 138
Douglas, Fred 178
Douglas, Mary 8
Douglass, Frederick 132–3
dowry system, rural Catalonia 85
dress, shelter, distinction 44
Dyck, Anthony Van 29

Eau de Cologne 103, 104, 106
    as male perfume 100
Elias, Norbert 77
Everett, Ron 185, 189
    formline motifs 173, **174**

fashion
    academic study of 1, 2–15
    and cultural theorists 8
    and quantitative history 9
    and Western art history 13
    and women's history 8
    Braudel on 11
    concept 41
    definition 10fn27
    Eurocentric bias 11–12, 13
    force of 14, 16, 18, 97
    gender bias 2, 3
    Islamic West Africa 13
    and luxury 75
    museum collections 4
    perceived triviality of 2–3
    perfume consumption as 100, 113
    pioneering studies 3–5
    role of tradesmen 22–3
    scope 1
    and self-esteem 180–81, 187
    Simmel on 101
    and social mobility 33
    and trade 17
    see also anti-fashion; French fashion;
        Native fashion
fashions, launch time 36
Female Specator 59

Finnane, Antonia 13–14, 15
floor coverings 56
Foley, Caroline 3
France
    perfumery market 98–9
    Universal Exhibition (1900) 99
Franklin, Benjamin 49
French clothing, Antwerp 25, 27
French culture, Antwerp 23
French fashion
    Antwerp 22, 25, 29
    textile anecdote 21
French theatre, Antwerp 25, **26**
Friedman, Jonathan 176
furniture
    for beverages 49
    items per household 53, 54
    recycling 61
    in Swedish houses 48
    textiles, association 47–8
    upholstered 53, **55**, 57
    wooden, absence in Ottoman Empire 47

Gallore, R.P.F. 30
Garland, John 42
Garrison, William Lloyd 132
Gonzales, Angela 181
Goody, Jack 13
Gordon, Beverly 116, 118, 138, 139
Grant, Dorothy 173, 185, 186, 188

Hagley Museum 9
hair pipe beads 173, 181
Hansen, Karen Tranberg 18
Harrison, William, *Description of England* 49
Harte, Negley 7
heiresses, consumption by 88
Hibernian Antislavery Society, Dublin 134
Hiler, David 81
Hiskett, Mervyn 146, 149
Hood, Adrienne 51
house, Chinese, interior **45**
Hubbard, Anny 177
Huguenot artisans, Antwerp 27
Hunt, Alan 16
hybridity 176
hygiene practices

    development 98, 100
    and perfume 100
identity
    and clothes 176, 177, 198
    intertribal 181, 188
    and Native fashion 182, 186, 188, 190
inventories, Catalan 71
    consumption evidence 77–9
    limitations 68–71
    post-mortem, and consumption patterns 68–9

Jones, Carla 198
Jones, David 183, 187
    design 180, **181**

Karim, Wazir 194
Kay, Allison 116
King, Gregory 42–3
Knight, Ann 133
Kramer, Jennifer 167
Kriger, Colleen 17

Latin America, women's cooperatives 196
Le Petit messager des modes 106
Lemire, Beverly 60
    Business of Everyday Life 135
Leshkowich, Ann Marie 198
Lewis, David 209
Lillethun, Abby *see* Welters, Linda
linen
    chests 64, **64**
    and cleanliness culture 63
    gender issues 64–5, **64**
    as heirloom 57
    sheets 49
    as space divider 62
Lipovetsky, Gilles 12
Lobo, Susan 172
Löfgren, Orvar 168, 169, 186
Louis XIV, King of France 23
Lundstrom, Linda 187
luxury/ies
    definition 72
    demand for 72, 74–5
    and depravity 73
    and fashion 75

necessity, distinction 71–2
perfume, association 111–12
purpose 72, 74
and sumptuary laws 73
and urban consumption 75–6
Veblen on 72, 73–4
and women 82–4, 90–91, 92

McCracken, Grant 8
McKendrick, Neil 33, 67, 74
   The Birth of a Consumer Society 10
Malanima, Paolo 76, 79
Marot, Daniel 27
Martin, Linda 173
Martineau, Harriet 133
Mauss, Marcel 8
Melchor de Macanaz, Don 73
middlemen, and consumers 36, 37, 38
Midgley, Clare 132
Milgram, Lynne 17–18
Miller, Daniel 8
Missoni, Vittorio 189
Moore, R.J.B. 221
   on African dress practice 218
Moses, D'Arcy 174, 175, 184–5, 188, 189
movable goods, real estate, distinction 47
Münster, peace treaty (1648) 28
musk, and good taste 104–5, 108–9

Nachtigal, Gustav 159
Nafata of Gobir, Sultan 143–4
Nantes, Edict of, Revocation (1685) 27
nation, concept 168
nation building
   in inner/spiritual realm 172
   intertribal 182, 186
   non-sovereign states 169
   role of culture 169
nationalism
   cultural 169–70
   economic 182–5
   enacting 185–9
nationhood
   indigenous constructions of 170–71
   intertribal 171, 172, 176, 185, 186, 189
   and Native fashion 189–90
Native Americans, occupation of Alcatraz
   Island 171

Native fashion 177–90
   appropriation of 177–9, **178**
   collaboration 186–7
   'Dances with Wolves' ensemble **180**,
      181–2
   designer strategies 183–4
   Dinawo company 183
   dress **179**
   formline designs 173, **174**
   fur designs 174, **175**
   government funding, problems 184, 186
   and identity 182, 186, 188, 190
   and 'Indianness' stereotype 173, 179,
      182, 189
   and nationhood 189–90
   shows, function 187
   tuxedo vests **181**
   'Winds of Change' show 186
necessity, luxury, distinction 71–2
needlebook 125, **126**
needles, manufacture of 125
needlework 124–5
   oppressive tendencies 125, 127
Niessen, Sandra 13
Nigeria, male dress 17
Nuttall, Sarah 233

Orlin, Lena 62
Ottoman Empire, absence of wooden
   furniture 47
Overton, Mark 43, 53
Owen, Mrs Henry, *History of Needlework*
   124–5
Ozbek, Rifat, 'Dances with Wolves'
   ensemble **180**, 181–2

Pan-Indianism 172
Pardailhé-Galabrun, Annik 50
Paris, fashion streets 36
Pasold, Eric 7
Pasold Research Fund 7
Paton, Catherine 135–6
Pease, Elizabeth 133
Pendleton Blanket Company 177
Pennsylvania, textile use 51–2
perfume
   bottle sizes 111
   boutique sales 111–12

as conspicuous consumption 102, 104, 112–13
consumption, as fashion 100, 113
and couture houses 113
as cultural communication 100, 110
display discourses 111, 113
ephemerality 100–101, 102, 104
heliotrope scent 107
high prices, strategy 112–13
and hygiene 100
labels 111
literary references 108, 109–12
luxury, association 111–12
market
    development 98–9
    and women 100
nineteenth-century fashions 104–9
packaging 111
products 99
synthetic 106–7
use, guidance on 103–4
violet scent, popularity 105–8
see also Eau de Cologne
periwig-makers, Antwerp 27
Philadelphia Antislavery Fair 118
Philip V, King of Spain 73
Picard, Fred 177
Platt Hall Gallery of Costume, Manchester 5
Plumb, J.H. 10
Poirters, A. 24
Ponsonby, Margaret 61
Ponting, Ken 7
porcelain manufactory, Sèvres 111
Powdermaker, Hortense 222
Powers Fashions 177, **178**
Prochaska, Frank 118
Pyrenees, peace treaty (1659) 28

Quarles, Benjamin 133

Ramos, Fernando 76
real estate, movable goods, distinction 47
Riello, Giorgio 17, 79
Roche, Daniel 74, 84, 110
    on clothes 97, 100
    La culture des apparences 97
Rosaldo, Renato 170, 172
Rubens, Peter Paul 29

Russell, John, *Boke of Nurture* 63

Saez, Barbara 117
Salikis, Ruta 168
Scott, Joan 137
self-esteem, and fashion 180–81, 187
Sèvres, porcelain manufactory 111
sewing circles 119–20, 127
Shammas, Carole 43
shelter, dress, distinction 44
Simmel, Georg 3, 108
    on fashion 101
smell/s
    images of 98
    and social imagination 98
    socially permitted 104
    see also musk; perfume
Smith, Adam 2
Smoke, Sue 183, 186
social class, and consumption 67
social imagination, and smell 98
social mobility, and fashion 33
Sokoto Caliphate
    creation 143, 149
    expansion 150
    map **144**
    robes
        Caliphate 145, 146, 152, 159, 160, **160**, 162, 163
        characteristics 151
        collections 152–3
        cotton 152
        economic role 157
        Frobenius robe 155–7, **156**
        of honour 145–6, 152, 153, 154, 161
        motifs 158–9, **160**
        price 158
        standard 152, 163
        Wilmot robe 152–3, **153**, 154, 161
    silk clothing 144–5, 152
        conflicted views on 146
        dan Fodio on 147–8, 160
        and gender 148
        in *hadith* literature 146, 147–8
        in the Quran 146
        types of 151–2
    sumptuary laws 144
    textile products 151, 157, 162

Sombart, Werner 72, 74, 79, 83
Southern Netherlands 21, 22, 23, 25, 27, 28
    fashion-changes 37
    sumptuary law (1679) 30
    see also Antwerp
space division, and textiles 62
Steel, Valerie 14
Stewart, Mary Lynn 14
Styles, John 58
sumptuary laws
    and luxury 73
    Sokoto Caliphate 144
Sweden
    furniture, value of 48
    textiles 48, 51, 52

tablecloths, Turkish carpets as 53, **56**
tapestries
    Auvergne 55
    Bergamo 54–5
Tappan, Lewis 132
taste, shaping of 101–2
Taylor, Alice 17
Taylor, Lou 7
tents, use as houses 46
textiles 78
    academic study of 41, 61
    accumulation of 52
    aesthetics 60
    agency concept 59
    care for 63
    in Chinese houses **45**
    and comfort 43–4, 60
    cotton 60
    furniture, association 47–8
    improvements 60
    inventories 58
    meaning of 58–60
    peasants' possession of 79
    in Pennsylvania 51–2
    social life of 61–5
    and space division 62
    stolen items 58
    storage for 48
    in Swedish houses 48
    as wealth indicators 51
    and women 59–60
Thirsk, Joan 6, 9, 10

Tour-à-la-mode 24, **24**
trade, and fashion 17
Turtle Concepts 180, **181**, 183, 187, 188

Veblen, Thorstein 3, 78, 83, 102
    on luxury 72, 73–4
Veblen-Simmel theses 32–3
Vickery, Amanda 2, 8, 84
Vigarello, Georges 63, 98, 100

wallpaper 55, 56
wardrobes 77–8
Weatherill, Lorna 43, 53, 57, 84
Welters, Linda, & Abby Lillethun, *Fashion Reader* 12
West Africa, Islamic, fashion 13
Weston, Anne 120, 128, 129, 139
Weston, Anne & Lucia 115
    journals 119
widows, consumption by 88–9
    rural Catalonia 89–90
Wiedmer, Laurence 81
Willett, Cecil 5
Williams, Patricia 168
Williamsburg, Colonial 4, 9
Willmott, Cory 17
Winterthur Museum 9
women
    African dress practice 219–20
    in business 136–7
        and charity bazaars 138–9
    cooperatives
        Latin America 196
        Southeast Asia 194
    fashions, Zambia 232–3
    and luxury items 82–4, 90–91, 92
    and perfume market 100
    and textiles 59–60
wood, use in buildings 46
wood panelling 55

Zambia
    Chitenge outfits 224, 226, **228**, 231, 232
    clothes
        'big look' style 230
        imports 221
        mail-order business 221–2

    men's fashions 229–31
    women's fashions 232–3
clothes consciousness 217, 233
dress codes, tv announcers 231
fashion sign **224**
jeans 230
new dress conventions 217

secondhand clothes
    consumer clothing competence 227–9
    imports 224–5, 233–4
    markets 225, 226, 227, **227**, 231
suit aesthetics 229–30